CHINESE

BUSINESS

NEGOTIATING

STYLE

INTERNATIONAL BUSINESS SERIES

SPONSORED BY
The Pacific Asian Management Institute, University of Hawaii

This series of books focuses on today's increasingly important phenomena: international business. Sponsored by the University of Hawaii's Pacific Asian Management Institute (PAMI), one of the key centers in the world for developing international business expertise, the series is devoted to international business, with an emphasis on the Asia-Pacific Region. Books in the series will help faculty, students, and business professionals acquire the knowledge and communication skills necessary for working in an ever-changing, international business environment.

Books in this series:

CHINA 2000: Emerging Business Issues
edited by Lane Kelley and Yadong Luo

TONY FANG

CHINESE

BUSINESS

NEGOTIATING

STYLE

SAGE Publications
International Educational and Professional Publisher
Thousand Oaks London New Delhi

For information:

SAGE Publications, Inc.
2455 Teller Road
Thousand Oaks, California 91320
E-mail: order@sagepub.com

SAGE Publications Ltd.
6 Bonhill Street
London EC2A 4PU
United Kingdom

SAGE Publications India Pvt. Ltd.
M-32 Market
Greater Kailash I
New Delhi 110 048 India

Printed in the United States of America

Library of Congress Cataloging-in-Publication Data

Fang, Tony.
    Chinese business negotiating style / by Tony Fang.
        p.   cm.—(International business series)
    Includes bibliographical references and index.
    ISBN 0-7619-1575-3 (acid-free paper)
    ISBN 0-7619-1576-1 (pbk.: acid-free paper)
        1. Negotiation in business—China.   2. Corporate culture—China.
    3. National characteristics, Chinese.   4. Business etiquette—China.
    I. Title.   II. Series: International business series (Thousand Oaks, Calif.)
    HD58.6 .F36   1998
    658.4'052'0951—ddc21   98-40121

This book is printed on acid-free paper.

99   00   01   02   03   04   05   7   6   5   4   3   2   1

Acquiring Editor: Marquita Flemming
Editorial Assistant: MaryAnn Vail
Production Editor: Sherrise M. Roehr/Diana E. Axelsen
Production Assistant: Patricia Zeman
Typesetter/Designer: Lynn Miyata
Cover Designer: Candice Harman

Contents

At fifteen my mind was set on learning.
At thirty my character had been formed
At forty I had no more perplexities.
At fifty I knew the Mandate of Heaven.
At sixty I was at ease with whatever I heard.
At seventy I could follow my heart's desire without
    transgressing moral principles.
                —*Confucius (551-479 B.C.)*

To Min, Fei, and David

Preface

I never imagined that I would someday write and publish a book about Chinese business negotiating style. I was born, brought up, and educated as a naval architect in China. From 1987 to 1991, I worked in Chinese shipping and shipbuilding industries in Shanghai, where negotiating with Western shipbuilders and marine suppliers was part of my routine work. Although my Chinese colleagues and I bargained relentlessly with Western business people at the negotiation table, we seldom reflected on our own negotiating style. Nor did we know much about the label that Westerners attached to us as "inscrutable" negotiators—toughest of all peers.

My academic journey in search of rational insight into Chinese culture and business style started after I came to the Linköping Institute of Technology as a graduate student in production economics in 1991 and became a PhD candidate in industrial marketing in 1992. It was in Sweden that I began to learn the Western management language and commenced my systematic study of Chinese culture, philosophy, social psychology, and business management.

From 1994 to 1995, I worked as an assistant export manager and visit coordinator in a Scandinavian forwarding company in Stockholm. I experienced, through my daily sea freight and air freight operations, how Western companies were elbowing one another in their enthusiastic rush to flock into China. Since then, I have also worked as a consultant for Scandinavian firms and served as an interpreter for approximately 25 Chinese delegations at various levels that visited government agencies, companies, and communities in Sweden, Denmark, Finland, and Germany. Because many of these visits are episodes in the processes of business negotiations between the Chinese visitors and their Western hosts, I had the chance to observe, as a "real-life" researcher, Chinese business negotiating style in situ.

We are witnessing a historical transition. The world's attention is shifting eastward as we approach the next millennium. The term *Far East* is being replaced by that of *East Asia*; China and East Asian countries with a Chinese cultural heritage are remolding much of our intellectual thinking about global politics and economy. It is within this framework that I returned to Linköping University in 1995 to continue my academic career at the newly established International Graduate School of Management and Industrial Engineering (IMIE). My life and my educational and working experience in both the East and West inspired me to write a book about Chinese business negotiating style. Focusing on this subject, I attempt to show broadly to Western readers the Chinese way of doing business. My commitment to writing this book also reflects my dissatisfaction with existing scholarship: There is a dearth of solid information in the West about Chinese business negotiating style. The existing studies, as I will discuss in detail in this book, suffer from a number of weaknesses, such as lack of a systematic model, lack of cultural analysis of Chinese negotiating tactics, lack of the presence of a Chinese voice, weak empirical description, and a predominance of U.S.-China negotiation literature.

Reality has painted a picture of the Chinese negotiator as bewilderingly complex. For example, I have met Western business executives who recalled their wonderful time in China. They said they loved to negotiate and work with the Chinese and were captivated by the harmonious Chinese style of negotiating. To them, the Chinese were sincere business gentlemen who worked at a very high level of mutual trust and respect. I have also met other Western business executives who narrated their terrible stories about China and complained that they hated to negotiate and work with the Chinese and were fed up with the tricky Chinese style of negotiating. According to them, the Chinese are "immoral" business people who can "cheat," "lie," or do whatever is necessary to knock you off balance.

I was struck by this contradictory picture and was myself very much a part of this Chinese phenomenon some years ago: The Chinese negotiator is both a sincere and a deceptive negotiator. Unfortunately, no previous studies provide a coherent framework to help readers to understand, systematically, the mechanisms underlying the complex personality of the Chinese negotiator. For example, the existing literature appears to have been remiss in answering the following: What constitutes the Chinese style of negotiating? Why do the Chinese negotiate both sincerely and deceptively?

Chinese negotiating tactics are another theme that motivated me to pick up my writing brush. There is an embarrassing problem in the existing scholarship. On the one hand, the uniqueness of Chinese negotiating tactics is postulated by thoughtful observers who have painstakingly prepared a long list of these tactics; on the other hand, no compelling cultural explanation of such tactics is provided. No previous work goes beyond various Chinese tricks and ploys to touch the very base of Chinese negotiating tactics by answering the following: What is the philosophical foundation of Chinese negotiating tactics? What is the "magic thread" that holds together all the Chinese negotiating "tricks," "ploys," and "tactics"?

Although complex, Chinese negotiating style is not unfathomable. The key lies in an in-depth and systematic understanding of Chinese business culture. I owe much of my inspiration to write this book to my previous life as a naval architect and seaman. One may marvel at the magnificent sight of the collection of ships sailing across the sparkling blue sea, wondering how anybody can design and operate such wonderful works, from meter-long small yachts to large tankers weighing hundreds of thousands of deadweight tons. Though complex indeed, all vessels are, nonetheless, built to a technical specification that merely consists of three parts: deck, engine, and electric parts. In the shipping industry, "deck," "engine," and "electric" are also the professional terms that define the work of crews: The deck department is responsible for navigating and operating the vessel, the engine department is responsible for providing the propulsion for the vessel and maintaining all on-board machinery equipment, and the electric department is responsible for supplying the electricity and furnishing all electric and radio connections for the operation of the vessel. A vessel is essentially a system in which deck, engine, and electric parts cannot be missing if the vessel is to be a vessel because each has its distinctive function; all three parts, however, are interrelated and interact with one another for the well-being of the entire vessel to navigate safely toward its destination. Having once been a seaman sailing from China to Europe and vice versa, I luckily derived a useful perspective from the sea: What are the deck, engine, and electric parts of life? Embarking on my research on Chinese business negotiating style, I asked myself: What are the deck, engine, and electric components of Chinese business culture and negotiating style?

This book is based on my licentiate dissertation *Chinese Business Negotiating Style: A Sociocultural Approach*, which I completed at IMIE in 1997. The purpose of the book is to provide an in-depth and systematic understanding of Chinese business negotiating style in a Chinese sociocultural context. The book reports my extensive investigations of the inscrutable Chinese negotiators during the past 7 years. In this book, I attempt to present the richness of Chinese business negotiating style by examining, systematically, how the three major components of Chinese business culture influence Chinese negotiating behavior: the PRC (People's Republic of China) condition, Confucianism, and Chinese stratagems. This book is empirically based on my interviews, during 1995 and 1996, with 71 Swedish and Chinese negotiators involved in various Sweden-China business negotiation practices.

This is an academic book, but the intended audiences include academics, students, managers, and general readers interested in the workings of Chinese business negotiating style. My writing style is tailored accordingly to attempt to satisfy the tastes of these groups of readers in a balanced manner. I hope the debates and models I present will be of value to scholars in culture, social psychology, international business, cross-cultural management, and so forth. In addition, I hope that MBA students and students of Chinese culture and business will find this book a useful textbook given its capacity to systematize Chinese business culture literature in a coherent fashion and to provide a large number of reader-friendly case illustrations for class-room jamming, and that Western business people, by following the cases, the managerial implications, and the list of Chinese negotiating tactics, will value my book as a useful "Chinese business culture and negotiating style" guidebook for negotiating and doing business effectively with China.

Writing a book of this magnitude involves strenuous work. I am not the only person behind the project, however. The book could not have been completed without the assistance of a variety of individuals and institutions. I thank, above all, the Chinese and Swedish managers and officials who appreciated my work and spent time discussing Chinese business negotiating behaviors with me. Although I chose to keep all the Chinese interviewees anonymous and fictitious in this book, I say to them: "*Zhongxin de ganxie nimen!*" Although it is impossible to list the names of all the Swedish managers with whom I discussed Chinese culture and negotiating skills during my research process, I acknowledge and thank, in particular, the following persons from various Swedish organizations for their insights and help, from which this study has greatly benefited (including a few local Chinese who are working or who have worked as managers for the Swedish companies): Lars-Erik Bröms, chief representative, Volvo Construction Equipment International AB, Beijing; Bo Bäckström, commercial counselor, Embassy of Sweden, Beijing; Che Wenjian, project manager, Market Operations China, Ericsson Radio Systems AB, Stockholm; Camilla Falk, controller, Joint Venture Cooperation, Ericsson Radio Systems AB, Stockholm; Hans Falk, human resources manager, Market Operations China, Hong Kong, Macao, Ericsson Radio Systems AB, Stockholm; Lars Edvardsson, president, Nanjing Ericsson Communication Co. Ltd., Nanjing; Ulf Gerbjörn, general manager, Sweden-China Trade Council, Stockholm; John Gilbertson, managing director, Ericsson Limited, Hong Kong; Mats Harborn, chief representative, Svenska Handelsbanken Beijing Representative Office, Beijing; Ulrica Holmberg, manager, Lotus Travel AB, Stockholm; Håkan Hu, financial controller, Ericsson (China) Co. Ltd., Beijing; Bengt Hult, managing director, Beijing Ericsson Mobile Communications Co. Ltd., Beijing; Thomas Kung, managing director, Atlas Copco (China) Ltd., Hong Kong; Billy Lau, managing director, United First Limited, Hong Kong; Olof Lenneman, president and chief representative, Ericsson (China) Co. Ltd., Beijing; Birgitta Lindgren, headmaster, Swedish School Beijing (SSB), Beijing; Tommy Liu, managing director, Chinese

Consulting in Scandinavia AB, Beijing; Janne Lundqvist, director of marketing, Mobile Networks (Guangdong, Hainan), Ericsson (China) Co. Ltd., Guangzhou; Robert Ma, executive assistant and interpreter, Ericsson (China) Co. Ltd., Beijing; Jan Malm, director, Market Operations China, Hong Kong, Macao, Ericsson Radio Systems AB, Stockholm; Håkan Osvald, assistant general counselor, Atlas Copco AB, Stockholm; Thomas Pleiborn, manager, Telefonaktiebolaget LM Ericsson, Stockholm; Britt Reigo, vice president, Head of Corporate Function Human Resources and Organization, Telefonaktiebolaget LM Ericsson, Stockholm; Michael Ricks, executive vice president, Ericsson (China) Co. Ltd., Beijing; Hans Sandberg, senior vice president, General Counselor, Atlas Copco AB, Stockholm; Jan Sjöberg, director, Joint Venture Cooperation, Ericsson Radio Systems AB, Stockholm; Michael Sundström, manager, Ericsson (China) Co. Ltd., Beijing; Christer Söderberg, area manager, Volvo Construction Equipment International AB, Eskilstuna; Lars Timner, vice president, AGA Aktiebolag, Stockholm; Conny Törnqvist, manager, Joint Venture Cooperation, Ericsson Radio Systems AB, Stockholm; Magnus Wennberg, export manager, Malmberg Water AB, Åhus; Patrick Wong, marketing director, Ericsson Limited, Hong Kong; Stephen Yeung, deputy managing director, Ericsson Limited, Hong Kong; Zhang Xingsheng, vice president, Ericsson (China) Co. Ltd., Beijing; Uldis Zervens, regional director, East Asia, Telefonaktiebolaget LM Ericsson, Stockholm.

A thousand thanks to my colleagues in the Department of Management and Economics, IMIE, Linköping University, especially to Professor Ove Brandes, my mentor, for his early trust in my potential to develop from being a ship engineer in China to a management researcher in Sweden and for his open-mindedness to my ideas, which enabled me to craft my perspectives creatively; Associate Professor Hossein Dadfar for his advice, questioning, and guidance; Professor Bengt Högberg, Per Åman, and Claes Moberg for their useful comments on my work; Professor Staffan Brege, Professor Sten Wandel, Dr. Helén Anderson, Dr. Roland Sjöström, Professor Staffan Gullander, and Associate Professor Peter Gustavsson for their encouragement; Brittmarie Genet and Saga Sedin for their professional secretarial assistance; Dr. Jörgen Dahlgren, the head of the department, and Christina Hansson, the administrative officer of the department, for their efforts in creating a fine working environment for me; Monica

Abrahamsson-Carton and Johan Holstrom for their stand-by Information Technology support; and Maurice Devenney for his skilled proofreading of the manuscript.

My deepest gratitude goes to Lucian W. Pye, Ford Professor Emeritus of Political Science at Massachusetts Institute of Technology, for his kind appreciation of my work and encouraging comments. Despite my critique, Pye's (1982) *Chinese Commercial Negotiating Style* remains the single most important work in the area, and Pye is one of the scholars and personalities I respect most. For their criticisms, comments, and encouragement, I am very grateful to the following: Michael J. Thomas, professor of marketing, the University of Strathclyde; Robert March, former professor of international business and management at Aoyama Gakuin University; Rosalie L. Tung, The Ming & Stella Wong Professor of International Business at Simon Fraser University; John Frankenstein, visiting professor at Copenhagen Business School; Michael Harris Bond, professor at The Chinese University of Hong Kong; Min Chen, associate professor at the American School of International Management in Arizona; Sally Stewart, former senior lecturer in marketing at the University of Hong Kong; Christian Scholz, professor of international management at the University of Saarland; and Harro von Senger, professor of sinology at Albert-Ludwigs University.

My special thanks and indebtedness go to Dr. Richard Brislin and Dr. Lane Kelley, both at The Pacific Asian Management Institute at the University of Hawaii, and to Marquita Flemming, senior editor at Sage Publications, for their vision and belief in the value of this book and their efforts in bringing it to publication. I also thank Sherrise Roehr, Diana Axelsen, MaryAnn Vail, Ravi Balasuriya, Jennifer Morgan, Dan Hays, and June Brewer at Sage for their efforts in the process of production and marketing of the book.

I acknowledge the generous permissions of the following authors and presses to use their materials in my book: Mun Kin-chok, The Chinese University of Hong Kong, "The Competition Model of Sun Tzu's *Art of War*," 1990; Wing-Tsit Chan, *A Source Book in Chinese Philosophy* (© 1963 by Princeton University Press; reprinted by permission of Princeton University Press); and Sun Tzu, *Sun Tzu on the Art of War* (S. B. Griffith, Trans., © 1963 by Oxford University Press, Inc.; used by permission of Oxford University Press, Inc.).

A thousand thanks go to Linköping University library for its professional librarian services, in particular to Ursula Nielsen, Anna Blad, Peter Karlsson, Magdalena Öström, and Per Eriksson working at "Kvartersbibliotek A," who have been hunting for "China literature" for me for years. My special thanks also go to Björn Böke for part of the artwork and Gunilla Jernselius for the map of China used in this book. I also thank Dr. Yong Luo, Xu Yang, Karin Timm, and Lotta Guan for their help.

I acknowledge and thank the following organizations for sponsoring my research: Swedish Foundation for Strategic Research, Sweden-China Trade Council, The Research Foundation of the Swedish Commercial Bank, Ericsson Radio Systems AB, Scandinavian Airline Systems, Aerocar-Spedman AB, Penta Shipping Group, and Svenska Handelsbanken Beijing Representative Office.

No graduates from Shanghai Jiao Tong University (Jiaoda), China's "Cradle of Engineers," could ever forget the university's fine old tradition: *Yin Shui Si Yuan* ("When you drink water, think of its source"). It was at Jiaoda in the early 1980s that I built up my knowledge about engineering and developed my interests in language and management. I owe my deep gratitude to Jiaoda.

I thank my parents, Fang Guoguang and Li Mingcai, both of whom have been humble intellectuals and dedicated all their lives to education in China, for their deep moral support and profound parental influences on my academic pursuits.

I thank my wife, Min Li, daughter, Fei Fang, and son, David Fang, to whom this book is dedicated. I simply could not have done my work without their consistent support, understanding, and love. To them, I owe the deepest debt of all.

Although I have acknowledged many individuals and organizations, this book is my own work and I alone am responsible for any errors that may exist in the book. A Chinese proverb and stratagem states, "Toss out a brick to attract a piece of jade." If my book happens in any way to serve as a "brick" to attract many "jade" publications on Chinese business negotiating style in the years to come, I shall be heartily satisfied.

Introduction

"The Chinese Are Coming"

China is the world's most populous country and its largest emerging market. To enter into China—the "Middle Kingdom"—to do business was a dream that had fascinated Western business people since the Industrial Revolution. A British writer (as quoted in Mann, 1989, p. 24) declared more than 150 years ago, "If we could only persuade every person in China to lengthen his shirttail by a foot, we could keep the mills of Lancashire working round the clock." China's "open-door" policy and unprecedented acquisition of foreign investment since the late 1970s has made the Western business people's dream a reality.

Today, China is the largest recipient of foreign direct investment among developing countries and the second largest in the world after the United States. By the end of 1995, China had accumulatively approved 258,000 foreign-invested enterprises with contractual foreign investment of $395.7 billion and actual invested capital of

AUTHOR'S NOTE: Throughout the book, the generic "he" and "gentleman" have been used for the sake of brevity. In all instances, it is my intention to imply both the male and the female gender.

$135.4 billion (Xu, 1996). Since 1978, China's real gross national product (GNP) has grown by an average of 9.5% per year, and its foreign trade has grown more than 16% per year. China's rank in world trade has risen steadily from 32nd in 1978, accounting for $20.64 billion, to 11th in 1993, accounting for $195.71 billion (Child & Lu, 1996), and it is currently ranked 10th ("Officials Outline Policies," 1998). When Zhu Rongji, China's premier, addressed the opening ceremony of the China Summit in 1996, he announced that during the next 15 years, China's economy will sustain its rapid growth, with an annual gross domestic product increase of 8% or 9%. He said that the world needs China and China needs the world (Wang, 1996). Various signs show that as we approach the next millennium, China is emerging as one of the most dynamic elements in world trade and international business (Child & Lu, 1996; Lardy, 1994).

China is currently the world's third largest economy in terms of purchasing power parity, after only the United States and Japan. The World Bank predicts that if China maintains its growing momentum, it will become the largest economy in the world in the Year 2020. In *Megatrends Asia*, the world's leading trend forecaster John Naisbitt (1996) holds that the notion of China's becoming the new world superpresence is not a question of "if" but "when." Naisbitt forecasts that the Chinese are on their way to catching up with the Japanese to drive much of the world economy in the years ahead:

> For some years it was the Japanese. The Japanese are coming. It appeared they were going to dominate the world economically. But now a remarkable transformation is taking place. The Chinese are coming. Asia and much of the world today is shifting from Japanese-dominated to Chinese-driven. (p. 17)

Why This Book?

The "Invisible Great Wall"

Although the Great Wall is no longer the physical symbol of resistance to foreign penetrations into the Middle Kingdom that it was previously, the Invisible Great Wall—that is, the gulf between the cultures of the East and West—remains. The People's Republic of China (PRC) differs from most other markets because it has the world's largest population, largest Communist bureaucracy, and oldest civilization. The Chinese market is still perceived as socioculturally so complex as to resist many Western efforts to penetrate it; also, the Chinese remain mysterious and, in many respects, confusing to Westerners. Numerous publications have reported that trading with the Chinese is difficult, negotiating with China is not easy, China is a demanding place in which to operate, and Western firms face a host of problems in the PRC (Blackman, 1997; Frankenstein, 1986; Mac-Dougall, 1980; Mann, 1989; Pye, 1982; Stone, 1992; Tung, 1982a, 1982b, 1989). The problems have been sharpened by the fact that, until recently, there has existed little China business research in the West, probably because the Middle Kingdom has been closed for a long time and there seems to have been little need to make a point of studying the Chinese market.

Embarking on their China ventures, Western business people often feel uncertain about Chinese business culture and negotiating style. They are often sent to China on the spur of the moment; China-oriented human resource training in many Western firms does not seem to keep pace with the explosive growth of China operations, and those who want to build up knowledge about China often find that there is a woeful dearth of solid information. A Swedish expatriate manager who was to move to China with his family remarked (as quoted in Granström, 1996, p. 6), "What I lacked was information about the culture, customs, negotiation technique, and the like, which is particular to the country one was going to move to." In doing business with the Chinese—a people whose "Yes" or "No" may not have the same meaning of a Western "Yes" or "No," whose mandate is nowhere but in the hands of the unseen officials beyond the negotiation table, and whose negotiating strategy is as elusive as "playing Tai Chi"—many Western business people end up feeling desperate and feeling pessimistic about their future commercial bonds with China; some would even go so far as to avoid dealing with the Chinese at all.

Business negotiation is a key dynamism of all business relationships. Inquiry into Chinese business negotiating style will encapsulate much of the truth about the Chinese style of doing business in

Sino-Western business relationships. Rosalie Tung (1982b) finds that the differences between the Chinese and American negotiating styles are among the most important factors responsible for the failure of business with China. Her follow-up study (1989) suggests that despite the increased contacts between American and Chinese negotiators between 1979 and 1987, marked differences in the Chinese and American negotiating styles persist and are believed to be "culture based." A study by Hakam and Chan (1990) of joint venture negotiations between the Singapore Chinese and the Mainland Chinese implies that mere cultural and linguistic affinities are no guarantee for the success of business negotiations with China; understanding the PRC's special needs and wants is equally important. In short, doing business and negotiating with China is both an economic transaction and a cultural activity.

The Chinese Negotiator: A Mixed Personality

During the past 7 years, I have had opportunities to listen to numerous real-life stories related by Western managers about Chinese business negotiating style, and a picture of bewildering complexity and uncertainty emerges: Negotiating with China can be both slow and quick, the Chinese can be both friendly and hostile, and Confucian ethics can be meticulously observed by a Chinese at one moment but openly violated by the same person at the other. Chinese negotiators are depicted as persons one both loves and hates to negotiate with. This high degree of complexity and uncertainty perplexes many Western business people, who keep asking "Why?"

Unfortunately, the existing scholarship has shown its failure to come to grips with the complexity and uncertainty of Chinese business negotiating style. Although existing studies, particularly Lucian W. Pye's *Chinese Commercial Negotiating Style* (1982), have generated many useful insights into our understanding of the subject, they have suffered from a number of drawbacks that prevent them from capturing the full richness of the Chinese business mind. For example, systems thinking is conspicuously lacking in the area of Chinese business negotiating style, Chinese negotiating tactics are left without cultural explanation, and there is a lack of Chinese voice in the literature. The area is in need of a coherent model that allows us to analyze systematically the complexity of Chinese business negotiating style and guides us to negotiate effectively with the Chinese. A close scrutiny of the existing literature will be presented in Chapter 2.

As a Chinese negotiator with many years of life and working experience in China, I recognized, and was myself very much a part of, the perplexing picture of Chinese negotiators; now a management researcher, I have been motivated by the "state of the art" of both business reality and scholarship to produce a work to undo the tangles confusing the minds of many Western business people. I intend to tell those who "love" to deal with the Chinese that a mere rosy picture of China and the Chinese is incomplete; China is so large that anything, both good and bad, can happen. More important, the Chinese, socio-culturally, are a blend of mixed personalities. Therefore, if something goes amiss in China, do not feel strange and never lose your confidence. I also show to those who "hate" to deal with them that the Chinese, despite their often-alleged "immoral" behaviors at the negotiation table, are nonetheless extremely moral-oriented creatures. The Chinese moral norms, deeply embedded in Chinese culture, are different from those of Westerners, and there are reasons for their "immoral" behaviors. Chinese culture is so encompassing that one should never miss the chance to experience and acknowledge that there exists genuine feeling in the Chinese mind so that even if one is placed in the darkest "Mayday" situation, one still does not allow the light of hope to be quenched.

Sociocultural Explanation

Culture defines people's behavior. Cultural explanation of management behavior has been increasingly favored in recent decades, especially since the 1980s (Adler, 1991; Adler & Bartholomew, 1991; Faure & Sjöstedt, 1993; Franke, Hofstede, & Bond, 1991; Fukuyama, 1995; Hofstede, 1980, 1991; Hofstede & Bond, 1988; Kahn, 1979; Mohamad & Ishihara, 1995; Naisbitt, 1996; Pye, 1985; Triandis, 1994; Trompenaars, 1994; Weinshall, 1977, 1993). An extensive survey of 28,707 articles appearing in 73 academic and professional management journals during the period of October 1985 to September 1990 shows that 70.6% of all international organizational behavior and human resource management articles included the concept of culture; of the articles including culture, almost all (93.8%) concluded that culture made a difference to the issue studied (Adler & Bartholomew, 1991, p. 558): "The overwhelming consensus, both inside and outside North America as well as in both the academic and professional communities, is that culture is important and does make a difference."

Another work (Huntington, 1996) argues that the world is moving into a period of "civilizational clash" in which the most important distinctions among people will not be ideological, political, or economic, as during the Cold War, but cultural. Although scholars differ in their definitions of "culture," "social system," and "society," the totality of their works suggests that a nation's sociocultural system provides an appealing explanation of its people's behavior. I shall discuss two broad approaches to the study of culture, that is, "etic" and "emic," under Methodology in this Introduction, and I shall also discuss culture and behavior in Chapter 2.

About This Book

The purpose of this book is to provide an in-depth and systematic understanding of Chinese business negotiating style in a Chinese sociocultural context. Three steps are taken to attain this purpose: (a) a review of existing literature in the area of Chinese business negotiating style, (b) the collection of empirical evidence in contemporary Sweden-China business negotiation practices, and (c) a proposal of a model to understand Chinese business negotiating style. Despite the growing importance of China in international business, insufficient research has been carried out on Chinese business negotiating style. A marked indication is that there has been no comprehensive survey of existing literature on the subject in international publications. To sow the seeds of new ideas, we must be aware of the climate and the state of the soil. Therefore, this book presents a state-of-the-art review of Chinese business negotiating style, summarizing the strengths and weaknesses of the existing contributions. In this book, I have collected empirical material by way of unstructured interviews with both Swedish and Chinese managers and officials involved in real-life Sweden-China business negotiation practices, with foreign technology transfer to China as a general background. I aim to construct, by way of inductive and deductive reasoning, a systematic model of Chinese business negotiating style to create a holistic picture of what is weighing on the mind of Chinese negotiators.

Given its purpose, the book is intended to answer three research questions: (a) What are the primary patterns of Chinese business negotiating behaviors?[1] (b) What are the fundamental Chinese sociocultural traits underlying Chinese business negotiating style? and (c) Why do the Chinese negotiate in different ways or how can Chinese negotiating style be understood in a Chinese sociocultural context? These questions are the key to understanding Chinese business negotiating style. I intend to seek insights into Chinese business negotiating style by tackling these questions one by one.

The scope of the book is limited based on a number of considerations. First, Chinese business negotiating style is examined at the national culture level. Culture possesses a number of levels, such as national, regional, organizational, gender, social class, and generation (Hofstede, 1991). Other levels of culture may be discussed only to the point that would help achieve the purpose of the book. Second, Chinese business negotiating style is explored within the general background of foreign technology transfer to China, with the Chinese party being the buyer and recipient of foreign technologies. The empirical materials are collected from Sweden-China business negotiation practices. Third, in this book, negotiation is viewed as part of the industrial marketing and purchasing process. It involves activities ranging from the initial contacts of partners to signing the final business contract. In this sense, Chinese business negotiating style can be broadly viewed as the Chinese way of doing business both at and beyond negotiation tables. Management problems in the implementation phase of executing a contract, though discussed occasionally, are not a major issue within the scope of this book. Finally, while keeping in mind that Hong Kong, since July 1, 1997, is part of the People's Republic of China, I use the term *Chinese* to refer to the Chinese of mainland China, where the socialist system governs.

This book distinguishes itself from most other works on doing business with China in general and Chinese business negotiating style in particular in the following respects:

- It constructs coherent systematic frameworks about Chinese business culture and Chinese business negotiating style.
- It penetrates into traditional Chinese culture to explain the uniqueness of Chinese negotiating tactics.
- It targets Chinese as well as Western business negotiators as informants.
- It collects empirical materials from Sweden-China business negotiations and provides many real-life empirical illustrations.
- It is written by a person who once was a Chinese business negotiator in his own right and has had life, educational, and working experience in both China and the West.

Conceptualization of Chinese Business Negotiating Style

Although the term *Chinese negotiating style* has frequently been used in the literature (Adler, 1991; Frankenstein, 1986; Kirkbride & Tang, 1990; Pye, 1982), it is a concept that has yet to be defined. I do not distinguish between the terms *style* and *behavior* in this book. A behavior can be viewed as any form of human action (Adler, 1991). Negotiating style can be broken down into four different types— interpersonal style, intergroup style, domestic style, and international style.[2] *Interpersonal style* occurs at the individual level; it involves the individual negotiators' communication style, use of influence strategies, cognitive or information processing style, role playing, and so on. *Intergroup style*, which may also be called organizational negotiating style, refers to the way groups or teams negotiate; it includes the mechanisms by which the need to negotiate arises, how the negotiating team is organized, how information is processed, how decisions are made, how rituals and ceremonies are arranged, and so on. *Domestic style* refers to the situation in which negotiation takes place between people from the same country. *International style* shows how people with different national cultural backgrounds negotiate with each other. This book examines how national sociocultural traits influence Chinese business negotiating style in international business negotiations. I have adopted the following formulation as the working definition of Chinese business negotiating style: Chinese business negotiating style is the way in which Chinese negotiators, both as individuals and as a group, behave and interact with foreign negotiating counterparts in Sino-foreign business negotiation processes.

Chinese style or behaviors can be further divided into "nontactical behaviors" and "tactical behaviors." The term *Chinese business negotiating tactics* refers to the tactical behaviors of Chinese negotiators displayed in Sino-foreign business negotiations. In this vein, Chinese business negotiating tactics is part of the term *Chinese business negotiating style*. I discuss the concepts of culture, sociocultural system, negotiation, and so on in Chapter 2.

Methodology

An Emic Approach

There are two basic approaches to the study of cultures: emic and etic (Berry, 1980; Brislin, 1983, 1993; Brislin, Lonner, & Thorndike, 1973; Gudykunst & Ting-Tommey, 1996; Triandis, 1994). The emic-etic distinction is borrowed by cross-cultural studies from psycholinguist Kenneth Pike's (1967) *Language in Relation to a Unified Theory of the Structure of Human Behavior.* In linguistics, the term *phonemics* refers to sounds that occur only in one language, whereas *phonetics* are sounds that can be heard in all languages. Pike therefore coined the terms *emic* and *etic* to refer to culture-specific and culture-general elements, respectively. In cross-cultural studies, the etic approach uses culture-general variables or dimensions of cultural variability, such as individualism versus collectivism (Hofstede, 1980, 1991; Triandis, 1988, 1995) and high- versus low-context communication (Hall, 1976/1981) to examine behavior patterns in one culture and compare them across cultures, whereas the emic approach employs culture-specific variables or idiosyncratic components of a specific culture to explain the behaviors in that culture. Both approaches are useful tools for understanding culture and human behavior:

Etics are used mostly by psychologists to develop "theories" or "scientific" generalizations in a quantitative manner, whereas emics are adopted mostly by anthropologists to achieve in-depth understanding of cultures in a qualitative fashion. Harry Triandis (1994, p. 68) holds that "if we are going to understand a culture, we must use emics." I am convinced that, regarding a sociocultural understanding of Chinese business negotiating style, the emic approach is particularly valuable, given the complexity of Chinese culture and the excessive focus on the etic approach in our current scholarships of cross-cultural management (Hofstede, 1980, 1991) and international business negotiations (Moran & Stripp, 1991).

In this book, I use an emic approach to analyze Chinese business negotiating style. In other words, I am committed to penetrating the idiosyncratic nature of China's sociocultural traits to seek explanations of Chinese business negotiating behaviors rather than using the established etic "dimensions" to frame these behaviors. My emic commitment reflects my discontent with the current scholarship in cross-cultural business studies: There has been too much etic talk since Geert Hofstede published *Culture's Consequences* in 1980; in-depth culture-specific writings are amazingly few. The etic bias should be complemented by more emic studies if our scholarship is to be developed along healthy lines. In this book, I aim to clarify what characterizes Chinese business negotiating style and, more important, why the Chinese negotiate in different ways through a close-up scrutiny of a number of indigenous Chinese concepts in the Chinese sociocultural system. The metaphor "A Middle Kingdom Perspective" could be used to describe the approach of this book.

Qualitative Method

My ultimate interest in the "whys" of Chinese business negotiating style allows me to use a qualitative case study method (Merriam, 1988; Yin, 1994) in my research. Qualitative reasoning is a powerful methodology in understanding culture and behavior: It is a "natural inquiry" (Patton, 1990) that is nonmanipulative, unobtrusive, noncontrolling, and open to whatever emerges; it studies "real-world" situations as they unfold naturally. Current research on culture and business negotiating style is dominated by the North American style of extensive use of simulation experiments, showing great interest in all sorts of figures (Adler, Brahm, & Graham, 1992; Francis, 1991; Graham, 1985a, 1985b, 1986; Graham, Kim, Lin, & Robinson, 1988; Graham, Mintu, & Rodgers, 1994; Tse, Francis, & Walls, 1994). Simulation, a quantitative research method, is valuable for generating knowledge about culture and negotiating style, especially in its capacity to control and manipulate the experimental environment to observe verbal and nonverbal behaviors of the "experimental negotiators." Simulation, however, is still simulation; it is "classroom game playing" rather than a serious investigation of real negotiation events. I believe a real-life portrayal of Chinese negotiating behaviors, though difficult to obtain, is far more exciting and valuable than playing simulation games in a classroom. In this book, I use direct citations of real negotiators, both Chinese and Western, to grasp their real-life experience, perspectives, and perceptions of Chinese business negotiating style. Forty "case-oriented" illustrations are provided in this book. These illustrations—long or short and process-related or situation-focused—present real-life episodes, events, phenomena, and conceptions in Sino-Western business negotiations, helping us understand Chinese business negotiating style holistically.

Another reason for my choice of the qualitative method is that my Chinese business culture framework contains many new constructs that need to be defined and discussed in a qualitative manner before they are to be exposed to any quantitative testing. For example, the concept of "Chinese stratagems"—a strategic component of Chinese culture and deeply rooted in the field of Chinese philosophy and folklore—is given little attention by scholars of Chinese business negotiating style. Much qualitative work needs to be done to introduce the concept to the field before it can be quantified meaningfully by way of, for example, survey and simulation.

Methodological Barriers

Chinese business negotiating style research is not a job for a Chinese-culture outsider; nor is it a destination for a halfhearted wanderer. As far as I am concerned, researchers face four methodological barriers: (a) lack of access to reality, (b) the "No tape recorder!" syndrome, (c) the sensitivity of the subject, and (d) the language barrier.

A word of explanation of these barriers is necessary to help us understand why existing scholarship has developed as it has. A value-adding work on Chinese business negotiating style must overpower these methodological challenges.

Lack of access to reality is the greatest challenge. According to Chinese regulations, foreign journalists are currently not allowed to interview Chinese citizens without permission from the foreign ministry or local government authorities; foreign researchers do not enjoy better treatment.[3] China's *neibu guiding* ("internal regulations") and *waishi jilü* ("disciplines concerning foreign affairs") often prevent Chinese interviewees from meeting foreign researchers in one-to-one settings. As a result, foreign researchers may find it difficult to know what is actually weighing on the mind of a Chinese interviewee when he is "forced" to converse in group settings. People with working experience in Chinese organizations know what *waishi wu xiaoshi* ("no foreign affairs are trivial") means. Fearing that they would make mistakes or lose face for China in front of foreigners, and consequently be criticized and punished internally, Chinese interviewees generally behave very cautiously and leave a great deal of leeway when talking face-to-face to a foreign investigator with whom they are not familiar. On the Western side, business deals with China often turn out to be so critical that some Western business people choose to keep quiet about troubles with their Chinese partners for fear of a negative effect on their China operations.

The "No tape recorder!" syndrome is common in the PRC and causes extra headaches even when circumstances happen to allow one to interview a Chinese in a one-to-one setting. "No tape recorder!" is requested almost 100% of the time by Chinese interviewees in the PRC. Political pressures (e.g., *neibu guiding*, old wounds from the Cultural Revolution) and cultural factors (e.g., Chinese distrust of strangers) make tape-recording of in-depth interviews with the Chinese very difficult, if not totally impossible (e.g., when there exists a high level of mutual trust). Although China is moving toward becoming a more open society, "a culture of fear," as Yang (1994) termed, is still part of the Chinese reality.

The sensitivity of the topic of Chinese business negotiating style poses another challenge. Due to the confidential nature of business negotiation per se (e.g., the existence of confidential clauses that do not permit the negotiating parties to disclose to any third party certain core information regarding the contract), particularly of Chinese business negotiations often involving transferring advanced foreign technology to China, both Chinese and foreign managers are understandably careful when talking to an "outsider." It is not uncommon within the context of China business studies that a researcher is regarded as a "spy" for either the Western or the Chinese side. Therefore, it seems necessary for a researcher to be prepared to explain to those "smart" people that he is not an "industrial spy" but an ambitious investigator who harbors no interest in "spying" for non-academic purposes.

Last, language complicates all the aforementioned problems. Chinese managers and officials, very often the senior and experienced ones, generally do not speak foreign languages. Although some of them are able to read technical documents in a foreign language (Russian, English, Japanese, German, etc.) with the help of a dictionary, their spoken ability in foreign languages is generally poor. If a researcher does not speak Chinese, interviews have to be conducted by involving a third person (the interpreter). This arrangement may negatively affect the data collection quality due to the reasons discussed previously. Moreover, Chinese culture is a high-context culture (Hall, 1976/1981) in which true meanings are often conveyed and perceived in implicit manners rather than in explicit and coded messages. To make matters worse, the Chinese do not communicate as deeply, openly, and sincerely with strangers as with family members because of their in-group orientation. Communication scholars Gao, Ting-Toomey, and Gudykunst (1996, p. 288) observe that "Chinese tend to become highly involved in conversation with someone they know, but they rarely speak to strangers." This suggests that the type of relationship between the researcher and the Chinese interviewees is also an important dimension in performing China business research in general. The high-context nature of Chinese communication also constitutes an obstacle to gaining access to the Chinese reality.

All these methodological barriers indicate that conducting Chinese business negotiating style research is far more involved than simply looking into a telephone directory to find interviewees' details, phoning them to make appointments, carrying an interview guide and tape recorder and stepping into the interviewee's office just in time, and heading back home to prepare reports—not to mention sending one-off questionnaires and waiting to calculate responding points in peace and quiet. Given the special PRC condition, I doubt the viability of these Western research procedures in approaching Chinese reality: They are destined to go amiss in China. A robust work on Chinese business negotiating style demands high quality on the part of researchers per se in terms of commitment, personality, Chinese language ability, cultural sensibility, and willingness to work hard. My experience shows that legitimate acceptance by negotiating parties is important so that issues can be discussed as openly, directly, and deeply as possible. High-level Chinese contacts, recommendations from influential Chinese organizations, and local networks will help obtain much access to the Chinese reality.

Sweden-China Empirical Context

Empirically, I chose to focus my analytical lens on the Sweden-China business negotiation context. The choice of Sweden is not merely a matter of my geographical access to this part of the world but also reflects my critical view toward the area of Chinese business negotiating style: It is based too much on U.S.-China business negotiation literature; empirical cases from outside the U.S.-China contexts need to be gathered to generate an energetic scholarship. Sweden is both a small and large country: It is small in terms of population but large by way of industry. Though a country with a mere 8.8 million inhabitants constituting less than 0.17% of the world population, Sweden ranks among the 12 largest trading nations in the world, contributing more than 1.5% of the world's total export; Swedish exports amount to 30% of the GNP, making Sweden 17th among the most export-dependent countries (Selmer, 1997). Sweden is also the home country for a number of world-class multinational corporations, such as Ericsson, ABB, Volvo, Saab, Electrolux, Atlas-Copco, Sandvik, Tetra Pak, Alfa-Laval, SKF, and IKEA. Statistics from the Swedish Trade Council indicate that Sweden-China trade increased by 30% during the first half of 1995—the largest increase among the countries within the European Community. Between 1979 and 1996, Swedish exports to China increased from SEK 0.4 to SEK 9.3 billion. Today, more than 100 Swedish companies, with Ericsson taking the lead, are operating in the Chinese market. So many Swedish-speaking Scandinavian expatriates and their families are now working and living in China that even a Swedish School (Swedish School of Beijing) was opened in Beijing in 1993.

The interviews on which this book is based were conducted in mainland China, Hong Kong, and Sweden during 1995 and 1996. My ambition was to collect the most salient features of Chinese business negotiating style from various business negotiation practices, such as those concerning joint ventures, licensing agreements, and sales contracts, by interviewing experienced negotiators, both Swedish and Chinese. The empirical objects (companies and interviewees) were selected purposely. The Swedish companies represent those very active Swedish export companies that, in various forms, are selling industrial goods or undertaking technology transfer or both to China in a number of industries, with telecommunications weighing heaviest. The Chinese organizations involved in this book are the Swedish companies' Chinese negotiating partners (e.g., local and national industrial corporations and the relevant Chinese government agencies).

My database consists of interviews with 71 persons, 56 "Swedish negotiators"[4] and 15 "Chinese negotiators," from more than 10 organizations. All the Swedish negotiators had been actively working with China for more than 3 years and had extensive experience in negotiating with the Chinese. Some had been working and living in China for more than 10 years. Most of the Chinese negotiators had been face-to-face negotiating opponents of the Swedish negotiators, whereas a few others were involved in large projects related to the Swedish companies' negotiations in China.

When interviewing the Swedish negotiators, I asked them to recall negotiation "events," "situations," and so on that they had experienced in negotiating with the Chinese or to give their personal comments on Chinese negotiating style based on their own negotiation experience with the Chinese. When I interviewed the Chinese negotiators, I paid attention not only to what was being said but also to what the Chinese interviewee really meant in the Chinese language. Instead of abruptly raising questions such as "What are your strategies in negotiating with the foreign companies?," I did the opposite. I always began by talking with the Chinese about "Swedish business negotiating style." As the conversation deepened, I found that much of the conversation concerned the Chinese business negotiating style as well.

A tape recorder was used in all my interviews with the native Swedish negotiators. Although the tape recorder could not be used in my interviews with most of the Chinese interviewees, I was allowed to tape-record some important interviews with several open-minded Chinese negotiators who trusted me and valued my project. I made quick notes during the interviews and recalled and completed them immediately after the interviews. The length of the interviews varied from 35 minutes to 3 hours, with the majority approximately 1 hour. Some key persons (e.g., chief negotiators) were interviewed more than once.[5] I used Swedish when interviewing the native Swedish negotiators[6] and Chinese when talking to the Chinese negotiators and those who spoke Chinese as a mother tongue.

The empirical data have been processed based on two criteria (Whetten, 1989): comprehensiveness (i.e., are all relevant factors included?) and parsimony (i.e., should some factors be deleted because they add little additional value to our understanding?). All 71 interviews were carefully listened to, noted, or both based on these criteria. They were also compared with each other so that the typical situations representing the most important features of the whole set of the empirical materials could be singled out. The scanning and filtering process led to a further concentration on 16 interviews, that is, my interviews with 16 persons[7]—6 Chinese negotiators and 10 Swedish negotiators. These 16 interviews were regarded as best representing the whole set of interview materials. They were transcribed into written form by me for those conducted in Chinese and by a secretary at my university for those conducted in Swedish.[8]

Then, I clipped a total of 40 citations out of these 16 transcribed interviews, translated them from both Chinese and Swedish into English, and presented them in the form of 40 "illustrations," as shown in Chapter 4. This 40-illustration arrangement is simply accidental. It appears as it is, even though the number 40 is not a favored number in Chinese culture. My choice was basically influenced by the ability of these 40 citations to illustrate, both comprehensively and parsimoniously, the most salient features and perspectives contained in the 71 interviews.

Each of the 40 illustrations is analyzed by referring to the framework of Chinese business culture proposed in Chapter 3. In other words, the Chinese negotiating behaviors and tactics are explained with reference to the three indigenous Chinese concepts: *Guoqing* ("the PRC condition"), *Rujia* ("Confucianism"), and *Ji* ("Chinese stratagems"). As a whole, these 40 illustrations reflect the central message that I intend to send to readers throughout the book: The Chinese negotiator is a blend of "Maoist bureaucrat," "Confucian gentleman," and "Sun Tzu-like strategist"; it is this "three-in-one" personality that constitutes the core of Chinese business negotiating style.

Structure of the Book

The book is divided into five chapters. This chapter introduced the general background within which this book is written and discussed the methodology of the research on which it is based. The purpose, research questions, scope, and main features of the book have been presented, and methodological approaches, challenges, and procedures were discussed.

Chapter 2 forms the theoretical foundation of the book. First, culture theory and negotiation theory are discussed. Next, a state-of-the-art review of Chinese business negotiating style is presented. Finally, using the existing literature as a point of departure, a framework of Chinese business culture—the PRC's sociocultural traits underlying Chinese business negotiating style—is proposed.

In Chapter 3, I discuss in great detail the framework of Chinese business culture proposed in Chapter 2. Three fundamental forces driving Chinese negotiating style, that is, the PRC condition, Confucianism, and Chinese stratagems, are identified, reasoned, and discussed. The framework provides a useful tool with which to understand, explain, and predict the idiosyncratic nature of Chinese negotiating behaviors, including Chinese negotiating tactics, in a Chinese sociocultural context.

Chapter 4 provides 40 empirical illustrations and analyses thereof. To facilitate the reading, each illustration is immediately followed by an analysis with reference to the Chinese business culture framework discussed in Chapter 3. Throughout Chapter 4, there is a basic assumption that to obtain a comprehensive understanding of Chinese business negotiating style we should try to seek explanations

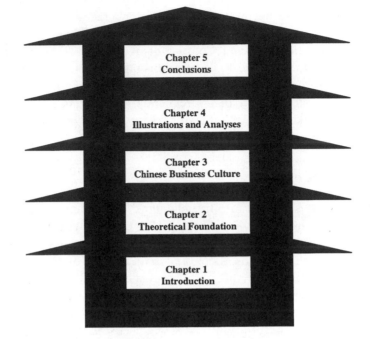

Figure 1.1. Structure of the Book

from a combination of the PRC condition, Confucianism, and Chinese stratagems perspectives.

   Chapter 5 concludes the book by presenting the theoretical and empirical findings as well as the managerial implications. Limitations of the book and suggestions for future research are also discussed in this chapter.

   As shown in Figure 1.1, these five chapters are linked together to broaden our vision of Chinese business negotiating style step by step, reminiscent of an artistic conception conveyed in a famous Tang Dynasty (618-906) Chinese poem "Climb the Stork Tower" by Wang Zhihuan (688-742):

> The sun beyond the mountains glows;
> The Yellow River seawards flows.
> If you want to enjoy a thousand-mile sight,
> Climb one more step in height.

▒ Notes

1. In this book, the terms *Chinese business negotiating style* and *Chinese business negotiating behavior(s)* are used interchangeably. For variation and simplicity, phrases such as "Chinese commercial negotiating style," "Chinese negotiating style," "Chinese behavior(s)," and "Chinese style" are also used.

2. I thank Professor Robert March for his constructive ideas about how to conceptualize "negotiating style." My conceptualization of Chinese negotiating style is inspired by March (1988) and his critique of an earlier version of this book.

3. See, for example, Yang (1994) and Leijonhufvud and Engqvist (1996) to gain insight into how adventurous it is to produce journalist and academic writings on China.

4. Included among these are a few local Chinese who are working or who had worked as senior business managers in the Swedish companies' local market organizations in China and Hong Kong.

5. In this book, interviews with one and the same person are counted statistically as one interview.

6. Swedish was used except for a few cases in which English was used. The advantage of using English as the interview language when conducting interviews with Swedish interviewees was recognized during the research. The Swedish interviewees are all able to speak English. English also remained the working and contracting language during the business negotiations investigated. The Swedish managers could therefore directly cite what the Chinese negotiators said to them in English (either directly or via an interpreter). In this way, the accuracy of translation is believed to be improved.

7. The total includes one interview in which three Chinese negotiators were actually involved. They are counted as one "Chinese negotiator" in this book.

8. One interview was done in English, and I did the transcription.

2 Theoretical Foundation

Culture Theory

What Is Culture?

Culture can be viewed as consisting of everything that is human made (Herskovits, 1955); everything that people have, think, and do as members of their society (Ferraro, 1990); communication (Hall, 1959, 1976/1981; Hall & Hall, 1989); a system of shared meanings (Geertz, 1973); the way of life of a group of people (Barnouw, 1979); collective programming of the mind (Hofstede, 1980, 1991); inherited ethical habit (Fukuyama, 1995); a "tool kit" of habits, skills, and styles from which people construct "strategies of action" (Swidler, 1986); one being composed of both "objective culture," such as chairs, tools, and jet planes, and "subjective culture," such as categories, norms, roles, and values (Triandis, 1994); a set of understandings shared among persons who have been similarly socialized (Terpstra & David, 1991); or a system consisting of subsystems, such as kinship, educational, economic, political, religious, association, health, and recreational systems (Harris & Moran, 1996).

21

Edward B. Tylor (1871, p. 1), the "father" of cultural anthropology, defines culture as the "complex whole" in his *Primitive Culture*: "Culture or Civilization, taken in its wide ethnographic sense, is that complex whole which includes knowledge, belief, art, morals, law, custom, and any other capabilities and habits acquired by man as a member of society." Root (1987, p. 238), a specialist in international business strategy, defines culture as "a unique lifestyle" in his *Entry Strategies for International Markets*: "Culture may be defined as the unique lifestyle of a given human society: A distinctive way of thinking, perceiving, feeling, believing, and behaving that is passed on from one generation to another." Lee (1995, pp. 4-5), in *Spectrum of Chinese Culture*, describes culture as involving many "parts," ranging from political institutions to philosophy and life values: "Culture is an institution of life and is a pattern of activities developed from the basic problems of environment. Social organization, political institutions, economic activities, law, art, science, religion, philosophy and life values are all parts of a culture." Kroeber and Kluckhohn (1952) provide a widely cited definition of culture based on their comprehensive review of a large number of conceptualizations of culture:

> Culture consists of patterns, explicit and implicit, of and for behavior acquired and transmitted by symbols, constituting the distinctive achievement of human groups, including their embodiments in artifacts; the essential core of culture consists of traditional (i.e., historically derived and selected) ideas and especially their attached values; culture systems may, on the one hand, be considered as products of action, on the other as conditioning elements of future action. (p. 81)

Although there is no agreement on the definition of culture, anthropologists generally agree on three common characteristics (Hall, 1976/1981, p. 16): (a) Culture is not innate but learned; (b) the various facets of culture are interrelated—if you touch a culture in one place, everything else is affected; and (c) culture is shared and, in effect, defines the boundaries of different groups. What we learn most from the previous discussion of culture is that culture, most basically, is a system consisting of various interrelated components shared by a group of people. This book is grounded in an understanding of culture as a sociocultural system.

Sociocultural System

The concepts of culture, social system, society, and sociocultural system have been a subject of much debate (Keesing, 1974; Kroeber & Parsons, 1958; Rohner, 1984). Keesing (1974, p. 82) calls, with "considerable precedent," the "patterns-of-life-of-communities" *sociocultural systems*—systems of socially transmitted behavior patterns that serve to relate human communities to their ecological settings. A sociocultural system thus includes technologies and modes of economic organization, settlement patterns, modes of social grouping and political organization, religious beliefs and practices, and so on. As such, Keesing views sociocultural systems as a part of the culture category (so-called "adaptive" culture as opposed to "ideational" culture as Keesing further explains in his article). Rohner (1984, p. 127), however, contends that culture is "but one among several concepts needed for understanding behavior in sociocultural contexts. Other constructs include social system and society." Differing from Keesing's standpoint, Rohner views culture as part of a sociocultural system that involves culture, social system, and society. Dadfar (1984, 1990) provides an "archetype" of a nation's sociocultural system, which conceives of sociocultural system as being made up of "local" culture/ religion and "adopted culture."

In this book, culture is perceived as a system of transmitted and created content and patterns of values, norms, and customs rooted in a country's philosophies or religions or both, and shaping human behavior and the artifacts produced through behavior (see Kroeber & Parsons, 1958). The sociocultural system is viewed as the "complex whole" that involves the culture and characteristics of the country's social system (political institutions, economic systems, technology development, education, population, etc.). The terms *Chinese sociocultural system* and *Chinese business culture* mean the complex whole of the traditional Chinese cultural values prevailing in all Chinese societies the world over and the basic characteristics of the social system of the People's Republic of China (PRC).

Influence of Culture on Behavior

Culture defines people's behavior (Adler, 1991; Brislin, 1993; Triandis, 1994). Adler (1991, p. 16) describes the influence of culture on behavior in a cycle chart, from culture to culture: culture → value → attitude → behavior → culture. *Value* is something that is implicitly or explicitly desirable to individuals or groups and influences their selection from available modes, means, and ends of action. Values can be both consciously and unconsciously held by people. *Attitude* is a construct that expresses values and disposes a person to act or react in a certain way toward something. *Behavior* is any form of human action. Individuals express culture through the values they hold about life and the world around them. These values in turn influence their attitudes about the form of behavior considered appropriate in given situations. Eventually, the continuously changing patterns of behavior influence the society's culture. Thus, the cycle begins again. Here, there is a more "ideational" (cognitive systems, such as values, norms, and attitudes) perspective of culture's influence on behavior, though an "adaptive" (ecological and patterns of life) perspective is also manifested in the running cycle (from behavior to culture).

Somewhat different from Adler's (1991) "value" explanation of behavior, Triandis (1994) argues that behavior is shaped by culture that, in turn, is shaped by ecology. Ecology refers to where people live; it consists of the objects, resources, and geography of the environment, and the ways one can make a living and survive. Therefore, the sequence of influence is ecology → culture → behavior. Here, there is an "adaptive" perspective of culture's influence on behavior. Similarly, Swidler (1986) argues that culture influences behavior (or "action" in Swidler's words) not by providing the ultimate values toward which a behavior is oriented but by shaping a "repertoire" or tool kit of habits, skills, and styles from which people construct "strategies of action." Here, the term *strategy* is broadly used by Swidler to refer to "a general way of organizing action . . . that might allow one to reach several different life goals" (p. 277). Swidler's tool kit explanation of strategies of action implies that when explaining the behavior of groups or societies, we should not only look for cultural values but also examine other distinctively cultural phenomena that may offer greater explanation power than values.

Therefore, whatever the perspectives, culture and behavior are closely linked to one another. Culture, whether in the form of "ultimate values" or a tool kit of habits, influences behavior.

Dimensions of Cultural Variability

Dimensions of cultural variability have been an extremely attractive topic in cross-cultural studies since Geert Hofstede published his monumental work *Culture's Consequences* in 1980. Searching for dimensions of cultural variability along which national cultures can be compared across borders belongs to the etic approach to the study of culture. To date, a number of culture dimensions have been isolated by theorists, such as Hofstede's (1980, 1991) power distance, uncertainty avoidance, individualism, masculinity, and Confucian dynamism; Hall's (1976/1981) high-context and low-context communication; Triandis's (1995) individualism versus collectivism; Trompenaars's (1994) relationships with people, universalism versus particularism, individualism versus collectivism, neutral versus emotional, specific versus diffuse, achievement versus ascription, attitudes toward time, and attitudes toward the environment; and Kluckholn and Strodtbeck's (1961) human nature orientation, man-nature (supernature) orientation, time orientation, activity orientation, and relational orientation.

These dimensions, with different focuses, all possess certain analytical power, especially high-context and low-context communication (Hall, 1976/1981), individualism versus collectivism (Hofstede, 1980, 1991; Triandis, 1995), and power distance (Hofstede, 1980, 1991). Therefore, it makes little sense to contend who is more authoritative or which number of dimensions is the correct one. The list of culture dimensions is bound not to be exhaustive. As Triandis (1982, p. 88) stated when reviewing Hofstede's (1980) first four dimensions: "My view is that the dimensions represent only a minimal aspect of the long list of dimensions that are needed. In my current thinking I use about 20 dimensions, including the ones presented by Hofstede."

Nevertheless, these dimensions all share a weakness inherently caused by the etic approach itself: failure to penetrate into a culture to discover the indigenous cultural values and norms that underpin people's behavior in that specific culture. This weakness can be overcome only by introducing an emic approach to the area of study because the emic approach, by definition, is able to sense the "sounds" that occur only in specific "languages." Therefore, in this book, I "ruthlessly" put aside many famous culture dimensions to enable me to turn to the emic approach for insights into Chinese business negotiating style. Despite my clear emic orientation in this book, I hold that the ultimate goal for culture theorists is to generate powerful theories that are able to combine both etic and emic approaches.

Chinese Culture

China is the world's "longest continuous civilization with the longest tradition of record-keeping and collection" (Ropp, 1990, p. x). Chinese people are proud of their culture, and a strong sense of cultural superiority is ingrained in the Chinese mind. The "xenophobic" Chinese view is evident even in the name "China," the character of which literally translates as the "Middle Kingdom," because the Chinese have always held themselves culturally in high esteem, viewing their culture and nation as lying in the center of human civilization.

"A Wonderful Way of Life"

Chinese culture has been molded by three philosophical traditions—Confucianism, Taoism, and Buddhism. Briefly, Confucianism deals with human relationship, Taoism deals with life in harmony with nature, and Buddhism deals with people's immortal world. For Chinese people, Confucianism, Taoism, and Buddhism are more philosophies than religions. Fung (1948/1966, p. 3) explains that "Chinese people have been less concerned with religion than other peoples are." He further elucidates that Confucianism is not a religion but a philosophy, whereas distinctions exist between Taoism and Buddhism as philosophies and religions. Lee (1995) clarifies that, for the Chinese, Confucianism, Taoism, and Buddhism are not religions but philosophical teachings. He calls this characteristic "a wonderful way of life" that makes the Chinese people "intensely practical":

This is a wonderful way of life which some Westerners cannot understand—how can a person follow the teachings of three teachers who have always been regarded by many Western and even Chinese writers as the founders of the three religions of China—Confucianism, Taoism, and Buddhism? The fact is they are not religions, and that is why the Chinese can follow all three teachings, each for one aspect of his life. This foundation of Chinese culture has made the Chinese intensely practical . . . and given them great power for absorbing all things that are good and beneficial, irrespective of their origin. Chinese culture has survived and has been enriched by this power. (p. 12)

Similarly, Hsu (1963) found that many Western observers of Chinese culture first imagined that the Chinese divided themselves into followers of Confucianism, Taoism, and Buddhism but then

were baffled by the fact that a Chinese easily might be all three and more at the same time while not caring too much about any of them. . . . The Western assumption of the desire on the part of believers for a religious schism which is common in Western culture . . . is absent in Chinese culture. (p. 67)

The Chinese have multiple moral standards in dealing with people, "behaving differently under contrasting sets of circumstances"; for them, "principles which are correct for one set of circumstances may not be appropriate for another at all, but the principles in each case are equally honorable" (p. 2). As will be discussed later in this book, this moral capacity of Chinese culture to follow different teachings and to behave differently in different circumstances is the key to understanding the complexity of Chinese business negotiating style.

The essence of traditional Chinese culture is considered to reside in the philosophical traditions of Confucianism and Taoism (Chan, 1963; de Bary, Chan, & Watson, 1960; Fung, 1948/1966; Kirkbride, Tang, & Westwood, 1991; Ren, 1986; Tang, 1991; Weber, 1919/1951), despite the great influence of Buddhism in Chinese society. Tang (1991, p. 62) states that "for Chinese culture, philosophy, art, and psychology the greatest influences have been Confucianism and Taoism." Fung (1948/1966, p. 19) calls Confucianism and Taoism "the two main trends of Chinese thought." Chinese scholars have used the phrase *"Ru Dao Zhi Zheng"* ("Contest between Confucianism and Taoism") to illustrate the most fundamental debates in Chinese culture.

Regarding Buddhism, which came to China from India in approximately the first century, Tang (1991, p. 70) writes, "Buddhism, acting like a catalyst, escalated the development of Taoism." In Chinese history, the propagation of Buddhism in China was greeted with protests by the bearers of the old Chinese cultural traditions. This defensive attitude acted as "a stimulus spurring the Chinese to strive even harder towards establishing an indigenous religion" (p. 71). It is generally held that Confucianism and Taoism have shaped Chinese culture insofar as human conduct in this "mortal world" is concerned, whereas Buddhism has provided the Chinese with a kind of "immortal food." The Buddhist doctrine of "reincarnation" has enabled many Chinese to endure hardship, suffering, and other vicissitudes in life and to look forward to a better life (Lee, 1995). The Chinese capacity to endure hardship and look to a better future, however, can also be well explained from the Yin Yang principle (see Yin Yang). Therefore, in this book, Chinese culture is viewed as being composed of two main trends of the Chinese thought: Confucianism and Taoism.

Confucianism

> If we were to characterize in one word the Chinese way of life for the last two thousand years, the word would be "Confucian."
>
> —de Bary et al. (1960, p. 17)

Confucianism (*Rujia* or *Rujiao* in Chinese) is a fundamental philosophical tradition that has shaped Chinese culture for 2,500 years.[1] Confucius (551-479 B.C.), a native of Qufu, Shandong province, is the founder of this philosophical doctrine. The core values or basic elements of Confucianism have been studied by scholars from various disciplines (Bond & Hwang, 1986; Child & Markoczy, 1993; Hofstede & Bond, 1988; Lockett, 1988, 1990; Shenkar & Ronen, 1987; Tan, 1990; Tu, 1984, 1990). Drawing on the existing studies, especially those on Confucian philosophy (Tu, 1984, 1990) and the influence of Chinese cultural tradition on Chinese management (Child & Markoczy, 1993;

Lockett, 1988, 1990; Tan, 1990), and relying on the authentic texts from the Confucian classics, *The Four Books*,[2] I identify the following six values of Confucianism for the study of Chinese business negotiating style: (a) moral cultivation, (b) importance of interpersonal relationships, (c) family orientation, (d) respect for age and hierarchy, (e) avoidance of conflict and need for harmony, and (f) concept of face. I discuss each of these values in great detail in Chapter 3.

Taoism

> Next to Confucianism the most important and influential native philosophy of the Chinese has undoubtedly been that of the Taoist school. No other doctrine of the ancient period except Confucianism has for so long maintained its vigor and attractiveness to the Chinese mind.
>
> —de Bary et al. (1960, p. 50)

The basic thinking of Taoism (*Daojia* or *Daojiao* in Chinese) can be found in Taoist classics, such as *Tao-Te-Ching* (or *Lao Tzu*), *I Ching* (or *Book of Changes*), and *Zhuang Tzu*. In particular, *Tao-Te Ching*, written by Lao Tzu before Confucius's *Analects*, is often called the only trend of Chinese thought that at least is comparable with Confucian philosophy. As Chan (1963) noted, Chinese civilization would have been utterly different if *Tao-Te Ching* had not been written, and no one could hope to understand the Chinese without a real appreciation of the profound philosophy taught in this work.

Taoism denotes simplicity, contentment, spontaneity, tranquillity, weakness, and, most important, Wu Wei. The key to understanding Taoism lies in understanding Taoist concepts: Tao, Yin Yang, and Wu Wei.

Tao. Tao literally translates as "Way." Lao Tzu, the founder of Taoism, defines Tao as follows (in Chan, 1963)[3]:

> There was something undifferentiated and yet complete,
> Which existed before heaven and earth.
> Soundless and formless, it depends on nothing and does not
>   change.

It operates everywhere and is free from danger.
It may be considered the mother of the universe.
I do not know its name; I call it Tao.

Lao Tzu continues (in Chan, p. 160):

Tao produced the One.
The One produced the two.
The two produced the three.
And the three produced the ten thousand things.
The ten thousand things carry the *yin* and embrace the *yang*,
    and through the blending of the material force (ch'i) they
    achieve harmony.

Therefore, Tao can be understood as the Ultimate One that shapes all in the universe. Tao is often described in its original Chinese meaning as Tai Chi—"the Great Ultimate" or "the great primal beginning" of all that exists. Tai Chi creates Yin and Yang.

Yin Yang. Probably the best known symbol of East Asia is that of the Chinese philosophical principle of dualism—Yin Yang—a circle equally divided by a curved line forming the black and white areas, as shown in Figure 2.1. Yin means female elements (the moon, water, weak, dark, soft, passive, etc.), and Yang means male elements (the sun, fire, strong, bright, hard, active, etc.). Yin and Yang represent qualities inherent in all things in the universe. Yin and Yang are both necessary and complementary if universal events are to be created, maintained, and developed in a harmonious way. As the two great regulating forces of cosmic order in the phenomenal world, Yin Yang becomes the cosmic symbol of primordial unity and harmony.

It is worth noting that Taoism highlights the power of Yin or weakness. Lao Tzu, the founder of Taoism, stated "Weakness is the function of Tao (in Chan, p. 160)." Cooper (1990) explains,

One of the outstanding teachings of Taoism is the strength of weakness. The *yin* power of passivity is more enduring than the *yang* force of direct action; the one has a controlled, sustained power, the other is quickly spent and dissipated. . . . This strength-in-weakness is also connected with the symbolism of the valley and

Figure 2.1. The Yin Yang Principle

the womb. It is that which receives and accepts all things, but from which, in turn, all things emerge. (p. 40)

Yin Yang exhibits two changing sides of the same phenomenon. In the appendices of *I Ching*, it is written (as quoted in Fung, 1948/1966, p. 19), "When the cold goes, the warmth comes, and when the warmth comes, the cold goes. . . . When the sun has reached its meridian, it declines, and when the moon has become full, it wanes."

Although Tao is absolute, unchanging, and pure, once it is manifested by way of the Yin Yang—the realm of duality—good can change to evil and vice versa. That is why Lao Tzu says "Reversion is the action of Tao" (Chan, p. 160). The reversion of Yin and Yang, love and hatred, good and bad, fortune and misfortune is well illustrated by the Chinese proverb, *Sai weng shi ma an zhi fei fu* ("The old man has lost his horse but who knows if this is a misfortune"). Behind the proverb is the following story about the "old man" and his "horse" (as quoted in Cooper, 1990):

The poor old man . . . lived with his son in a ruined fort at the top of a hill. He owned a horse which strayed off one day, whereupon the neighbours came to offer sympathy at his loss. "What makes you suppose that this is misfortune?" the old man asked. Later the horse returned accompanied by several wild horses and this time the neighbours came to congratulate him on his good luck. "What makes you think this is good luck?" he enquired. Having a number of horses now available, the son took to riding and, as a result, broke his leg. Once more the neighbours rallied round to express sympathy and once again the old man asked how they could know that this was misfortune. Then the next year war broke out and because he was lame the son was exempt from going to the war. (p. 39)

Fung (1948/1966) maintains that this "theory" of reversion has had a great effect on the character of the Chinese people and enabled them to overcome difficulties that they have encountered in their long history. The Chinese "remain cautious even in time of prosperity, and hopeful even in time of extreme danger. . . . It was this 'will to believe' that helped the Chinese people to go through the war" (p. 19).

Wu Wei. Wu Wei literally translates as "inaction," "nonaction," or simply "doing nothing." Just a superficial examination of the term, however, can miss the philosophical profoundness Wu Wei embraces. A true Taoist is not doing nothing but rather is dedicated to life with great passions. In *Tao-Te Ching,* one can find what I call the "Rule of Lao Tzu": Lao Tzu talks about doing nothing only in the first half of the sentences, not in the next half. For example, Lao Tzu (in Chan, p. 167) writes,

> I take no action and the people of themselves are transformed.
> I love tranquillity and the people of themselves become correct.
> I engage in no activity and the people of themselves become prosperous.
> I have no desires and the people of themselves become simple.

Therefore, I view Taoism essentially as a strategic teaching. Wu Wei may be better rendered as "actionless activity," "to act without acting," "noninterference," or "letting-go"; doing nothing virtually refers to "doing things strategically." We can further arrive at this strategic message of Taoism from Lao Tzu's words (in Chan, 1963):

The softest things in the world overcome the hardest things in
the world.
Non-being penetrates that in which there is no space.
Through this I know the advantage of taking no action. (p. 161)

Operate the army with surprise tactics. Administer the empire by
engaging in no activity. (p. 166)

The strategists say:
"I dare not take the offensive but I take the defensive;
I dare not advance an inch but I retreat a foot."
This means:
To march without formation,
To stretch one's arm without showing it,
To confront enemies without seeming to meet them,
To hold weapons without seeming to have them. (p. 172)

Explaining Wu Wei, Cooper (1990) quotes Lin Yutang as saying,

It is the secret of mastering circumstances without asserting oneself against them; it is the principle of yielding to an oncoming
force in such a way as it is unable to harm you. Thus the skilled
master of life never opposes things . . . he changes them by acceptance, by taking them into his confidence, never by flat denial . . .
he accepts everything until, by including all things, he becomes
their master. (p. 80)

Therefore, Wu Wei nurtures a calmness of mind that empowers
one to swallow all the confronting forces and then become their master
in the end. It offers what Lin (1939, p. 54) describes as "certain defense
tactics which can be more terrible than any tactics of aggression." Wu
Wei and Yin Yang principles form the philosophical platform on which
the concept of "Chinese stratagems" is based (see Chapter 3).

To summarize the quintessence of Taoism, I cite Lin Yutang's
(1996, p. 108) poem:

There is the wisdom of the foolish,
The gracefulness of the slow,
The subtlety of stupidity,
The advantage of lying low.

Confucianism Versus Taoism

Confucius is probably better known in the West than any other single Chinese or East Asian. Confucius, however, "was primarily a teacher, and certainly a great one, but far from being the only teacher" in Chinese history (Fung, 1948/1966, p. 47). The emergence of Confucianism can be understood as one of several responses to the decline and fall of a major civilization, *Zhou*, which developed and flourished for a number of centuries prior to the birth of Confucius (Tu, 1984). Other approaches include Taoism (*Daojia*), Moism (*Mojia*), and Legalism (*Fajia*).

Taoism is fully the equal of Confucianism in terms of doctrines on government, on cultivating and preserving life, and on handling things (Chan, 1963). Taoism is a severe critic of Confucianism on many grounds. The Taoists blamed the Confucianists for introducing hypocrisy or artificiality into life. For example, Lao Tzu (in Chan, 1963) writes,

> Only when Tao is lost does the doctrine of virtue arise.
> Only when virtue is lost does the doctrine of humanity arise.
> Only when humanity is lost does the doctrine of righteousness
>   arise.
> Only when righteousness is lost does the doctrine of propriety
>   arise.
> Now, propriety is a superficial expression of loyalty and
>   faithfulness, and the beginning of disorder. (p. 158)

The Confucian advocacy of such values as humanity, righteousness, filial piety, loyalty, and propriety (*li*) is therefore considered by Lao Tzu as either the result or the cause of a decline in the Tao. In modern Chinese history, "anti-Confucianism" campaigns were waged during the May Fourth Movement in 1919, the New Culture Movement in the early 1920s led by Chen Duxiu, Hu Shih, Lu Xun, and so on, and the Cultural Revolution (1966-1976). In his famous essay "Diary of a Madman," Lu Xun (1990) described a "madman" who believed that people wanted to kill and eat him. The madman tried to find the answer in a history book:

There were no dates in this history, but scrawled this way and that across every page were the words BENEVOLENCE, RIGHTEOUS-NESS, and MORALITY. Since I couldn't get to sleep anyway, I read that history very carefully for most of the night, and finally, I began to make out what was written between the lines; the whole volume was filled with a single phrase: EAT PEOPLE! (p. 32)

Taiwan-based Chinese writer Bo Yang (1992) also blames the "Ugly Chinaman Syndrome"—"crass," "arrogant," "noisy," "uncivilized," "uncooperative," "boastful," "dirty," and "unforgiving"—largely on the legacy of Confucianism.

Taoism and Confucianism, however, are generally regarded as the two complementary streams of Chinese thought crafting the two sides of the Chinese character, just like Yin and Yang. As Lin Yutang (1937/1996, p. 111) says, the Chinese "are all born half Taoists and half Confucianists." My view of Confucianism is a kind of "idealism" focusing on moral development, relationship, and social order, whereas Taoism is a sort of "practicalism" focusing on artistic conception, mystic element, and, above all, creativity of life.

To summarize my discussions of culture, it has been shown that culture is a system that consists of various interrelated components. The essence of traditional Chinese culture resides in the philosophical traditions of Confucianism and Taoism. The Chinese are "intensely practical" people who can follow different teachings at the same time. These understandings are vital to the modeling of the Chinese business culture framework later in this chapter.

Negotiation Theory

What Is Negotiation?

There is an abundant negotiation literature in the West. Negotiation, a basic human activity, has been approached by scholars from diverse disciplines, such as political science (Iké, 1964/1968), social psychology (Rubin & Brown, 1975), organization (Sheppard, Bazerman, & Lewicki, 1990), cross-cultural marketing (Ghauri & Usunier, 1996; Graham, 1985a; McCall & Warrington, 1984), and communications

(Firth, 1995). Although there is no agreed conceptualization of negotiation, Iké's (1964/1968) two elements of negotiation are widely cited:

> To begin with, two elements must normally be present for nego-
> tiation to take place: There must be both common interests and
> issues of conflict. Without common interests there is nothing to
> negotiate for, without conflicting issues nothing to negotiate about.
> (p. 2)

Therefore, negotiation may be understood as a process of two or more
parties combining their conflicting points of view into a single decision
of mutual interest (Zartman, 1978). Negotiation literature can be
classified into two broad theoretical perspectives: game theory and
social exchange theory.

Game Theory

Game theory aims at a deeper understanding of rational behavior
in real conflict situations and focuses on maximizing the party's
substantive outcomes in negotiations; it has the character of a mathe-
matical theory that deals with the problem of rational decision making
in interpersonal conflict situations in general (Raiffa, 1982; Siebe,
1991). Rationality and common knowledge are two prerequisites for
game theory to be applied in practice. Game theory views relationships
between negotiating parties as manipulative and competitive in nature, the so-called "zero-sum" or "win-lose" game: One party's gain is
the other's loss. Contemporary game theorists Barry Nalebuff and
Adam Brandenburger (1996) used game theory to link competition
with cooperation by coining the term *co-opetition*, which suggests that
the game can be manipulated to create a business relationship characterized by both competition and cooperation.

Social Exchange Theory

Social exchange theory views negotiation as a social exchange
process; it emphasizes the interactions of the negotiation parties that
influence each other in a problem-solving manner to reach a "win-win"
agreement (Angelmar & Sten, 1978; Bagozzi, 1978; Bonoma &

Johnston, 1978; Ghauri, 1983; Graham, 1986; McCall & Warrington, 1984). Here, relationships between negotiating parties are cooperative in nature. The parties try to maximize the benefits for everyone to succeed and maintain a positive relationship during the negotiation process. Game theory and social exchange theory lead to two generic negotiation strategies, respectively: competition and cooperation.

Negotiation Strategies

The term *negotiation strategy* is used in this book to refer to the means used by one party to influence the other party's perception and behavior in negotiations. Strategies therefore can be both tactically and non-tactically oriented. Two universal negotiation strategies— competition and cooperation—can be summarized from negotiation literature (Fisher & Ury, 1981; Graham, 1986; Hall, 1993; Pruitt, 1981, 1991; Pruitt & Rubin, 1986; Putnam, 1990; Usunier, 1996; Walton & McKersie, 1965).

Competition, also known as contending or distributive bargaining, is a strategy used by a negotiator to pursue his goals by persuading his opponent to concede. On the basis of game theory, competition strategy entails "efforts to maximize gains and minimize losses within a 'win-lose' or self gain orientation" (Putnam, 1990, p. 3). This win-lose approach highlights the negotiating tactics and tricks to be employed to overpower the other party and ensure victory. Fisher and Ury (1981) use the terms *tricky tactics, tricky bargaining,* and *dirty tricks* to refer to tactics, tricks, and ploys that a negotiator employs to take advantage of his counterparts. There are three types of dirty tricks: (a) deliberate deception (phony facts, ambiguous authority, and dubious intentions), (b) psychological warfare (stressful situations, personal attacks, the good-guy/bad-guy routine, and threats), and (c) positional pressure tactics (refusal to negotiate, extreme demands, escalating demands, lock-in tactics, a calculated delay, and "take it or leave it"). Tricky tactics are one-sided proposals about the negotiating game that the parties are going to play. The purpose of employing tricky tactics is "to help the user 'win' some substantive gain in an unprincipled contest of will" (Fisher & Ury, 1981, p. 134).

Cooperation, also referred to as problem solving, collaboration, or integrative bargaining, "aims to reconcile the interests of both parties, reach joint benefits, or attain 'win-win' goals" (Putnam, 1990, p. 3). The parties work together to find solutions that satisfy their common goals. The reason for the immense popularity of Fisher and Ury's (1981) *Getting to Yes* is its teaching on win-win, or the so-called "principled negotiation": (a) Separate the people from the problem; (b) focus on interests, not positions; (c) invent options for mutual gain; and (d) insist on objective criteria. According to Fisher and Ury, the principled negotiation employs no tricks and no posturing. It helps one obtain what one is entitled to and still be decent and enables one to be fair while protecting oneself against those who would take advantage of one's fairness. The problem-solving strategy is regarded as having a positive influence on both the seller's profit and the buyer's satisfaction (Graham, 1986).

A weakness in the current academic modeling of negotiation strategies is that it severs competition from cooperation and vice versa. For example, Fisher and Ury (1981) draw only a dark picture of competition or tricky bargaining: One party uses dirty tricks to become the "winner," leaving the other party as the "loser"; a "decent" negotiator must not employ tricks and "posturing." Thus, competition has somewhat negative connotations of being illegal, unethical, or unpleasant. My stance, however, is that competition forms an important part of our life; nations, industries, firms, social groups, and individuals all have to face, cope with, and can benefit from competition. Cooperation does not exist in a vacuum; rather, it interacts intimately with competition. Nalebuff and Brandenburger's (1996) *Co-opetition* suggests that business is both war and peace; tactics can also be used to create long-term prosperous business relationships characterized by both competition and cooperation. Jarillo and Ricart (1987) also find that the use of competition strategy such as the threat of breaking off the relationship would actually serve as the "main deterrent to non-cooperation."

In addition, the term *win-win* lacks definition and debate. Dawson (1995) raises a number of interesting questions related to win-win: What do we mean when we say win-win? Does it really mean that both sides win, or does it mean that both sides lose equally so that it is fair? What if each side thinks that they won and the other side lost—would that be win-win? I do not believe win-win is as simple as two parties sitting at the negotiation table and talking about cooperation from beginning to end. The win-lose competition and the related influence tactics have their parts to play in creating the ultimate win-win cooperation atmosphere in negotiations. I view win-win as a situation in which both parties perceive that the deal is beneficial to them.

Moreover, the existing notions of negotiation strategies are products of the etic approach; very few works tell us how patterns of competition and cooperation appear in specific cultures. My thesis is that there exists certain emic elements in every culture that contribute to the shaping of competitive and cooperative negotiation strategies of people in that culture. A deeper understanding of the workings of Chinese negotiation strategy requires us to go beyond conventional wisdom to examine what is unique with Chinese competition and cooperation strategies in Chinese culture.

Cross-Cultural and Marketing Approach to Business Negotiation

As international business becomes increasingly cross-cultural, the cross-cultural and marketing approach to international business negotiation has attracted increasing academic attention (Cohen, 1991; Fayerweather & Kapoor, 1976; Fisher, 1980; Graham 1985a, 1996; Graham & Herberger, 1983; Hendon, Hendon, & Herbig, 1996; Herbig & Kramer, 1992; Hofstede & Usunier, 1996; McCall & Warrington, 1984; Moran & Stripp, 1991; Salacuse, 1991; Tung, 1982a, 1982b; Usunier, 1996; van Zandt, 1970; Weiss, 1994a, 1994b). This approach accentuates essentially the environment analysis of business negotiations and cultural sensitivity in negotiating business contracts internationally. Here, *environment* is a term borrowed from marketing literature that refers to institutional (e.g., political, economic, legal, and technological) and cultural factors, or in my terminology in this book, the "business culture" or "sociocultural system." Although different opinions exist (e.g., Harnett & Cummings, 1980), national culture is generally believed to have influence on national negotiating style. People negotiate in different styles. If not managed well, such differences can lead to frustration and disappointment and can even jeopardize business relationships. For example, Rosalie Tung (1982b) finds that the differences between the Chinese and American negotiating styles are one of the most important factors responsible for the failure of U.S. business with China.

Stephen Weiss's (1994a, 1994b) "Negotiating With 'Romans'" deserves a special remark. His thesis is that every negotiator has his own cultural "script" for behavior; simply adapting to the counterpart's script is no guarantee for resolving conflicts. The variation of familiarity with each other's script calls for more than one responsive strategy in negotiation. Differing from many cross-cultural negotiation experts who generally advise "When in Rome, do as the Romans do," Weiss goes deeper to analyze various conditions under which one should or should not do as the Romans do. Eight culturally responsive strategies for cross-cultural negotiations are presented based on familiarity (low, moderate, or high) with the counterpart's culture: (a) Employ an agent or adviser (low), (b) involve a mediator (low), (c) induce the counterpart to follow one's own script (low), (d) adapt to the counterpart's script (moderate), (e) coordinate the adjustment of both parties (moderate), (f) embrace the counterpart's script (high), (g) improvise an approach (high), and (h) effect symphony (high). Weiss's thesis offers useful insights into my formulation of some of my responsive strategies for negotiating effectively with Chinese (see Chapter 4 and 5).

This book follows the direction of a cross-cultural and marketing approach to international business negotiation but with a new coloration: It digs deeply into the indigenous soil of China business culture to explain the uniqueness of Chinese business negotiating style.

Dimensions of Business Negotiation

Dimensions of business negotiation as part of the industrial buying-selling process have been explored by researchers (Dadfar, 1988, 1990; Hillier, 1975). Hillier tackles the complexity of the industrial buying-selling process by defining its "three elements": technical complexity of the product, commercial complexity of the negotiations, and behavioral complexity of human interactions. Dadfar further develops these three elements into "three dimensions" of business negotiating style or behavior: *Technical behavior* refers to the way that technical specifications and standards are developed and discussed; *commercial behavior* is demonstrated in price preference and bargaining, contracting, payment, financial terms, delivery terms, attitudes toward economic obligations, and so on; and *social behavior* refers to the establishment of trust and confidence, patterns of communication, the way that personal contacts are made, preference for the media of communication, social interaction within the organization and between the buyer's and seller's personnel, attitudes toward social institutions (i.e., family, tribe, and friends), and so on. This dimensional thinking of business negotiation and negotiating style is useful to structure findings of Chinese business negotiating style (see Chapter 5).

Negotiation Phases

Negotiation phases address how negotiation behavior changes over time as parties interact. Holmes (1992) provides a review of research on phase structures in negotiation and synthesizes three phases: initiation, problem solving, and resolution. In cross-cultural business negotiation studies, a number of scholars have worked out various conceptual phase models, such as pre-negotiation, negotiation, and post-negotiation (Ghauri, 1996); non-task sounding, task-related exchange of information, persuasion, and concessions and agreement (Graham & Lin, 1987; Graham & Sano, 1986, 1989); and pre-negotiation, face-to-face interaction, and post-negotiation (McCall & Warrington, 1984). Researchers in Chinese business negotiating style generally follow the opening, substantive sessions, and closing phase model (Frankenstein, 1986; Pye, 1982; Seligman, 1990).[4] Drawn from these lines of thought, I use pre-negotiation, face-to-face interaction, and post-negotiation phases to structure the Chinese business negotiation process.

Pre-negotiation corresponds to what Graham and Sano (1986, 1989) call "non-task sounding." The phase involves all those initial activities that may be described as establishing a rapport or getting to know one another socially, often in an informal manner. Pre-negotiation does not include information related to the "core contents" of the formal meetings. This is the phase in which the parties prepare and plan negotiation, collect information, determine objectives, make initial contacts, define negotiating issues, seek necessary permits from government authorities, and so on. Face-to-face interaction is the phase in which formal face-to-face negotiation sessions take place. It is characterized by the parties' exchange of information, recognition and definition of conflicting issues and common interests, debate, distributive and integrative bargaining, persuasion, bartering, concession or adjustment of position, and movement toward a joint solution. Post-negotiation concerns drawing up a final contractual agreement that reflects the established understanding and realities of legal interpretation where appropriate. The phase is featured by the parties' formulating a final contract text, seeking necessary permits, business licenses, or both from the government authorities concerned for the operation of the business, and actually executing the agreement. Although an examination of how Chinese business negotiation phases unfold is not a major issue here, the three-phase model is useful for my constructing a model of Chinese business negotiating style (see Chapter 5).

In summary, Western negotiation literature has provided many etic concepts and models. We need both to follow and to discard them when approaching Chinese business negotiating style from the emic perspective. The marketing and cross-culture approach to business negotiation is appealing to me because it takes "environment analysis" (i.e., political, economic, legal, and sociocultural factors) into account where factors influencing business negotiation are examined. I am not going to transplant mechanically the buzzwords of Western negotiation strategies, such as "cooperation," "competition," "win-win," and "win-lose," into the domain of Chinese business negotiation. Instead, I attempt to penetrate Chinese business culture to discover its indigenous cooperation, competition, win-win, and win-lose elements.

Review of Chinese Business Negotiating Style Literature

The following is a Chinese proverb: "A thousand-mile journey is started by taking the first step" (*Qian li zhi xing shi yu jiao xia*). Any academic writing should take into consideration previous works in the same area to avoid pursuing a trivial topic, duplicating a study already done, and being caught in an earlier trap. The task of this section is to overview previous studies on Chinese business negotiating style. It begins with my classification of the existing literature. Then, efforts are directed toward identifying the "what" and "why" questions regarding Chinese negotiating style: A list of Chinese business negotiating behaviors (including Chinese negotiating tactics) is provided, and two schools of thought, that is, "Chinese bureaucracy school" and "Confucian school," are singled out. This section concludes with a critique of previous works, dissecting their theoretical and methodological weaknesses. The ultimate goal of the survey is to form a platform on which sharper approaches to the subject can be crafted.

Classification of Literature

Curiosity about Chinese "communist" or "political" negotiating style began in the 1960s (J.-L. J. Chang, 1991; Lall, 1968; Solomon, 1985, 1987; Young, 1968). Chinese "business" or "commercial" negotiating style, however, did not emerge as a special subject of inquiry until the beginning of the 1980s with the advent of China's active acquisition of foreign investment and the upsurge in interest in China by foreign business communities. The literature that can be subsumed under the rubric of Chinese business negotiating style can be classified into three categories as shown in Table 2.1.[5]

Lucian W. Pye

The single most influential authority on Chinese business negotiating style is Lucian Pye, Ford Professor Emeritus of Political Science at Massachusetts Institute of Technology. Pye has gained the position as the founder of, and most authoritative voice in, the area of Chinese business negotiating style through his widely acclaimed book *Chinese Commercial Negotiating Style,* published in 1982. This work, a Rand Corporation study, emerged as the first comprehensive report on Chinese business negotiating style ever published in the West. The bulk of the growing body of Chinese business negotiating style literature by far simply revolves around this masterpiece. *Chinese Commercial Negotiating Style* has already become, as it indeed deserves, a "must read" on which Western business executives and expatriates often rely when seeking recipes for negotiating with the PRC, as many

TABLE 2.1   Classification of Literature on Chinese Business
Negotiating Style

Literature on Chinese business negotiating style
This category is composed of authors who directly target Chinese business nego-
tiating style as the subject. Influential writings include the following: Adler,
Brahm, & Graham (1992); Blackman (1997); Brunner & Taoka (1977); Brunner
& Wang (1988); Chang (1987); Chen (1993); Deverge (1986); Eiteman (1990);
Frankenstein (1986); Hendryx (1986); Hoose (1974); Kazuo (1979); Kindel (1990);
Kirkbride & Tang (1990); Kirkbride, Tang, & Westwood (1991); Knutsson (1986a,
1986b); Lavin (1994); Lee & Lo (1988); Lieberthal & Oksenberg (1986); Lubman
(1983); Pye (1982, 1986); Sheng (1979); Shenkar & Ronen (1987); Stewart &
Keown (1989); Stone (1992); Tse, Francis, & Walls (1994); Warrington & McCall
(1983); Withane (1992); and Yuann (1987).

**Literature on Chinese business negotiation practices
and foreign technology transfer to China**
In this category, the authors' major interest is in the practices, procedures, and
outcomes of Sino-foreign business negotiations against a background of foreign
technology transfer to China. Explicitly or implicitly, the "Chinese style" issue
forms part of the authors' contributions. Impressive works include the following:
Campbell & Adlington (1988); Davidson (1987); de Keijzer (1992); de Pauw
(1981); Goldenberg (1988); Hakam & Chan (1990); Lewis (1995); Schnepp, von
Glinow, & Bhambri (1990); Tung (1982a, 1982b, 1989); and Wang (1984).

Handbooks and popular writings
Contributions in this category appear in the form of handbooks, novels, news re-
leases, and other types of popular writings. The authors are concerned mainly
with Chinese business etiquette and the Chinese way of doing business, but
Chinese business negotiating style is also discussed. Important contributions include the following: de Mente (1992); Hinkelman (1994); Hu & Grove (1991);
Mann (1989); and Seligman (1990).

writings suggest (Brislin & Hui, 1993; Hu & Grove, 1991; Mann,
1989; Schnepp, von Glinow, & Bhambri, 1990).

Writing in a rather popular style, Pye (1982) describes how the
Chinese maneuver for position at the inception of negotiations, what
procedures they tend to follow, their ploys and strategies, their expectations of concluding agreements, and how one can avoid probable
pitfalls. Pye also includes a psychological interpretation of the motivations that impel the Chinese negotiators. The work is empirically
based on Pye's informal interviews and conversations with Americans

engaged in China trade and, to adjust for American biases, also with Japanese business people.

Pye (1982) discovered that there have been three principal sources of difficulty in Sino-Western business negotiations: (a) problems that arise from the newness of the relations and the lack of experience on both sides, (b) problems inherent in capitalist enterprises seeking to do business with the socialist economy in uncertain transition and reform, and (c) cultural characteristics of both Chinese and Americans. He draws attention to two basic propositions about Chinese negotiators: (a) Chinese business negotiating style is fundamentally influenced by what he calls "Chinese political culture" and (b) Chinese business negotiating style is characterized by the Chinese fascination with employing a variety of negotiating tactics and ploys. According to Pye, the Chinese are the win-lose type of negotiators:

> Most Chinese officials tend instinctively to believe that everything is a zero-sum game. They are convinced that in any situation there must be a winner and a loser. Even when both are benefiting one will benefit more than the other, hence there is still a loser. (p. 71)

Pye (1982) divides the Chinese business negotiation process into the "opening moves" and the "substantive negotiating session." During opening moves, the Chinese insist on reaching a "general agreement" that will later be used by them to their own advantage; they use the tactic of inducing the other party to show its hand first, and then they cause "the long wait." In the substantive negotiating session, the Chinese often display a great fascination for a variety of tactics (see the next section, A Bird's-Eye View of Chinese Business Negotiating Style). Finally, Pye cautions that "nothing is ever final" in negotiating with the Chinese. There is no finality for either agreements or disagreements when negotiating with the Chinese.

To negotiate more effectively with the Chinese, Pye (1982, p. xii) advises the following six "most elementary rules": (a) practice patience, (b) accept as normal prolonged periods of no movement, (c) control against exaggerated expectations and discount Chinese rhetoric about future prospects, (d) expect that the Chinese will try to influence by shaming, (e) resist the temptation to believe that difficulties may be caused by one's own mistakes, and (f) try to understand Chinese cultural traits but never believe that a foreigner can practice them better than the Chinese.

In 1986, Pye published his article "The China Trade: Making the Deal" in *Harvard Business Review*. In 1992, the new edition of his 1982 book was released (Pye, 1992b), this time under the new title *Chinese Negotiating Style: Commercial Approaches and Cultural Principles*. Because Pye's 1982 and 1992 editions remain almost identical to one another in both layout and text, I choose to refer mostly to his old edition (Pye, 1982) when I need to cite and comment on Pye's works (1982, 1992b).

Among writings on Chinese business negotiating style, two other works also stand out:[6] Scott D. Seligman's (1990) "Negotiating with the Chinese" (a chapter in his book *Dealing With the Chinese*, pp. 113-140) and Carolyn Blackman's (1997) *Negotiating China*. Seligman observes that the Chinese seldom give up anything without a fight, and he singles out the 10 most common Chinese negotiating tactics: (a) controlling the location and schedule, (b) exploiting vulnerabilities, (c) guilt-tripping, (d) instilling shame, (e) playing off competitors, (f) using intermediaries, (g) feigning anger, (h) revisiting old issues, (i) invoking the law, and (j) raising and lowering expectations. Blackman discovers that the popular Western win-win negotiation model is not popular in China. She uses six case studies to highlight the haggling atmosphere of the China scene. Twelve "Chinese influence tactics" are identified: (a) using false authority, (b) psychological pressure, (c) "left-field" tactic, (d) time pressure, (e) using competitors, (f) changing negotiators and location, (g) pushing to find the bottom line, (h) reopening closed issues, (i) changing levels and specialists, (j) standing on fixed positions, (k) concentrating on price, and (l) needing guarantees or conformity to bureaucratic codes.

A Bird's-Eye View of Chinese Business Negotiating Style

There is an international consensus that the Chinese are "inscrutable," "skillful," "tough," "shrewd," and "tenacious" negotiators with a unique negotiating style (Deverge, 1986; Kazuo, 1979; Lee &

Lo, 1988; Mann, 1989; Pye, 1982, 1986; Stewart & Keown, 1989; Tung, 1989; Warrington & McCall, 1983)—this despite their isolation for many years from the rest of the world and lack of international business experience. Pye (1986, p. 74) points out that, "for centuries," the Chinese have had no equal in the "subtle art of negotiating":

> The Chinese may be less developed in technology and industrial organization than we, but *for centuries* [italics added] they have known few peers in the subtle art of negotiating. When measured against the effort and skill the Chinese bring to the bargaining table, American executives fall short. (p. 74)

In *Beijing Jeep* (Mann, 1989), which documented a joint venture romance between American Motors Corporation and Chinese organizations, Mann (pp. 79-80) describes the Chinese as the world's toughest negotiators: "Clare [chief negotiator from American Motors Corporation] came to feel that the Iranians, whom he had once called the world's toughest negotiators, were second-rate compared with the Chinese." A study (Kazuo, 1979, p. 552) of diplomatic and trade negotiations between China and Japan—often referred to as the two "inscrutables"—concludes, "The Chinese are skilful [sic] negotiators. They are skilful [sic] not only in extracting maximum concessions from foreigners but also in creating the appearance of their own generosity."

Reportedly, the Chinese tend to display an array of rather persistent negotiating styles, both tactical (negotiating tactics) and nontactical, in Sino-Western business negotiations. Table 2.2 is a summary of the Chinese business negotiating behaviors that are most frequently mentioned in the existing literature, a brief discussion of which is given as follows:[7]

> *Large team, vague authority, the presence of technical people, often with incompetent interpreter:* The Chinese negotiating team tends to be large, but lines of authority can be diffuse and vague. Technical people from end-users take part in discussions aggressively but turn out not to have a strong influence on final decisions. The interpreter provided by the Chinese side may not be competent in special terminology (Pye, 1982).

TABLE 2.2 A Bird's-Eye View of Chinese Business Negotiating Style

Large team, vague authority, the presence of technical people, and often with
    incompetent interpreter

Exploit "agreed principles"

Play home court

Buy the best technology but show no appreciation for monetary value of
    knowledge

Mask interests

Price sensitive

Stalling, delays, and indecision

Hierarchical

Nonlegalistic versus legalistic approach

Play competitors off against each other

"Sweet and sour" approach

Attrition

Shaming technique

Exploit vulnerabilities

Take surprising actions

Show anger

Friendship means obligation

Double standards

"Richer bears heavier burden"

Mixed feelings toward foreigners

Renegotiate old issues

Exploit "agreed principles": The Chinese insist on opening negotiations with general principles without clarifying details. Then they
will press the other side to live up to the "spirit" of these general
principles (Pye, 1982).

Play home court: Most negotiations take place on Chinese soil. Chinese are skilled at using their role as hosts to control the timing,
location, and pacing of negotiations. The Chinese are able to posture
that it is the foreign business people who come to China to ask
favors of the Chinese (Pye, 1982; Seligman, 1990).

Buy the best technology but show no appreciation for monetary value of knowledge: The Chinese buy only the best technologies, but they do not seem to appreciate the monetary value of knowledge (Pye, 1982).

Mask interests: The Chinese insist that the other party show its hand first while masking their own interests and priorities. They remain surprisingly passive and restrained, expecting the other party to take the initiative in proposing concrete deals (Pye, 1982).

Price sensitive: Price is uppermost in the minds of Chinese negotiators (Frankenstein, 1986; Pye, 1982).

Stalling, delays, and indecision: The Chinese are masters of the art of stalling, all the while keeping alive the other side's hope. Indecision and prolonged delays are common (Pye, 1982).

Hierarchical: The frontline negotiators perform the roles of questioners, reporters, and agents, whereas the unseen officials behind the negotiators are the real authorities (Davidson, 1987; Mann, 1989; Pye, 1982). Chief Chinese executives are usually involved at the beginning and the final phases of negotiations; the higher the ranking, the greater the flexibility (Pye, 1982).

Nonlegalistic versus legalistic approach: On the one hand, the Chinese take a nonlegalistic approach to negotiations. They look more for a commitment to working together to solve problems than for a water-tight legal package (Seligman, 1990); they try to avoid legal settlement of nonfulfillment of contracts (Wang, 1984); and they emphasize friendship, sincerity, mutual benefit, and mediation, not adjudication (Sheng, 1979). On the other hand, the Chinese know that records are vital in determining career promotions; they are meticulous about legalistic documentation that could be used to protect themselves from would-be criticism in the future (Pye, 1982).

Play competitors off against each other: The Chinese have been known to invite competing companies to China at the same time for negotiations, often in the very same building (Seligman, 1990). They move around from one competitor to the other, suggesting to each rival firm that the others are making more attractive offers (Pye, 1982).

"Sweet and sour" approach: The Chinese use the sweet and sour approach to remind the other party that friendship is not the only thing they know; they can be "sour" when necessary. Often, some

members on the Chinese team are less friendly than their colleagues, which makes one more dependent on the friendlier persons (Pye, 1982).

Attrition: Chinese negotiators are patient and can stretch out negotiations to wear one down. Excessive entertaining in the evening can also take the edge off a foreign negotiator's attentiveness (Hinkelman, 1994).

Shaming technique: The Chinese are quick to point out any "mistakes" by the other party; they genuinely believe that people can be devastated by the shame of their mistakes (Pye, 1982; Seligman, 1990).

Exploit vulnerabilities: The Chinese identify areas of vulnerability in either one's position or one's personality, and then they use them to their advantage. They may also use their own vulnerability to their best advantage (Seligman, 1990).

Take surprising actions: Compared with Western teams, Chinese negotiating teams take far more surprising actions, putting the opposite party in disadvantageous positions (Stewart & Keown, 1989).

Show anger: Although public expression of anger is a clear violation of Confucian ethics, the Chinese may pack up their papers with a flourish and storm out of the negotiation room (Chen, 1993; Seligman, 1990).

Friendship means obligation: The driving purpose behind much of Chinese negotiating tactics is the creation of friendship, in which the foreign party ends up finding strong and imprecisely limited bonds of obligation toward the Chinese (Pye, 1982).

Double standards: The Chinese seem to have two different standards for judging themselves and other parties. They tend to get specific and deal with concrete matters only if these affect the Chinese, whereas issues of concern to foreigners are dealt with on a general level (Frankenstein, 1986). In joint-venture negotiation, the Chinese team might push hard to get one to guarantee to export a fixed percentage of the product, but for its own part may only promise to make its "best effort" to have things done (Seligman, 1990).

"Richer bears heavier burden": The Chinese are fully convinced that it is only fair for the richer party to bear the heavier burden. They use the advantage that a weaker party has to extract favors from the strong, without losing in dignity (Pye, 1986).

Mixed feelings toward foreigners: Chinese negotiators seem to have mixed feelings toward foreigners; they are torn between a distrust of foreigners and fascination with foreign technologies (Pye, 1982).

Renegotiate old issues: The Chinese do not view the signing of a contract as the end of negotiation; they attach great importance to long-term relationships and will not hesitate to suggest adjustments immediately on the heels of an agreement (Frankenstein, 1986; Pye, 1982).

Two Explanations

Chinese business negotiating style has fascinated thoughtful observers and invited a variety of attempts to arrive at explanations. Although authors do not label their contributions as belonging to certain schools of thought, I dare to classify them into two major trends of current thought on the subject: the "Chinese bureaucracy school" and the "Confucian school."

The Chinese Bureaucracy School

The Chinese bureaucracy school centers on explaining Chinese business negotiating style with reference to bureaucratic or institutional factors in the PRC (Davidson, 1987; Lavin, 1994; Lieberthal & Oksenberg, 1986; Pye, 1982). Decades of "Chinese communist culture" or "Chinese political culture" (Lavin, 1994; Pye, 1982) and China's complex "internal bargaining system" (Lieberthal & Oksenberg, 1986) have left an indelible imprint on Chinese business negotiating style. As a result, Chinese negotiators avoid taking responsibility, fear criticism, show indecision, and have no final say, among other things.

Pye is a major exponent of the Chinese bureaucracy school. Capacitated by his profound political science background with many publications on the topic of contemporary Chinese politics (Pye, 1981, 1988, 1992a), Pye is dedicated to a political analysis of Chinese negotiators. His basic assumption is that business negotiations with China could not be isolated from China's domestic political development. Pye (1992b) clarifies how he approached Chinese business negotiating style as follows:

The approach in this study is . . . to investigate the deeper cultural and institutional factors that are important for understanding Chinese negotiating practices. The cultural tradition is a strange mix. It of course is founded on basic Chinese culture, but it has been profoundly influenced by decades of Marxism-Leninism, and more recently by ambivalent reactions against that orthodoxy and uncertainty about the reforms. (p. viii)

Chinese culture, in Pye's (1982, p. 20) study, means largely "the all-pervasive influence of politics in Chinese Communist culture." Pye attributes the distinctiveness of Chinese style to decades of Chinese communism: "In almost all cases, what makes Chinese practices distinctive is that they reflect Chinese culture as it has responded to three decades of Communism" (p. 81). In the same vein, Lavin (1994) writes,

> Especially in dealing with China, political cultures and political systems matter. They shape expectations, the interests of negotiators, and the desirability of outcomes. A careful review of prior trade negotiations with the Chinese should help explain not only the persistence of the trade imbalance and China's barriers to U.S. businesses, but also the broader difficulty of dealing with a political culture that often works from an entirely different set of assumptions. (p. 17)

Pye (1982) gives the following pungent depiction of Chinese bureaucracy, which has considerable bearings on Chinese negotiators:

> The Chinese system . . . is in its essence a bureaucratic process in which the critical art is to avoid responsibilities, diffuse decisions, and blunt all commands that might later leave one vulnerable to criticisms. . . . In Chinese political culture there is no assumption that power must be tied to responsibility; on the contrary, in the ranks of the powerful, proof of importance lies precisely in being shielded from accountability. . . . Hence, at all times Chinese officials have to practice the bureaucratic art of "covering their tails," in the American vernacular. (pp. 16-17)

Pye (1982) observes that the Chinese tend to display both "stubborn" and "accommodating" behaviors as a result of Chinese bureaucracy:

> The Chinese also quickly adopt a stubborn posture whenever they are confronted with propositions that go beyond the scope of their authority. Usually Chinese negotiators are given little authority and therefore questions must be repeatedly referred back to their superiors. . . . If their superiors authorize them to go ahead they can suddenly become most accommodating. (p. 68)

The meticulous Chinese attitude toward wording a contract reflects the Chinese need to escape from bureaucratic punishment. The Chinese can be "legalistic" enough in negotiations despite their traditional nonlegalisic orientation (Pye, 1982):

> Whatever may be the influences of traditional Chinese culture on law, cadres now engaged in negotiations have learned that records are critical in determining career advancements. They appreciate the significance of written reports and legalistic documentation, yet realize that they can be protected when something is not included in the written record. In short, most Chinese officials are well aware of the advantages of avoiding precise written commitments as to their part of an agreement, and of inserting precise commitments for the foreigner. (p. 22)

Chinese business negotiations are so starkly colored by political or bureaucratic features that Chinese negotiators are found to be simply rehearsing "theater" in which all the Chinese lines are prepared (Lavin, 1994, p. 19): "Talks sometimes took on the air of theater in which the Chinese lines were all scripted. The Chinese were not actually negotiating anything, at least not as Americans understand the term."

The Chinese are tough negotiators; Chinese bureaucracy is one important reason. Pye (1982, p. 17) writes, "The universal fear within the Chinese bureaucracy of being charged with not upholding China's national interests contributes to making Chinese negotiators exceptionally meticulous, astute, and tough, people who have extraordinary endurance and the ability to negotiate seemingly forever." Chinese bureaucracy boasts a complex internal bargaining system, and there has been an ongoing process of bargaining among various organizations and departments. In their own system, the Chinese feel totally comfortable trying to negotiate and renegotiate and interpret and reinterpret policies, regulations, and agreements as conditions change.

In other words, bargaining is a way of life in Chinese bureaucracy. The patience that the Chinese exhibit toward their foreign counterparts may indicate much about internal consensus-building among various interests. As Lieberthal and Oksenberg (1986) stated,

> Negotiations, bargains, and exchange, in short, are essential ingredients of the Chinese system. It is no wonder that many Chinese are tough and effective negotiators with foreigners. They have gained a lot of experience at home, dealing with one another. (p. 28)

Business negotiations in China are known to be more time-consuming than is common in the West. Chinese bureaucracy is one major reason. Davidson (1987) discovered that the frontline Chinese negotiators only perform the role of "questioner" or "reporter," whereas the unseen officials behind the negotiators are the real "authorities." He goes on to explain vividly why Chinese business negotiation often takes time by using the metaphor of "an electrical series circuit":

> A variety of factors contribute to delays in forming joint ventures, but the most important and pervasive factor is the administrative structure of the Chinese government, which slows the negotiation process. Negotiators for the Chinese side generally possess little or no actual decision-making authority. They must review any proposals or agreements with a host of interested ministries, committees, and bureaus at the municipal, provincial, and federal level. Even if the Chinese negotiator is highly skilled and there are no fundamental conflicts between all the Chinese interests party to the negotiations, it will take considerable time to run through the loop of multiple review, concurrence, and approval procedures. The set of many Chinese stakeholders to the negotiations functions like an electrical series circuit. All the bulbs must light up at the same time in order for the circuit to function. (pp. 78-79)

China's active participation in international business is a new phenomenon. Therefore, many of the misunderstandings, problems, and frustrations that have plagued negotiations between Chinese and Western business people can be attributed to what Pye (1982) calls the "problems of novelty"—the lack of precedence and experience on both sides.

Given China's poor infrastructure, its still strongly centralized state economic planning system, the devastating legacy of the Cultural Revolution on a generation that should have provided today's middle managers, and so on, Hendryx (1986) warns that negotiating the contract is not a real problem; the real problems start after one signs the contract.

In short, the Chinese bureaucracy school decodes Chinese negotiating style from Chinese bureaucratic or institutional factors in the PRC. The school attributes the distinctive features of Chinese behavior to contemporary Chinese political culture and the internal bargaining system. Why does Chinese business negotiation take time? The Chinese bureaucracy school scholars answer: because dealing with Chinese bureaucracy takes time.

The Confucian School

The Confucian school interprets Chinese business negotiating style from human relationship-oriented Confucian traditions (Brunner & Wang, 1988; Deverge, 1986; Kindel, 1990; Seligman, 1990; Shenkar & Ronen, 1987; Withane, 1992). The scholars often label their interpretation as a "cultural" explanation. They view, either explicitly or implicitly, the essence of Chinese culture as residing in the Confucian values, so much so that they believe Chinese negotiating style is solely embedded in the Confucian tradition. For example, in Shenkar and Ronen's (1987) "cultural context" of Chinese negotiations, there is nothing more than "the influence of Confucius."

According to the Confucian explanation, Chinese negotiators look more for a sincere commitment to working together to solve problems than for a neatly decorated legal package (Seligman, 1990). They place great emphasis on reputation, sincerity, credibility, personal character, and quality on the part of both the Western firm and its negotiators (Frankenstein, 1986; Hoose, 1974; Kindel, 1990). As Confucian "gentlemen," Chinese negotiators "generally keep their commitments" (Seligman, 1990) and do not "tear apart a contract or refuse to implement it without good reason" (Chen, 1993, p. 13). Because of the Confucian aversion to law, Chinese negotiators prefer mediation and conciliation to adjudication (Sheng, 1979). Imbued with the Confucian tradition of family and kinship affiliation (Kindel,

1990; Shenkar & Ronen, 1987) and due to the Chinese concept of face (Brunner & Wang, 1988), Chinese negotiators demonstrate a strong preference for meeting in groups rather than in one-to-one settings. Because of the Confucian need for moral cultivation and harmony, the Chinese show a high degree of emotional restraint in business negotiations (Shenkar & Ronen, 1987).

The most prominent characteristic of the Confucian school is its assertion that Chinese negotiating style is not the product of Chinese manipulation of strategies, tactics, and ploys. Rather, it is the rational manifestation of Confucian ethics. For example, Deverge (1986), a prominent figure of the Confucian school, writes,

> There is an international consensus (including the Japanese) that the Chinese are skilful [sic] negotiators possessing a unique negotiating style. Among the factors most often mentioned are the slow pace of negotiation, the seriousness and determination of the negotiators, along with a strong tendency to sentimentalise and to appeal to general principles. These are not [italics added] tactical practices but stem directly from Confucian philosophy and the Chinese bureaucratic culture it created. In other words, Chinese negotiating skills are deeply rooted in their cultural and social values. (p. 34)

Deverge decodes the Chinese style—such as behaving obstinately, asking questions a hundred times, doing homework carefully, and writing down everything—from the Confucian legacies, such as face and group orientation:

> Negotiators [Chinese] will be very serious, writing down everything, forgetting nothing, doing their homework very nicely because it is not only their face [italics added] which is at stake but also that of the consensus-reaching group. [italics added] They will be obstinate and not afraid of repeating the same thing with the same conviction a hundred times. The objective is to ensure maximum security for the negotiators, but serves also to break the nerve of the other party who, if foreign, is more than often in a hurry. (p. 35)

The Confucian school assumes that Chinese negotiators are of the win-win type of negotiators, seeking mutual benefit and compromise.[8] As Deverge (1986, p. 35) stated, for the Chinese "negotiations are not seen as a win/lose battle but as a dignified process of compromise."

In short, the Confucian school explains Chinese business negotiating style from one of the most important Chinese philosophies or cultural traditions—Confucianism. Why does negotiation with the Chinese take time? The Confucian school points to the complications of "Chinese culture" or Confucian traditions. For example, Brunner and Wang (1988) and Kindel (1990) attribute the time-consuming characteristic of the Chinese business negotiation process to the impact of the Chinese concept of face.

Both explanations—the Chinese bureaucracy school and the Confucian school—possess strengths; neither, however, is satisfactory in a comprehensive sense. In addition, neither school has given any cultural explanation of Chinese negotiating tactics. Despite their limitations, the Chinese bureaucracy school and the Confucian school sparked much of my thought when I conceptualized the major components of Chinese business culture, that is, PRC condition, Confucianism, and Chinese stratagems.

Critique of Existing Literature

The existing studies with the foregoing two explanations have generated many useful insights into understanding Chinese business negotiating style. They have also propelled my thinking immeasurably. The research area suffers from a number of theoretical and methodological weaknesses, however. It is a pity that no previous works can be found that place the existing thought under close scrutiny, a sign that also indicates that the area lacks research. In this section, I examine the area critically by addressing five problematic issues.

Lack of a Systematic Model

The first and overriding problem of the area is the lack of a systematic model with which to analyze Chinese business negotiating style in a Chinese sociocultural context. Amazingly few studies approach the subject by scanning systematically different components of China's sociocultural system that underpin Chinese negotiating behaviors. The area seems to have inherited much of Pye's (1982) writing style in *Chinese Commercial Negotiating Style*, which lacks systems thinking. Pye's contribution to the area is very admirable and has greatly inspired subsequent studies, including mine. Unfortunately, Pye does not provide any coherent model for a systematic understanding of Chinese negotiating behaviors. In addition, almost no visual model can be found in the existing literature on Chinese business negotiating style. Although not all writings must contain figures with boxes and arrows, a visual model, as David Whetten (1989) argues, often clarifies the author's thinking and enhances and reinforces the reader's comprehension.

The need for a systematic model arises because the empirical world of Chinese business negotiating style is characterized by a high degree of complexity and uncertainty. Chinese negotiators are described as cooperative or win-win negotiators by some authors (Adler et al., 1992; Deverge, 1986) but as competitive or win-lose negotiators by others (Blackman, 1997; Pye, 1982); the Chinese are considered very "honest" at one moment and "not honest" at all the next (March, 1994); and the Chinese view a cosignatory to an agreement as establishing a relationship between friends and adopt a positive problem-solving attitude toward business transactions, but at the same time they do not hesitate to employ a daunting array of ploys and tactics to knock their partners off balance (Seligman, 1990). My personal experience as a Chinese negotiator and my observations as a real-life investigator also confirm this picture of bewildering complexity. Systems thinking is a major concern in the science and art of management; it helps us see wholes and structures underlying complex situations (Churchman, 1968; Deming, 1993; Senge, 1990). To tackle the complexity of the subject, we need systems thinking and systematic models.

Pye (1992b) says that given the "constant change" in China, he is not searching for "fixed formulas" for negotiating with the Chinese, and what is needed instead is "alertness to Chinese tendencies and proclivities" (p. viii). The changing situation in China, however, does not necessarily contradict the necessity to build models to understand Chinese negotiating behaviors systematically. The task of scientists "is to build viable models of the empirical world that can be comprehended by the human mind" (Dubin, 1978, p. 2). Powerful models can advance our knowledge and help achieve a genuine alertness to Chinese negotiating tendencies and proclivities.

A review of the subject reveals that existing propositions are rather narrowly devised, each concentrating on one part of the picture rather than mapping out the landscape of a larger whole. For example, although Pye's (1982) "bureaucratic" diagnosis of the Chinese is incisive, his cultural analysis of the Chinese is rather weak (Fang & Timm, 1995). Although Deverge's (1986) Confucian interpretations of the Chinese are informative, his bureaucratic and tactical understandings of the Chinese are rather blunt. The existing schools have generated useful insight into our understanding of the subject. Nevertheless, they are incomplete because they merely touch on separated components of a larger system.

Frankenstein's (1986) "spiral model of Chinese business practices and negotiating style" is perhaps the only visual model in the field. The model indicates that Chinese business negotiation process is divided into four stages: opening moves, assessment, end-game, and implementation. It also insightfully notes that the Chinese never stop negotiating; these four stages tend to reappear in a spiral way. The model does not, unfortunately, contain any sociocultural variables that would otherwise allow us to systematically analyze Chinese business practices and negotiating style.

The more closely I examine the subject, the more profoundly I become convinced, given its high level of complexity, that we need systems thinking to approach the subject. We need both to synthesize the existing thinking and to develop new thinking to generate greater analytical power. Chinese business negotiating style is defined by Chinese business culture that consists of different components. To understand Chinese business negotiating style, we need to study these components and find how they influence the Chinese style respectively. Without a systematic look at these different components, our knowledge will remain only as "the blind men perceiving the elephant," leaving our advice about doing business with China at best incomplete and at worst misleading. A systematic model will not only offer in-depth knowledge about the negotiating style of the PRC Chinese but also provide hints for us to understand the negotiating style of the Chinese living in Chinese societies outside the PRC.

In short, the subject calls for a systematic model for under-standing Chinese business negotiating style in a Chinese sociocultural context. In this book, I attempt to construct a model of this kind that is able to answer both the whats and the whys of Chinese business negotiating style in a systematic fashion.

Lack of Cultural Study of Chinese Negotiating Tactics

The second problem is the lack of a cultural study of Chinese business negotiating tactics. This is a rather embarrassing problem. On the one hand, the uniqueness of Chinese negotiating tactics has been agreed on by authors, and many have prepared impressive lists of these tactics (Blackman, 1997; Hinkelman, 1994; Pye, 1982; Seligman, 1990). On the other hand, no compelling cultural explanation of Chinese negotiating tactics has ever been provided. Chinese negotiating tactics have proved to be a fascinating topic. Throughout the years, authors seem to have reached a tacit understanding that no writing on Chinese business negotiating style can be complete without dipping into the sea of Chinese negotiating tactics; terms such as *Chinese negotiating tricks, ploys,* and *tactics* never fail to catch one's eye. Nevertheless, no previous academic writing can be traced that penetrates beneath various Chinese tricks, ploys, and tactics to touch the cultural or philosophical base of Chinese negotiating tactics; nor can previous "How to do business with China" guides be found that tackle Chinese negotiating tactics by demonstrating to readers the very "magic thread" that binds all the Chinese negotiating tricks, ploys, and tactics together.

The Confucian school simply denies the existence of Chinese manipulation of tactics in negotiations, which no doubt would be a violation of the noble Confucian virtues. The Chinese bureaucracy school explains the peculiarity of Chinese negotiating behaviors from "Chinese political culture" and the "internal bargaining system." The scholars, however, have still not dug the cultural soil deeply enough to answer why Chinese negotiating tactics are culturally peculiar and what kind of rationale underpins various patterns of Chinese negoti-ating tactics.

For instance, the more we read Pye's *Chinese Commercial Negotiating Style* (1982), the more we see that Pye leaves the Chinese negotiating tactics he has discovered—a significant contribution he has made to the area—culturally unexplained. Pye writes (p. x), "The Chinese believe that patience is a value in negotiation, particularly with impatient Americans, and they freely use stalling tactics and delays." I wonder how patience, a Confucian virtue, could be reduced to a tactical move of stalling tactics?

Seligman (1990) falls into the same trap: He states, "The position of the individual in Chinese society cannot be fully understood without a discussion of the thought of the sage Confucius (551-479 B.C.) and his disciples" (p. 40). Accordingly, he refers only to Confucianism when explaining Chinese negotiating style. As a piece of evidence of the Chinese following the Confucian tradition, Seligman observes that Chinese negotiators look for "a commitment to work together to solve problems," "accord and harmony," "expression of mutual interests," and "mutual obligations" (p. 114). This Confucian mode of thought, however, disappears when Seligman substantiates the Chinese manipulation of a variety of negotiating ploys, tactics, and "insincere behavior." Seligman (p. 136) finds that "they [the Chinese] seldom give up anything without a fight, even if it is unimportant to them. It can always be used to extract something from you." As such, Chinese negotiators under Seligman's pen suddenly become "fighters," and the properties of Confucian gentlemen have completely vanished. Moreover, Seligman describes Chinese negotiators as controlling negotiation location and schedule, exploiting the other party's vulnerabilities, using guilt-tripping and shaming techniques, playing off competitors, manipulating intermediaries to their advantage, feigning anger, revisiting old negotiation issues, invoking the law to their advantage, and so on. Self-evidently, this picture of Chinese negotiators does not fit the profile of a Confucian gentleman at all. This is where the theoretical paradox of Seligman's reasoning lies; he refers solely to Confucianism as the theoretical foundation to explain Chinese negotiating style, but the Chinese negotiating ploys and tactics he observed are diametrically opposed to Confucian values. I presume Seligman (p. 131) also noticed his paradox when he explained the Chinese behavior of showing anger in business negotiation: "Although public expressions of anger, as clear violations of the Confucian ethic . . . are frowned on by the Chinese, they consider it acceptable to commit such solecisms in negotiations as a means to an end." This is but an awkward explanation. I could hardly believe the sage Confucius would forgive such "solecisms" as showing anger in negotiation. Seligman fails to move a step further to find out other more pertinent cultural explanations of Chinese negotiating tactics.

Blackman's (1997) *Negotiating China*, further elucidating the issue of Chinese negotiating tactics, certainly makes her another influential name in the area of Chinese business negotiating style. Blackman grounds her cultural analysis of Chinese negotiating tactics on the Confucian in-group and out-group mentality, the concept of face, and so on coupled with bureaucratic pressure. Still, Blackman has not answered the burning question: What is the philosophical principle underlying all the Chinese negotiating tactics she has discovered?

It seems that the Chinese often display a kind of tactical behavior that can hardly be explained if reference is made solely to Confucianism. I contend that if the Chinese have really known few peers in the subtle art of negotiating "for centuries," they must have been equipped with a kind of theory of negotiation tactics deeply rooted in traditional Chinese culture with which Westerners have not been very familiar. This line of thought led me to write my first article on the subject in 1995 to introduce the Chinese concept of *ji* to the area of Chinese business negotiating style (Fang, 1995) and further develop the thesis in my subsequent writings (Fang, 1996, 1997b, 1997c). In this book, I intend to show that all the secrets, myths, and mysteries of Chinese negotiating tactics can be traced back to a single most important Chinese word that is unknown to the West: *ji* (Chinese stratagems). *Ji* provides the cultural explanation not only for Chinese negotiating tactics but also for strategic thinking in the whole East Asia.

Lack of the Presence of a Chinese Voice

The third weakness is the lack of the presence of a Chinese voice in the current workshop of Chinese business negotiating style. The area is almost purely based on the Western, mostly American, perception of China and the Chinese. First, Western authors have dominated the forum. Western contributions, though inspiring and informative, are still Western contributions; they represent only one side of the coin. To obtain a comprehensive and in-depth understanding of the workings of Chinese business negotiating style, contributions from native and ethnic Chinese authors need to be encouraged. Being nurtured in Chinese culture, Chinese authors may provide perspectives that help deepen and broaden the existing knowledge.

Also, very few studies target Chinese managers as informants.[9] The existing research grounds itself largely on Western managers' perceptions of marketing and negotiating in the PRC. For example, Pye's (1982) *Chinese Commercial Negotiating Style* is purely based on the stories provided by the American and Japanese business people, without any Chinese voice being audible in the debate.

Very often, Western views and explanations of the Chinese are true only in a piecemeal sense, as Edward Hall (1976/1981) noted:

> Such [Western] pictures and explanations are real in one sense, because they are constructions of the human mind and they tell us a lot about how that mind works as a product of a given culture. But they are *not* the mind and they are not the real world either. . . . The ideas and concepts of the Chinese philosopher Confucius mean one thing to the Chinese, something else to Westerners. (p. 214)

There has been no dearth of well-documented studies that demonstrate that purely Western-derived models or research instruments fail to produce a valid and reliable description of Chinese behaviors when they are used in China (Adler, Campbell, & Laurent, 1989; The Chinese Culture Connection, 1987; Hofstede, 1991; Hofstede & Bond, 1988).[10] The PRC scholars may have somewhat different perceptions of the same phenomena compared with Western scholars (Stewart, 1994). This suggests that only when research is based on the harmonious balance of Eastern and Western minds can it produce powerful knowledge (see also Bond, 1996).

Because more than 20% of all humans are Chinese, the "Chinese voice" should be heard if a healthy and energetic scholarship is to be developed. I use the Yin Yang metaphor to illustrate the point of inviting the Chinese to join the debate: The perspectives of Chinese and Western managers are both necessary and complementary, and both need to be strenuously voiced if a powerful and harmonious knowledge about Chinese business negotiating style is to be produced for the same reason that Yin and Yang are both necessary and complementary if universal events are to be created, maintained, and developed in a harmonious way. Therefore, this book targets both Chinese and foreign managers as sources of information.

Weak Empirical Descriptions

Although studies on Chinese business negotiating style appear occasionally, few offer rich empirical descriptions. Most writings are characterized by prescriptive accounts, often of a speculative and commanding nature, with little documented empirical evidence. This problem of weak empirical descriptions reflects the methodological barriers, for example, the lack of access to reality, facing the area that I discussed in Chapter 1. The lack of access to reality also explains, at least in part, why the current workshop of Chinese business negotiating style has few Chinese participants. As far as I am concerned, methodological issues, or more specifically the empirical access to the Chinese reality and ability to offer thick descriptions, are vital to the quality of Chinese business negotiating style research.

The existing studies divide methodologically into questionnaire sampling and qualitative reasoning. Questionnaire studies (Davidson, 1987; Frankenstein, 1986; Lee & Lo, 1988; Stewart & Keown, 1989) do not make the following point clear: whether the respondents' information was based on real-life personal experience or simply secondhand. Qualitative studies, however, do not actually match the basic feature of qualitative research method: description. For example, Kindel's (1990) list of Chinese negotiating behaviors is impressive but, unfortunately, there is no empirical evidence attached to it. Without an empirical base, qualitative studies are but "castles in the air," offering no rich insights. I believe in the power of "thick description," a concept proposed by anthropologist Clifford Geertz (1973), in sociocultural understanding of Chinese business negotiating style. An overview indicates that few studies are of the thick-description type—offering real-life descriptions to enrich readers' heuristic understanding of the subject.

Blackman (1997), Knutsson (1986a, 1986b), Schnepp et al. (1990), and Tung (1982a) are among only a few exceptions who try to provide readers with real-life empirical descriptions of Chinese business negotiation practices and negotiating style. These works have provided hints for my empirical orientation. Still, however, very few works use direct quotations from real negotiators, both Chinese and Western, telling their true stories about Chinese negotiating style to enrich readers' self-understandings, as this book does.

Predominance of U.S.-China Negotiation Literature

The field is overwhelmingly dominated by U.S.-China business negotiation literature (Brunner & Taoka, 1977; Davidson, 1987; de Pauw, 1981; Frankenstein, 1986; Lavin, 1994; Lee & Lo, 1988; Pye, 1982, 1986; Tung, 1982a, 1982b).[11] To label this a problem might not be appropriate; it does reflect the relative importance of U.S.-China bilateral relations in the countries' global chessboards. Judged from an academic point of view, however, the American dominance is not favorable for the healthy development of scholarship.

Culturally, Edward Hall (1976/1981) finds that American culture is placed toward the lower end of the low- and high-context scale but still "considerably" above Scandinavian culture, whereas Chinese culture is on the high-context end of the continuum. Ideologically, Sweden was the very first Western country to recognize the PRC on May 9, 1950, followed by other Scandinavian countries. All this implies that the United States does not represent all Western countries; nor does American culture equal Western culture. Therefore, even the Western perception of Chinese behavior should include perceptions from Westerners other than Americans.

Although Scandinavian firms' investment in China still constitutes a relatively small proportion of all foreign investment in China, it has increased rapidly since the late 1980s. Unfortunately, researchers in Chinese business management in Scandinavian countries lag far behind their business colleagues. Few significant reports on Chinese business culture and business style have been published by Nordic researchers.[12] Too little research has been conducted on Scandinavia-China business interactions (Tung & Worm, 1997). Because Sweden is often perceived as representative of the Scandinavian countries (Worm, 1997), this book aims to add a Scandinavia-China texture to the existing fabric of knowledge of Chinese business negotiating style by examining Sweden-China business negotiations.

Furthermore, future research needs to examine Chinese negotiating style beyond the Sino-Western negotiation context. I hypothesize that the Chinese may negotiate differently with countries other than "Western powers." Although this book does not probe in this direction, the hypothesis finds some initial backing. I will return to this point in the discussion of future research in Chapter 5.

Conceptualization of Chinese Business Culture

The literature survey shows that the existing studies on Chinese business negotiating style possess both strengths and weaknesses. They have inspired me to develop my lines of thought considerably. By adopting the strong points and overcoming the shortcomings of the previous studies, as well as by developing new approaches to the subject, I am able to build emic models to understand Chinese business negotiating style in a Chinese sociocultural context.

In this section, I provide a conceptual framework of Chinese business culture: the PRC's sociocultural traits underlying Chinese business negotiating style.[13] This framework forms part of the model of Chinese business negotiating style to be constructed in Chapter 5. As shown in Figure 2.2, Chinese business culture is conceptualized as consisting of three fundamental forces: the PRC condition, Confucianism, and Chinese stratagems. As I detail in Chapter 3, the *PRC condition* refers to the basic political and social characteristics of the PRC that have evolved since 1949, *Confucianism* refers to the values and norms of Confucian traditions, and *Chinese stratagems* refers to the cultural fountainhead of strategic Chinese thinking. Together, these sociocultural forces exert fundamental influences on Chinese business negotiating style. My conceptualization of Chinese business culture is inspired by the following theoretical inputs:

1. Culture theory: Culture as a "sociocultural system" or "complex whole" that involves components ranging from political institutions to philosophies and social customs; it is a unique lifestyle shared

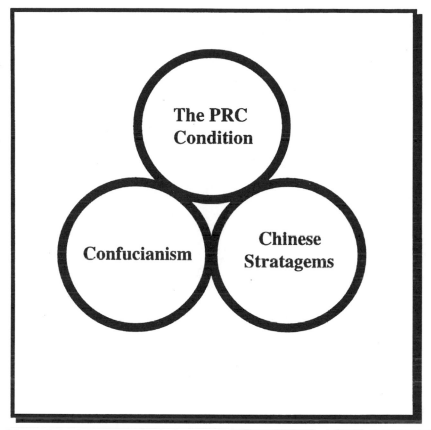

Figure 2.2. A Framework of Chinese Business Culture

among people who have been similarly socialized (Barnouw, 1979; Hall, 1976/1981; Kroeber & Kluckhohn, 1952; Lee, 1995; Root, 1987; Terpstra & David, 1991; Tylor, 1871). Moreover, culture influences human behavior by both values (Adler, 1991) and tool kit skills from which people construct strategies of action (Swidler, 1986).

2. The essence of Chinese culture has been shaped by Confucianism and Taoism—the two indigenous Chinese philosophies (Chan, 1963; de Bary et al., 1960; Fung, 1948/1966; Ren, 1986; Tang, 1991; Weber, 1919/1951). Chinese stratagems are a strategic component in Chinese culture that is rooted in the Taoist Yin Yang and Wu Wei principles.

3. The management problems in the PRC reflect the impact of a combination of traditional Chinese culture and contemporary Chinese politics and socialist economy (Campbell & Adlington, 1988; Child, 1990, 1994; Hsiao, Jen, & Lee, 1990; Lockett, 1988; Porter, 1996). The "whole" of the PRC condition, Confucianism, and Chinese stratagems represents this combination.

4. The sociocultural "archetype"—that is, the contemporary sociocultural system of a nation—is composed of both "local" and "adopted" cultures (Dadfar, 1984, 1990). From this perspective, China's sociocultural system may be seen as involving both the local forces, such as Confucianism and Chinese stratagems, and the adopted forces, such as Marxist ideology and Western cultural influence as seen in the PRC condition.

5. The existing schools of Chinese business negotiating style, that is, the Chinese bureaucracy school and the Confucian school: The PRC condition deals with Chinese bureaucracy as the central theme; Confucianism embraces the thinking of the Confucian school by associating the core values of Confucianism with Chinese negotiating style. The Chinese stratagems deal with the cultural explanation of Chinese negotiating tactics that existing studies have discovered but failed to provide convincing answers for.

6. The rationale that Confucianism and Chinese stratagems, two strikingly contrasting components in Chinese culture, can be put together to explain Chinese negotiating behavior is that the Chinese view Confucianism and Taoism not as religions but as philosophical teachings. The Chinese follow each of them to handle situations practically.

7. The whole framework can also be understood as using a marketing or environmental approach (McCall & Warrington, 1984; Terpstra & David, 1991) to Chinese business negotiating style, with the environmental factors (political, economic, legal, technological, cultural, etc.) being placed in the center.

The Chinese business culture framework allows us to examine, in a systematic fashion, how various Chinese sociocultural forces influence Chinese business negotiating style. This framework is discussed in further detail in Chapter 3.

▨ Notes

1. The term *Confucianism* involves not only the thought of Confucius and Mencius but also neo-Confucianism, which thrived from the twelfth to the sixteenth century.

This interpretation of Confucianism is based on the Confucian classics *The Four Books,* which were compiled by a Chinese philosopher Chu Hsi (1130-1200) in 1190.

2. *The Four Books (Si Shu)* involves (a) *Great Learning (Da Xue),* (b) *Doctrine of the Mean (Zhong Yong),* (c) *Analects (Lun Yu),* and (d) *The Book of Mencius (Meng Zi).*

3. Chan, W.-T, *A Source Book in Chinese Philosophy,* p. 152. Copyright © 1963 by Princeton University Press. Reprinted by permission of Princeton University Press.

4. The closing phase is implicitly suggested by Pye (1982), who observes that "nothing is ever final" in negotiating with the Chinese (p. 78).

5. There is a body of literature on Chinese political negotiating style that is not included here. Interested readers are referred to J.-L. J. Chang (1991), Davies (1984), Kreisberg (1995), Lall (1968), Solomon (1985, 1987), and Young (1968). My previous works (Fang, 1993, 1995, 1996, 1997b, 1997c), on which this book is based, are not included in Table 2.1.

6. Richard Solomon is another influential writer on Chinese negotiating style who focuses on Chinese political negotiations. Although Solomon is not particularly mentioned here, his work (1987) is a must read for anyone who is interested in Chinese business negotiating style.

7. More extensive discussions of Chinese negotiating tactics are provided in Appendix A.

8. The exception is that several writers from the Confucian school, for example, Brunner and Wang (1988) and Seligman (1990), regard the Chinese as the win-lose type of negotiators.

9. Schnepp et al.'s (1990) study of U.S.-China technology transfer is an exception, in which the Chinese perspective on negotiation and foreign technology transfer to China is studied as opposed to that of Westerners. The section on Chinese negotiating style, however, is presented in only a very limited fashion. Methodological barriers (see Chapter 1) are believed to be the reason.

10. The Chinese Culture Connection is a team of researchers, led by Michael Bond at the Chinese University of Hong Kong, who are interested in Chinese values and behaviors.

11. The phenomenon can also be found in Chinese political negotiating style literature (Lall, 1968; Solomon, 1985, 1987; Young, 1968).

12. I use "Scandinavian countries," "Scandinavia,", "Nordic countries," and "Northern Europe" anonymously to refer to Denmark, Finland, Norway, and Sweden. The first comprehensive study of Sino-Scandinavian business interactions available in Northern Europe was provided by Verner Worm (1997). Knutsson (1986a, 1986b) wrote reports on Chinese negotiation behavior.

13. I use the term *Chinese business culture* loosely to refer to China's sociocultural system or "the PRC's sociocultural traits" that define values and codes for conduct in Chinese business settings.

3 Chinese Business Culture

Chinese business culture is the key to the Chinese way of doing business and their style of negotiating. This chapter deals with three components of Chinese business culture: the PRC condition, Confucianism, and Chinese stratagems. To negotiate and do business effectively with the People's Republic of China (PRC), Western managers must ensure that their contemporary China business lexicon contains not only familiar terms, such as *face* and *guanxi*, but also new concepts, such as *guoqing* ("the PRC condition") and *ji* ("Chinese stratagems").

The PRC Condition

The first fundamental force that makes China different from most other markets is manifested in the Chinese word *guoqing*, which can be heard everywhere in the PRC. The Chinese character *guo* translates as "state," "nation," or "country"; *qing*, in this context, translates as "condition," "situation," or "characteristics." *Guoqing* can be understood as "China's situation," "Chinese characteristics," "the special situation in China," and "Chinese condition." China's great size, large population, and practice of one-child-per-family policy are examples of China's *guoqing*. Borrowing its contemporary usage in the PRC, I translate *guoqing* as the PRC condition to refer to the unique practices in the PRC since it was founded in 1949.

Although the term *guoqing* is little known in the West,[1] the unique practices that evolved in the Communist PRC have been noted by many authors. For example, MacDougall (1980) observes that

> trading with the Chinese is difficult, even for the initiated. Not only is there the difference in organization of trade that exists between a planned and a market economy, but also there is a host of other dissimilarities which arise from the gulf between the cultures of east and west. *On top of that there are the unique practices evolved by the Chinese since 1949* [italics added]. (p. xiii)

Deng Xiaoping's "open-door" policy was based on the "integration" of Marxism with China's *guoqing* ("Chinese conditions"; Deng, 1985, 1987). A recent study (Yan, 1994) of *guoqing* published in the West reports that

> in 1984, Deng Xiaoping issued a Communist Party directive that said, "Western cultures and ideas should be adopted only if they fit *guo qing*. Good ideas applicable in China should be promoted; corrupted and inapplicable ideas should be discarded."
> The Chinese use the expression "does not meet China's *guo qing*" to criticize methods and ideas that they believe foreign governments or corporations may be imposing on them. (p. 67)

I conceptualize the PRC condition as consisting of the following variables: politics, economic planning, legal framework, technology, great size, backwardness, and rapid change. The central theme of the PRC condition is Chinese bureaucracy.

Politics

Article 1 of *The Constitution of the People's Republic of China* (1982, p. 359) reads as follows: "The People's Republic of China is a socialist state. . . . The socialist system is the basic system of the

People's Republic of China." *The Constitution of the Communist Party of China* (1982) stipulates that

> the Communist Party of China is the vanguard of the Chinese working class . . . and the force at the core leading China's cause of socialism. . . . The Communist Party of China takes Marxism-Leninism and Mao Zedong Thought as its guide to action. (p. 382)

First to be borne in mind about *guoqing* is that the PRC is a socialist state with Marxism-Leninism and Mao Zedong Thought as its political ideology and the Communist Party of China as its ruling party. As Huang (1996) stated,

> Political power in China has always resided firmly with the central government, and with the Chinese Communist Party. This feature of the Chinese political system has remained fundamentally unaffected by the economic reforms. It is obviously still a one-party system, and it can be extremely repressive and brutal when the political authority of the Chinese Communist Party is challenged. (p. 3)

Chinese politics is grounded in Marxism-Leninism, but its concrete rhetoric is found in Mao Zedong Thought or so-called "Maoism." Lucian Pye (1984) condenses "fundamentals of Maoism" into the following points:

Contradiction and struggle: The major difference between Mao Zedong Thought and Confucian tradition is that the former does not view social disorder and conflict in a negative way, whereas the latter emphasizes social order and harmony.

Class struggle and class attitude: Individuals were distinguished by their class backgrounds in Mao's time. The ideology dictates that the working class has the innate ability to understand political situations better than all others.

Human spirit over machines: Another distinctive feature of Mao Zedong Thought is a belief in the superiority of the willpower of people over machines. Mao transferred political ideology to a sort of morality and used "correct thoughts" and "right spirit" to motivate the masses; the Maoist glorification of human motivations strikes chords in harmony with the Confucian notions of "self-cultivation" and "correct behavior."

Self-reliance: Self-reliance, not dependency on foreign powers, is valued in Mao Zedong Thought, which is consistent with Mao's value of human motivations.

Distrust of specialization: "Mao Zedong himself . . . remained throughout his life deeply distrustful of intellectuals" (p. 208). The rationale is that political attitude ("red") is more important than specialized knowledge ("expert").

Rural over urban: Mao's distrust of specialization is also manifested in his idealization of rural values, viewing city settings as sources of moral and political corruption. This ideology led to millions of high school graduates being sent to the countryside to receive re-education from the peasants during the Cultural Revolution (1966-1976).

The collective over the individual: A final important theme in Maoism is its "deep distrust of individualism and an unquestioning belief that the interests of all individuals should yield to the interests of the group or collective" (p. 209). Mao Zedong Thoughts "are simple, moralistic principles stressing the need for self-sacrifice and heroic self-destruction in favor of collective interests" (p. 203). The same spirit is also spelled out in Confucian philosophy, in which the interests of the family and kinship networks outweigh those of the individuals. The difference, however, is that, in Maoism, "the collectivity has become the larger concept of the 'state' and the 'people' as a whole" (p. 209).

Post-Mao Chinese leadership has certainly put aside certain aspects of Maoism, such as class struggle and idealization of conflict, and modified some others, such as self-reliance and distrust of specialization, thereby ideologically paving the way for massive absorption of foreign investment in China today. Marxism-Leninism and Mao Zedong Thought, however, are still proclaimed by the regime as the fundamental ideology of the PRC as seen in the so-called Four Cardinal Principles (*si xiang ji ben yuan ze*: adherence to the socialist road, to the people's democratic dictatorship, to the leadership of the Communist Party, and to Marxism-Leninism and Mao Zedong Thought), despite the fact that

China today appears to be extremely different from what it was in Mao's time.

One of the most significant implications of Chinese politics consists in the mechanisms through which behavior is controlled by ideology. First, in the PRC there is an interlocking structure of the party (*dang*), the state (*guojia*), and the government (*zhengfu*), with the party commanding the ultimate leadership. The party is "an omnipresent, omniscient, criss-crossed, interwoven force controlling the entire system of political organization" (Rohwer, 1992, p. 20); the party "controls and directs the complex system of government machinery," and it is "through the agencies of the government that the policies and programs approved by the party are implemented" (Constitution of the Communist Party of China, 1982, p. 114).

Mao (1966, p. 135) states, "Political work is the life-blood of all economic work." The "party-government" is a predominant player in economic life in China. China began to absorb foreign investment only after the party-government had set forth the reform and open-door policy in 1978. Politics is a powerful factor influencing Chinese business decision making, which can be either "crazily quick" or "tremendously slow." Huang, Leonard, and Chen (1997) noted,

> Of course, as political considerations have an impact on business decision making, the timing could be either crazily fast or tremendously slow. That is to say, in some cases, the timing of business decision making will be based on political needs, not economic laws. For example, before President Bill Clinton decided whether or not to extend the status of Most Favored Nation (MFN) of China in 1994, because of the Chinese human rights situation, China quickly organized a huge business delegation with billions of U.S. dollars of orders to visit the United States in May. At that time, whether or not the Chinese status of the Most Favored Nation could be extended would be determined by the U.S. Congress and President Bill Clinton. On the other hand, because of the U.S. visit of Lee Teng-hui, President of Taiwan, many Sino-American business decisions were delayed. Particularly, the negotiation about three openings, the opening of navigation and air traffic, and opening of postal communication, and the opening of trade association between the mainland and Taiwan, were put off again. (pp. 137-138)

The importance of Chinese politics to Chinese business does not seem to be clearly comprehended by many Western business people. For example, Tung (1996) noted the cases in which mayors from Chinese cities are assigned the seat of honor, whereas the party secretary, who is usually the more powerful person in China's system, is relegated to a position of lesser honor during visits to American cities. "The Chinese government is the biggest boss"—a theme demonstrated by Illustration 1 in Chapter 4—is the key to understanding the essence of Chinese business reality. Illustration 8 in Chapter 4 tells a story about a provincial party secretary's visit to Sweden, showing the role that the party-government plays in Chinese business negotiation processes.

Second, the party attracts a number of talented people to join the web of the party by offering better career and promotion opportunities and then, through these people, the party's image and control over bureaucratic power are reinforced. de Keijzer (1992, p. 32) explained why more than 2.4 million people have joined the Communist Party of China since the Tiananmen Square incident, increasing membership to 50.3 million: "If two talented young people are competing for the same job, the senior official may still feel it's 'safer' to give it to the one who has joined the Party."

Third, the Chinese are controlled through *jilü* (discipline), a term blending ideology indoctrination with moral obligations; no PRC officials can afford to "violate the discipline" (*weifan jilü*). Mao (1966) wrote,

> We must affirm anew the discipline of the Party, namely: (1) The individual is subordinate to the organization; (2) the minority is subordinate to the majority; (3) the lower level is subordinate to the higher level; and (4) the entire membership is subordinate to the Central Committee. Whoever violates these articles of discipline disrupts Party unity. (p. 255)[2]

Fourth, *danwei* and *dang'an* limit the physical mobility of the Chinese and exert psychological pressure and fear on the Chinese mind. I discuss these under Chinese Bureaucracy, later in this chapter.

The political movements in the PRC's history, such as the Anti-Rightist (1957-1958), the Great Leap Forward (1958-1960), and the Cultural Revolution (1966-1976), have left indelible traumas on the Chinese mind, contributing to making today's PRC Chinese less candid and honest than they would be otherwise. The Cultural Revolution, which lasted from May 1966 to October 1976, constitutes what the post-Mao Chinese leadership formulated as the "most severe setback and the heaviest losses" suffered in the PRC's history ("Resolution," 1981, p. 32). During the Cultural Revolution, many Chinese were persecuted; China's young legal system was destroyed; and Confucius was attacked, academic learning was abolished, and intellectuals were stigmatized and called *chou lao jiu* ("stinking ninth category"). It was also during the Cultural Revolution that the personality cult of Mao reached its peak. "More than any Chinese emperor, Mao was revered, eulogized, and glorified" (Pye, 1984, p. 202). Mao's "Little Red Book" was fanatically memorized and sloganized by the PRC Chinese. Mao's words, such as "Political power grows out of the barrel of a gun" (Mao, 1966, p. 61), are not "gentle" at all. Mao also states,

> A revolution is not a dinner party, or writing an essay, or painting a picture, or doing embroidery; it cannot be so refined, so leisurely and gentle, so temperate, kind, courteous, restrained, and magnanimous. A revolution is an insurrection, an act of violence by which one class overthrows another. (p. 11)

The impact of Mao's "non-dinner-party" style on today's middle-aged PRC managers should not be underestimated, as Seligman (1990) observes:

> The Cultural Revolution of 1966-1976 had devastating effects on interpersonal relationships that are felt even to this day. Chinese in the PRC who lived through this period tend to be less trusting and friendly towards people they do not know and less likely to express unorthodox political opinions in their presence. (p. 4)

Given Mao's great influence on life in the PRC, any discussion about Chinese politics without reference to Mao's personality would be incomplete. Mao's thinking is not totally separated from Confucian traditions as is shown from the previous discussion about the "fundamentals of Maoism." Furthermore, I view Mao Zedong as a person full of stratagems. The post-Mao leadership ("Resolution," 1981) summarized Mao Zedong Thought into "six assets," two of which (i.e., "On the building of the revolutionary army and military strategy" and "On policy and tactics") are directly related to his theories on strategies and tactics. The name of Sun Tzu, a great ancient Chinese strategist, and his strategies frequently appear in Mao's writings. Talking about the importance of tactics, Mao (1966, p. 7) straightforwardly states: "Policy and tactics [in Chinese, Mao uses the word *celue*] are the life of the Party; leading comrades at all levels must give them full attention and must never on any account be negligent." Mao's tactical personality can be seen in two influential books about his private life: *Mao Zedong: Man, Not God* written by Quan Yanchi based on stories by Li Yinqiao, Mao's bodyguard during the period from 1947 to 1962, and *The Private Life of Chairman Mao* written by Dr. Li Zhisui, Mao's personal physician from 1955 to 1976. I shall discuss Mao's strategic character later.

Economic Planning

State planning is one of the most important characteristics of the Chinese economy. China's state enterprises must operate under the state plan, as Article 16 of *The Constitution of the People's Republic of China* (1982, p. 361) stipulates that "State enterprises have decision-making power in operation and management within the limits prescribed by law, on condition that they submit to unified leadership by the state and fulfil [sic] all their obligations under the state plan."

China has gradually developed a multieconomic structure involving the state-owned, collective, private, and foreign-invested economic elements, with the state-owned economy being the leading force and other economies complementary ones. The leading status of state-owned enterprises (SOEs) and public ownership in the Chinese economy is still emphasized by the party. Jiang Zemin (as quoted in Frankenstein, 1993) said,

> In China's economic growth we shall persist in taking public ownership as the main body and developing diverse economic sectors, bringing into play the beneficial and necessary supplementary role of the individual economy, the private economy, Chinese-

foreign joint ventures, cooperative enterprises and foreign-owned enterprises. . . . This doesn't mean in any way weakening or eliminating the position of public ownership as the main sector. . . . Large and medium-sized enterprises under public ownership are the mainstay of China's socialist modernization. [Our policy toward other sectors] is, first to encourage them to develop vigorously within limits specified by the state; and second, to strengthen management and guidance over them by economic, administrative [code words for Party and state political regulation] and legal means so as to give effect to their positive role and to restrict their negative aspects that are harmful to socialist economic development. (pp. 15-16)

China's centralized economic planning structure is still very much part of the reality, and reforms to date aim to "modify" rather than "replace" it (Child, 1990). A fundamental problem with China's economy is the lack of concrete definition of *gongyouzhi* (public ownership) in Chinese industrial governance. Nominally, "the people" are the owners of China's industry. In practice, however, the specific owners of industrial properties remain unidentified. John Child (1994) writes,

Who actually owns Chinese "state-owned" enterprises is a particularly vexed question which has not been resolved, but which is extremely germane to proposals now being discussed for issuing shares in these enterprises to members of the public and/or to employees, or even privatizing them entirely. (p. 20)

As a consequence, the Chinese government becomes de facto owner of Chinese industry and holder of industrial property rights in the PRC, and the government's planning steers much of the economy.

Zhou (1992) points out that China's centralized economic planning suffers from four drawbacks. First, enterprises lack decision-making power and become simply appendages of state administrative agencies at various levels. The government agencies (often referred to by the Chinese as "mother-in-law") give mandatory instructions top down to the lowest level regarding the standards to be instituted. Second, the management is carried out vertically through the central and regional administrative systems, and the lateral economic relations among organizations, industries, and regions are severed. This results in self-sufficient organizations, industries, and regions. Third, the mandatory planning does not meet the changing demand of society. Finally, there is no relationship between the profit of the enterprise and the quality of its operation or between the income of its employees and their efforts and contributions made at work. This gives rise to low efficiency and lack of accountability.

The vague definition of public ownership also contributed to egalitarianism and the *daguofan* phenomenon ("Everyone eats in the same big rice pot"); workers believe they deserve a *tiefanwan* ("iron rice bowl")—a guaranteed lifetime employment and salary—regardless of whether they are doing a good job or not or whether the enterprises need their services. Wall (1990, p. 22) notes, "In the past, they have been granted these, regardless of their efforts and as a result, many do not choose to work hard; they are indifferent to quality standards; they avoid responsibility; and they consider customers a nuisance." *Daguofan* goes hand in hand with the punishment-oriented corporate policies in PRC organizations. Björkman (1994) observes that whereas Western management stresses the value of incentives, Chinese organizations emphasize punishment rather than rewards. Employees may lose their monthly bonus if they make mistakes, but they are rarely rewarded for their outstanding performance.

China's SOEs account for the larger part of China's industrial output and represent China's key industries; they are most often the ones that Western firms face in negotiations, especially regarding large industrial projects. In terms of numbers, the SOEs account for a mere 2.8% of the national total. They contributed 74% of China's total treasury income in 1995, however (Lu, 1996b). The government "controls its infrastructure of railways, telecommunications, and other industries" (Lu, 1996a, p. 5). Jiang Zemin, the Communist Party of China's (CPC) general secretary and China's president, reaffirmed at the 8th National People's Congress (NPC) that "state-owned enterprises are the backbone of China's national economy and serve as the force leading the socialist market economy" ("Jiang: State Run," 1996, p. 1).

Nevertheless, the "backbone" of China's economy is suffering great losses today. One third of the SOEs are definitely operating at a loss, and another one third suffer hidden losses. The government subsidized losses of $4.93 billion in 1995, a 20.5% increase compared with 1994 (Lu, 1996b). The reinvigoration of the SOEs is high on the agenda of the government's Ninth Five-Year Plan (1996-2000).

With regard to management of China's SOEs, a number of scholars have provided highly constructive insights (Boisot & Xing, 1992; Child, 1990; Child & Lu, 1990; Hunt & Yang, 1990; Jackson, 1992; Laaksonen, 1984; Li & Murray, 1992; Lockett, 1988; Walder, 1989; Zhou, 1992). Walder (1989) describes four "facts of life" in Chinese management. First, the enterprise is a "political coalition" in which management continues to rely on the support of other enterprise officers, particularly the party secretary. Second, the enterprise is a "sociopolitical community" in which management is judged on social criteria by both the party and the trade union. Third, Chinese management is characterized by the continued importance of vertical relationships with the government bureaucracy. Finally, non-market exchange relationships exist, particularly in the area of securing shortage supplies and trade credit.

In a replication of Mintzberg's (1973) study of how a group of American managers spent their day, Boisot and Xing (1992) time analyzed the behavior of six Chinese directors during a period of 6 days. The following were the marked differences between Chinese and American managers: The Chinese spent much more time with their superiors and much less time with outsiders and peers than did the Americans, the Chinese received five times as much written materials from their superiors as did the Americans, and the Chinese submitted to their superiors less than one tenth as much as did the Americans. The top-down hierarchical Chinese management style is seen in this comparative study.

Child (1990) points out that although Chinese management is characterized by vertical dependency and authority, horizontal relationships are less evident. All Chinese enterprises are subordinate to a number of higher authorities on which they rely for information on the external environment. These government authorities normally have complementary dependent subunits located within the enterprise itself. Therefore, multiple lines of control are in place. Many departments are loyal to their superiors in the government at the expense of their colleagues in other functional departments within their own enterprise, which gives rise to what the Chinese refer to as a mother-in-law relationship. Child (1990) writes,

> It is not surprising that among the managerial problems most
> frequently mentioned in China are poor communication and co-
> operation between departments, slow decision making due in part
> to this poor integration, and limited identification by members of
> the enterprise with corporate goals. (p. 139)

The centralized planning system that has dominated Marxist China for decades is still a reality that foreign marketers have to face, despite the economic reform carried out since 1978. Gao (1993) provides two reasons. On the one hand, China's effort to build up a new economic model cannot be accomplished in one move; on the other hand, the market economy that China intends to establish will retain the basic features of socialism. The state will exercise a much greater control over the economy than does the government of a market economy. This control is effected through plans, thus explaining why China's new economic model is labeled "the socialist market economy."

De Anzizu and Chen (1991, p. 58) summarize Chinese economic planning after reforms into three features. First, the mandatory plans have been significantly reduced at the national level. Nevertheless, the government still controls some scarce raw materials and resources. Second, with varying degrees, depending on the industry, the provincial and local governments, as well as the enterprises, have acquired more power in the decision-making process. Third, although the freedom of the enterprises is increasing as they depend less on mandatory plans and more on market mechanism, "the average enterprise is still not a truly independent economic entity." Since 1978, the title of "Chinese economy" has been changed several times from "socialist planned economy" to "socialist planned commodity economy" and, currently, "socialist market economy." Whatever the terms, strong governmental control and planning are the Chinese reality.

Government planning and control also extend to foreign business in China. For example, under Chinese law, all joint ventures contracts and articles of association must be approved by the Ministry of Foreign Trade and Economic Cooperation (MOFTEC) and local government authorities (Foreign Economic Relations and Trade Commissions) depending on the scale (e.g., dollar ceiling) and importance (e.g., key and priority industries) of the projects (Chang, 1987; Chen, 1996; Wang, Zhang, He, & Zhang, 1995). Pye (1982, p. 15) notes that despite a degree of apparent decentralization, "the Chinese system is still highly centralized in that any significant allocation of foreign exchange is controlled by the Bank of China, which must review most contract negotiations." Similar views are also expressed by Huang et al. (1997) in *Business Decision Making in China.*

Given the inherent political and economic structures and despite changes brought by reforms, the state enterprises in the PRC share many operational characteristics: dependency on overall planning by the state, lack of independent identity and managerial autonomy, low mobility of employees, low incentives for better performance, high risk of punishment, and poor economic returns. Illustrations 1 through 6, 8, 20, and so on in Chapter 4 provide insights into how state planning and bureaucracy influence Chinese negotiating behavior.

Legal Framework

Since 1979, China has embarked on a course of building a substantial body of laws and regulations. More than 300 laws have been promulgated by the NPC, and more than 400 regulations have been issued by the State Council (Brown, 1993). Three basic laws on foreign direct investment in China have been issued (Ministry of Foreign Economic Relations and Trade [MOFERT], 1992): (a) The Law of the People's Republic of China on Chinese-Foreign Equity Joint Ventures (adopted on July 1, 1979), (b) The Law of the People's Republic of China on Chinese-Foreign Cooperative Joint Ventures (adopted on April 13, 1988), and (c) The Law of the People's Republic of China on Wholly Foreign-Owned Enterprises (adopted on April 12, 1986). Furthermore, "Regulations on the Administration of Technology Import Contracts" was promulgated by the State Council on May 24, 1985, to regulate foreign technology transfer to China.

Despite progress, the Chinese legal system is young and unstable. It is burdened by six major weaknesses. First, in the PRC, it has always been the party and government leaders' *zhishi* (instructions) and *yijian* (opinions) that guide Chinese law. For example, after the then paramount Chinese leader Deng Xiaoping's tour to Shenzhen in January 1992, many previous taboos became nonexistent (Tan, 1993). This means that there are many human factors placed above the Chinese legal system.

Second, the government agencies' administrative measures and regulations function as de facto law. All the *guiding* (regulations), *mingling* (orders), *jueyi* (decisions), *zhishi* (instructions), and *faling* (decrees) of the Chinese government (the State Council, ministries, commissions, etc. at the central and local levels) have the force of law (*falü*) and are applicable throughout China (Brown, 1993). The relationship between Chinese enterprises and external government agencies is not established by law but by administrative regulations (Boisot & Xing, 1992). The Chinese government is also a primary instrument in deciding the contents of a contract. Campbell and Adlington (1988, p. 25) noted, "The government influences the detailed content of contracts through its approval process in order to prevent the Chinese partner from accepting clauses which the government considers unfavorable." To make matters more complicated, business in China is often regulated by the government's unpublished or so-called *neibu* (internal) regulations that are unavailable to foreigners (Carver, 1996; Chang, 1987; Roehrig, 1994a). The Chinese government's approach to law is fundamentally instrumentalist; laws and regulations are enacted to achieve immediate policy objectives of the government. Consequently, Chinese laws and regulations are intentionally ambiguous and remain open to interpretation (Potter, 1995).

Third, there are still many loopholes in the Chinese legal system. For example, China is weak in economic laws covering market structure, market activities, market order, macroeconomic control, social insurance, and so on, which urgently need to be enhanced (Ma, 1996a).

Fourth, implementation of existing laws is weak. The Chinese reality is more law on paper than in practice (Li, 1980). The Chinese legal regime is featured by formalism that emphasizes content over performance (Potter, 1995). Tian Jiyun, vice-chairman of the NPC Standing Committee, China's highest legislation body, admitted that "law implementation is still a weak link in the judicial sector" (Ma, 1996b, p. 1).

Fifth, the average education level of the Chinese population is low. In China, where only a small percentage of youth have a chance to receive formal higher education, and several hundred million people are illiterate or semi-illiterate, it takes time for the people to gain the required legal awareness and for the legal concept to take root in the society. Li (1980, p. 39) adds one more reason in this regard by observing that "none of the major past or present Chinese Communist leaders received any training in law or had much experience with law."

Finally, it is common that existing laws are subject to constant changes due to the experimental nature of China's reform, which was described by Deng Xiaoping as "crossing the river by feeling the stones underfoot" (*mo zhe shi tou guo he*). Campbell and Adlington (1988, p. 23) observed, "There is a regular stream of Implementing Regulations which clarify and extend existing legislation."

China's lax legal system is found to be responsible, in part, for "economic crime," "rampant fraud," "counterfeit" practices, and "illegal" trading in the PRC (Z. L. Liu, 1996; Silk, 1994; Sun, 1995). These problems are acute, especially when China today is "crossing the river by feeling the stones under her feet."

Having discussed many weaknesses of China's legal system, it should be noted, however, that because of the deep Confucian aversion to law, there has been a lack of a well-functioning legal system in Chinese society since ancient times. The Confucian notion that law alone does not solve problems and people's behavior must be influenced by their own use of self-regulating moral mechanisms (e.g., face and shame) seems to have been deeply rooted in the Chinese mind. It is not necessarily a negative notion; it can be positive as well (see Confucianism). Therefore, although there have been encouraging changes brought into the PRC's legal framework in recent years, it must be understood that the real changes in the people's mind will take time—decades or even centuries. Illustration 4 in Chapter 4 indicates that the Chinese legal awareness was blunt; Illustrations 9, 10, and 11 show the typical Chinese aversion to law and lawyers.

Technology

The gap between China and Western countries lies most prominently in China's backward technology, both hardware and software. To import foreign technology to close the gap and enhance people's living standard is the major rationale behind China's open-door policy (Simon, 1989).

China's industrialization suffers from such problems as lack of technological innovation, low productivity, poor economic returns, antiquated production facilities, energy waste, and environmental pollution. Due to the neglect of technological innovation, Chinese enterprises, particularly SOEs, are poorly equipped. For example, only one third of China's mechanical and electronic products can meet the international standard of the 1960s and 1970s, and only 5% meet current international standards (Shen, Guo, & Li, 1995). As a result, key technologies and equipment for new and emerging industries depend largely on import. Therefore, when teaming up with foreign companies, the Chinese are looking for what they call "big mountains" that they can rely on technologically, as shown in Illustration 15 in Chapter 4.

Although the import of foreign technology in the form of turnkey projects was practiced from 1950 to 1962 (from the former Soviet Union, etc.), from 1963 to 1968 (from Japan, the former West Germany, etc.), and from 1973 to 1978 (from the United States, Japan, the former West Germany, etc.), China's real takeoff in acquisition of foreign technology in a wide variety of forms has occurred since 1978, when China embarked on her Four Modernizations (i.e., modernizations in industry, agriculture, science and technology, and national defense). According to Deng Xiaoping, of the Four Modernizations, modernization in science and technology is the "key." China is interested in advanced rather than outdated technology. The second paragraph of Article 5 of the Joint Venture Law reads as follows (MOFERT, 1992):

> The technology and equipment contributed by a foreign party as its investment must be advanced technology and equipment which is truly suited to the needs of China. In case of losses caused by deception through the intentional provision of outdated technology and equipment, compensation shall be paid for such losses. (p. 18)

Not all transfers of technology will be approved as qualified transactions. According to "Regulations on the Administration of Technology Import Contracts," a technology transfer must be able to meet at least one of the following requirements to be approved by the Chinese government authorities (Moser, 1986): (a) The transfer must enable the Chinese party to develop and produce new products; (b) the transfer must be able to improve product quality and performance, reduce the cost of production, and save energy or raw materials; (c) the transfer must be conducive to making full use of local Chinese resources; (d) the transfer must enable the Chinese party to expand exports and increase foreign exchange earnings; (e) the transaction must be conducive to environmental protection in China; (f) the transaction must be conducive to safety in production; (g) the transfer must allow the Chinese party to improve business management; and (h) the transfer must help raise the level of science and technology in China generally.

Although there are various channels for technology transfer to China by foreign firms (e.g., turnkey project, licensing, coproduction, equity joint venture, cooperative joint venture, and wholly foreign-owned enterprise), equity joint venture (EJV) is generally preferred by the Chinese government and is the most widely used method for technology transfer (de Bruijn & Jia, 1993; Tsang, 1994). Wang et al. (1995) provide four major reasons for the Chinese preference for EJV. First, because of joint share in profits (or losses), risks, and management in proportion to the parties' equity contribution, the EJV can make the foreign partner an active partner in terms of transferring advanced foreign technology and upgrading Chinese products. Second, the marketing and distribution channels of the foreign party can be used to obtain market information and spur export. Third, foreign management know-how can be learned. Finally, because the parties jointly share profits, losses, and risks, the EJV will not increase the financial burden of the Chinese government, thereby helping the development of China's economy. In short, the continuous or ongoing transfer of advanced foreign technology to the EJV is what the Chinese expect most.

An EJV, however, is not the only way to enter the Chinese market. Vanhonacker (1997, p. 131) holds that because Chinese and foreign partners generally have the "same bed" but "different dreams," and "divorce" is difficult, EJVs often operate unsatisfactorily. By contrast, a wholly foreign-owned enterprise, which provides flexibility and managerial control to the foreign side and jobs, technology, and foreign exchange to the Chinese side, may offer a better, win-win alternative.

Regarding technology protection, China recently passed laws on patents and copyrights. Nevertheless, pitfalls exist. Chen (1996) notes that "Regulations on the Administration of Technology Import Contracts" allow a Chinese recipient to use simultaneously other foreign suppliers' technology so that when the Chinese recipient cooperates with a direct competitor of the foreign supplier, it is more difficult to maintain trade secrets. Most foreign business people are unsure just how much protection they will receive given the Chinese tradition of "socialist responsibility"—that is, the copying and distribution of protected technology within any given industrial bureaucracy. Some (in Frankenstein, 1986, p. 152) complain that once a technology is in China, there is no way to protect company rights—"It's just gone!" Illustration 4 in Chapter 4 provides insight into the weakness of the Chinese system in protecting foreign technology around 1990 and 1991.

China has been improving its record steadily in recent years regarding intellectual property rights (IPRs). The Memorandum of Understanding signed in 1992 between China and the United States concerning IPRs has laid an important legal foundation for protection of foreign intellectual property in China (Chen, 1996). Until the late 1980s, any identified Chinese student could easily purchase a large collection of pirate copies of foreign-language dictionaries and other publications in the state-owned Foreign Languages Bookstore in Shanghai. Now, however, this type of open state-backed pirate selling is rarely seen in China. Therefore, I view this issue as essentially a development one with which China will be more able to come to grips in the future.

Great Size

China is often compared to a continent (Figure 3.1). With a land area of 9.6 million square kilometers, occupying 6.5% of the world total, and 1.2 billion people, accounting for approximately one fifth of the whole human population, China is no doubt the world's largest emerging market. Although China's family planning program has been rather successful, with only 1.5% population growth, its population still increases by about 15 million each year. The huge number of people in China is the very first thing that strikes Western visitors. A senior business executive of a Swedish company said in an interview, "When I landed in Sweden after months of working in China, I felt as if there had been a war in Sweden—there were almost no people to be seen here compared with vastly populated China."

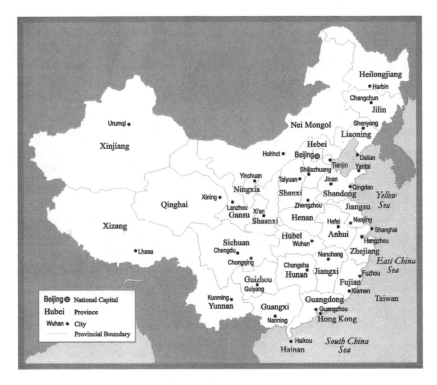

Figure 3.1. Map of China

SOURCE: Drawing by Gunilla Jernselius; copyright 1998 by Tony Fang.

Tapping the vast Chinese market is the primary motivation behind foreign firms' China operations. China is fully aware of its "market advantage," on the one hand, and its capital and technology disadvantage on the other hand. In the early 1980s, Deng Xiaoping made explicit his view that China is a large market and China must make good use of this advantage when developing foreign economic cooperation. Deng Xiaoping considered it a "strategic issue" that China's market advantage can be exchanged for the capital advantage of the developed countries on the basis of equality and mutual benefit. To exchange the Chinese market for foreign technology is an important state policy for utilizing foreign investment in China (see Chapter 4, Illustration 16). It is also stated in the party's "Resolution" adopted in 1993 at The Third Session of the 14th CPC Central Committee

(Li, 1995, p. 31) that "[We shall] bring the resources and market advantage of our country into play to attract foreign capital and technology in order to promote economic development."

China's large population also remains a chief obstacle to China's modernization. In the 1950s, Mao attacked professor Ma Yinchu, who had been the first leading Chinese economist to advocate family planning in China, because Mao (1966, p. 35) believed that "[m]ore people mean a greater ferment of ideas, more enthusiasm, and more energy." Professor Ma was criticized nationwide and labeled as a "rightist." As a result, several hundred million "extra" Chinese have been born since the 1950s. Mao's mistake has proved to be so monumental that it cannot be remedied by any one-off family planning policy, not even the one-child per family policy that took hold in China in the 1980s—the greatest demographic experiment in the history of humankind. The population problem constitutes a major challenge for the heightening of the average living standard in China. This conclusion can be drawn by any educated Chinese who have visited the West or have been living in the West for some time. As Bo Yang (1992) remarks,

> People say that the living standard in the USA is very high. But the U.S. has a population of only 260 million people. Can you imagine what life would be like in the USA if a billion Chinese people moved there? The population problem is a critical one. (p. 54)

A challenge to China in the future is how to turn its population from an enormous burden into a huge amount of human capital for China's economic development.

A close examination of China's geography shows that China's arable land is only 12% of its territory. More than 90% of the population is crowded into the eastern third of the mainland, whereas China's "wild west" remains very sparsely populated. Although China has a wealth of natural resource in absolute terms, its resource per capita is far below the world average. For example, China's freshwater resource per capita is only one fourth that of the world average (Shen et al., 1995). The lack of resource per capita contributes considerably to the people's competitive behavior, which can be observed in Chinese life in the PRC. The extremely high density of the Chinese population also contributes to making many universal cultural traits, such as face, interpersonal relationship, and tactics in handling relationships, particularly salient in China.

China is administratively divided into 23 provinces,[3] five autonomous regions, and four municipalities (i.e., Beijing, Shanghai, Tianjin, and Chongqing) directly under the central government. Due to differences in geographical location, natural conditions, and the pace of economic development, the character of Chinese people varies to a certain extent from region to region. Hu (1994, p. 238) provides a list of the character of Chinese people from different regions (Table 3.1).

Although Table 3.1 certainly provides a grain of truth, folk sayings probably offer better illustrations. A popular saying in the PRC regards a Chinese traveler's impressions:

> [It is] in Beijing that you realize you are *guan xiao* ["low ranking," suggesting that Beijing is a political city with many high-ranking bureaucrats]; in Shanghai, you understand the meaning of *qiliang xiao* ["narrow-minded," suggesting that Shanghai people can be too clever to be wise]; in Guangdong, you realize you are *dan xiao* ["timid," meaning that Guangdong people are brave in actions, doing things often not in line with the central government]; in Shenzhen, you find you are *qian shao* ["lacking money," implying that Shenzhen appears to be a Westernized moneymaking society]; in Hainan, you come to know the importance of *shengti hao* ["keeping fit," suggesting that prostitution in Hainan is commonplace].

In short, the Chinese can be different from place to place, given the regional cultural influences (see Chapter 4, Illustrations 7 and 30).

My thesis, however, is that China's national cultural homogeneity outweighs regional differences so much so that we can capture much of the workings of the Chinese mind at the national culture level. A limitation of the regional perspective also lies in the fact that, today, one actually meets many southern Chinese in north China and vice versa, given the increased mobility of the population. For example, Shenzhen, China's most successful and publicized economic model city in Guangdong province, is composed of "immigrants" largely from northern and central China. This makes the definition,

TABLE 3.1 Regional Characters of Chinese People

- Beijing people are straightforward
- Shanghai people are clever and farsighted
- Tianjin people are capable and seasoned
- The people of Guangdong, Zhejiang, and Anhui are decisive and full of stratagem
- Fujian people are honest and sedate
- Shandong people are forthright and generous
- The people of Liaoning, Jilin, and Heilongjiang are reasonable and loyal
- The people of Henan, Hebei, Hunan, and Hubei are open and direct
- The people of Sichuan, Shannxi, Jiangxi, and Shanxi are upright
- Those in Yunnan, Hainan, Guangxi, Guizhou, and Qinhai always behave in an unhurried manner
- The people of Inner Mongolia, Xinjiang, and Tibet are warmhearted but dubious

SOURCE: Based on Hu (1994, p. 238).

operationalization, and measurement of regional culture and its influence on people's behavior difficult, if not totally unworkable.

China's absolute scale, by virtue of population and economy, implies that China's success and failure affect everyone on the planet. For example, China's refugee flows, even a tiny fraction of China's population, would cause disasters for the whole world. Brown (1995) warns that there may not be enough food in the world to meet the ever-demanding appetite of China's 1.2 billion consumers. China's energy crisis, environmental problems, and so forth are essentially global issues. China is the world's fourth largest contributor to the annual increase in the greenhouse effect (Kennedy, 1993). Some draw a pessimistic picture about China's ambition to equip every family with a refrigerator by the Year 2000, which they believe would result in a huge increase in chlorofluorocarbons, further depleting the ozone layer. Kristof and Wudunn (1994, p. 388) noted, "The upshot is that Chinese peasants get cold drinks, and we get skin cancer."

I am of the stance that China's challenges and opportunities are not only China's but everyone's. China's stability and harmonious development benefit not only China but also the rest of the world. Therefore, policies aimed at preventing China from becoming a full member of the world community would be at best shortsighted and at worst dangerous. Genuinely caring about China's development process and integrating it into the global chessboard is of strategic and ecological importance to the peace and progress of the whole of humanity.

Backwardness

China has lagged behind the West since the Industrial Revolution, which began in England about 1750. Prior to this point, China was more advanced than the West in almost all areas: The Chinese level of technology in the Year 1500 was higher than that prevailing in Europe (Needham, 1954); the Chinese Han empire (206 B.C.– A.D. 220) "had been contemporary with and bigger than the Roman Empire" (Fairbank, 1992, p. 2); and from 1000 to 1500 A.D., "no comparison of agricultural productivity, industrial skill, commercial complexity, urban wealth, or standard of living (not to mention bureaucratic sophistication and cultural achievement) would place Europe on a par with the Chinese empire" (Feuerwerker, 1990, p. 235).

The limited progress of science and technology in China is a result of cultural, social, and political factors. Tu (1984) explains that, in the Confucian tradition, the energies of Chinese intellectuals were channeled into humanistic areas or social sciences instead of natural sciences. Deng Xiaoping (1987, p. 56) assumes that "China's past backwardness was due to its closed-door policy" and uses it as a key rationale for opening up China to the rest of the world.

China's improved economic strength and figures of absolute terms often distract people from recognizing the fact that China is still a developing country and is backward in many respects. Western business people must realize that backward or even primitive physical infrastructure, unreliable transportation networks, serious shortages in some basic utilities, such as electricity and drinking water, and so on are still very much part of the Chinese reality. China is also an unevenly developed market in which several million millionaires and a large number of middle-class consumers live alongside approximately 350 million country people who live in poverty, that is, living on less than $1 dollar per day (the United Nations poverty level; The World Bank, 1996).

Most prominently of all, China is short of capital to develop its economy and to revitalize its enterprises.[4] The PRC's shortage of foreign currency is the most important reason for the failure of negotiation with the Chinese (Stewart & Keown, 1989). In the mind of Chinese negotiators, there is one overriding concern: to reduce the cost and thus minimize their expenditure of foreign currency (Blackman, 1997). Having observed the financial reason behind the "marriages" of many Chinese-foreign joint ventures, one Western business executive joked during a conversation with me, "You know what 'Chinese-foreign joint venture' means? It means Chinese *join* and foreigners *venture!*"

The Chinese seem to be torn between their past greatness and increasing international importance, on the one hand, and the lack of modern technologies and large transnational Chinese corporations, on the other. Chinese vice premier Wu Bangguo (as quoted in "Managing Big," 1997) said,

> Our country's steel output already boasts 100 million tons, not to mention our 10 million tons extra production capacity, making us the world's number one. We may be called the largest steel producing nation, but not the strongest because we do not have any iron and steel enterprise which can be numbered internationally. . . . In Northern Europe, Finland is but a small country with a mere 5 million people; but it has Nokia, which holds a 25 percent share of the world's telecommunications market. Sweden is also a small country with 8 million inhabitants. But it has Volvo, which tops the world in heavy duty trucks and busses; it has Ericsson, whose mobile hand-set can be so small as to allow you to put it in your shirt pocket, and whose R&D cost amounts to 18 percent of the company's total sales; and it has ABB, which is very competitive in power generation equipment and transformers. . . . Only after

we have found some 10 to 30 Chinese enterprises in the list of the world's top 500, can we say that our economic quality is greatly improved. (p. 1)

Therefore, studying and making use of Western firms' advanced experience and expertise to heighten the international competitiveness of Chinese firms is a matter of great concern for Chinese leaders. Chinese managers generally lack rich international business experience, given China's long isolation from the rest of the world. To the Chinese, learning whatever is useful for China from advanced foreign nations thus becomes an important dimension of contemporary Sino-Western business relationships.

Although Chinese education has been improved historically since 1949, it is unevenly developed, and the Chinese people's average education level is low. Literacy—the basic educational index—shows the extent of the problem: China has a purported adult literacy rate of 69%; this means, however, that approximately 220 million Chinese are illiterate, almost three fourths of them women (Kennedy, 1993). Given this PRC condition, it is not strange that few Chinese can communicate in English, and that even vulgar behavior can be found in China.

All these problems of a human resource nature limit China's absorptive capacity to digest foreign technology (Kosenko & Samli, 1985; Tung, 1994b) and will slow its pace of economic development in the twenty-first century (Rohwer, 1996). They also contribute, at least in part, to the Chinese mentality of relying on intangible relationships rather than tangible systems and infrastructures to get things done. This no doubt influences Chinese bargaining behaviors. Roehrig (1994a) points out that chronic resource shortages and less developed infrastructure make bargaining beyond legal boundaries "a fact of business life." Their lack of confidence in tangible infrastructures and the rapid change of Chinese life also contribute considerably to the fact that the Chinese do not believe in any planning on paper (ironically, the Chinese economy is highly planned by nature!). What they do believe is that anything can happen in China: Problems of various natures can crop up anywhere at any time. This mentality in turn contributes to making the Chinese an "impatient" people who seem to have a great hurry when doing things in reality. The harsh and, in many places, primitive or even chaotic living and working conditions in China also contribute to making the Chinese an extremely enduring people who are prepared and able to cope with all hardships.

Rapid Change

China has been undergoing tremendous changes since the late 1970s; it is on its way to lifting one fifth of humanity out of poverty, moving toward modernization. The Chinese society is developing so rapidly that data acquired yesterday often need to be updated tomorrow. The changing feature of Chinese society results in the fact that things can hardly be fully planned at the operational level. One Swedish negotiator told me about the problems of his ongoing negotiations with the Chinese: "The most difficult problem in negotiating with China is that things cannot be planned in advance. You get change, change, and change."

Reform is the most important force behind the changing facade of contemporary China. It has been observed that now every noun in the Chinese managers' vocabulary has "reform" attached to it (Wall, 1990). Rohwer (1992) notes,

> No matter where you travel in China today, the most emphatic sensation you get is the intensity of the desire to modernize and to grow. Governors, party secretaries, party representatives on boards of directors: Their only interests seem to be foreign investment, trade, and economic reform. (p. 22)

Due to the experimental nature of China's reform—crossing the river by feeling the stones underfoot—changes are not strange at all.

China's reforms are largely confined to the sphere of economy, which reflects the Chinese tradition of min yi shi wei tian ("For the people, food is heaven").[5] Chinese leaders realized the serious consequences of a poor economy. On the eve of the collapse of Communism in the former Soviet Union, Deng Xiaoping (as quoted in Stewart, Cheung, & Yeung, 1992, p. 35) made the views of the Chinese leaders abundantly clear when saying, "One major factor [for the collapse] is that they did not manage their economies well. They failed to turn the superiority of socialism into reality." China is currently trying to make good use of capitalism in whatever area is necessary to build socialism with China's *guoqing* (Fang, 1992).

One of the features of China's reform program is decentralization of decision making from the central government to local governments (Deng, 1987) and from administrative bodies to enterprises and, by extension, the delegation within enterprises of specific decisions to a trained body of managers (Child & Lu, 1990). Decentralization of government control of both the domestic economy and the foreign trade sector is designed to stimulate rapid growth while encouraging controlled competition between regions, bureaucratic divisions, organizations, and individuals (Gorman, 1986). By way of various mechanisms, such as the "Director or Manager Responsibility System" that is practiced in Chinese industries, Chinese managers secure additional autonomy to make decisions of strategic significance. As Child and Lu (1990, p. 321) observed, however, "this autonomy is uncertain and bounded. It is liable to be rescinded as the result of sudden changes in government policy and it is bounded by local relational obligations."

The most important characteristic of China's reform is the birth of a competition mechanism in Chinese economy. Rohwer's (1992) analysis shows that Chinese reforms have succeeded thus far because they introduced much competition into the economy: competition between regions, firms, foreign investors, and industrial organizations. A large-scale survey of Chinese cities (Tan, 1993) shows that despite complaints, 85% of the interviewees agreed that reform has provided unprecedented opportunities for people to demonstrate individual talents.

China's foreign trade system is an example. Before 1978, China's import and export trade was handled by a dozen national import and export corporations or foreign trade corporations (FTCs) under MOFERT (now known as MOFTEC) in line with plans by the State Planning Commission and financed by the Bank of China. Reform has broken down MOFERT's monopoly over China's foreign trade, however, and given rise to the emergence of a large number of FTCs run directly by individual ministries and even the People's Liberation Army. Now there are a variety of agencies, companies, and organizations in each province and municipality with whom foreign firms can do business directly. It is not uncommon for Chinese companies from different ministries to compete in business areas far beyond their traditional jurisdiction.

To attract foreign investment more efficiently, the Chinese government has several times simplified formalities with regard to project approval. For example, currently, the coastal provinces and municipalities have a mandate to approve manufacturing projects with total investment capital under $30 million, whereas the power of inland provinces and municipalities is within $10 million. Non-manufacturing projects, except for energy, transportation, and raw material projects, are at the disposal of local government regardless of contract value.

MOFTEC, however, still represents the highest power controlling foreign transactions in China. For example, under Chinese law, all joint venture contracts and articles of association must be approved by MOFTEC's Foreign Investment Administration before becoming legally effective. Chang (1987) points out that "government approval" is still a Chinese characteristic, although MOFERT delegates authority to approve contracts under certain dollar ceilings to local government authorities. Given this characteristic, some suggest the decentralization and local autonomy are superficial. For example, Stewart (1990) holds that although authorized ceilings for foreign exchange spending were notified to lower authorities, ostensibly delegating powers from ministries to provinces to enterprises, the disbursement of foreign currency and control of imports remain firmly in the hands of Beijing. Stewart stated, "Whatever the theory of local autonomy, no deal requiring major foreign exchange can be concluded without Beijing becoming involved through the Ministry of Foreign Economic Relations and Trade (MOFERT) and the Foreign Exchange Administration" (p. 55).

As a result of the open-door policy and introduction of Western technology, Western values and lifestyle have been introduced to China and influence the people's behavior. Today, social and ideological controls are considerably loosened. China is flooded with pop cultures of the commercial world. The Chinese are now consumers of McDonald's and listeners of ABBA, Roxette, and even Spice Girls! "Parts of this [Chinese] culture are being threatened," wrote Feng Jicai (Feng, J. C., 1996, p. 9), a well-known Chinese writer, in an article about culture and the Chinese New Year, and Feng explains why. First, young Chinese are becoming more interested in Western culture. Second, Chinese increasingly turn to leisure whenever they have holidays and grow impatient with overelaborate festival customs. Third, the traditional cultural connotations of the New Year run largely counter to people's concepts of life today. Finally, important aspects of the New Year festival, such as firecrackers and ancestral sacrifice, are fading from the scene, leaving only the family reunion dinner, the nationwide spring festival entertainment show on TV, and New Year calls—often done by telephone.

China's opening to the outside world has left the Chinese staring wide-eyed at Western material life. Clearly, today's Chinese are becoming more money-oriented than they were in Mao's time. Frankenstein (1993, p. 11) observes that after decades of enforced poverty, the Chinese took the slogan "To get rich is glorious" seriously, perhaps too seriously: Foreigners were "struck by the spread of a grasping, money-seeking mentality that was a far cry from the 'serve the people' sloganeering of previous periods, or even what passes for normal, competitive business ethics in the West."

The language barrier is a daunting challenge in dealing with the Chinese. That very few Chinese speak English is a reality. It must be noted, however, that the Chinese are learning quickly. Chinese students actually spend much more time studying English than Westerners spend studying Chinese. We will soon meet more Chinese business people who are able to communicate effectively in English. We must also not conclude from the common Chinese inability to speak foreign languages that they cannot read, write, or understand foreign languages. Very often, the opposite is true: The Chinese do read, write, or understand foreign languages well but are not good at speaking them because they have been socialized in a culture that does not encourage speaking out. Communication researchers Gao, Ting-Toomey, and Gudykunst (1996) call Chinese communication a "listening-centered communication" (*tinghua*) and point out that most Chinese schools emphasize listening skills, memorizing skills, writing skills, and reading skills but rarely give importance to speaking skills. In fact, a Western-educated Chinese can easily be differentiated from a Chinese-educated Chinese simply by way of oral presentation. Illustration 39 in Chapter 4 shows that the Chinese ability to understand but inability to verbalize English gives them a significant bargaining advantage at the international negotiation table.

Chinese negotiating style is currently in transition; Chinese managers are becoming increasingly experienced, professional, or "modern" at the international negotiation table. The reasons are many: For example, ideology has declined gradually in importance in China; Chinese business norms are becoming more compatible with international ones; and many Chinese have traveled abroad and studied at Western universities, thereby obtaining frequent glimpses into international practices and standards, which in turn allow them to imagine other solutions than just those using the Middle Kingdom mentality.

A comparative examination of the works of Tung (1982b) and Stewart and Keown (1989) shows that the Chinese have become more "mature" throughout the years in the sense that "nonpersonal factors, such as product and financing, are becoming more important than personal and cultural factors" (Stewart & Keown, 1989, p. 72). Some change in Chinese negotiating style can be expected given the emergence of younger, more technically competent officials who emphasize economic performance (Frankenstein, 1986). An increasing number of lawyers from Chinese law firms participate in negotiations with foreign companies. They "often play a helpful role as far as contract language is concerned," and "many of the younger Chinese lawyers realize the need for precision and completeness in contract language" (Chang, 1987, p. 10). In short, a modern style of Chinese negotiating will take shape more clearly as time elapses. This changing aspect of Chinese business can be discerned in Illustration 13 in Chapter 4.

Chinese Bureaucracy

Chinese bureaucracy is the central theme in the PRC condition. The Chinese market is vast—so is Chinese bureaucracy. Recognition by social scientists of the existence of bureaucracies and bureaucrats dates back to Max Weber and Karl Marx. In this book, *bureaucracy* means more a "rational legal authority" (Weber, 1947/1964, p. 330), "an organizational structure characterized by hierarchy" (Garston, 1993, p. 5), and "a particular form of organization comprised of bureaus or agencies" (Jackson, 1982, p. 121) than the now popularized meaning of "red tape" and "inefficiency." Historically, the Chinese have confronted the frustrations of bureaucracy for thousands of years. Max Weber (as quoted in Bond, 1991, p. 73) called the Chinese bureaucracy a "patrimonial bureaucracy" to which China's stability and resilience were attributed.

Figure 3.2 shows Chinese bureaucracy—the government structure and planning hierarchy. Although the CPC is not included in the chart, it should be understood that the CPC is everywhere in the background. The major institutions responsible for providing overall strategic planning and guidance for Chinese economy and trade are the CPC, the State Council, the State Development Planning Commission, the State Economic and Trade Commission, and the various ministries.[6]

Lieberthal and Oksenberg (1986) provide a theoretical analysis of Chinese bureaucracy and identify a number of unique structural features; the key to Lieberthal and Oksenberg's (1986) analysis is the thesis that Chinese bureaucracy is "a complex internal bargaining system:"

> *Personalized rule at the top:* At the apex of Chinese bureaucracy are the top leaders who rule China and who are the key to setting the political climate for negotiations and for approving very large projects.
>
> *Fragmented, segmented, and stratified bureaucracy:* Below the apex, there is a bewildering number of ministries, national agencies, and provincial and local units. Each has command over a distinctive set of resources and is charged with a specific mission that gives it a measure of autonomy. Each tends to disregard injunctions from agencies outside its command hierarchy.
>
> *Complex internal bargaining system:* At the core of the Chinese bureaucracy lies an ongoing process of bargaining among agencies, each of which commands resources that other units need but cannot obtain simply by demanding or purchasing them. Negotiation or bargaining is an essential ingredient of the Chinese system. It is no wonder that the Chinese are tough negotiators with foreigners; they have simply gained much training at home dealing with one another.
>
> *Ambiguities in domestic deal making:* Typically, ambiguities are deliberately preserved so that much is exposed to bargaining. Bargains

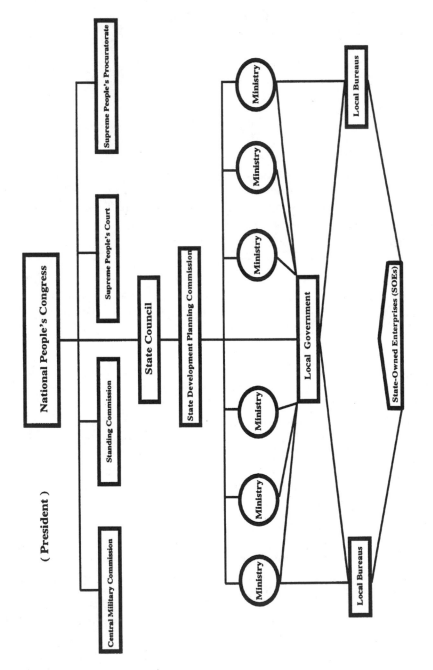

Figure 3.2. Chinese Bureaucracy: The Government Structure and Planning Hierarchy

among Chinese bureaucracies are wide-ranging, flexible, and subject to constant adjustment. The Chinese often feel comfortable with contracts that exhibit the same qualities of ambiguity and flexibility.

Professional negotiators: Chief Chinese negotiators are usually not important executives or decision makers but rather career negotiators. They do not earn plaudits for a job well done, but they are vulnerable to censure should the contract not adequately protect the interests of China. They usually have little incentive to bring their discussions to an end.

Chen and Faure (1995) provide a follow-up case study showing how a Chinese company (BHTC) "negotiated" with the Chinese government. To implement the government policy of a "contract management responsibility system," which was introduced in China in the mid-1980s, Chinese companies were asked to sign contracts with local (municipal) bureaus that in turn signed contracts with the central government. The contract in the case covered three key issues: the fixed amount of remitted profits to the government for the period of 1987 to 1990, the investment for upgrading the company's technology level and improving its management, and the wages and bonuses scheme subject to the company's performance. Six local (municipal) bureaus representing the government were involved in the 3-month negotiation beginning in the autumn of 1990: the High-Tech Bureau, the Labor Bureau, the Financial Bureau, the Local Branch of China Industrial and Commercial Bank, the Tax Bureau, and the State-Asset Administrative Bureau. This case implicitly suggests that in negotiating with its government, a Chinese company has virtually no negotiating power. Chinese enterprises must use many informal contacts to grasp the overall picture of the game and to devise languages to manipulate between various bureaus and agencies to gain only a marginal footing.

One of the most important changes that the Chinese Communists have brought to Chinese society is the creation of *danwei* (work unit) or *zuzhi* (organization). The traditional predominance of the Chinese family as the basic social unit has been broken down to give new authority to the party and the state. "The communists rightly saw that the authority of the family was a threat to their own and engaged in an extended struggle to subordinate the family to the state" (Fukuyama, 1995, p. 86). At the organizational level, *danwei* or *zuzhi* is but one example. Far different from Western organizations, Chinese *danwei* influences, regulates, and controls most aspects of the employees' life through regular ideological sessions, allocation of housing, arrangement of jobs for children of retiring employees, family planning control, medical care, the pension system and other welfare programs, and so on. In a certain sense, China is not big at all: One simply cannot move from one province to another if one does not have approval from one's *danwei* or be transferred from one company to another if one's *danwei* refuses to release one's *renshi dang'an* (personnel file). Every *danwei* keeps the employee's *dang'an* (or *renshi dang'an*), which is called by a Chinese author (as quoted in Dutton, 1992, p. 222) "the secret information held on each individual in a unified and concentrated form and taken care of by the personnel departments of each work unit at every level." Various kinds of information, such as family background and kinship networks, career paths and work evaluations, political attitudes, and past promotions and punishments, are documented in *dang'an*. If a PRC official or manager is denounced for having violated the party's *jilü* (discipline), his *dang'an* is certain to be inked with his mistakes, and his chances of finding another decent job will be very small, if not nonexistent. The following remark by Foster and Tosi (1990) demonstrates the authoritarian and commanding way in which the Chinese government exerts control over the PRC Chinese:

> The Chinese government feeds, clothes, shelters, educates, finds work, assigns housing, promotes, retires, and buries its citizens. Having all the guns and all the butter, the state controls and influences an individual's life in areas and to degrees not paralleled in the West. (p. 24)

The Chinese *danwei* is not without positive implications. I have seen that, in certain circumstances, the Chinese can be motivated to direct their loyalty outside their traditional family and kinship networks; the Chinese concept of family can be transferred to the larger concept of the state as a whole. Therefore, I cannot totally accept the thesis of Francis Fukuyama (1995) that the Chinese will never be able to develop professional management or large multinational corporations because of the extreme family-centeredness in the Chinese personality. I believe that the Chinese are learning, and their strong international presence is not a question of "to be or not to be" but "when."

The Chinese bureaucracy and its implication for Chinese business negotiations are discussed in a number of studies (Campbell & Adlington, 1988; Deverge, 1986; Lieberthal & Oksenberg, 1986; Stewart, 1990). Deverge (1986, p. 34) depicts the foremost cardinal principle governing the Chinese bureaucracy as follows: "He who does nothing makes no mistakes." A telling local Chinese saying popular in recent years about Chinese bureaucracy is the following:

> [If leaders] say you are capable then you are capable even if you are in fact incapable; [if leaders] say you are incapable then you are incapable even if you are in fact capable [in either case] you are incapable of not obeying [leaders].

Cultured in the Chinese bureaucracy, Chinese negotiators fear taking risks or making mistakes, show indecision, avoid taking responsibility, and have no final say. For a Chinese negotiator, the rewards for good performance are minimal, whereas the penalties for making a mistake are great. Therefore, nothing is as reassuring to the Chinese negotiator as evidence that other Chinese organizations or negotiators have used the same or similar contract provisions. The precedent can serve to cover the "bureaucratic tail" of the Chinese negotiator and may miraculously break negotiation deadlocks. This bureaucratic picture of Chinese negotiators is presented in a foreign manager's report on Chinese negotiators (as quoted in Schnepp, von Glinow, & Bhambri, 1990):

> Another problem occurred when I insisted that there be two versions, both official, one in Chinese and one in English. They insisted that the only official version would be in Chinese and there would be a translation into English. I said, "No. I don't know Chinese. I won't sign an agreement unless I can sign an official version in a language in which I'm more fluent." It went round and round for several days. On the third day, my secretary came across a press report on the first U.S.-China trade agreements that said there would be two versions of this agreement, both official, both formal, and one would be in English and one in Chinese. These people didn't know that. They were in the United States at the

time, so they could not easily pick up the phone and say, "Is that all right?" So when they came in, I asked their interpreter to read the report in Chinese to the group. Then they all smiled and said, "Ah, we have wasted two days. But now it's OK, we will have two versions." (p. 51)

It must be noted that problems intrinsic to Chinese bureaucracy are also noticed and criticized by the Chinese themselves. For example, Deng Xiaoping (1987, p. 192) says, "China is burdened with bureaucratism." Similarly, Zhu Rongji ("Zhu Charts," 1998) said the following at his first press conference as China's premier:

But why can't this [the government's program to revitalize China through science and education] be implemented well? Because there is no money. Where has all the money gone? We have very unwieldy government institutions. We call it an "eating budget." A large proportion of the budget has been earmarked for paying salaries of government functionaries. All the money has been eaten up. (p. 2)

The first impressive action that Premier Zhu took, to the satisfaction of the people, was to slash the ministries and commissions of the state council from 40 to 29 and cut in half the staff of government institutions to free money to support the development of science and education.

I believe that Western writings on Chinese bureaucracy focus too much on the red tape, which is blamed for delays in Chinese business negotiations, thereby overlooking the "planning" or "commanding" feature of Chinese bureaucracy. Gao (1993) provides the following fresh insight into the nature of Chinese bureaucracy by identifying its "quick buying":

Take 1988 for example. In that year China imported goods worth more than U.S.$40 billion. This was a pretty large sum in view of the fact that all the buying was done in one short year. To import goods worth so much, the Chinese businessmen could not afford to lose much time. They had to act fast, and they did act fast for they knew well that if they failed to do so, they could not possibly import all the things needed within a comparatively short time. In fact, there are numerous examples of the rapidity of the Chinese in taking action. For instance, people often find Chinese purchasing-missions buying things abroad worth millions of dollars within a couple of weeks. Evidently, in this process neither bureaucracy nor the cultural tradition has any role to play. . . . The centralized planned economy . . . is still a reality a marketer has to face. All China's purchasing activities are guided by an annual plan. This means that there is little likelihood for China to buy anything that is not included in the plan. Should it happen that there is a need for a product not envisaged in the plan, the need will be subjected to a long process of examination. . . . However, if a product is included in the plan, it must be bought quickly, because it is not permissible not to fulfill the plan, which is a mandate. So here we have two conflicting sides of a picture: On the one hand, there is a lot of *stalling* [italics added]; on the other, there is a lot of *quick buying* [italics added]. (pp. 227-228)

Gao (1993) accentuates the need on the part of foreign marketers to study the plans (e.g., Five-Year Plan) and policies of the CPC and the Chinese government. On the basis of the previous discussion, it can be understood that that Chinese bureaucracy has two facets: red tape, on the one hand, and "quick buying," on the other hand (see the Politics section earlier in this chapter).

The quick buying facet of Chinese bureaucracy, together with Confucian traditions, explains, in part, the strength of China's romantic attraction. Mann (1989) observes the contrast between China and India. With 800 million people, India is the world's second most populous nation, and some demographers believe that if China's family planning program is successful, India's population will overtake China's in the early part of the twenty-first century. Mann notes, however, that "American business leaders rarely talked or dreamed of getting in position to capture the vast Indian market" (p. 57). China's "authoritarian" traditions have somehow helped to reinforce the foreign perception that China is controllable and may be "changed quickly by orders from the top" (p. 58).

I have discussed the PRC condition (*Guoqing*), the contemporary social force that makes China different from most other markets. The PRC condition changes; it represents the changing element of Chinese business culture as opposed to the enduring traditional elements, such as Confucianism and Chinese stratagems. Recently, Zhu Rongji, a straightforward reform-minded technocrat, became China's fifth premier. Zhu's government will certainly bring many changes to the Chinese life that in turn will have an impact on Sino-Western business relations and negotiations. Whatever the government, however, I, as a person who has lived in the PRC for approximately three decades, am quite optimistic about China's overall development. The single most important reason for my optimism is that, since the reforms started in 1978, the Chinese people have indeed tasted the good sides of life, experienced increased freedom, and have heard and seen the rest of the world, so much so that they will by no means accept any historical move to set the "China clock" back. Lee Kuan Yew (as quoted in Rohwer, 1996), the former prime minister of Singapore, made the following important remark that supports my thesis:

> These are not ordinary people, you know. They are products of a very self-conscious civilization—self-conscious because they know they once did it and now they are out of the race, and they must get back into the race. . . . Anyway, it's no longer a question of what the leaders want. If the leaders don't bring progress and prosperity to replace backwardness and poverty, there will be a revolution in China, a real one in which armies will change sides and will shoot ministers. That's part of Chinese tradition. The people now know that it's the system that is at fault. They see the Taiwanese. Look at them bringing all their gifts to relatives. They look at Hong Kong. If people in Singapore can make it and people in China cannot, then it has to be the stupidity of the Soviet system that Mao adopted. Then let's get rid of it. (pp. 165-166)

Confucianism

The second major component of Chinese business culture is Confucianism. Confucianism (*Rujia* or *Rujiao*) is a Chinese philosophical tradition that has fundamentally shaped not only Chinese but also East Asian mentality for 2500 years. Many contributions to the area of Chinese business negotiating style belong to the Confucian school (Deverge, 1986; Kindel, 1990; Seligman, 1990; Shenkar &

Ronen, 1987; Withane, 1992). Few, however, have adopted a clear orientation to identify the key elements or values of Confucian traditions.[7] To generate a theoretically sound Confucian explanation of Chinese business negotiating style, we must start with a knowledge of the key Confucian values. As noted in Chapter 2, Confucianism can be conceived as involving six core values: (a) moral cultivation, (b) importance of interpersonal relationships, (c) family orientation, (d) respect for age and hierarchy, (e) avoidance of conflict and need for harmony, and (f) concept of face.

Moral Cultivation

Confucianism can be understood, first of all, as a form of moral ethic (Tu, 1984). The term *junzi* ("gentleman," "profound man," "superior man," "cultivated man," "princely man," or "noble man") has appeared 107 times in Confucius' *Analects.* In some cases, it refers to the ruler; in most cases, however, it means a morally superior person who embodies many virtues. One major concern of Confucianism is how people learn to become human through lifelong learning and moral cultivation.

Confucianism advocates *Wuchang* ("Five Constant Virtues"): *ren* (human-heartedness and benevolence), *yi* (righteousness and justice), *li* (propriety, rituals, and rules of conduct), *zhi* (wisdom), and *xin* (trust) (Fung 1948/1966). Above all, Confucianism emphasizes sincerity (*cheng*). It is written in *Doctrine of the Mean* (in Chan, 1963)[8] that

> Sincerity is the Way of Heaven. To think how to be sincere is the way of man. . . . Sincerity means the completion of the self, and the Way is self-directing. Sincerity is the beginning and end of things. Without sincerity there would be nothing. Therefore the superior man values sincerity. Sincerity is not only the completion of one's own self, it is that by which all things are completed. (pp. 107-108)

Trust features preeminently in Confucianism. According to Confucius, a gentleman must keep his word and be sincere to his friends. It is worth noting that the Confucian moral thinking is not a universal one but closely related to family or group. It is the family or group that demarcates the borderline between trust toward insiders and distrust toward outsiders, not necessarily foreigners. In *Trust: The Social Virtues and the Creation of Prosperity*, Francis Fukuyama (1995) calls Chinese society a "familistic" or "low-trust" society in which trust is high inside but low outside family borders. Fukuyama argues that the Chinese have been unable to create large, professional, durable economic organizations between family and the state (the so-called "missing middle") because of the relatively low degree of trust in voluntary associations outside kinship in the Chinese society.

Next, the Chinese trust is more an interpersonal trust than organizational. Jansson (1994) calls trust in Chinese society a group-based "individual trust" that differs from the Western "organizational trust" based on professionalism. The Chinese culture makes individual trust more important than organizational trust, with the latter frequently being a consequence of the former. This, together with the theme shown in Illustration 24 in Chapter 4—"Chinese do business with you, *not* with your company"—implies that to do business successfully with China, foreign firms must understand the importance of cultivating and developing a trusting relationship with the Chinese at the interpersonal level.

Finally, trust, in Chinese culture, takes time to cultivate between people who do not know each other. Typically, Chinese business people find themselves in a perplexing quandary: On the one hand, they do business only with people they trust (if you are not trustworthy, a Chinese will never buy from you even if you offer the cheapest price); on the other hand, business partners cannot always be relatives and ready friends but must extend to outsiders and strangers whose records of sincerity and trustworthiness contain no ready-made answers. The only test is time. A Chinese proverb says, "The stamina of a horse is tested by distance; the heart of a person is tested by time" (*Lu yao zhi ma li, ri jiu jian ren xin*). Therefore, culturally, doing business with the Chinese tends to take time and calls for patience.

Legal power does not figure at all in Confucianism. In Confucian terms, government is about governing by moral forces: A ruler should rule by virtues rather than law; the ruling power comes from the ruler's superior moral example rather than coarse resort to law and punishment. In *Analects*, Confucius elaborates (in Chan, 1963),

A ruler who governs his state by virtue is like the north polar star, which remains in its place while all the other stars revolve around it. . . . Lead the people with governmental measures and regulate them by law and punishment, and they will avoid wrong-doing but will have no sense of honor and shame. Lead them with virtue and regulate them by the rules of propriety (*li*), and they will have a sense of shame and, moreover, set themselves right. (p. 22)

The Confucian message is clear: Law does not eradicate problems; people's behavior can be influenced effectively only by a set of self-regulating moral mechanisms, for example, by *li* (ritual propriety, etiquette, etc.) and by instilling "a sense of shame" into people's minds. The Confucian moral notion of shame lays much of the philosophical foundation for the Chinese concept of face. The Chinese preference for using moral mechanisms instead of legal measures to regulate people's conduct has its strong belief in the original goodness of human nature, one of the fundamental ideas of Mencius's philosophy. Because of the deep Confucian aversion to law, legalism has never had a lasting influence in Chinese history. Law, in Chinese culture, had always been equated with lack of trust, trouble, coercion, and tyranny and thus treated as a less effective means of affecting behavior.

Tu (1984) elaborates that Confucianism can be and has been employed as a form of political ideology. The highest personality ideal in the Confucian tradition is the "sage-king": One must cultivate oneself to the point of becoming an exemplary moral teacher to become a king or a ruler and to gain the respect and support of the people. The sage-king uses moral influence to further his political purposes. Tu notes, however, that throughout Chinese history many leaders have not been sages at all. They have been so-called "king-sages": "A king who is not an exemplary moral figure and who has come to power by means other than moral persuasion wants to assume the role of a sage" (p. 28); they thus turn the Confucian ideal of moral government into a coercive method of control. In this sense, Confucianism as a political ideology can be a dark doctrine, diametrically opposed to democracy.

Moral-oriented education and training are emphasized in the entire Chinese socialization process, from childhood to adulthood. Chinese parents pay special attention to training children to develop "a moral character, such as respecting elders, cooperating, and maintaining harmonious social relations" (Wu, 1996, p. 154). In the PRC, for example, role models have become a major means used to influence people's behavior. "Models" (*mofan*) are chosen and publicized at various levels every year: model workers, model teachers, model party members, model families, model husbands, and even model foreigners. Regarding the last category, Murray (1983) writes,

> One American student at a large Chinese university didn't know whether to laugh or cry when he discovered that several weeks previously he had been chosen "model foreigner"; the institution's Foreign Affairs Office had advised everyone in his department to observe him, to emulate his diligence, and to learn from his example how a foreigner ought to behave in Chinese society. (p. 24)

To examine whether a person's behavior is appropriate, the Chinese first consider whether it *he qing he li* ("complies with human feeling and reason"). Recently, because of economic reforms, a new phrase has come into use, *he fa* ("complies with law"), and the Chinese have begun to use the saying *he qing he li he fa*. The sequence of importance, however, is suggested by the Chinese: The law always comes last.

Confucius does not think of profit; instead, he is concerned with righteousness and human-heartedness. In *Analects,* Confucius says (in Chan, 1963), "The superior man understands righteousness; the inferior man understands profit" (p. 28).

Confucianism honors knowledge and scholarship and discredits trade and commerce. In traditional Chinese society, professions were divided into four distinctive classes: (a) scholars (*shi*), (b) farmers (*nong*), (c) artisans (*gong*), and (d) merchants (*shang*). Scholars ranked first because they produced knowledge, and they were the educated people who formed the ruling class; farmers followed because they produced what the Chinese believed to be the most important means of living—food; artisans were third because they produced useful tools for production; and merchants ranked last because they produced nothing. Today, this classic view of social class is reputed to hold truth in Chinese societies in the sense that education, knowledge, and diligence are greatly valued. Rich Chinese business people always see to it at any cost that their children receive the best education possible.

Despite the Confucian contempt for profit, the Chinese have often been described as people who care very much about money. Ironically, this Chinese "money behavior" also has to do with Confucianism: the concept of the Chinese family as an "insurance company" (see the Family Orientation section later in this chapter).

Confucius is a gentleman who takes no unfair advantages. In *Analects* (Chan, 1963), it is documented that "Confucius fished with a line but not a net. While shooting, he would not shoot a bird at rest" (p. 32). Moreover, Confucius is not concerned with tactics, let alone deception. It is also recorded (as quoted in Szuma, 1979, p. 14) that "Duke Ling consulted him [Confucius] about warfare. 'I know something about sacrificial vessels,' said Confucius, 'but have never studied military science.' "

One's moral potential also includes the ability to control overt expression of thoughts and emotions. Showing restraint is the responsibility of the gentleman, who, in the Confucian tradition, is a cultivated and learned person situated above all others (Shenkar & Ronen, 1987). I elaborate on this point in the discussion about the Confucian "need for harmony."

The Confucian gentleman or superior man is depicted by Confucius (in Chan, 1963) as follows:

> The superior man has nine wishes. In seeing, he wishes to see clearly. In hearing, he wishes to hear distinctly. In his expression, he wishes to be warm. In his appearance, he wishes to be respectful. In his speech, he wishes to be sincere. In handling affairs, he wishes to be serious. When in doubt, he wishes to ask. When he is angry, he wishes to think of the resultant difficulties. And when he sees an opportunity for a gain, he wishes to think of righteousness. (p. 45)

The Confucian value of moral cultivation can be seen in Chinese business negotiating style. Chinese business is governed less by the legalistic concept of contract than by the moralistic notion of sincerity and trust. When negotiating with foreign business people, the Chinese first think "Are you and your company sincere?" (Hoose, 1974, p. 464). In the Chinese view, as Pye (1982, p. 32) observes, "all successful negotiations call for a high level of mutual trust and respect." The Chinese place high value on reputation, credibility, personal character, and quality on the part of both Western firms and their negotiators (Frankenstein, 1986; Kindel, 1990). "Honesty is probably the most important factor in negotiating in China because it builds trust, a major consideration in the Chinese decision" (Yuann, 1987, p. 52). Chinese negotiators "generally keep their commitments" (Seligman, 1990, p. 114). "As a rule, Chinese parties will not tear apart a contract or refuse to implement it without good reason" (Chen, 1993, p. 13). Victor Li (1980, p. 38) finds that "even during the serious economic disruptions of the Great Leap Forward and the Cultural Revolution, foreign debts were paid on schedule and trade contracts were generally carried out" by the Chinese. All this shows that morality and trust are important dimensions in the Chinese business process.

As noted earlier, Chinese negotiations can take considerable time because trust takes time to build up between people who do not belong to the same family or group. It has been found that the Chinese do not rush into formal contract discussions (Kindel, 1990), and the first meeting is usually not a sales meeting (Hoose, 1974). "Pre-negotiation" is involved in the Chinese business negotiation process, in which the Chinese tend to collect much information (Seligman, 1990; Stewart & Keown, 1989) to assess the "trustworthiness" of the foreign partner early on (Chen, 1993). If the Chinese sense a lack of sincerity or commitment on the part of the foreign party at this stage, they are quite likely never to proceed with face-to-face meetings (Seligman, 1990).

Chinese business is built on trust and not law. One can negotiate a deal with the Chinese most effectively when there is enough trust between the parties, and a verbal agreement is as good as a written contract (Roehrig, 1994b). The Chinese tend to feel embarrassed and insulted when confronted with clauses spelling out the penalties or remedies if the Chinese partner cannot make good on its commitments (Lubman, 1983; Mann, 1989). Chinese are generally reluctant to resort to adjudication or go to court. Instead, they prefer mediation and conciliation. This is a direct manifestation of the moralistic rather than legalistic frame of the Chinese mind. Sheng (1979, p. 21) reports that "rather than turn to third parties such as arbitration committees or courts, the Chinese expect the two sides to discuss their differences and to arrive at a mutually acceptable solution by adjusting price, delivery terms, and so forth."

Given the nonlegalistic Confucian tradition, Roehrig (1994a) suggests that a non-lawyer with substantial knowledge of the Chinese legal system and familiarity with Chinese culture may be able to conduct the negotiation more effectively. Campbell and Adlington (1988) report that some foreign firms never allow lawyers to participate in their negotiations because they recognize that everything is negotiable and that there is no need for legal interpretations. Others do use lawyers but more as business consultants who have gained experience in previous negotiations. Increasingly, Chinese lawyers are beginning to appear at negotiating sessions. This presence, however, is a relatively novel phenomenon. Seligman (1990) notes that Chinese lawyers who participate in negotiating sessions typically come from independent law organizations other than the negotiating Chinese organization, and they may or may not have the respect of the chief Chinese negotiator. Chinese lawyers (as quoted in Chang, 1987, p. 10) also admit that they are in the ambivalent position of acting both as the lawyer for the Chinese party and as an officer of the government: "From a bureaucratic perspective, the lawyer's neck is on the line." See Illustrations 9, 10, 11, 14, 21 through 24, and 26 in Chapter 4 for further discussion of the topics covered in this section.

Importance of Interpersonal Relationships

Confucianism can also be viewed as a practical philosophy of human relationships and conduct or simply as a "philosophy of daily life" (Fung, 1948/1966; Lee, 1995). Confucianism may be called a "this-worldly" philosophy because it has little to do with the spiritual world. When asked about the meaning of death, Confucius says (in Chan, 1963), "If we do not yet know about life, how can we know about death?" (p. 36).

In the Confucian tradition, self is an open system—the sum of its relationships. Tu (1984, p. 5) notes that "Confucianism conceives of the self neither as an isolated atom nor as a single, separate individuality, but as a being in relationship." Self-cultivation does not refer to any single separate action. Tu (1985) states,

A distinctive feature of Confucian ritualization is an ever-deepening and broadening awareness of the presence of the other in one's self-cultivation. This is perhaps the single most important reason why the Confucian idea of the self as a center of relationships is an open system. (p. 232)

Confucianists view the world through the lens of Five Cardinal Relationships known as *Wulun* (in *Doctrine of the Mean*, in Chan, 1963):

There are five universal ways [in human relations]. . . . The five are those governing the relationship between ruler and minister, between father and son, between husband and wife, between elder and younger brothers, and those in the intercourse between friends. These five are universal paths in the world. (p. 105)

All five relationships are characterized by reciprocity. It is true that Confucianism preaches the junior's loyalty, filial piety, obedience, and respect. The senior, however, must be self-righteous, benevolent, charismatic, and loving to enable the subject to become loyal, filial, obedient, and respectful. If not, the junior can disobey and even rise up to choose a better senior. This revolutionary, and often called "democratic," message of Confucianism is clearly spelled out by Mencius (in Chan, 1963), a great Confucian philosopher second only to Confucius:

If a ruler regards his ministers as his hands and feet, then his ministers will regard him as their heart and mind. If a ruler regards his ministers as dogs and horses, his ministers will regard him as any other man. If a ruler regards his ministers as dirt and grass, his ministers will regard him as a bandit and an enemy. (p. 105)

Hence, the Confucian view of relationships is highly reciprocal. There is a Chinese concept that highlights this notion of reciprocity: *bao*. According to Yang (1957), *bao* (or *pao* in the original text) has a wide range of meanings, including "to report," "to respond," "to repay," and "to retaliate." Yang explains,

The center of this area of meanings is "response" or "return," which has served as one basis for social relations in China. The Chinese believe that reciprocity of actions (favor and hatred, reward and punishment) between man and man, and indeed between men and supernatural beings, should be as certain as a cause-and-effect relationship, and, therefore, when a Chinese acts, he normally anticipates a response or return. Favors done for others are often considered what may be termed "social investments," for which handsome returns are expected. (p. 291)

There are many Chinese sayings that concern the meaning of reciprocity—for example, *Ni jing wo yi chi, wo jing ni yi zhang* ("If you honor me a foot, I shall honor you 10 feet in return"). Another—*li shang wang lai*—translates as (a) "courtesy demands reciprocity" and (b) "deal with a man as he deals with you" or "pay a man back in his own coin" (*A Modern Chinese-English Dictionary*, 1994, p. 543). The principle of reciprocity applies to the Chinese concepts of *guanxi, renqing, li,* and *keqi,* which will be discussed later.

Hence, Chinese morality belongs to two diametrically different constellations: If you are good to me, I will be 10 times better to you, but if you are bad to me, I will be 10 times worse to you. According to this morality, relationship is not a universal notion but highly reciprocal, situational, dynamic, and context-related. Francis Hsu (1963) calls the Chinese a "situation-centered" people: The Chinese have multiple moral standards, "behaving differently under contrasting sets of circumstances" (p. 2). Once a Chinese has sensed that you are treating him like a "dog and horse" or "dirt and grass," he will be morally justified to look down on you and deal with you as a "bandit and enemy." Most important, one's influencing power must come from one's own moral examples rather than coarse foisting of governing and control over the other party. This Confucian morality can be discerned from a series of harsh criticisms of Western powers unleashed recently by some Asian leaders—for example, "You must be flagrantly self-righteous—have no doubts about the superiority of your ways—to try to civilize foreigners" (Mohamad & Ishihara, 1995, p. 93).

The reciprocal feature of Chinese interpersonal relationships makes the impression from the first contact extremely critical from the Chinese point of view. It is largely based on the "feeling at the first sight" and the adjustment gradually made during later contacts that the Chinese calibrate their degree of trust and sincerity and choose influence strategies toward the other party in a dyadic relationship. Therefore, the Chinese give great importance to, and spend much time in, preparing and studying the first-round meetings with the other party, the atmosphere of which exerts considerable influence on the whole relational process (see Chapter 4, Illustrations 21, 22, 24, and 26).

The Confucian emphasis on the importance of interpersonal relationships is logically correlated with its disregard of legal systems. According to Lee Kuan Yew (as quoted in Yeung & Tung, 1996, p. 56), the founding father of Singapore, Chinese use interpersonal relationships "to make up for the lack of the rule of law and transparency in rules and regulations." John Kao (1993, p. 25) holds that given China's long history of political upheaval, natural disasters, waves of emigration, and, most important, economic scarcity, the well-defined Confucian relationships have often helped keep social chaos at bay. Therefore, Confucian relationships are of a distinctive Middle Kingdom flavor.

Guanxi

The Chinese term for relationship is *guanxi*, one of the most important cultural traits of Chinese people the world over. The term may be better translated as "personal contacts" or "personal connections." *Guanxi* can be understood as "reciprocal obligation" (Seligman, 1990, p. 45), "a special relationship individuals have with each other in which each can make unlimited demands on the other" (Pye, 1982, p. 89), "friendship with implications of a continual exchange of favors" (Chen, 1996, p. 224), or "the establishment of a connection between two independent individuals to enable a bilateral flow of personal or social transactions" (Yeung & Tung, 1996, p. 55).

Guanxi derives essentially from the Chinese family system. In the traditional Chinese family, whether immediate or extended, members are mutually obligated to help one another. In the Confucian tradition, a person is morally expected to improve the welfare of his less fortunate relatives and friends through his influence and contacts. *Guanxi* is strongly colored by this Confucian reciprocal obligation toward family members. Through the establishment of *guanxi*, people bond with each other with expected obligations toward each other. *Guanxi* is essentially a network. The absence of caste in the Chinese society has also helped spin the web of *guanxi*. Lin (1939) writes,

> Through marriage, or through acquaintance, there is hardly a family in China that cannot find a distant cousin who knows the teacher of the third son of Mr. Chang whose sister-in-law is the sister of a certain bureaucrat's wife, which relationship is of extreme value when it comes to lawsuits. (p. 180)

Guanxi is usually established among people who share a commonality of certain identities—for example, *tongxue* (schoolmates), *laoxiang* (fellow villagers), and *laopengyou* (old friends). China is not a free market economy, which makes it difficult to allocate resources through market mechanisms; therefore, *guanxi* is a major means of resource allocation in contemporary China. Without *guanxi*, one "simply cannot get anything done" (Davies, Leung, Luk, & Wong, 1995) or "gets half the result with twice the effort" (Chen, 1996). Making extensive use of *guanxi*, or going through the "backdoor" to get things done, has been legitimately criticized by the Chinese government. *Guanxi* is everywhere, however. Chen (1995) observes that, in China, hardly any aspect of social life is not touched by *guanxi*.

   Guanxi pervades the whole Chinese business process. Hsieh and Liu (1992) argue that *guanxi* strategy is helpful for seeking background information about potential Chinese business partners, negotiating prices and terms of payment, and implementing the contract. Hu (1994) emphasizes that doing business in China is not just a matter of price and product. To succeed in the Chinese market, foreign business people must rely on friendship or good personal relationships (*guanxi*), which often take time and patience to build. Schnepp et al. (1990) hold that a fine *guanxi* with high-level officials in Chinese bureaucracy can facilitate market penetration and smooth negotiation and generate good business.

   On the basis of their empirical study of 19 Hong Kong and non-Hong Kong firms that have business dealings in China, Yeung and Tung (1996) have drawn several conclusions about *guanxi*. First, *guanxi* is a necessary but insufficient condition for long-term business success in China. Second, in the established phase of business operations in China, technical competence gains importance. Third, to be successful, it is important to build strong relationships with the right individuals. Fourth, *guanxi* relationships are person specific and cannot be transferred. Fifth, non-Chinese firms often must resort to intermediaries to gain the proper connections in China. Sixth, the tendering of favors, particularly the offer of short-term gains, is essential but not powerful enough to maintain long-term *guanxi* relationships alone. To maintain long-term relationships, an integrated approach is more effective. Finally, trust is essential to long-term *guanxi* maintenance. This can only come about if there is a genuine attempt on the part of the foreign investor to understand Chinese culture. These findings imply that trust is an important dimension in keeping long-term *guanxi*; *guanxi* is important, but it is not everything. This latter thesis has also been proved recently by the highly publicized case of the Beijing Oriental Plaza Project, a $1.5 billion 760,000-square-meter modern complex of shops, offices, and apartments to be erected on Wangfujing, the busiest street in Beijing. The project has been delayed many times since it was started in 1994, despite the fact that the developers involved two Hong Kong companies with impeccable *guanxi* with the central government: Cheung Kong Holdings Ltd., run by Hong Kong billionaire Li Ka-shing, and Orient Overseas International Ltd., led until recently by Tung Chee-hwa, Hong Kong's chief executive. The reasons for the delays include a discovery of Stone Age relics on the site, the fast-food giant McDonald's Corp.'s refusal to vacate the spot, and the environmental concern that the complex would dwarf the nearby Tiananmen Square and Forbidden City (Roberts, 1997b).

Renqing

Closely intertwined with *guanxi* is *renqing,* an important vehicle in Chinese social exchanges. *Renqing,* which literally translates as "human feelings," is defined by Yang (1957, p. 292) as "covers not only sentiment but also its social expressions such as the offering of congratulations or condolences or the making of gifts on appropriate occasions." Hwang (1987, pp. 953-954) describes "the rule of *renqing*" as follows: "If you have received a drop of beneficence from other people, you should return to them a fountain of beneficence." A Chinese who has done a favor for you automatically feels that he is owed a favor from you in return. Hence, *renqing* follows the Confucian notion of reciprocity. There are many Chinese expressions that are associated with *renqing*, such as giving somebody a *renqing* (*song renqing*) and owing somebody a *renqing* (*qian renqing*). See Illustration 3 in Chapter 4 to understand *renqing* in Chinese business negotiations.

Li

Renqing is related to another Confucian concept: *li*. *Li* translates as "etiquette," "decorum," "protocol," "rites," "propriety," "ceremony," "rules of conduct," "courtesy," "politeness," and so on. In Confucius's time, however, the term *li* originally referred to "the social hierarchy and order of the slavery system of the Zhou Dynasty (dating back to 1100 B.C.), which was regarded by Confucius as an ideal model of any society" (Gu, 1990, p. 238). It was not until the publication of the book *Li Ji* (*On Li*)[9] 200 or 300 years after Confucius that the current meanings of *li* came into use.

Confucianism stresses the social responsibility of individuals, who must behave according to certain prescribed principles of *li*. *Li* dictates the manner in which Chinese position themselves in the hierarchical society and perform their roles accordingly. Therefore, *li* can be understood as doing the proper things with the right people in the appropriate relationships (Bond & Hwang, 1986). *Li* embraces a set of principles or standards governing proper etiquette and conduct in human interactions, such as marriage, funerals, greetings, meetings, eating, ancestor worship, reward, and promotion. Confucius was a person of fine feeling, particular about *li*. For example, his meticulous eating manner is recorded as follows (from *Analects* as quoted in Lin, 1981a):

> When the food's flavour was changed, he would not eat. When the smell was not right, he would not eat. When the colour of the food was not right, he would not eat. When it was not cooked just right, he would not eat. When a thing was out of season, he would not

eat. When the meat was not cut squarely, he would not eat. When a thing was not accompanied by its proper sauce, he would not eat. Wine that was not home-brewed and cooked meat purchased from the shops, he would not eat. (pp. 153-154)

China has been known as a "land of etiquette," or *li yi zhi bang* as the Chinese refer to it. Seligman (1990, p. 1) observes that though keenly aware of their need to learn from the West in technological areas in which their country lags behind the rest of the world, "the Chinese people have never felt the need for instruction from anyone in the area of decorum and protocol." *Li* is also a way of expressing one's sincerity. I use "gift-giving" (*songli* or "to give *li*": here *li* refers to gift) as an example. In Confucian gift-giving, the exchange of gifts is an expression of sincere friendship. Tu (1984) notes that in Chinese tradition, the gift of even a goose feather, totally without value, brought from thousands of miles away is considered most rewarding and precious.

Gu (1990) provides four notions underlying the Chinese conception of politeness (*li* or *limao*): respectfulness, modesty, attitudinal warmth, and refinement. Self-denigration and other-elevation is the major feature of the Chinese politeness. The following interaction, in which a mainland Chinese (M) and a Singapore Chinese (S) introduce themselves to each other, is typical of Chinese:

M: *nin guixing?*
[Your precious surname?]

S: *xiaodi xing Li.*
[Little brother's surname is Li.]

nin zunxing?
[Your respectable surname?]

M: *jianxing Zhang.*
[My worthless surname is Zhang.] (p. 246)

Keqi

Li is closely related to another Chinese term: *keqi*. In Chinese, if someone is said to be particular about *li* (*jiang li*), then he is very *keqi*. In Chinese, *ke* means "guest," and *qi* means "air" or "behavior"; together, the term *keqi* means "behavior of guest" or, in a generalized sense, "polite," "courteous," "modest," "humble," "understanding," "considerate," and "well-mannered" (Yao, 1983). Politeness, or *keqi*, is a basic principle observed by the Chinese in their everyday communication (Gao et al., 1996). The Chinese concept of politeness is rooted in the Confucian notion of self as the sum of harmonious relationships with others. The basic rule of *keqi* is to denigrate self and respect others in social interactions.

Gu (1990) provides a telling example of *keqi* shown in a typical Chinese inviting transaction between A, a prospective mother-in-law, and B, a prospective son-in-law:

> **A:** *mingtain lai chi wanfan (ar).*
> [tomorrow come eat dinner]
>
> **B:** *bu lai (le), tai mafan.*
> [not come too much trouble]
>
> **A:** *mafan shenme(ya),*
> [trouble nothing]
>   *cai dou shi xiancheng(de).*
> [dishes all are ready-made]
>
> **B:** *na yedei shao(wa)*
> [that still cook]
>
> **A:** *ni bu lai women yedei chifan.*
> [you not come we all the same have meal]
>   *yiding lai(ar), bu lai wo ke shengqi(le).*
> [must come not come I shall feel offended]
>
> **B:** *hao(ba), jiu shuibian yidian.*
> [all right just potluck] (pp. 252-253)

Here, the host demonstrates *keqi* by inviting the guest to dinner in a way that a Westerner would find harshly imposing, whereas the guest returns *keqi* by turning down the invitation in the first place, showing his concern for not wishing to cause even the least trouble to the host in a way a cultural outsider would find sheer hypocrisy. According to the Chinese norms, however, both are well mannered. The sincerity of the host and guest is seen in this back and forth interaction—through the host's "imposing" invitation and the guest's caring and concern for the incurred cost to the host.

Other examples of Chinese *keqi* behaviors include the following: When praised by others, a Chinese is bound to say, "No, I am not worthy"; and at the dinner table, the host usually opens even a lavish dinner party by saying to the guests, "Today you are invited to a very simple meal, just help yourself please." The Chinese etiquette and *keqi* behavior are one of the areas to which foreign business people need to pay special attention when negotiating with the Chinese (see Chapter 4, Illustration 29).

Chinese Social Customs, Taboos, and Symbolism

Related to the concepts of *guanxi* and *li* are distinctive Chinese social customs, taboos, and symbolism that also define and condition the social behavior of the Chinese people. Violations of these customs and taboos have a negative influence on the harmony of interpersonal relationships.

The Chinese are not religious people, but they are extremely superstitious people who have long been worshippers of nature and ancestors and believe in all kinds of supernatural powers. Feng Shui, which literally translates as "wind water," is a frequently talked about supernatural Chinese notion. Feng Shui "is about living in harmony with the natural environment and tapping the goodness of nature to benefit man (Lip, 1995, p. iv); it is "the art of adapting the abodes of the living and the graves of the dead so as to cooperate and harmonize with the local currents of the cosmic breath, the Yin and Yang" (Williams, 1941, p. 178). Feng Shui reflects the emotional Chinese conception of nature that there exists a "golden chain of spiritual life [*qi*] running through every form of existence . . . that subsists in heaven above or on earth below" (Eitel, 1873/1984, p. 4) and that "people and their activities are affected by the layout and orientation of their workplaces and homes (Adler, 1991, p. 25).

Although certainly influenced by the Taoist Yin Yang doctrine, Feng Shui also has part of its philosophical roots in the Confucian tradition. Lip (1995) observed that the Confucian ideals and ancient Chinese social and political hierarchy were reflected in the plans of ancient Chinese cities. Ernest Eitel (1873/1984) wrote,

> The deepest root of the Feng-shui system grew out of that excessive and superstitious veneration of the spirits of ancestors, which, though philosophical minds like that of Confucius might construe

it on an exclusively moral basis as simply an expression of filial piety, was with the mass of the Chinese people the fruitful soil from which the poisonous weed of rank superstition sprang up in profusion. (p. 51)

In their daily life, the Chinese, especially those from southern China, go to great lengths to see to it that their offices, homes, meeting venue, and ancestors' graves have a favorable Feng Shui. According to the rules of Feng Shui, as noted by Williams (1941), houses and graves should face south because the annual animation of the vegetable kingdom with the approach of summer comes from that quarter, whereas the deadly influences of winter come from the north.

Chinese taboos are many. In gift-giving, for example, it is important to know what to give and what not to give. One traditional prohibition concerns the "clock." It is taboo to give a clock as a gift. The Chinese expression "to give a clock" (*song zhong*) sounds exactly the same as another Chinese expression "to attend a dying person" or "to watch someone dying" (*song zhong*), though these two "*zhong*" terms are different in writing. Similar examples are found in giving "shoes" (*xie*, which sounds exactly the same as "evil") and "pears" (*li*,[10] which sounds exactly the same as "separation") as gifts.

The Chinese are a people who are gifted with vivid imaginations. The Chinese imaginative powers are evident in Chinese symbolism that has been handed down from generation to generation. In recent years, as East Asia has become increasingly attractive in international business, studies relating to the symbolic Chinese value of words, sounds, numbers, colors, and so on have emerged in the literature (Baker, 1993; McDonald & Roberts, 1990; Pan & Schmitt, 1996; Schmitt, 1995; Schmitt & Simonson, 1997).

Although Americans customarily use assorted colorful flowers for funerals, reserving all-white arrangements for weddings, the Chinese custom is the opposite (Yao, 1987). Red is the most lucky color for Chinese. A red and yellow combination is mostly favored by Chinese people.

The Chinese adore the number 8 because 8, in Chinese, sounds like the word meaning "get rich." On August 8, 1988—that is, 8-8-88—an unprecedented number of new businesses were registered or opened in Hong Kong, including the Bank of China's new Hong Kong office.

Baker (1993, p. 274) observes that, in Hong Kong, "the Government makes large sums for charity by organising auctions of 'lucky' car registration numbers—8888 fetched a record price." By contrast, the number 4 is often avoided by the Chinese because it sounds like the word for "death" in Chinese. Particularly, the number 14 as a brand name or product number must be avoided at any cost because 14 sounds similar to the expression "going to die" or "sure death" in colloquial Chinese. The number 9413 is shunned because it sounds like "90 percent likelihood of death and 10 percent likelihood of survival" (Baker, 1993) in Chinese. Therefore, one should never use 9413 to number products to be marketed in the Chinese culture. Although 8 is the most favored number for the Chinese, 3, 6, and 9 are also positive numbers, suggesting "growth," "wealth" or "going through smoothly," and "longevity," respectively. When Beijing was bidding for the right to host the Olympic Games in the Year 2000, Ms. Gao Min, known as the world's "Queen of Diving" donated 66,666 Yuan to the state to show her support—the figure symbolized "smoothness" and "sailing."

Some PRC and overseas Chinese I have met said that they chose to carry Ericsson's mobile telephones simply because the telephones bear the number 8. At Ericsson's mobile telephone series exhibit at the recent CeBIT '97 fair (Lindén, 1997), all phones were "8-numbered": GF 788, GH 688, and GA 628. I can imagine the significance these 8-numbered products have for Ericsson at a time when China is steadily becoming Ericsson's largest market,[11] and Asian countries will account for one third of Ericsson's sales by the end of this century (Landin, 1996). Because China and East Asian markets are becoming increasingly important for Western business communities, the language and visual effect of corporate identity in China and East Asia constitute an issue of strategic importance for Western marketers.

The Confucian emphasis on interpersonal relationship can be found in the Chinese style of business. Seligman (1990) observes that, in China, it is strong personal relationships that provide some assurance that an agreement can come to fruition; Chinese negotiators look more for a sincere commitment to working together to solve problems than for a neatly decorated legal package. In other words, the Chinese rely on a network of relationships to solve problems that may crop up at any time in China. Kirkbride, Tang, and Westwood (1991) found that Chinese negotiators tend to expect and desire a level of personal relationship with their counterparts that would be viewed as unnecessary in the West. The Chinese view a foreign cosignatory to an agreement as having established himself as a "friend" who has an obligation to help his Chinese friends in case of difficulty (Chen, 1993; Seligman, 1990). A team of Japanese negotiators commented that "the Chinese respect courtesy very much"; without paying an informal "courtesy" or "friendly" visit to China prior to the formal meeting, the Japanese offer was "quickly rejected" (March, 1994, p. 10). Though both the Chinese and foreign parties typically agree in the contract to use arbitration if the need arises, "the Chinese are generally loath to resort to legal proceedings" because "the Chinese see the settlement of a dispute either in the courts or through arbitration as a failure of the relationship, which reflects badly on both sides" (Chen, 1993, p. 16). This view toward business transaction, which I call "Confucian problem solving," implies that the Chinese do not treat a contract as something fixed and unchangeable. Rather, they view the contract essentially as a joint problem-solving process or a relationship in which the parties' mutual understanding, trust, and exchange of favors are called for. Therefore, renegotiation of old issues based on high mutual trust and for good reasons is positive and reasonable from the Confucian point of view. The Chinese preference for seeking initial agreement on general principles can be more a matter of courtesy and of showing goodwill to establish a working relationship between the parties than a Chinese negotiating tactic as identified by Pye (1982). Of course, the initial agreement may also be employed as a potential weapon by the Chinese if negotiations turn sour.

In Confucian terms, *guanxi* is reciprocal in nature. Therefore, "equality and mutual benefit" is reiterated in China's joint venture law, which may be one of the most commonly read phrases in Chinese business contracts. Lewis (1995) finds that Chinese negotiators love to see this phrase worded in business contracts. Chinese negotiators do not want to accept terms that are not reciprocal, as also observed by Lavin (1994).

Family Orientation

Family is the root of Chinese society and Chinese civilization, of which Confucianism is the rational and theoretical justification. Confucianism sees a direct transition from *jia* (family) to *guo* (state).

It considers *xiu shen* (moral cultivation of personality), *qi jia* (orderly regulation of family), and *zhi guo* (governing of state) as interrelated processes. The following Confucian aphorism appears in *Great Learning* (in Wu, 1990):

> If you want to rule the state, first put your family in order; if you want to put your family in order, first cultivate your morality; if you want to cultivate your morality, first set your heart right; and to set your heart right, you must be sincere. (p. 1)

The Confucian explanation of the linkage between personal character, family, and state is the following (from *Great Learning*, as quoted in Chan, 1963): "What is meant by saying that in order to govern the state it is necessary first to regulate the family is this: There is no one who cannot teach his own family and yet can teach others" (p. 91). Regarding the aforementioned Confucian aphorism of *xiu shen*, *qi jia*, and *zhi guo*, Lee Kuan Yew (as quoted in Zakaria, 1994) made the following remark:

> We have a whole people immersed in these beliefs. My granddaughter has the name Xiu-qi. My son picked out the first two words, instructing his daughter to cultivate herself and look after her family. It is the basic concept of our civilization. Governments will come, governments will go, but this endures. (p. 114)

Lee Kuan Yew and other Asian leaders share more or less the same thesis: The emphasis on the roles family plays in a society is the fundamental source of the East Asian renaissance; the diminishing respect for family and the precedence of individual rights over the family and communal interests are the reasons for the breakdown of Western civil society.

The intimate relationship between family and state explains the existence of a standard Chinese phrase *guojia* (literally, "state-family"), which is the nearest equivalent to the notion of "country" and "society." As such, "state" should always exist together with "family." The Chinese believe that a person with too many personal and family problems cannot become a good leader and teacher. Therefore, shaming and attacking personal moral weaknesses have become a common

Chinese tactic to challenge the legitimate status of the person being targeted. In Chinese, the word *jia* (family) is widely used to also describe "all of us" (*dajia*, "big family"), "expert" (*zhuanjia*, "special family"), or "a corporation" (*yi jia gongsi*). In their social life, the Chinese extend kinship terms, such as "grandpa," "grandma," "uncle," "aunt," "brother," and "sister," to address people outside their family and kinship networks.

The Confucian relationships are essentially family-centered. Of the Five Cardinal Relationships (*Wulun*), three—that is, father-son, husband-wife, and elder brother-younger brother—are direct family relationships, whereas the remaining two—that is, ruler (sovereign)-minister (subject) and friend-friend—can also be perceived as kinds of family relationships. Relationships independent of family do not exist in Confucian parlance. Self is defined by family networks. As Tu (1984, p. 5) writes, for the Chinese, the "family is seen as an enriching and nourishing support system, a vehicle for the true realization of the self in its center."

In Confucian society, remaining single without establishing a family and bearing a child is unthinkable, as a Chinese saying demonstrates: "Of the three offenses against filial piety, having no heir is the worst" (*Bu xiao you san, wu hou wei da*). Lin (1937/1996) notes that a Chinese parent's greatest concern is to see his sons and daughters properly married before he dies; if the daughters-in-law and sons-in-law are satisfactory, he can "close his eyes without regret." Lin (p. 189) states, "The net result of such a conception of life is that one gets a lengthened outlook on everything, for life is no more regarded as beginning and ending with that of the individual." More important, marriage is not a personal affair but that of a large family, as Lin (1939) notes:

> For it must be remembered that a marriage in China is not an individual affair but a family affair; a man does not marry a wife but "marries a daughter-in-law," as the idiomatic expression goes, and when a son is born, the idiomatic expression is "a grandson has been born." (p. 141)

Therefore, a Chinese is the "role" of the family rather than the "self" of the individuality. In Chinese, the terms *individual* (*geren*) and

individualism (*geren zhuyi*) have acquired almost only negative connotations (e.g., selfish). The word *individualism* was used by Mao
(1965) in his work "On Individualism" to refer to "retaliation," "small
group mentality," "the employee mentality," "pleasure-seeking," "passivity," and "the desire to leave the army." The strong Chinese family
orientation can also be seen, for example, in the idle topics that they
usually talk about when meeting each other for the first time; the
Chinese are bound to engage in discussion of their families within
3 minutes! This contrasts strikingly with a phenomenon commonly
found in Western societies: People work side by side for many years
without knowing each others' family backgrounds. This is why
Chinese culture is often referred to as a typical "collectivistic culture"
(Hofstede, 1980, 1991; Triandis, 1995).

There is economic rationality behind the origin of the Chinese
family system if it is examined from a historical perspective. Fung
(1948/1966) explains that China was traditionally a farming country,
and farmers had to live on their land, which was immovable. The
family in a wider sense had to live together for economic reasons.
Thus, the Chinese family system developed what is one of the most
complex and well-organized systems in the world. Even today, China
is largely an agrarian society, with more than 80% of the people living
in rural settings. The farmer's mentalities, such as "The more children, the more happiness" (*duo zi duo fu*) and "Bearing a son to protect
the old" (*yang er fang lao*), hold truth in the eyes of many country
people.

The Confucian ideal of the husband-wife relationship is not
romantic love but caring for one another in the "division of labor" for
the family: The husband should take care of matters outside of the
family, whereas the wife should be responsible for domestic affairs (Tu,
1984). Tu notes that Confucianism contains "an implicit male orientation, favouring male dominance" in the sense that

> much emphasis is placed on the father-son relationship and not
> enough on the mother-daughter relationship. Too great an empha-
> sis rests on the importance of the husband as a stabilizing force in
> the family rather than on the importance of the wife or the husband
> and wife together. (p. 106)

This implicit male orientation can also be discerned from numerous Chinese poems, proverbs, and expressions in which the word *er* ("son") is found to be universally used to refer either implicitly to *ernü* ("son and daughter") or explicitly to *erzi* ("son"). For example, a line that Chinese officials often quote when resigning from office reads, "Having sons, I am content with life; Without office, my body is light" (as quoted in Lin, 1996, p. 189).

In the traditional Chinese society, in which there had been no well-functioning legal framework, no established property rights, and no formal social security and welfare systems, a strong Chinese family system became a predominant social unit that contributed greatly to Chinese social stability. It was within the Chinese family and through the closest kinship networks that the Chinese people received care, protection, insurance, jobs, and, most important, security. Fukuyama (1995, p. 88) regards the Chinese family as "an essentially defensive mechanism against a hostile and capricious environment," whereas Lin (1939) calls it a system of "insurance":

> The family system must be taken as the Chinese traditional system of insurance against unemployment. Every family takes care of its own unemployed, and having taken care of its unemployed, its next best work is to find employment for them. (p. 173)

Despite the Confucian indifference to profit discussed previously, the Chinese have gained a wide reputation for their shrewd money-making and money-saving capacities; they can calculate money and haggle about price to the extremes. Bo Yang (1992) offers the following poignant sarcasm of the Chinese haggling behavior in *The Ugly Chinaman and the Crisis of Chinese Culture*:

> Chinese people are very clever. No ethnic group in the world, not even the Jews, are as shrewd as the Chinese. So shrewd are they, in fact, that once they've been sold off for the kill, they continue haggling over the price of their own flesh all the way to the slaughterhouse. If they can earn five extra bucks before the knife passes through their necks, they will die in ecstasy, knowing they had not lived in vain. (p. 56)

Note also that China's private saving rate is the highest in the world: Household saving is about 23% of disposable income in China compared with 21% in Japan, 18% in Taiwan, 16% in Belgium, 13% in the former West Germany, and 8% in the United States (The World Bank cited in Cao, Fan, & Woo, 1997).

Ironically, the Chinese money-oriented behavior also results essentially from the Confucian doctrine per se: its disregard of legal institutions and its family predominance. The behavior reflects the deep-seated Chinese psychological craving for security given the long-lasting lack of powerful legal and social welfare frameworks in Chinese society. For a Chinese, a sense of security can only be secured by the incessant accumulation of family wealth, which in turn enables family members to help one another in case of difficulties. As Jung Chang (1992, p. 22) stated in her best-seller *Wild Swans*, "Being an official brought power, and power brought money. Without power or money, no Chinese could feel safe from the depredations of officialdom or random violence."

Therefore, I view Chinese money-oriented behavior essentially as a by-product of Confucianism or a result of the Chinese family as an "insurance company" rather than a manifestation of "Chinese materialism." In this insurance company of the Chinese family, those with wealth and power have moral obligations to help less fortunate family members and relatives to overcome difficulties. Hence, Confucianism, though distrustful of the profit motive and commercial activity, can hardly prevent many a Chinese from becoming merchants who are hell-bent on making money. The Chinese have been shrewd traders for centuries. Ebrey (1993, p. 213) remarks, "Merchants thrived in almost all periods of peace" in Chinese history.

The Chinese family system has molded Chinese character. It is a mistake to view the traditional Chinese family as a harmonious and unified whole, as it is sometimes perceived to be from the outside (Lin, 1939). "The *jia* was in fact fraught with a number of inherent tensions" (Fukuyama, 1995, p. 90). Patience is a noble virtue of the Chinese people; Lin (1939) points out that the big Chinese family is the "training school" for developing such virtue:

> The training school for developing this virtue is, however, the big family, where a large number of daughters-in-law, brothers-in-law,

fathers, and sons daily learn this virtue by trying to endure one another. In the big family, where a closed door is an offense, and where there is very little elbow-room for the individuals, one learns by necessity and by parental instruction from early childhood the need for mutual toleration and adjustments in human relationships. (p. 45)

The Chinese language offers vivid illustration of the meaning of patience or tolerance: The Chinese character for "patience" or "tolerance" is made up of two other characters—"the edge of a knife" (*ren*) on top of "heart" (*xin*), as shown in Figure 5.2, suggesting an immeasurable capacity to endure hardships and misfortunes.

The Chinese have also gained a reputation for being an "individualistic" people, ironically also because of the strong Confucian family-centeredness. Lin (1939) describes the traditional Chinese society as "a tray of loose sands" (p. 177), with each grain being not an individual but a family, and the Chinese as "a nation of individualists" (p. 164). Fukuyama (1995, p. 86) remarks similarly: "Competition between families makes Chinese societies seem individualistic." The Chinese are too family-oriented to be social-minded. "Society" does not exist as an idea in Chinese thought. Teamwork is unknown to Chinese, who are born "uncooperative" (Bo, 1992). The Chinese like to play mah-jongg, a card game in which each party plays for itself; they do not like bridge, in which cooperation between parties is called for. Through the Chinese fondness for mah-jongg, Lin (1939) sees "the essence of Chinese individualism." Lin also observes that the relationship toward "strangers" or "others" is not among the Five Cardinal Relationships; the Chinese family is a "walled castle," and the family border serves as the indicator of the Chinese behavior:

> The family, with its friends, became a walled castle, with the greatest communistic cooperation and mutual help within, but coldly indifferent toward, and fortified against, the world without. In the end, as it worked out, the family became a walled castle outside which everything is legitimate loot. (p. 172)

Fukuyama (1995) regards China and other East Asian societies with a Chinese cultural heritage (i.e., Hong Kong, Taiwan, Singapore, and

South Korea) as "familistic" and "low-trust" societies in which the path to "sociability" is based on "family and kinship." There is a strong distrust of outsiders (non-family members) in these Chinese societies. The borderline between family and nonfamily is sharply drawn. Kao's (1993) study of Chinese entrepreneurship in familial businesses shows that

> a non-Chinese professional manager can't expect the same level of trust he or she would have as a family member in the company. Outsiders can never know family insiders as well as they know each other. And non-Chinese professionals often have to work doubly hard to understand the reasons underlying certain decisions. (p. 27)

Worm (1997) compares Chinese culture with Scandinavian culture and finds that trust and solidarity is low in the former but high in the latter. At the same time, Worm (1997, p. 55) also finds that "one can count on genuine Chinese friends to do much more to help than we are accustomed to in the West." These writings point to the reality that the Chinese family is the ultimate answer to Chinese trusting and distrusting behaviors.

Fukuyama (1995) and Kao (1993) assume that, as Chinese family companies start to grow, the conventions of traditional Chinese business, especially caution toward outsiders, will become a clear competitive disadvantage. "The lack of trust outside the family makes it hard for unrelated people to form groups or organizations" (Fukuyama, 1995, p. 75). Triandis (1996) maintains that Chinese culture has a collectivist-hierarchical quality or tendency. This tendency has the effect of increasing the probability of harmony-seeking and interpersonal relationships among in-group members but also increases the probability of distrustful or even hostile behaviors toward those who are perceived as belonging to out-groups. Shenkar and Ronen (1987) observe that the Chinese are uniformly cautious, at times reluctant, to request assistance from those outside their kinship groups. All this means that, in Chinese societies, it takes a considerable amount of time to build trust between non-family members.

Management researchers (Child & Markoczy, 1993; Lockett, 1988) use the term *group orientation* to describe the management style in the PRC. Although overseas Chinese businesses are regarded as family-oriented, businesses in the PRC seem to possess many "group-oriented" features. For example, *danwei* in the PRC has, to a large extent, replaced many functions of the traditional Chinese family, thereby institutionalizing the people to cooperate with one another outside their nuclear families. *Danwei* may be called a "quasi-family" structure, unique in the PRC, which helps contribute to the Chinese managers' social-minded behavior. At this point, I view *danwei* in a good light because it serves to pull the Chinese out of their nuclear family circles toward commitment to professional institutions in the society.

In business negotiations, a Chinese negotiating team is essentially a consensus-reaching group (Deverge, 1986). It stands for the positions agreed on by a large number of people inside the negotiating organization. Chinese negotiators are mutually dependent on one another in their decision making. Internal consultations and discussions are frequent. The Chinese also show a strong preference for meeting in groups rather than in one-to-one settings (Kindel, 1990; Shenkar & Ronen, 1987). The Chinese family awareness that those with wealth and power have moral obligations to help less fortunate family members and relatives explains, at least in part, why the Chinese often feel that investors from "rich" industrialized countries should help "poor" developing countries by bearing the heavier burden. See Illustrations 9, 21, 23, 27, and 32 in Chapter 4 to further understand this section's discussion.

Respect for Age and Hierarchy

One important hallmark of Confucianism is its teaching on respect for age and hierarchy. In *Analects*, Confucius says (in Chan, 1963),

> At fifteen my mind was set on learning.
> At thirty my character had been formed.
> At forty I had no more perplexities.
> At fifty I knew the Mandate of Heaven.
> At sixty I was at ease with whatever I heard.
> At seventy I could follow my heart's desire without transgressing
>   moral principles. (p. 22)

Through this immortal saying, Confucius is believed to highlight the character-building of a great personality through lifelong learning and self-cultivation. At the same time, the words clearly convey an important Confucian message that age means wisdom.

Instead of social equality and individual freedom, Confucianism emphasizes social hierarchy and order. This teaching can be seen in Confucius' aphorism *jun jun, chen chen, fu fu, zi zi* as follows (from *Analects*, in Chan, 1963)

> Duke Ching of Chi asked Confucius about government. Confucius replied, "Let the ruler *be* a ruler, the minister *be* a minister, the father *be* a father, and the son *be* a son" (p. 39)

According to Confucianism, social order has precedence over individual rights. Social stability and harmony—the very foundation of individual rights—can be realized only through everyone's wholeheartedly doing their duty as defined by their positions in the hierarchical society. Chinese socialization is characterized by training for obedience, proper conduct, impulse control, and acceptance of social obligations instead of independence, assertiveness, and creativity (Wu, 1996). At this point, the Western conception of democracy finds no logical footing in Confucianism.

Hierarchy and ordering relationships are also expressed in the Five Cardinal Relationships—that is, between ruler and subject, father and son, husband and wife, elder and younger brothers, and senior and junior friends. In each case, the former ranks above the latter. Eberhard (1971) notes that these five relationships involve three principles of ranking: (a) age (older ranks above younger), (b) social status (ruler above subject), and (c) sex (male above female). These three principles can usually be reduced to one, namely, age.

Chinese society is apt to have a certain contempt for young enthusiasm; the young are taught early to hold their tongues while their elders are speaking (Lin, 1939). Gao et al. (1996, p. 285) call Chinese communication a listening-centered communication (*tinghua*): "In Chinese culture, there are conditions associated with speaking, and not everyone is entitled to speak. . . . A spoken 'voice,' thus is equated with seniority, authority, experience, knowledge, and expertise. As a result, listening becomes a predominant communication activity." In the Chinese culture, good children (*hao haizi* or *guai haizi*) are those who "listen talks" (*tinghua*) and do not interrupt (*chazui*).

Traditionally, young people in Chinese society are not considered dependable, experienced, or capable of doing good business. This attitude can be seen in the Chinese proverb *Zui shang wu mao ban shi bu lao* ("No beard, no business"). The older are specially honored in Chinese culture; the "honored places" must be reserved for the people with "white hair," as Confucius says (in Chan, 1963),

> In the pledging rite the inferiors present their cups to their superiors, so that people of humble stations may have something to do. In the concluding feast, honored places were given to people with white hair, so as to follow the order of seniority. (p. 103)

The Confucian respect for age and hierarchy is evident in Chinese social life. The Chinese language has a large vocabulary used to distinguish people in terms of generation, age, and so on. For example, in Chinese, there are specific terms for elder uncle (*bofu* or *bobo*) and younger uncle (*shufu* or *shushu*) and elder brother (*xiong* or *gege*) and younger brother (*di* or *didi*). Further distinction is made between members from paternal and maternal sides. Chinese children are taught early to address guests differently according to their age, which is in stark contrast to the universal "Hi!" to address everyone used by their counterparts in many Western societies.

Consider the Chinese forms of address. The first name is seldom used and is reserved exclusively for family members, close relatives, and extremely intimate friends; the family name plus occupation-linked title is a very popular form of address in Chinese social life, such as "Professor Wang," "Director Li," "Manager Liu," and "Teacher Zhang." Very often, the Chinese use an occupational title without adding any family name to it. For example, one will hear "Teacher, Good Morning!" in every Chinese school. This usage is different from that of many Western countries. The following is a cross-cultural joke about a Chinese student (C) meeting his English lecturer (E) for the first time (Gu, 1990, p. 250):

C: Teacher, how do you do?

E: How do you do? Where do you teach?

C: No, I'm not a teacher, I'm a student.

Another very popular form of address is to add an age-linked prefix to the family name of the person to be addressed: *xiao* ("young" or "junior") for those younger and *lao* ("old" or "senior") for those older than the addresser. This form of address is used when people know one another very well. Note that *xiao* and *lao* may be used with both men and women, although the current trend is that *lao* is used more frequently with men. Therefore, one will hear Chinese addressing each other as, for example, "Lao Wang" and "Xiao Li." *Lao* can also be used after the family name if the person is of senior age and an exceptionally venerable personality, such as "Wang Lao."

Other examples of the Chinese respect for age and hierarchy include the following: In China's state-owned organizations, age (*nianling*) and ranking (*jibie*) are people's two most important assets regarding rating of professional titles (*ping zhichen*), allocation of housing (*fen fangzi*), increments in salary (*jia gongzi*), and so on; when keeping an appointment, the Chinese visitor may arrive 15 to 20 minutes early if the host is a person of senior age and high status simply because the visitor wants to show respect for the host by not keeping him waiting even a second; and business and professional titles are extensively printed on Chinese business cards. One of my favorite teaching materials in this regard is a business card of a Chinese professor that contains a total of 16 titles and positions on both sides, ranging from professor, editor, and researcher to president, managing director, and management adviser!

The Confucian value of respect for age and hierarchy has important implications for foreign negotiators. First, foreign negotiators' age and rank will determine the attitude of the Chinese host organization toward the foreign company. For example, if your rank is low, the Chinese may feel insulted and doubt your "sincerity" to do business (Chen, 1993; Seligman, 1990). Second, because hierarchy is so important to the Chinese, you must not forget to put your business title on your business card to be presented to the Chinese business people. The Chinese would feel uncertain and, at worst, insulted when meeting a foreign business person whose title is blank. Third, you must not feel strange when Chinese negotiating partners do not talk as much as you do. In business negotiations, the well-known Chinese "listening" approach can be both non-tactical and tactical. On the one hand, the Chinese listening-centeredness (*tinghua*) can make the Chinese behave reserved in front of Western business people, who are assumed to have higher status by the Chinese and are expected to talk more about their advanced technology and products. On the other hand, this Chinese listening approach may also be employed as a Chinese negotiating stratagem. As Pye (1982) observes, by talking less, the Chinese can mask their interests and priorities while stimulating the other party to show its hand first. Finally, forget the stereotype that Chinese managers are poor at English. Given their listening-centered socialization, the Chinese may not be able to orally "show off" their English language ability, but they most probably understand English well. Snow (1980, p. 65) observes that "many more [Chinese] can understand English than can speak it." See Illustrations 25, 29, and 39 in Chapter 4 for a more in-depth understanding of some of the topics discussed in this section.

Avoidance of Conflict and Need for Harmony

A basic tenet of Confucian philosophy is the principle of harmony, which reflects an aspiration toward a conflict-free, group-based system of social relations (Shenkar & Ronen, 1987). In the Confucian tradition, social harmony is achieved when the Five Cardinal Relations are fulfilled (Deverge, 1983). Confucianism stresses the need to achieve harmony in society through moral conduct in all relationships: adapting to the collectivity, controlling emotions, avoiding confusion, competition, and conflict, and so on. Scholars (Bond & Wang, 1983; Shenkar & Ronen, 1987) find that the principle of harmony has not been challenged by modern Chinese ideologies, either in the PRC or in the non-Communist Chinese societies, and seems to have persisted in modern Chinese communities in Western countries.

The Chinese avoidance of conflict and the need for harmony is a product of the Confucian notion of *Zhong Yong* (literally, "moderation," "compromise," "harmonization," and "Mean"; the Confucian classic *Zhong Yong* is translated as *The Doctrine of the Mean*). Wu (1990) maintains that *Ren* (humanity and benevolence), *Li* (propriety, ceremony, rites, and rules of proper conduct), and *Zhong Yong* form the foundation of Confucian philosophy. A Confucian gentleman does not quarrel. If circumstances compel him to be in a contest, he will then contend like a gentleman. Confucius says (from *Analects* as quoted in Wu, 1990),

> A gentleman has no squabbles. If he really needs to contend, it would be like an archery contest: he bows politely and goes up the hall; he comes down and drinks the penalty wine if he loses. This is a gentleman's contest. (p. 69)

A Confucian gentleman is patient, maintaining self-control whatever the situation. The Chinese avoid passing harsh judgment or criticism and find it difficult to have frank dialogues except among trusted friends (Tan, 1990). Direct and open conflict upsets interpersonal relationships and causes the people involved to lose face. Therefore, conflict is frequently resolved by bringing in a third-party mediator who has respected status and is accepted by both parties.

Pacifism is a fundamental characteristic of the Chinese people. The Chinese are traditionally a self-contained continental people; the defensive properties of the Chinese blood are engraved in the building of the Great Wall itself. The Middle Kingdom boasts an 18,000-kilometer-long coastline; nevertheless, it has never managed to cultivate a people whose sights have been set on foreign conquests. Fairbank's (1974) study of the Chinese style of warfare shows that the Chinese prefer *wen* (the arts of peace and the sagehood of the ruler) to *wu* (brute force and conquest). An old Chinese saying reveals the "cowardliness" of the Chinese personality: "Good men are not made to become soldiers, and good iron is not used for making nails" (*hao nan bu dang bing, hao tie bu da ting*). Regarding Chinese pacifism, Lin Yutang (1939) provides a short but thorough analysis:

> The Chinese are the world's worst fighters because they are an intelligent race, backed and nurtured by Taoistic cynicism and the Confucian emphasis on harmony as the ideal of life. They do not fight because they are the most calculating and self-interested of peoples. (p. 56)

Although the Chinese are not an outward fighting people, they have been known for their "infighting" or *wolidou*, a term coined by Bo Yang (1992). A popular saying reveals a marked difference between the Chinese and Japanese (see also Bo Yang, 1992, p. 11):

> A Chinese all by himself is as awesome as a dragon [*long*], but three Chinese together are no better than a worm [*chong*]; a Japanese all by himself is no better than a worm [*chong*], but three Japanese together are as awesome as a dragon [*long*].

Strong family orientation is the main reason behind the Chinese inability to cooperate (see the section on Family Orientation earlier in this chapter).

The Chinese avoidance of conflict and need for harmony can be seen everywhere in the Chinese life. "Suggestiveness, not articulateness, is the ideal of all Chinese art, whether it be poetry, painting, or anything else" (Fung, 1948/1966, p. 12). The level of suggestiveness is the reason why Chinese poems, sayings, and philosophical works are often very difficult to translate exactly into foreign languages. The traditional Chinese medicine (Veith, 1972) and theory of love (J. Chang, 1991) emphasize harmony and discourage excessive expression of emotions, such as grief, fear, pity, anger, joy, and love.[12] The following is from *The Yellow Emperor's Classic of Internal Medicine* (as quoted in Veith, 1972):

> The sages attained harmony with Heaven and Earth and followed closely the laws of eight winds. They were able to adjust their desires to worldly affairs, and within their hearts there was neither hatred nor anger. (p. 101)

> The emotions of joy and anger are injurious to the spirit. Cold and heat are injurious to the body. . . . When joy and anger are without moderation, then cold and heat exceed all measure and life is no longer secure. Yin and Yang should be respected to an equal extent. (p. 117)

People familiar with Chinese music can hardly fail to notice that phrases such as "making love," "having sex," and so on, which are ubiquitous in Western music, cannot be heard in the Chinese counterpart, whether it be classical or modern, soft or rock, or romantic or nonromantic music. In the West, a common phenomenon can be seen at any airport or train station: People, on parting with each other, kiss each other good-bye. This is seldom seen at the Chinese airport or train station. Do the Chinese lack the feeling of love? No. The Chinese are great lovers (note that China has the world's largest population)! If one observes the Chinese more carefully, one finds their tears framed in their eyes and their hands gripping each other's hands, bags, and clothes. The Chinese do have a strong feeling of love but express it in an implicit manner.

This is why Hall (1976/1981) defines Chinese communication as a high-context communication. Often, genuine Chinese meanings do not exist in coded and transmitted messages. As a famous Chinese saying goes, "The drinker's heart is not in the cup" (*Zui weng zhi yi bu zai jiu*). Marketing is about satisfying the customers' needs and wants. This Western definition, however, does not attend to the implicit way in which the Oriental people tend to express their needs and wants. I always challenge my students of international business and marketing by asking, How can we satisfy the Chinese customers' needs and wants when they are expressed in an implicit manner? My advice is the following: To succeed in the Chinese culture, a marketer must move beyond the explicit Chinese wishes to discover those unspoken needs and wants that the Chinese customers really mean to imply. In other words, we need to find out what is actually weighing on the Chinese drinker's heart.

Pye (1982) observes that the most striking personal characteristic of Chinese negotiators is their ability to separate whatever emotions they may show from the actual progress of the negotiations: The Chinese "never telegraphed their next moves through a show of emotions" (p. 80). As "cultivated men," the Chinese negotiators master prudently the opportunities available through self-control. They consider negotiation as a simultaneous discussion of issues that leads to integrative solutions and adopt a slow but steady approach, through collaborative measures, to win their opponents' heart (Withane, 1992).

The Chinese need for harmony seems to be a contradiction to the prevalent Chinese practice of bargaining or haggling for a mutually agreeable price. Tan (1990) argues that bargaining is a Chinese way of life, especially in the traditional marketplace. According to Tan (1990), the Chinese bargaining process is seldom a win-lose contest or winner-takes-all situation. Rather, a successful bargaining interaction gives everyone a sense of satisfaction even though compromises have been made by both sides. The state of harmony is maintained, and no one suffers any loss of face (see the following discussion of face). Therefore, Chinese negotiators seek compromise (Kirkbride & Tang, 1990; Kirkbride et al., 1991) and behave carefully (Deverge, 1986), slowly (Deverge, 1986), prudently (Withane, 1992), less emotionally (Shenkar & Ronen, 1987), and patiently (Pye, 1982).

Concept of Face

Although a universal human nature and a ubiquitous concept that occurs in all cultures (Goffman, 1955; Ting-Toomey, 1988), face is particularly salient for Chinese culture (Hu, 1944; Lin, 1939; Redding & Ng, 1982; Stover, 1974). In fact, the concept of face is Chinese in origin. The term is a literal translation of the Chinese word *lian*. In the *Shorter Oxford English Dictionary on Historical Principles* (1933/1975, p. 716), "to lose face" is rendered directly from the Chinese phrase *tiu lien* (*diu lian*)—"to lose one's credit, good name, or reputation."

Face is described as "the positive social value a person effectively claims for himself by the line others assume he has taken during a particular contact" or "an image of self delineated in terms of approved social attributes" (Goffman, 1955, p. 213); "one's dignity, self-respect, and prestige" (Hofstede & Bond, 1988, p. 8); "the most delicate standard by which Chinese social intercourse is regulated" (Lin, 1939, p. 190); and by Ho (1976) as

> the respectability and/or deference which a person can claim for himself from others, by virtue of the relative position he occupies in his social network and the degree to which he is judged to have functioned adequately in that position as well as acceptably in his general conduct. (p. 883)

A Chinese saying states that "every person has a face, for the same reason that every tree has a bark" (*Ren you lian, shu you pi*); losing one's face is compared to a tree being stripped of its bark—an endangering situation. Hofstede and Bond (1988, p. 8) also observe that losing face, in the Chinese tradition, "is equivalent to losing one's eyes, nose, and mouth."

The Chinese concept of face is explored in an early article written by Hsien Chin Hu (1944). Hu argues that societies may have formed different conceptions of even the most universal aspects of human life; often, this difference in conception is reflected in the indigenous vocabulary. Hu then penetrates beneath the Chinese concept of face by distinguishing two Chinese words, both of which mean face: *mien-tzu* (*mianzi*) and *lien* (*lian*). Because he has written lucidly on this topic, Hu (1944) is worth quoting at length:

> Verbally the two sets of criteria are distinguished by two words which on the physical level both mean "face." One of these, *mien-tzu*, stands for the kind of prestige that is emphasized in this country [America]: a reputation achieved through getting on in life, through success and ostentation. This is prestige that is accumulated by means of personal effort or clever maneuvering. For this kind of recognition ego is dependent at all times on his external environment. The other kind of "face," *Lien*, is also known to Americans without being accorded formal recognition. It is the respect of the group for a man with a good moral reputation: the man who will fulfill his obligations regardless of the hardships involved, who under all circumstances shows himself a decent human being. It represents the confidence of society in the integrity of ego's moral character, the loss of which makes it impossible for him to function properly within the community. *Lien* is both a social sanction for enforcing moral standards and an internalized sanction. (p. 45)

By this definition, face involves (a) the respect of the group for a person with a good moral reputation and (b) the person's prestige. It should be noted that the difference between *mianzi* and *lian* is rather sharp in Hu's analysis. In Chinese, the concept of *mianzi* is not altogether devoid of a moral element. Hu (1944), however, has captured the essence of the Chinese concept of face by pointing out its moral orientation and family-centeredness: Face is not only a person's private affair but also, more important, a concern of the person's whole family, social networks, and community at large. Explaining loss of face, Hu (1944) writes,

Ego almost always belongs to a closely integrated group on which is reflected some of his glory or shame. His family, the wider community of friends, and his superiors, all have an interest in his advancement or set-backs. So a person does not simply "lose his own face." Public disgrace or ridicule of a serious nature is bound to have an effect on the reputation of the family. (p. 50)

The Chinese concept of face is embedded in the Confucian notions of shame and social harmony. Harmony is found in the maintenance of an individual's face (Hofstede & Bond, 1988, p. 8). Confucius teaches a kind of statesmanship that advocates governing people by instilling "a sense of shame" into their mind, thereby using shame or face as a regulating mechanism for people's self-adjusting social behavior. Mencius, one of the outstanding transmitters of Confucian traditions, characterized the way of being human in terms of four basic moral qualities known as "Four Beginnings" or "Four Germinations." According to Mencius, the feeling of shame is the germination of righteousness. Shame provides the incentive for a human being to behave morally. Mencius says (in Chan, 1963),

A man without the feeling of commiseration is not a man; a man without the feeling of shame and dislike is not a man; a man without the feeling of deference and compliance is not a man; and a man without the feeling of right and wrong is not a man. . . . Men have these Four Beginnings just as they have their four limbs. (p. 65)

The Chinese face has several distinctive dimensions. First, it ties together one's status. Second, there exist certain limits of face that determine whether one is to lose or gain face. Lu Xun (1980), a famous Chinese writer, wrote a splendid essay on the Chinese concept of face:

But what is this thing called face? It is all very well if you don't stop to think, but the more you think the more confused you grow. There seem to be many kinds: Each class in society has a different face. There are certain limits to face, and if you fall short of the limit you lose face, if you don't mind losing face you are shameless, while if you rise above that limit you gain face. Different people lose face in different ways. For example, we think nothing of it if a

> rickshaw man sits by the roadside stripped to the waist to catch
> lice, whereas if a rich man's son-in-law sits by the roadside stripped
> to the waist to catch lice he loses face. It is not that a rickshaw man
> has no face, only that he does not lose it in this case; but if his wife
> kicks him and he lies down to howl, he loses face. (pp. 131-132)

Given these characteristics of face, persons in subordinate positions
can use the fact that their superiors must maintain their face at a high
level to exploit an economic advantage without offending moral standards (Hu, 1944). This implies that face can be employed as an
influencing tactic in interpersonal relationships.

Finally, reciprocity is inherent in the Chinese face behavior
(Brunner & Wang, 1988; Ho, 1976; Hwang, 1987). The Chinese face
may not only be saved or lost but also be "traded"—to give and be
given. Chinese commonly use the term "giving face to someone" to
mean doing a favor for someone. The person who has been given face
is expected to give face in return—a face trading thus begins. Therefore,
the Chinese concept of face is inextricably linked to other Chinese
concepts such as *guanxi, renqing, li,* and *keqi.*

Face is evident in all aspects of Chinese life. The Chinese often
avoid saying the word "No" to save face for both parties. Words such
as *inconvenient (bufangbian), too difficult (taikunnan),* and *maybe
(huoxu)* are often synonyms of "No" in Chinese culture. The Chinese
"Yes" *(shi)* can also be elusive—a word that has little meaning because
it is used to respond to almost everything, such as "Yes, but it is
inconvenient."

Recent years have witnessed many Chinese dissidents who received permission to leave China because of their "health problems."
Devising a face-saving reason to resolve negotiation deadlocks was
found to be an effective negotiating tactic employed by foreign negotiators in these cases. Fang Lizhi, China's foremost dissident, left
China on June 25, 1990, after a year-long negotiation between China
and the United States. Schell (1992) stated,

> It was not long before negotiations with the United States began
> to center on a face-saving device for resolving the matter. In May
> a perfect opportunity presented itself when Fang reported experi-
> encing some minor heart palpitations. Although he was checked

out by a Western doctor who found no serious medical problems, and although Fang himself later dismissed his chest pains as being the result of "drinking too much coffee," U.S. negotiators were not so quick to dismiss the matter. After news of how Fang was "stricken" had been leaked in Washington to the San Francisco *Examiner*, where it quickly garnered a front-page headline reading, "China Dissident Suffers Heart Attack," the year-long deadlock began to break in the Beijing negotiations. (p. xxxvi)

Face is also evident in a Chinese business negotiation context. It is observed as a decisive reason for the Chinese preference of doing business with large companies with worldwide reputations. As Chu (1991, p. 197) states, "The Chinese do not want to be seen by their colleagues as ones who do business with second-rate companies. When they do business with the largest and best-known international companies, it causes them to gain face."

Brunner and Wang (1988) explain Chinese negotiating style—for example, meeting in a group, proceeding cautiously and slowly—from the face perspective. They also explain the Chinese face behavior at the dinner table as follows:

> If the occasion is a formal dinner, innumerable toasts will be given with emphasis upon the importance of an enduring and deep friendship and mutual respect and cooperation. One should not refuse to drink a toast as this would indicate that he does not want "to give face." Further, one should not eat all the food and wine served as this will also cause the Chinese to lose "face." (p. 38)

It would be difficult for a Chinese negotiator to make concessions because of his face consciousness, as a report describes ("Negotiating in China," 1986):

> The Chinese negotiators would refuse to back down. They acted as if the issue was theirs to decide and if we did not yield, the negotiations were at an impasse. They would then ask their higher levels to intervene and overrule them. They therefore did not lose *face* [italics added] by being the one to yield. (p. 29)

It is also reported (Schnepp et al., 1990) that the Chinese frequently reopen negotiations to press out additional profit. The Chinese propensity to renegotiate also has much to do with face; the Chinese negotiators want to look "good."

To deal with Chinese face in negotiations, authors universally advise that we must give face to the Chinese and avoid actions that will cause them to lose face. For example, Pye (1982, p. 89), a chief representative of the "Chinese bureaucracy school," advises that we must help the Chinese gain face: "As a result, a great deal can be gained by helping the Chinese to win face and a great deal will be lost by any affront or slight, no matter how unintended." Brunner and Wang (1988), the "Confucian school" authors, also advise that

> foreigners involved in negotiations with the Chinese must be cognizant of the patterns of face behavior, and endeavor to "give face" to the Chinese, and avoid actions which will cause them to "lose face." To do otherwise, is to ignore the importance of the face behavior, its pervasiveness in social interaction, and its role in successfully negotiating with the Chinese. (p. 42)

See Illustrations 11, 15, 28, 31, and 34 in Chapter 4 for more discussions of face.

I have discussed six basic values of Confucian tradition. I emphasize that each of these values has its "good" and "evil" faces, just as Yin and Yang exist in every universal phenomenon. First, the Confucian value of moral cultivation is positive with regard to its advocacy of people's lifelong learning, commitment, and self-regulation of behavior. The value can also be a negative value, however, because it rebuts any rationality in legalism, resulting in a more than 2,000-year lack of an effective legal framework and the people having had a feeling of social insecurity for an equally long time period. The Confucian morality (e.g., trust and sincerity) and notion of relationships are highly reciprocal, situational, dynamic, context-related, and family centered rather than a principled moral thinking applicable to the society at large. As a political ideology, Confucianism is positive when the sage-king uses his exemplary moral influence to govern this country and people; it is negative when the king-sage abuses the power of the king in the name of the sage.

Second, the Confucian mentality of relying on informal inter-personal relationships, not formal prescribed systems, to get things done allows the Chinese to be a flexible and innovative people who believe there is no problem that cannot be solved in China. The same mentality, however, also makes it difficult for modern political and economic institutions to take firm root in Chinese society. This problem of "weak institutions" is not unique to China but common to all Asian societies.

Third, the strong Confucian family orientation explains why Chinese culture is so enduring and why the Chinese have been able to survive innumerable hardships throughout history. Again, the destructive and creative aspects of Confucianism are a package. If the Chinese *jia* (family) is interpreted solely as a cohort of nuclear family and kinship, then the Confucian family orientation can degenerate into corruption, nepotism, and vulgarization and result in the destruc-tion of individuals' personality and creativity. If *jia* is viewed as a larger concept, however, that includes, for example, professional organiza-tion, community, and society, then the Confucian *jia* offers an inno-vative and energetic approach to life: It encourages people's total com-mitment to communal activities to achieve genuine self-realization and harmony in the society.

Fourth, the Confucian value of age and hierarchy is positive in the sense that it encourages the younger to learn from the older, and, as a result, fine tradition and far-seeing wisdom can be handed down from generation to generation, making culture a lasting one. The value is also positive because it emphasizes the people's commitment to doing their own duties and their own jobs well. The same value can be negative, however, because it is too tradition oriented, allowing little room for new ideas, risk-taking spirits to burgeon, and younger voices to speak out, thereby stifling personality, innovation, creativity, free-dom, and democracy.

Fifth, the Confucianism principle of harmony is obviously a positive value for handling conflicts not only at the interpersonal relationship level but also at the organizational and global levels. It encourages the participation of individuals in a larger system and facilitates a holistic approach to solving problems. The same principle, however, views individual rights as inferior to collective harmony, thereby going against concepts such as freedom, liberty, and, most important, democracy. Too much emphasis on harmony also makes Chinese communication too implicit to understand and the Chinese people too difficult with which to communicate.

Finally, face, as a self-regulating moral mechanism, is positive simply because if one does not mind losing face one is shameless. Face entails a deep moral connotation that enables a Chinese to fulfill his obligations regardless of hardships and behave as a decent human being whatever the circumstances. Moreover, face is not only a person's private affair but also, more important, a concern of the person's whole family, social networks, and community at large. Chinese people are widely known as ambitious and hardworking people. A deep psychological answer is face: Without any achievements, the Chinese would feel faceless (*wulian* or *wuyan*) standing before the pictures of their ancestors. Many overseas Chinese adapt themselves to new societies very quickly, and face is a major reason. The following is from a story (as quoted in Huang et al., 1997), "My Daughter Played the National Anthem of China on the Piano," told by Zhang Xiaoming about how her 7-year-old daughter adapted successfully to her new life in Japan:

> The daughter who was a first grade pupil, came to Japan without knowing any Japanese. The parents worried that she could not adapt to changes in the Japanese school system. The girl made great achievements after only six months. The girl often said to her parents: "If I cannot do a good job, they (her Japanese classmates) will think that Chinese people are unable to achieve. I must gain a respectful 'face' for our Chinese people." (p. 224)

What a lovely girl and what a positive effect of face! Examining the Chinese history, I believe that had the Chinese people not had a deep face consciousness or keen sense of shame, China, a country traditionally lacking effective legal and social frameworks, would have become a disunited or conquered nation long ago.

Nevertheless, face can be a negative value as well; it serves as an "invisible knife" to kill the Chinese ability to demonstrate their genuine feeling of love for life, making the Chinese an extremely elusive character. Cheng (1990) finds that, given the common Confucian traditions, the Chinese and other East Asians share three

"behavioral traits": lack of personality, lack of principled moral thinking, and lack of assertiveness. Li Yutang (1981b, p. 127) states more
sharply, "Not until everybody loses face in China, will this country
ever become a democratic nation." At this point, I note that the
Chinese, just like other East Asians, may not be called a "frank" people,
because they are too preoccupied with the family-centered and context-
related Confucian morals and too self-conscious about *li, keqi,* and,
most important, face to be natural and straightforward human beings.

Given the previous discussion, I am dismayed at some cross-
cultural theories that group Confucian values into two poles: "long
term," "future-oriented," or "positive," on the one hand, and "short-
term," "past and present oriented," or "negative," on the other hand.
The fact is that every Confucian value has its Yin and Yang. This is
why I believe that there exists a philosophical flaw in Hofstede's fifth
national culture dimension, Confucian Dynamism (Fang, 1998).

Chinese Stratagems

The third major component of Chinese business culture is what
I term *Chinese stratagems.* Chinese stratagems are a strategic component of Chinese business culture. They form the very core of the
strategic Chinese thinking and offer a cultural explanation of the
strategic patterns of Chinese negotiating style—that is, Chinese negotiating tactics.

Many previous studies of Chinese business negotiating style were
very useful because they drew attention to the haggling characteristics
of the Chinese negotiation process and, especially, provided lists of
Chinese negotiating tactics (Blackman, 1997; Pye, 1982; Seligman,
1990). These influential reports, however, unfortunately failed to
explore the cultural or philosophical foundation of the various Chinese
negotiating tactics they discovered. Here, a philosophical perspective
is crucial because it will allow us to go beyond a wide variety of Chinese
ploys, tricks, and tactics to reach the essence of strategic Chinese thinking
that welds together all Chinese negotiating tricks, ploys, and tactics.

My line of thought is simple: If the Chinese "for centuries" really
have been superb negotiators knowing few peers in the subtle art of
negotiating as postulated by Lucian Pye (1986, p. 74), they must have

been equipped with a kind of Chinese theory of negotiating tactics deeply rooted in the traditional Chinese culture with which Westerners are not very familiar. My past working experience as a Chinese business negotiator and my "insider" knowledge of Chinese culture, especially Chinese folklore and ancient Chinese military literature, have led me to discern the indigenous Chinese concept of *ji*, a word unknown to the West, to better understand the workings of Chinese negotiating tactics.

A Chinese Word Unknown to the West

There is a Chinese word that is unknown to the West but appeared as early as 2,300 years ago in the world's earliest treatise on warfare strategy, *Art of War* (*Sun Zi Bing Fa*), written by the great ancient Chinese military strategist Sun Tzu: The word is *ji*. Of a total of 13 chapters contained in *Art of War*, Sun Tzu begins with the "Chapter of *ji*," in which the art of war is described as the manipulation of various *ji*'s rather than resorting to absolute military forces. *Ji* is the general commander's key to victory. Sun Tzu (1963/1982, p. 66)[13] writes, "If a general who heeds my strategy [*ji*] is employed, he is certain to win. Retain him! When one who refuses to listen to my strategy [*ji*] is employed, he is certain to be defeated. Dismiss him!"

The Chinese word *ji* unfortunately has not been introduced in its original form in any published foreign language translations of *Art of War* that I have traced. Despite the fact that *Art of War* was first published in the West in 1772 (Griffith, 1963/1982) and has since been translated into approximately 10 different foreign languages (Wu, 1991), the Chinese concept of *ji* is still unknown to the West. Consequently, very few Western business people know *ji*; the concept at the center of Sun Tzu's *Art of War* has also been neglected by many Western and even Chinese authors on the subject of Sun Tzu and business management.

What Is Ji?

Ji is diversely translated in various English versions of *Art of War*. For example, *ji* is translated as "laying plans" and "counsel" by Giles (Sun Tzu, 1910); as "estimates" and "strategy" by Griffith (Sun Tzu,

Figure 3.3. The Chinese Character *Ji*
SOURCE: Calligraphy by Tony Fang; copyright 1998 by Tony Fang.

1963/1982); and as "estimation," "strategy," "tactics," and "strategic plan" by Sawyer (Sun Tzu, 1994). In *A Modern Chinese-English Dictionary* (1994, p. 412), *ji* is defined as follows: (a) to count, compute, calculate, number (as a verb); (b) meter and gauge (as a noun); and (3) idea, plan, ruse, stratagem, and tactics (as a noun). In Chinese, the character *ji* is a combination of two other characters: *yan* to the left and *shi* to the right (Figure 3.3). Literally, *yan* means "to speak, say, tell"; *shi* means "ten." Taken together, the two parts imply "speak to ten," "count to ten," "count from A to Z," or "think through the whole situation."

Harro von Senger (1991a, p. 2), a Swiss sinologist, explains the word *ji* at two different levels: (a) a tactic or ruse of war and (b) artifice in political or private life or both. Chien Chiao (1981, p. 429),[14] a Hong Kong-based scholar, provides the following definition of *ji*: "It [*ji*] is defined as a socially allowed though not necessarily encouraged scheme with which an individual or a group of individuals try to acquire certain benefits or avoid disasters."

Recently, *ji* has been translated into English as *stratagem* and into German as *strategeme* by many authors in connection with the introduction to the West of a compendium of ancient Chinese wisdom titled *Sanshiliu Ji* (*The Thirty-Six Stratagems*; Gao, 1991; Lip, 1991; von Senger, 1991a, 1991b). Harro von Senger, who spent many years in mainland China, Taiwan, and other East Asian countries systematically studying the ancient Chinese wisdom, assumes that *stratagem* is the best English translation of the Chinese concept of *ji*.

The English word *stratagem* originates from the Greek word *strategema*, which means (Wheeler, 1988)

> a strategic or tactical act of trickery, deceit, or cunning in military affairs and especially war, whereby one attempts to gain psychological or material advantage over an opponent, to neutralize some part of an opponent's superiority, to minimize one's own expenditure of resources, or to restore the morale and physical state of one's own forces. (p. xi)

Although this Western definition of *stratagem* is basically suitable for an application in the Chinese context, I emphasize stratagem as a human wisdom or psychological weapon in Chinese culture. In Chinese, *ji* is a neutral word that can convey both positive and negative meanings depending on how it is used. It is more a sophisticated wisdom of life than a sheer act of trickery and deceit. There exist numerous Chinese sayings that are related to *ji*, including the following: "The *ji* for the whole year lies in the spring; the *ji* for the whole day lies in the morning; the *ji* for the whole family lies in harmony; the *ji* for the whole life lies in diligence" (*Yi nian zhi ji zai yu chun; yi ri zhi ji zai yu chen; yi jia zhi ji zai yu he; yi sheng zhi ji zai yu qin*). When a Chinese has done something resourcefully, others would ask somewhat humorously, "What kind of *ji* have you used to accomplish this marvelous work?"

Ji is neither strategy nor tactic but rather encompasses the meaning of both. This is why *ji* is often translated as *strategy* (Chiao, 1981; Chu, 1991; Pheng & Sirpal, 1995; Sun, 1991). I deem *stratagem* a better translation and prefer it to *strategy* for two reasons. First, *ji*, a classical Chinese word (*wen yan wen*), contains the meaning of both *strategy* and *tactics*. If *ji* could be rendered into *strategy*, could it also be rendered into *tactics*? Second, in modern Chinese, the words *strategy* and *tactics* have equivalents that are widely used by the

Chinese—that is, *zhanlue* or *celue* (strategy) and *zhanshu* (tactics).[15] Therefore, *stratagem*, an English word combining *strategy* and *tactics*, seems to offer a linguistic match with the Chinese word *ji*. Furthermore, I prefer to use the full term *Chinese stratagem(s)* to translate *ji* to emphasize its Chinese cultural characteristics.[16]

It is worth noting that *ji* is not the only Chinese word that conveys the meaning of strategic Chinese thinking. Other Chinese words often used to designate a similar meaning include *zhi, mou, ce, zhao,* and *lue* (Chiao, 1981; von Senger, 1991a, 1991b). *Ji*, however, is the chief representative in this body of vocabulary. In modern Chinese, *ji* is often combined with *mou* and *ce* in such formulations as *jimou* and *jice* to mean Chinese stratagems. Other formulations that mean *ji* are *zhimou,*[17] *moulue, celue,* and so on. Two classic works on Chinese stratagems, *Art of War* and *The Thirty-Six Stratagems*, are the best introductions to the Chinese concept of *ji*.

Art of War

Sun Tzu's *Art of War*, a 13-chapter ancient Chinese military treatise, is heralded by Liddell Hart (1963/1982, p. v), a famous military historian in the West, as "the earliest of known treatises on the subject, but has never been surpassed in comprehensiveness and depth of understanding." *Art of War* has been interpreted in many publications, Chinese and Western. If asked to compress the wisdom of Sun Tzu's strategic thinking into one sentence, I point to Sun Tzu's admonition: "Subdue the enemy without fighting." According to Sun Tzu, physical military force is the last of several means to subdue the enemy: A skillful strategist should be able to conquer the enemy without fighting it, to take the enemy's cities without laying siege to them, and to overthrow the enemy's state without bloodying swords. Hart maintains that the world civilization would have been spared much of the damages suffered in the world wars of this century if Sun Tzu's voice, an Oriental wisdom, had been better heard in the West: "There has never been a protracted war from which a country has benefited" (Sun Tzu, 1963/1982, p. 73). Therefore, I view *Art of War* as essentially a work on the "art of non-war": One should use mental wisdom instead of physical force to win a war.

A Visual Model of Art of War

Although an increasing number of writings within marketing and strategic management refer to Sun Tzu's name, words, and thoughts (Davidson, 1995; George, 1972; Ho, 1997; Ho & Choi, 1997; Hsiao, Jen, & Lee, 1990; Kotler, 1994; Li, Yang, & Tan, 1986; McNeilly, 1996; Mintzberg, 1990; Mintzberg, Quinn, & Voyer, 1995; Mun, 1990; Wu, 1991), only a few provide a comprehensive visual model to help us understand Sun Tzu's strategic thinking in a holistic way. Kin-chok Mun (1990), from The Chinese University of Hong Kong, offers a "Competition Model of Sun Tzu's *Art of War*" for use in management studies (Figure 3.4). The model involves "15 principles" that may be understood as the 15 Chinese stratagems refined from *Art of War*. This model may be called a Chinese model of competition as opposed to Michael Porter's (1980) Western one (five competitive forces). In the following, I list the 15 principles based on Mun (1990) and explain each of them by referring to the original text of *Art of War*. Quotations below are from Sun Tzu's (1963/1982) *Art of War*,[18] translated by S. B. Griffith.

Principle 1: Comparison

Know the enemy and know yourself, in a hundred battles you will never be in peril. When you are ignorant of the enemy but know yourself, your chances of winning or losing are equal. If ignorant both of your enemy and of yourself, you are certain in every battle to be in peril. (p. 84)

Sun Tzu emphasizes the importance of benchmarking in terms of *Wushi* ("Five Matters"): moral influence, climate, terrain, generalship of commander (i.e., wisdom, sincerity, humanity, courage, and strictness), and discipline (organization, control, logistics, and management system).

Principle 2: Leadership

By moral influence I mean that which causes the people to be in harmony with their leaders, so that they will accompany them in life and unto death without fear of mortal peril. (p. 64)

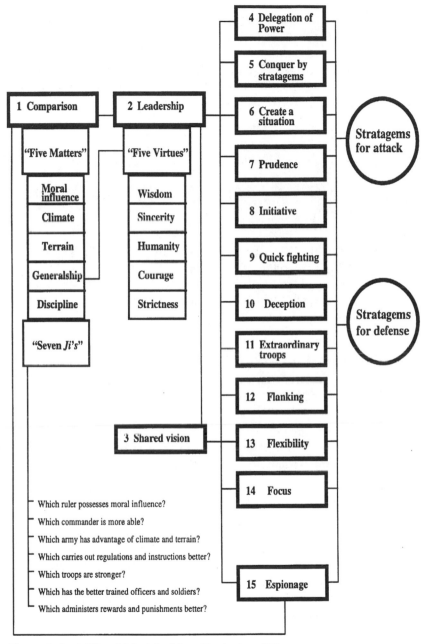

Figure 3.4. A Visual Model of Sun Tzu's *Art of War*
SOURCE: Mun, 1990, p. 931; reproduced with permission.

It is the business of a general to be serene and inscrutable, impartial, and self-controlled. (p. 136)

Sun Tzu underscores the importance of generalship and the moral influence of the commander. Through his moral influence, a general is able to make soldiers accompany him in life and death, fighting with the same "heart."

Principle 3: Shared Vision

He will win whose army is animated by the same spirit throughout all its ranks. (p. 24)

Sun Tzu (1963/1982, p. 135; see also Sun Tzu, 1910, pp. 128-129) also uses "*Shuairan* snake" in *Chang* Mountain as a metaphor to describe a well-coordinated army with a shared vision: "When struck on the head, its tail attacks; when struck on the tail, its head attacks; when struck in the center both head and tail attack."

Principle 4: Delegation of Power

He whose generals are able and not interfered with by the sovereign will be victorious. (p. 83)

A sovereign of high character and intelligence must be able to know the right man and delegate the responsibility down to him.

Principle 5: Conquer by Stratagems

[T]o win one hundred victories in one hundred battles is not the acme of skill. To subdue the enemy without fighting is the acme of skill. Thus, what is of supreme importance in war is to attack the enemy's strategy; Next best is to disrupt his alliances; The next best is to attack his army; The worst policy is to attack cities. Attack cities only when there is no alternative. (p. 77)

The highest form of victory is to conquer the enemy by using stratagems without bloodshed—victory without fighting.

Principle 6: Create a Situation

Thus, those skilled at making the enemy move do so by creating a situation to which he must conform. . . . Therefore a skilled commander seeks victory from the situation and does not demand it of his subordinates. . . . He who relies on the situation uses his men in fighting as one rolls logs or stones. Thus, the potential of troops skillfully commanded in battle may be compared to that of round boulders which roll down from mountain heights. (p. 95)

Here, "situation" is the English translation of the Chinese word *shi,* which may also be translated as "energy" and "power." A good commander avoids direct confrontation. Instead, he creates or borrows outside forces to his advantage.

Principle 7: Prudence

He who knows when he can fight and when he cannot will be victorious. (p. 82)

He who is prudent and lies in wait for an enemy who is not, will be victorious. (p. 83)

Sun Tzu highlights prudence and the need for thorough planning. *Art of War* begins with the opening statement, "War is a matter of vital importance to the State; the province of life or death; the road to survival or ruin. It is mandatory that it be thoroughly studied" (Sun Tzu, 1963/1982, p. 63).

Principle 8: Initiative

Generally, he who occupies the field of battle first and awaits his enemy is at ease; he who comes later to the scene and rushes into the fight is weary. And therefore those skilled in war bring the enemy to the field of battle and are not brought there by him. (p. 96)

Close to the field of battle, they await an enemy coming from afar; at rest, an exhausted enemy; with well-fed troops, hungry ones. This is control of the physical factor. (p. 109)

A skilled commander knows how to take initiative. He acts as the first mover, controlling the timing and location of the battlefield.

Principle 9: Quick Fighting

We have not yet seen a clever operation that was prolonged. For there has never been a protracted war from which a country has benefited. (p. 73)

Hence what is essential in war is victory, not prolonged operations. (p. 76)

Therefore at first be shy as a maiden. When the enemy gives you an opening, be swift as a hare and he will be unable to withstand you. (p. 140)

The stratagem of quick fighting reflects Sun Tzu's realism and moderation regarding war.

Principle 10: Deception

All warfare is based on deception. Therefore, when capable, feign incapacity; when active, inactivity. When near, make it appear that you are far away; when far away, that you are near. (p. 97)

Subtle and insubstantial, the expert leaves no trace; divinely mysterious, he is inaudible. Thus he is master of his enemy's fate. (p. 97)

According to Sun Tzu, war is more a contest of the wit of minds between the confronting parties than a match of sheer military force. "Deception," or manipulation of stratagems, is vital to victory.

Principle 11: Extraordinary Troops

Generally, in battle, use the normal force to engage; use the extraordinary to win. (p. 91)

This stratagem stresses the importance of taking surprising actions and using unexpected force to win.

Principle 12: Flanking

> Nothing is more difficult than the art of manoeuvre. What is difficult about manoeuvre is to make the devious route the most direct and to turn misfortune to advantage. Thus, march by an indirect route and divert the enemy by enticing him with a bait. . . . One able to do this understands the strategy of the direct and the indirect. (p. 102)

When the enemy is strong, one can turn disadvantage to advantage by avoiding direct confrontation and by outflanking him.

Principle 13: Flexibility

> Although everyone can see the outward aspects, none understands the way in which I have created victory. Therefore, when I have won a victory I do not repeat my tactics but respond to circumstances in an infinite variety of ways. (p. 100)

> An army may be likened to water, for just as flowing water avoids the heights and hastens to the lowlands, so an army avoids strength and strikes weakness. And as water shapes its flow in accordance with the ground, so an army manages its victory in accordance with the situation of the enemy. And as water has no constant form, there are in war no constant conditions. Thus, one able to gain the victory by modifying his tactics in accordance with the enemy situation may be said to be divine. (p. 101)

Sun Tzu's message is the following: Stratagems must be flexibly employed based on concrete situations in the battlefield. Sun Tzu also states,

> When ten to the enemy's one, surround him, When five times his strength, attack him; If double his strength, divide him; If equally matched, you may engage him; If weaker numerically, be capable

of withdrawing; And if in all respects unequal, be capable of eluding him. (pp. 79-80)

The highest principle of Chinese stratagems is flexibility (Gao, 1991).

Principle 14: Focus

In war, numbers alone confer no advantage. Do not advance relying on sheer military power. It is sufficient to estimate the enemy situation correctly and to concentrate your strength to capture him. (p. 122)

Another important tenet of Sun Tzu's strategic thinking is to use your strength to attack your enemy's weakness.

Principle 15: Espionage

Of all those in the army close to the commander none is more intimate than the secret agent; of all rewards none more liberal than those given to secret agents; of all matters none is more confidential than those relating to secret operations. . . . Delicate indeed! Truly delicate! There is no place where espionage is not used. (p. 147)

As early as 2300 years ago, Sun Tzu (1963/1982, pp. 145-146) defined five kinds of secret agents: "native" (yinjian), "inside" (neijian), "double" (fanjian), "expendable" (sijian), and "living" (shengjian), all of which can be used for the purposes of obtaining intelligence information. Note that expendable agents are those to whom false information is deliberately leaked so that when they are later caught, tortured, and confess, their leakage will mislead the enemy. According to Sun Tzu, secret agents are among the most honorable people and must be the best rewarded.

Sun Tzu Versus Carl von Clausewitz

It is interesting to compare Sun Tzu's *Art of War* with von Clausewitz's *On War* (1832/1984), the only comparable Western statement on strategy (Handel, 1992; Hart, 1963/1982). Although both share a number of similarities regarding "whats" (e.g., what matters is to win a war, the extension of state politics and diplomacy), they differ greatly in "hows" (e.g., how to win a war). Whereas the former teaches us to gain victory without fighting, the latter teaches us to win by using the "absolute" forces. For example, von Clausewitz writes,

> Kind-hearted people might of course think there was some inge-nious way to disarm or defeat an enemy without too much blood-shed, and might imagine this is the true goal of the art of war. Pleasant as it sounds, it is a fallacy that must be exposed. (p. 75)

> To introduce the principle of moderation into the theory of war itself would always lead to logical absurdity. (p. 76)

> War is an act of force, and there is no logical limit to the application of that force. . . . The aim of warfare is to disarm the enemy. . . . The worst of all conditions in which a belligerent can find himself is to be utterly defenseless. . . . If you want to overcome your enemy, you must match your effort against his power of resistance, which can be expressed as the product of two inseparable factors, viz. *the total means at his disposal* and *the strength of his will.* (p. 77)

> The best strategy is always *to be very strong;* first in general, and then at the decisive point. (p. 204)

I believe that *Art of War* and *On War* are telling examples of Chinese and Western strategic thinking that form the foundations for Chinese and Western business strategies, respectively. Strategy as a concept dates back to ancient military strategies. Signs of interest in military metaphor also appear in Western marketing literature (Kotler & Singh, 1981; Levinson, 1995; Ries & Trout, 1986). Western "marketing warfare" authors, however, did not appear to have studied Sun Tzu's strategic thinking when launching their theories. For example, Ries and Trout (1986) turn to von Clausewitz's *On War* (1832/1984) for the formula of marketing strategy. In Ries and Trout's best-seller, *Marketing Warfare,* von Clausewitz is called "one of the greatest marketing strategists the world has ever known," and the book is also dedicated to him. I profoundly believe, however, that Western marketers or negotiators who blindly follow Ries and Trout's advice to prepare a direct confrontational marketing warfare in China would find their Chinese counterparts not susceptible to their style because the Chinese do not confront directly at all; they follow what Sun Tzu advised—to subdue the enemy without fighting.

The Thirty-Six Stratagems

The Thirty-Six Stratagems (also known as *Secret Art of War: Thirty-Six Stratagems*) was written by an anonymous Chinese writer in the late Ming (1368-1644) or early Qing (1644-1911) dynasties. It is a condensed compendium containing 36 pieces of Chinese stratagems. Although entirely consisting of a mere 138 Chinese characters, it has systematically crystallized the Chinese nation's wisdom and personality. von Senger (1991a) maintains that the Chinese have compressed into *The Thirty-Six Stratagems* much of their thousands of years of experience in dealing with enemies and overcoming difficult and dangerous situations. "For westerners, knowledge of the 36 stratagems can provide a key to much of Chinese thinking" (von Senger, 1991a, p. 12). Gao (1991, p. 16) holds that these stratagems "provide a means for comprehending other people's behavior, including both deliberate and inadvertent actions."

Why was *The Thirty-Six Stratagems* born in China? China's long history, many wars, and difficult situations are reasons given by Lee Siow Mong (1995), a Singapore-based Chinese scholar who calls *The Thirty-Six Stratagems* "the stratagems of life":

> The long history of China with its many wars, conquests by foreign powers, trickeries, and difficult situations in which the people have found themselves in times of trouble and unrest has taught them good stratagem to take advantage of and use to get out of a difficult situation, or to find a solution to what would otherwise be an insoluble problem. From the time of the Warring States in particular, some two to three thousand years ago, right through the centuries, various stratagems have been used and proven. Some of these are quoted like Common Sayings or proverbs in short pithy forms and widely known, though no one knows all. These have

been reduced and condensed into the famous Thirty-Six Stratagems, which every Chinese can mention, but none can say what
they are, except the last one, which they all know will solve when
the other thirty-five have failed. (p. 254)

Chinese stratagems are a distinctive product of Chinese society also
because of China's demographic features and Confucian traditions.
Stratagems (wisdom, strategies, tactics, tricks, ploys, etc.) in handling
interpersonal relationships are of the utmost concern for the Chinese,
a people who, for centuries, have lived so densely together with one
another and attach such great importance to their relationships owing
to the Confucian influence. For example, stratagems may be used not
only to skillfully cultivate and develop a set of *guanxi* but also to subtly
avoid and discontinue another set of *guanxi*.

The list of the 36 Chinese stratagems is provided in Table 3.2
and Appendix A. Given the limited space, the detailed historical and
legendary origins of the stratagems are omitted.[19] The 36 stratagems
are structurally divided into the following six categories: (a) *Shengzhan
ji* ("stratagems when commanding superiority"; Nos. 1-6), (b) *Dizhan
ji* ("stratagems for confrontation"; Nos. 7-12), (c) *Gongzhan ji* ("stratagems for attacking"; Nos. 13-18), (d) *Hunzhan ji* ("stratagems for
confused situations"; Nos. 19 24), (e) *Bingzhan ji* ("stratagems for
gaining ground"; Nos. 25-30), and (f) *Baizhan ji* ("stratagems when
being inferior", Nos. 31-36). In reality, however, these stratagems can
be flexibly used in any situation. Although appearing in different
forms, all 36 stratagems follow Sun Tzu's philosophy of subduing the
enemy without fighting, using a borrowed external force to deal with
the opponent psychologically instead of engaging in a head-on fighting
physically. Stratagems contained in *The Thirty-Six Stratagems* and in
Sun Tzu's *Art of War* can, in most cases, be directly coupled with one
another. For example, the essence of Stratagems 1, 2, 3, 4, 8, 29, 33,
and 36 in *The Thirty-Six Stratagems* can also be found in Principles
10, 14, 5, 8, 11, 6, 15, and 13, respectively, in Sun Tzu's *Art of War.*

In summary, at the heart of Chinese stratagems lies Sun Tzu's
admonition to subdue the enemy without fighting. Chinese stratagems assert the superiority of using human wisdom rather than
engaging in pitched battle to cope with various situations and gain

TABLE 3.2 The 36 Chinese Stratagems

Strategem 1:   Cross the sea without Heaven's knowledge
Strategem 2:   Besiege Wei to rescue Zhao
Strategem 3:   Kill with a borrowed knife
Strategem 4:   Await leisurely the exhausted enemy
Strategem 5:   Loot a burning house
Strategem 6:   Clamor in the east but attack in the west
Strategem 7:   Create something out of nothing
Strategem 8:   Openly repair the walkway but secretly march to Chen Cang
Strategem 9:   Watch the fire burning from across the river
Strategem 10: Hide a knife in a smile
Strategem 11: Let the plum tree wither in place of the peach tree
Strategem 12: Lead away a goat in passing
Strategem 13: Beat the grass to startle the snake
Strategem 14: Borrow a corpse to return the soul
Strategem 15: Lure the tiger to leave the mountains
Strategem 16: In order to capture, first let it go
Strategem 17: Toss out a brick to attract a piece of jade
Strategem 18: To capture bandits, first capture the ringleader
Strategem 19: Remove the firewood from under the cooking pot
Strategem 20: Muddle the water to catch the fish
Strategem 21: The golden cicada sheds its shell
Strategem 22: Shut the door to catch the thief
Strategem 23: Befriend the distant states while attacking the nearby ones
Strategem 24: Borrow the road to conquer Guo
Strategem 25: Steal the beams and change the pillars
Strategem 26: Point at the mulberry tree but curse the locust tree
Stratagem 27: Play a sober-minded fool
Strategem 28: Lure the enemy onto the roof, then take away the ladder
Strategem 29: Flowers bloom in the tree
Strategem 30: The guest becomes the host
Strategem 31: The beautiful woman stratagem
Strategem 32: The empty city stratagem
Strategem 33: The counterespionage stratagem
Strategem 34: The self-torture stratagem
Strategem 35: The stratagem of interrelated stratagems
Strategem 36: Running away is the best stratagem

NOTE: I have chosen to translate the 36 stratagems from Chinese to English in a way that I consider best conveys their meaning to Western readers. Other English translations include those by Chu (1991), Gao (1991), Sun (1991), and von Senger (1991a).

advantage over opponents. They teach us how to win the biggest victory at the lowest cost.

Taoist Influence

Chinese stratagems are permeated with Taoist philosophy. The Taoist Yin Yang principle that the interaction of Yin and Yang determines the harmonious development of universal phenomena can be found in the myriad patterns of the Chinese stratagems. Chinese stratagems, often planned and implemented in secrecy, may be understood as belonging to Yin (Gao, 1991). Taoism, however, emphasizes the strength of Yin. Given appropriate circumstances, Yin can conquer yang, weak can defeat strong, and small can overpower big (see discussion of Yin Yang in Chapter 2).

The strategic Chinese thinking of subduing the enemy without fighting also reflects the Taoist Wu Wei principle (see discussion of Wu Wei in Chapter 2). Sun Tzu's aphorism (Sun Tzu Principle 5), "To win one hundred victories in one hundred battles is not the acme of skill. To subdue the enemy without fighting is the acme of skill" (Sun Tzu, 1963/1982, p. 77), can be understood as another version of the Wu Wei principle.

Legacy of Confucianism?

The relationship between Confucianism and Chinese stratagems has been too little studied. Some authors view Chinese stratagems as directly opposing Confucianism. For example, Ma and Zhang, coauthors of *The 36 Stratagems With Examples From Times Past and Present* (as quoted in von Senger, 1991a) write,

> Stratagems are the exact opposite of "Confucian" humanity and virtue. But he who treats his enemy with humanity and virtue only harms himself. . . . Using the rhetoric of virtue to maintain a pretense to others . . . is acceptable. But you must not fool yourself [with such rhetoric], at least not when engaged in combat, whether with the weapons of reason or of force. . . . Our age boasts of being civilized. Yet the more civilized a society, the more rampant are lies and deception. In such an environment, the 36 Stratagems are

the perfect means of offense and defense. They constitute a body of practical knowledge which is far more valuable than empty moralistic phrases. (p. 12)

The following story about Duke Hsiang of Sung (also known as Song Xiang Gong) is well-known in Chinese history. Duke Hsiang of Sung was badly defeated in a battle when he confronted his enemies as a Confucian gentleman (Mao, 1967):

> Duke Hsiang of Sung ruled in the Spring and Autumn Era. In 638 B.C., the state of Sung fought with the powerful state of Chu. The Sung forces were already deployed in battle positions when the Chu troops were crossing the river. One of the Sung officers suggested that, as the Chu troops were numerically stronger, this was the moment for attack. But the Duke said, "No, a gentleman should never attack one who is unprepared." When the Chu troops had crossed the river but had not yet completed their battle alignment, the officer again proposed an immediate attack, and once again the Duke said, "No, a gentleman should never attack an army which has not yet completed its battle alignment." As a result, the Sung troops met with a disastrous defeat and the Duke himself was wounded. (p. 267)

Mao Zedong (1967) mocked Duke Hsiang of Sung's stupid morality as follows:

> We are not Duke Hsiang of Sung and have no use for his asinine ethics. In order to achieve victory we must as far as possible make the enemy blind and deaf by sealing his eyes and ears and drive his commanders to distraction by creating confusion in their minds. (p. 240)

The proposition that Chinese stratagems are the "exact opposite" of Confucianism, however, does not seem to be completely sound. Chinese stratagems can actually be associated with Confucianism on several grounds. First, a link can be made between Chinese stratagems and Confucianism if Chinese stratagems are viewed broadly as a system of strategic Chinese thinking rather than narrowly as a collection of specific tactical "recipes." Unlike most Greek and Roman writers, Sun

Tzu is not purely fascinated with stratagems or superficial and transitory techniques; his purpose is to develop a systematic theory to guide rulers and generals in the intelligent prosecution of successful war (Griffith, 1963/1982). In fact, in *Art of War,* Sun Tzu not only prescribes "deceptive" stratagems but also elaborates, to a considerable extent, the art of managing leadership, organization, human resources, and so forth. For example, according to Sun Tzu, a general commander must possess "Five Virtues": wisdom (*zhi*), sincerity (*xin*), humanity (*ren*), courage (*yong*), and strictness (*yan*). Through his good moral influence, the general commander is able to make his soldiers accompany him in life and unto death without fear of mortal peril (Sun Tzu's Principle 2). Here, we see a thread of the Confucian moral persuasion running through Sun Tzu's Five Virtues. This is probably why Mun (1990, p. 930) maintains that *Art of War* has actually assimilated the "quintessence" of Confucianism as well as Taoism.

Second, one can discern a glimpse of the Confucian gentleman from the core of the Chinese stratagems. War is viewed, above all, by the Chinese as contending at a high mental level. The superior man (*junzi*), a person with a high level of wisdom and moral control, should be able to attain his ends decently without violence. As Fairbank (1974, p. 5) stated, "Placed beside its contemporary the *Mencius,* the Sun-tzu's emphasis on unsettling the mind and upsetting the plans of one's opponent obviously shares the early Confucian assumption as to the primacy of mental attitudes in human affairs." In this vein, I view Sun Tzu's subduing the enemy without fighting as a doctrine that guides people to obtain their goals in a subtle way, without transgressing the principle of harmony.

Third, Chinese stratagems can also be associated with Confucian notions such as *guanxi* and family. As noted earlier, Chinese stratagems reflect thousands of years of Chinese wisdom about interpersonal relationships or *guanxi*. Yang (1994, p. 109) defines the "art" of guanxi as being composed of three elements—ethics, tactics, and etiquette—that intertwine with and merge into one another in the Chinese practice of *guanxi*. Thus, *guanxi* possesses a tactical dimension. Yeung and Tung (1996) assert that 2 of the 36 stratagems (i.e., Stratagem 11, "Let the plum tree wither in place of the peach tree," and Stratagem 17, "Toss out a brick to attract a piece of jade") can be associated with the building and maintenance of *guanxi*: They "describe the distribution of favors to gain even bigger advantages or successes" (p. 62). Earlier, I discussed that, given the Confucian tradition, Chinese morality is highly reciprocal, situational, context-related, and family centered. If the ruler is not righteous and loving, the subject can revolt and choose a better one (see the Confucianism section earlier in this chapter). Therefore, the use of Chinese stratagems, as a "tit-for-tat" strategy against the insincere and unrighteous counterparts, can be morally justified from the Confucian perspective. Before a trusting "family"-type relationship is established, the Chinese use of Chinese stratagems to gain the advantage against the "nonfamily" negotiating counterpart seems to be inevitable. Chen and Ying (1994) write,

> If a Chinese negotiator does not establish a personal relationship with a potential investor, he does not feel obligated to be fair to the investor. Following this line of reasoning, the Chinese party would not view fishing [unethical deception of foreign investors] as an immoral act, but rather as a part of the negotiation process. (p. 27)

Chinese stratagems can also be related to the Chinese notion of family. In light of his family's face and interests, a Chinese can be morally motivated to try to "defeat" his opponent by employing whatever deceptive stratagems are required by the circumstances. Tung (1994a) observes that, like "the empty city" stratagem, many of the Chinese stratagems involve "deceptive tactics or devices," such as creating an illusion that an attack will be launched from the east when the real offensive will start in the west. Tung provides an analysis of the moral basis on which Chinese and East Asians use deceptive tactics:

> Because of the Judeo-Christian influence, westerners consider such deception immoral. On the other hand, East Asians, who have no indigenous religion akin to Judaism and Christianity, consider deception a neutral term—it is amoral and acceptable if it results in a greater good. From the East Asian perspective, "the greater good" embraces the well-being of the nation-state, the clan (the geographic region from which a person's ancestors came), the extended family, the nuclear family, the corporation (employer), and the self. Their order of importance, however, varies among East Asian countries. . . . In China, Hong Kong, and Taiwan, the family is usually considered paramount. (p. 60)

Given the previous discussion, I believe that Chinese stratagems have their philosophical roots basically in Taoism, although Confucianism also contributes to the strategic Chinese thinking in a broad sense.

A Strategic Component of Chinese Culture

The Chinese believe that *shangchang ru zhanchang* ("The marketplace is like a battlefield"). In the view of the Chinese, business competition and military warfare share many common traits (Chen, 1995; Chu, 1991; Mun, 1990). First, both enterprises and armies strive for a favorable position to protect themselves and to defeat the opponents. Second, enterprise competitions and wars are confrontational activities. Third, both organizations must be well organized and managed. Fourth, both require strategies and tactics. Fifth, the leadership of both an army and an enterprise plays a decisive role in obtaining success. Sixth, both rely on high-quality and committed people. Seventh, both require a supply of resources and logistics. Finally, both attach importance to intelligent gathering of information.

That Chinese culture has a strategic component (*ji* or other terms) is noted by many scholars in Chinese culture and business studies (Chen, 1995; Chiao, 1981; Chu, 1991; Gao, 1991; Lee, 1995; Liu & Zhu, 1991; Shi, 1993; von Senger, 1991a, 1991b). Shi (1993) assumes that if the ancient Chinese "war culture" had not existed, the value of Chinese culture would have been considerably discounted. Sun Tzu's *Art of War* is on the list of 30 books that are considered to represent the traditional Chinese culture best (Pang & Liu, 1994). Chinese stratagems as an everlasting Chinese tradition prevail in all Chinese societies, regardless of whether they are Communist or non-Communist. In his research on social and political strategies in Chinese culture, Chiao (1981) developed the following "hypothesis":

> The main hypothesis of this study is that social and political strategies form a highly sophisticated, extensive, and enduring tradition in Chinese culture; what are manifested by the contemporary Chinese, Communist or non-Communist alike in this regard are basically the continuation of this everlasting tradition. (p. 429)

Although little known in the West, recipes of Chinese stratagems are *jia yu hu xiao* ("known to every household") in China. *Ji* is a cultural phenomenon that permeates the socialization process of the Chinese people. The great popularity of Chinese stratagems is due mostly to Chinese folk literature as well as the form in which they are preserved. Through TV, radio, theater, and even grandfather's bedtime stories, Chinese children, in early childhood, learn various kinds of Chinese stratagems. In China, the folk novel *Three Kingdoms* (Luo, 1994) is commonly called the "textbook of *ji*," in which various ancient Chinese stratagems can be found in real historical contexts. Jin (1994) selected and analyzed 381 Chinese stratagems from *Three Kingdoms*. Zhu Ge Liang (Kong Ming), a figure from the *Three Kingdoms* period and the strategist behind the story of "The Empty City Stratagem" (see Stratagem 32 in *The Thirty-Six Stratagems*; see also Appendix B), is one of the most beloved heroes in Chinese folk literature. Hsu (1963) and Yau (1994) describe the Chinese "situation-oriented" or "pragmatic" behavior and believe it has to do with child-rearing practices in which Chinese children are taught by and exposed to the views of a large number of people within a family. Although I agree with this explanation, I add one point to it: The Chinese are flexible, practical, pragmatic, or situation oriented because they have been reared and socialized in a culture in which Chinese stratagems are an important theme.

Chinese stratagems are preserved and expressed in a simple and condensed form of Chinese idioms, most of which consist of no more than four Chinese characters arranged so that when recited they produce a rhythmic effect, making it easy even for children to remember them. For example, in *The Bank of Stratagems* (Chai, 1992), of a total of 470 pieces of Chinese stratagems analyzed, 400 are composed of four or fewer Chinese characters. In Jin's (1994) book, all Chinese stratagems are four-character idioms.

Deeply rooted in Taoist Wu Wei and Yin Yang principles, Chinese stratagems may be viewed as having offered a "cultural value" explanation of Chinese behavior. From Swidler's (1986) "tool kit" perspective, however, we may also view Chinese stratagems as a "repertoire" or tool kit of skills from which people construct strategies of action (see Chapter 2). Whatever the perspectives, Chinese stratagems are an indigenous Chinese cultural force that forges what I call the "Sun Tzu-like Chinese strategists." I have previously discussed the Confucian gentleman (see the Moral Cultivation section earlier in this chapter). By contrast, the sketch of a Sun Tzu-like Chinese strategist is diametrically different. Chiao (1981) provides the following description:

> He waits patiently for the right opportunity with full alert, constant observation, and investigation on the situation. When he moves, his actions tend to be deceitful and indirect, and often he tries to achieve his goal by making use of a third party. He may exaggerate or fabricate occasionally, but always feigns. He does his best to stop his opponent's advance. He may allure, prod, and warn his opponent, but unless it is absolutely necessary, he will not have a real direct confrontation with him. If he has to, he will move fast and try to quickly put his opponent under control. He is always ready to abandon or withdraw, that is only a step for coming back. (p. 436)

Chinese Stratagems and Chinese Negotiating Tactics

Applying Chinese stratagems in business settings is not a new invention. To my knowledge, however, no one has tried to interpret Chinese business negotiating style from the Chinese stratagems (*ji*) perspective in international publications.[20] This book attempts to fill this scholarly gap.

Chinese Negotiating Tactics: A New List

Inspired by the indigenous Chinese concept of *ji* and, especially, by the ancient Chinese wisdom *The Thirty-Six Stratagems*, I provide a new list of Chinese business negotiating tactics by classifying those Chinese tactics that are commonly talked about in Sino-Western negotiation literature under the 36 pieces of Chinese stratagems, as shown in Appendix A. This classification presents a picture of the Sun Tzu-like Chinese negotiators. It also provides a practical guide for Western negotiators to identify various Chinese negotiating ploys, tricks, and tactics so as to achieve an alertness to Chinese tactical tendencies and proclivities. The Chinese negotiating tactics contained in Appendix A may also be employed by the Chinese in nonbusiness negotiation settings as many writings have suggested (J.-L. J. Chang, 1991a; Davies, 1984; Kreisberg, 1995; Lall, 1968; Solomon, 1985, 1987; Young, 1968).

From the list, it can be seen that all Chinese negotiating tactics share a prominent theme that reminds us of Lao Tzu's Wu Wei and Yin Yang principles or Sun Tzu's (p. 77) admonition: "To subdue the enemy without fighting is the acme of skill" (Sun Tzu, 1963/1982). The subtlety of Chinese negotiating tactics lies in the Chinese capacity *to bargain without bargaining*—for example, by borrowing an external force, creating a favorable situation, playing a sober-minded fool, opening the "empty-city" door, and even running away. In a word, the Wu Wei and Yin Yang principles lay the philosophical foundation of Chinese negotiating tactics; Sun Tzu's wisdom—subdue the enemy without fighting—is the magic thread that holds together all the Chinese negotiating tricks, ploys, and tactics.

Rational Versus Strategic Patterns of Chinese Negotiating Style

In an interview in 1995, a chief negotiator of a Swedish multi-national corporation gave his impression of Chinese negotiating style, based on his ongoing negotiations with the Chinese, as follows: "The most significant Chinese negotiating style is that they merely put the competitor's proposals on the table before your eyes." Other empirically based reports also confirm that the Chinese tend to use the tactic of pitting competitors against each other (see Chapter 4, Illustrations 37 and 38). This widely remarked Chinese negotiation tactic of playing competitors off against each other, however, never appears in the reports from the Confucian school; nor does the Chinese bureaucracy school furnish compelling explanations. From the Chinese stratagems perspective, however, this strategic Chinese behavior typifies the strategic Chinese thinking of subduing the enemy without fighting and can be culturally understood as "Kill with a borrowed knife" (see Appendix A, Stratagem 3).

The existing schools—that is, the Chinese bureaucracy school and Confucian school (see Chapter 2)—describe what I call the rational patterns of Chinese business negotiating behavior. By contrast, Chinese stratagems shape the strategic patterns of Chinese business negotiating behavior—that is, Chinese business negotiating tactics. The Chinese use of language in negotiation can be used to illustrate this point. The rational patterns involve, for example, the phenomena that few Chinese are able to speak foreign languages (see the PRC Condition section earlier in this chapter) and that the Chinese do not like to say "No" (see Confucianism), whereas the strategic patterns refer to, among other things, the Chinese use of translation to gain strategic advantage over the opponent (see Chapter 4, Illustration 39; see also Appendix A, Stratagem 29). Chinese stratagems are an important reason behind the "illogical" or "irrational" Chinese behaviors at the negotiation table.[21] The rational and strategic patterns together explain why Chinese business negotiation abounds with contradictions and why Chinese are known as tough, shrewd, tenacious, contradictory, and inscrutable negotiators. To understand Chinese negotiating style in a comprehensive way, we need to study not only rational patterns but also strategic patterns.

Why Do the Chinese Use Stratagems?

There are a number of reasons why Chinese stratagems are relevant for the study of Chinese business negotiating style and why PRC managers and officials can employ Chinese stratagems deliberately or inadvertently or both in business negotiations. First, the Chinese believe that the marketplace is like a battlefield. They believe the wisdom that guides the general in battle is the same that guides all of us in our daily lives, including business life (Chu, 1991). Because the marketplace is like a battlefield, Chinese stratagems can be reasonably employed to gain competitive advantages over the opponents. Therefore, Chinese negotiators seldom give up anything without a fight (Seligman, 1990). They perceive business negotiations as a "zero-sum game" (Lavin, 1994; Pye, 1982).

Second, Chinese stratagems can be reasonably used by the Chinese even from the Confucian perspective. Once the Chinese have sensed that one is treating them like "dog and horse" or "dirt and grass," they will then be morally justified by Mencius to deal with one as "bandit and enemy" by using whatever tit-for-tat Chinese strategies and tactics are necessary (see the Confucianism section earlier in this chapter). In this context, the word *moral* has little meaning in the

Chinese vocabulary. As noted earlier, Chinese stratagems can be employed by the Chinese to promote the interest of their families or groups and protect them from being encroached on by outsiders. Apart from this tit-for-tat mentality and family centeredness, Confucianism, broadly speaking, provides a cooperation-oriented Chinese negotiation strategy. By contrast, Chinese stratagems offer a competition-oriented Chinese negotiation strategy. Cooperation does not exist in a vacuum, however, but rather interacts inextricably with competition in business processes. Therefore, the Chinese may use the competitive Chinese stratagems as a means to create conditions and positions for reaching an ultimate win-win agreement for both parties (see Chapter 2).

Third, merchants (*shang* or *shangren*) were not held in high esteem in the traditional Confucian society. They belonged to the lowest class in the Chinese social hierarchy (after scholars, farmers, and artisans) and were regarded as corrupt, obedient, treacherous, and selfish (Fung, 1948/1966; see Confucianism). Traditionally, *shangren* (merchant) was almost a synonym of *jianshang* ("unscrupulous merchant" and "dishonest trader"). In present-day China, in which a fair-play market mechanism is far from being established, the market is full of unethical "fishing hooks" (Chen & Ying, 1994), and counterfeit products and economic crime are becoming commonplace (Silk, 1994; Sun, 1995), this traditional Chinese distrust of business people is hard to remove. An old Chinese saying still seems to apply today: "There is no merchant who is not evil" (*wu shang bu jian*). In this sense, Chinese stratagems can be adopted by even decent people as a defensive weapon to try to keep the evils, real or suspected, at bay.

Fourth, middle-aged Chinese managers and officials, many of them middle school students in the 1960s who had no chance to receive formal and qualified higher education because of the Cultural Revolution, were in their youth and childhood imperceptibly influenced by Chinese legend and folklore in which manipulation of Chinese stratagems to cope with various situations is a primary theme. During the Cultural Revolution, "class struggles" among various factions proved to have trained many a Chinese to put Chinese stratagems to practical use for various purposes. Thus, the Chinese naturally carry with them an "inborn" strategic thinking as a result of their socialization process, regardless of their formal education backgrounds. The Chinese may employ Chinese stratagems deliberately or inadvertently or both in every aspect of their social life, positively or negatively. For example, Chinese stratagems find their daily applications within Chinese bureaucracy, as exemplified by a popular saying in the PRC: "Where there is a policy from above, there is a counter-tactic from below" (*Shang you zheng ce, xia you dui ce*). In China, the recent renaissance of the *Thick Black Theory*—a book written by Li Zongwu in 1912 advising people to use stratagems to live a successful life by simply having a "thick face" and "black heart" (Chu, 1992; Li, 1997)—reinforces my thesis that *ji* pervades Chinese life, including business negotiation settings.

Fifth, Chinese managers, especially middle-aged ones, have been attentive students of Mao Zedong. Even today, many Chinese adore Mao more than a god; the following title of a book about Mao's private life officially published in China actually serves to confirm this phenomenon: *Mao Zedong: Man, Not God* (Quan, 1992). Mao's bodyguard, Li Yinqiao (as cited in Quan, 1992), recalled that Mao was an ardent fan of traditional Chinese plays and operas. One of Mao's favorites was the "Defenseless City" (or "The Empty City"), a famous Chinese stratagem story about how Zhuge Liang (or Kong Ming, Kung Min) defended his "empty city" when his greatest enemy, Sima Yi (or Si Ma), approached it unexpectedly (see Appendix B).

Pye (1984, p. 210) states that Mao showed his revolutionary prowess in his early childhood by being an "unfilial" son who dared to challenge his father's authority. Mao read everything except the Confucian classics. His mind was filled with the exploits of the heroes and clever bandits in the *Three Kingdoms* (*Sanguo Yanyi*) and the *Water Margin* (*Shuihuzhuan*). Pye noted, "He was fascinated by stratagems and deceptions and moved by the struggles of the poor and the dispossessed" (p. 210). In Li's (1994) *The Private Life of Chairman Mao*, Mao's tactical character is demonstrated in his later years. Mao was a voracious reader of ancient Chinese stories of stratagems and deceptions and liked to play mah-jongg. All his strategic talents, however, could be traced to *Art of War* and *Three Kingdoms* (Li, 1994):

> Mah-jongg is indeed a game of strategy, and Mao was both China's great strategist and a superb mah-jongg player. But I think his strategic brilliance came from other sources—from Sun Zi's ancient *Art of War*, from his reading of Chinese history, from the *Romance of the Three Kingdoms*. (p. 83)

In 1957, during the party's "Rectification Movement," Mao used a stratagem called "To coax the snakes out of their holes" to identify the "rightists".[22] Mao blatantly criticized the party bureaucracy and urged members of the "democratic parties" and other intellectuals to speak out their own criticisms of the party's mistakes. In the beginning, the intellectuals remained reluctant and kept silent. Mao repeated his messages, however, and asked them to overcome their hesitations. Only after hundreds of thousands of intellectuals had poured out their grievances and criticisms did Mao turn harshly against them, which led to countless Chinese intellectuals being labeled "rightists" (youpai) and persecuted accordingly.[23] Mao (as quoted in Li, 1994) explained his stratagem as follows:

> We want to coax the snakes out of their holes. . . . Then we will strike. My strategy is to let the poisonous weeds grow first and then destroy them one by one. Let them become fertilizer. . . . I handle opportunities by letting them attack first. . . . Only later do I strike back. . . . I follow the ancient philosopher Laozi. I, the father, do not initiate action.[24] When under attack, I retreat, doing nothing, remaining silent. We let the enemy feel he has scored a few points. If we were to answer enemies immediately . . . they would not dare to show their true face. (pp. 201, 203, 204)

Zhou Enlai, the late Chinese premier in Mao's time, has been widely acclaimed in China as a legendary diplomat who was skillful at employing stratagems. Huang et al. (1997) provided a story of Mr. Zhou "playing Taiji boxing" (Tai Chi) with the Red Guards during the Cultural Revolution:

> During the Cultural Revolution, thousands of Red Guards surrounded the Great Hall of the People, and their representatives were arguing with Mr. Zhou about the Minister of Foreign Affairs, Mr. Chen Yi. Mr. Zhou explained his opinions to the representatives of the Red Guard neither superciliously nor obsequiously. As long as the representatives of the Red Guard could not persuade Mr. Zhou on a certain topic, they changed to another one; nevertheless, no matter what topics they changed or they wanted to change, eventually they were surprised to find out that they still came back to the original issue Mr. Zhou wanted to discuss. After

ten hours of arguments, the representatives of the red Guard fell asleep one after another until Mr. Zhou was the only one who was awake. People jokingly said that Mr. Zhou was playing Taiji boxing by being slow, gentle, but tough with the Red Guard. (p. 272)

Henry Kissinger (1979, p. 744) also recalled that Zhou Enlai "was a figure out of history. He was equally at home in philosophy, reminiscence, historical analysis, tactical probes, humorous repartee." It is reported that Zhou Enlai once employed strategies (*ji*'s) in his meeting with Henry Kissinger (Chu, 1991):

> In a meeting between Henry Kissinger and Zhou Enlai, Secretary Kissinger made a comment that demonstrated an awareness of the strategies that Zhou was employing with him. Zhou complimented him by saying, "You are very smart." Kissinger replied, "You mean, smart for an American." Zhou smiled and said nothing. (p. 17)

Given the great influence of Mao Zedong and Zhou Enlai in the PRC's history, it follows logically that the PRC managers can imitate their style of stratagems in doing things, including negotiating contracts with foreign business people.

Sixth, the Western concepts of negotiation and marketing are new "imported goods" to the Chinese. An examination of the references in Chinese scholars' writings on negotiation (Fan & Yan, 1990; G. Liu, 1996) indicates that the Western negotiation theories (see, e.g., Nierenberg, 1968/1981) were introduced to China during the 1980s. Chinese management training and foreign management courses in China became popular only after 1979 (Warner, 1991). Western marketing theory has been developed in China since the late 1970s and the early 1980s (Mei & Zhang, 1990). There is not a single Chinese word that corresponds to the Western term marketing.[25] If the Chinese really have for centuries found no peers in the subtle art of negotiating, they must have their own marketing theory, negotiation theory, and so on that are perhaps "superior" in some ways to the Western ones. The traditional Chinese culture does have a Chinese negotiation theory to offer: Confucianism provides the Chinese with a cooperation-oriented strategy, and Chinese stratagems provide a competition-oriented strategy. Chinese stratagems shape the strategic patterns of Chinese business negotiating style.

Finally, Chinese managers are educated to make use of *Art of War* and *The Thirty-Six Stratagems* to deal with foreign business people (Chen & Xiao, 1992, pp. 445-459; Li et al., 1986). For example, in their widely acclaimed book, *Sun Tzu's Art of War and Enterprise Management* (actually, the first report of this kind appeared in mainland China), Li et al. (1986) write,

> Our country is pursuing the policy of opening to the outside world. It is necessary to do business with foreign capitalists in order to import advanced foreign technology and capital for our use. But, in order not to be tricked in dealings with capitalist countries and also for the purposes of winning business in competition with foreign business people and making our products enter into the international market, we need to study Sun Tzu's *Art of War*: Use this magic weapon handed down from our ancestors to defeat them. (p. 12)

Currently, many Chinese still believe that a capitalist society is full of acts of blackmail and deception. Capitalists are but unethical money-earners, and they come to China to make money on the Chinese people. Therefore, using whatever Chinese stratagems are necessary to outwit the capitalists can be morally justified. Li et al. (1986, p. 183), for example, advise that deception as a technique "can and should be employed in dealing with business people from capitalist countries." Chen and Ying (1994) observe that the local Chinese officials and enterprise managers often work hand-in-glove to "fish" foreign investors:

> Local officials often work hand-in-glove with State-owned enterprises, which probably have the most to gain from "fishing." . . . Local managers, often acting in concert with local officials, or at least with their tacit approval, thus may try nearly any tactic to attract a foreign partner. They will take pains to cover up existing problems at a given enterprise while exaggerating the competitive advantages the facility can provide. The least scrupulous managers may manipulate facts—even though they are well aware that they are doing something unethical—in the hopes of attracting foreign

investment. In some cases, the enterprise keeps two sets of accounting records: one for the enterprise itself and another, which makes the enterprise appear highly profitable, for use in negotiations with potential investors. (p. 27)

If terminology from Western negotiation theory is used, Chinese negotiating tactics may be called "dirty tricks" (see Chapter 2, Negotiation Strategies). It should be borne in mind, however, that the term *dirty tricks* disappears from the Chinese negotiators' lexicon once they perceive that their negotiating partners are not considerate, fair, or following the Confucian rule of reciprocity to do business. This Chinese perception may not always be correct given a host of sociocultural barriers between the cultures of the negotiating parties.

The Uniqueness of Chinese Negotiating Tactics

People with experience in international business negotiations will notice that many Chinese negotiating tactics listed in Appendix A are not a monopoly of the Chinese but apply to negotiations between Western firms as well. The Chinese, however, as Chen (1993, p. 16) observes, "are generally more adept than westerners at gaining the upper hand." Kazuo's (1979, p. 540) observations from negotiations between the Chinese and the Japanese, who are often referred to by Westerners as two inscrutables, also show that the frequency and intensity with which the Chinese use their tactics against the Japanese appear to be "unusually high." In China, a familistic society in which trust is low among non-family members and a socialist state in which the top-down hierarchical pressure is high on Chinese officials, the traditional Chinese wisdom of *ji* plays an important part in helping the Chinese negotiators deal with Chinese-culture outsiders. Different cultures may have shared some universal concepts and phenomena; often, the difference in their intensity, frequency, and flavor can be found in the indigenous vocabulary of a culture. Given the distinctiveness of *ji* as a strategic component of Chinese culture, we have reason to assume that the frequency and intensity with which the Chinese adopt the negotiating tactics in Appendix A will be higher than those of other cultures.

Chinese negotiating tactics are culturally distinctive because they are based on the Chinese concept of *ji*, a more than 2,000-year-old Chinese cultural heritage. *Ji* is an indigenous Chinese concept that makes Chinese negotiating tactics unique. All the Chinese negotiating tricks, ploys, and tactics have their philosophical foundation in the Taoist Wu Wei and Yin Yang principles and are all welded together by Sun Tzu's strategic thinking—to subdue the enemy without fighting. The secret of Chinese negotiating tactics lies in, as mentioned earlier, the Chinese ability to bargain without bargaining—to kill with a borrowed knife.

I do not mean to imply, however, that all the tactics listed in Appendix A will be adopted by Chinese negotiators deliberately. Chinese negotiators may employ the tactics inadvertently during the process of negotiations, given the all-pervasive influence of Chinese stratagems on the socialization process of Chinese people in Chinese culture. Nor do I mean that these tactics have all been verified against rich empirical settings. Actually, the Chinese negotiating tactics in Appendix A are based purely on China-Western business negotiation settings, with a strong influence of U.S.-China business negotiation literature. The empirical illustrations in this book indicate that some purported Chinese negotiating tactics need to be corrected with a special remark. In the future, we need to answer, for example, whether the Chinese also use those tactics employed on Western business people to deal with other Third World business people (see the section in Chapter 5 on Limitations and Future Research).

Moreover, I do not imply that Chinese negotiators will always behave exactly as suggested in Appendix A. As discussed earlier, a Chinese can be not only a Sun Tzu-like strategist but also a Confucian gentleman. The strategic orientation of Chinese negotiators may be viewed as a continuum ranging from a pure Confucian gentleman without any tactics in mind to a pure Sun Tzu-like strategist full of stratagems of life. For the former, no stratagem recipes contained in Appendix A apply, whereas for the latter, even more thick-faced or black-hearted Chinese tactics can be discerned and added to the list. The Chinese guide for behavior depends on the depth of trust between negotiating partners, given the reciprocal and context-related Chinese morality in dealing with people (see the Confucianism section).

Finally, as noted earlier, Chinese stratagems are a neutral concept; whether they are good or evil depends on how they are used. In everyday life, there are many cases of evil exploitation of Chinese stratagems. A recent case concerned a local car distributor in Macao who, immediately after Princess Diana's tragic car accident, produced a "clever" advertisement for Volvo cars in a local Chinese newspaper by placing beside it a smiling photo of the Princess, thus "borrowing" Princess Diana's misfortune to reinforce the safety image of Volvo cars. This action was denounced by the Swedish company Volvo as immoral and shameless. The case suggests that there exist Chinese business people who are too clever to be wise. Too many *ji*'s may not be good.

How to "Fight Back"

Although specific tactical moves and countermoves can be worked out based on the list provided in Appendix A, the most effective and rewarding counterstrategy for Western negotiators is to negotiate beyond all Chinese stratagems. To fight back most effectively, Western business people should try to negotiate with the Chinese within the Confucian working environment by nurturing a trusting family-like business relationship with their Chinese partners, giving the Chinese no reason to employ tactics, ploys, and stratagems. The bottom line is that the Chinese seldom use evil stratagems or dirty tricks in dealing with their family members and genuine friends. Within a Confucian working environment, the Chinese tend to use a problem-solving, cooperation-oriented negotiation strategy.

At this point, I appreciate Robert March's (1997) "becoming family" metaphor for developing long-term business relationships with China and East Asia. I consider becoming family a very useful metaphor for also understanding the mechanism of neutralizing various Chinese negotiating tactics. Trust and honesty are vital in negotiating with the Chinese, whatever the negotiation situations— Confucian or non-Confucian (see Chapter 4, Illustrations 10, 11, and 34).

Another useful counterstrategy that Western business people can put to use is to attract the Chinese to play the Western rules of the game or, as Stephen Weiss (1994a, 1994b) mentioned, induce the counterpart to follow one's own script. In Chapter 5, I detail this thinking into a concrete strategy: Invite the Chinese to negotiate abroad.

The PRC Condition, Confucianism, and Chinese Stratagems: An Interplay

Chinese business negotiating style is highly complex and uncertain because the PRC negotiators are driven by the interplay of the three different yet intertwined components of Chinese business culture: the PRC condition, Confucianism, and Chinese stratagems. I previously discussed the relationships between Confucianism and Chinese stratagems (see the section, Legacy of Confucianism?). Chinese stratagems can also be coupled with the PRC condition. For example, as noted earlier, one of the fundamental aspects of Mao Zedong's thought is *celue* (strategy, stratagems, and tactics). By definition, Chinese stratagems involve an "artifice" in political life (von Senger, 1991a). Pye's (1981, 1988, 1992a) in-depth analyses of the dynamics of Chinese politics provide many hints to link Chinese stratagems with the art of Chinese officialdom. Using various stratagems to defeat the opponents can help the Chinese gain face in front of their superiors and prevent them from being accused of incompetence in Chinese bureaucracy. As noted earlier, China's demographic features (e.g., dense living ambience) make stratagems in handling interpersonal relationships an important theme in Chinese social life.

The PRC condition is also interrelated with Confucianism. Maoist "glorification of human motivation" and advocacy of "the collective over the individual" find their ultimate roots in Confucian philosophy, although Mao extended the Confucian notion of "collectivity" from nuclear family to *danwei*, the state, and the party. Nevertheless, Maoist distrust of intellectuals and the practice of egalitarianism run counter to the Confucian respect for scholarship and hierarchy (Pye, 1984). The Maoist style—"A revolution is not a dinner party"—is both opposed to the Confucian notion of *li* ("etiquette," "propriety," etc.) and in line with the "democratic message" of the Confucian notion of *bao* ("to repay," "to retaliate," "to retribute," etc.). Although Confucian teachings were condemned as feudal practices in the PRC in Mao's time, the Confucian family prototype has always been at work in the Chinese organizational structure and in the personalized style of Chinese management. The top-down economic planning hierarchy and the lack of a well-functioning legal framework also owe much to the traditional influence of the Confucian traditions. With the opening up of China since the end of the 1970s, Confucius has been honored, and the relevance of the Confucian classics has been reemphasized in the PRC. Confucian values can be found, for example, in a post-Mao government campaign known as *Wu Jiang Si Mei* ("The Five Stresses and the Four Beauties"),[26] and in Article 49 of the Chinese Constitution (Constitution of the Communist Party of China, 1982), part of which reads, "Parents have the duty to rear and educate their minor children, and children who have come of age have the duty to support and assist their parents." Despite the evident Confucian influence on the PRC condition, I attribute the notorious Chinese fear of making decisions, taking responsibility, and having no final say largely to the inherent cause of the Chinese bureaucracy. This is why I later use the term *Maoist bureaucrats* as a metaphor to capture part of the mixed personalities of the Chinese negotiators.

The Chinese business culture framework provides a useful tool for us to answer the "whys" of Chinese business negotiating style. It suggests that a Chinese negotiator is a mix of different personalities, and we need a combination of different perspectives to understand a Chinese negotiating behavior. For example, it has been widely reported that the Chinese prefer to carry out negotiations on Chinese soil, the so-called "play home-court" tactic (Pye, 1982; Seligman, 1990). To gain a more comprehensive understanding of this Chinese negotiating behavior, we must systematically examine the PRC condition, Confucianism, and Chinese stratagems and how these sociocultural forces shape the Chinese behavior.

From the vantage point of the PRC condition, if negotiation takes place in China, it will satisfy the need of Chinese bureaucracy because the frontline Chinese negotiators tend not to be the decision makers. Negotiation in China would make the frequent Chinese internal upward reporting possible, as Schnepp et al. (1990) observe:

> From the outset of negotiations in 1979, it became clear to Bob Murphy [American negotiator] and the other Westinghouse executives that the only appropriate venue for commercial contract negotiations was on Chinese turf: Chinese negotiators had to

frequently consult their superiors since they had limited authority
to make on the spot decisions. (p. 95)

From the Confucian perspective, negotiation taking place in China
will enable Chinese negotiators to have more time and opportunities to
become socially familiar with foreign negotiators to establish the trusting interpersonal relationship that any successful business agreement
requires (see the Confucianism section).

From the Chinese stratagems perspective, conducting negotiations in China is a strategic action to help Chinese negotiators gain
advantage in climate, terrain, and people (see Sun Tzu Principle 1
under A Visual Model of *Art of War* or Stratagem 4 in Appendix A).
Being the host, the Chinese side is in a favorable position to play such
games as those that Pye (1982, pp. 28-29) discovered: control the
agenda and the pace of negotiations, exacerbate the problem of American impatience and Chinese patience, gain the advantages of surprise
and uncertainty in agenda arrangements, establish recognizable standards of favoritism and play off competitors against each other, and
make foreign negotiators the travelers from afar who are naturally cast
in the role of supplicants asking for Chinese beneficence.

I now provide another example. Chinese business negotiation is
generally considered a time-consuming process. Why? We should
try to seek a more comprehensive answer from the PRC condition,
Confucianism, and Chinese stratagems, respectively. From the perspective of Chinese stratagems (e.g., Stratagem 9 in Appendix A), the
Chinese are "masters of the art of stalling" who can use time to wear
the other party down. Furthermore, the PRC condition and Confucianism also provide reasonable explanations, as is manifest in the following report (Schnepp et al., 1990):

> The Chinese offered two reasons for the lengthy two-year period
> to negotiate the contract with C-E. First, it takes time to obtain
> approvals from various PRC government officials. Second, it takes
> time to become acquainted with the U.S. company before any
> agreements are signed, a necessary process to the Chinese. (p. 209)

Furthermore, a systematic approach to Chinese negotiating style
also indicates that negotiating with the Chinese may not always be a

slow, boring process; it can be quick as well. The reasons are a result of a combination of the PRC condition, Confucianism, and Chinese stratagems—for example, the "quick buying" facet of Chinese bureaucracy; access to the right *guanxi*, which helps one penetrate the Chinese family border and foster a trusting relationship with the Chinese partners; and quick and surprising actions by the Chinese out of strategic considerations. Therefore, blindly saying that "time is not money in China" or "negotiating with China takes time" is senseless. The Chinese are, in effect, a people who value time, as demonstrated in the following famous Chinese saying: "An inch of time is like an inch of gold, but an inch of gold will not buy an inch of time" (*Yi cun guang yin yi cun jin, cun jin nan mai cun guang yin*).

Chinese Business Culture and East Asian Economic Miracles

Within only a short time period (1950s-1990s), East Asian economies have been developed to levels that have often been referred to as "miracles."[27] Economists and business leaders generally predict that the East will replace the West as the hub of economic growth in the twenty-first century. The framework of Chinese business culture discussed previously has relevance for our understanding of the rapid growth of the East Asian economies. Simply stated, Confucianism, Chinese stratagems, and market conditions together provide the answer.

Confucian Heritage

The intellectual perception of the impact of Confucianism on the economic growth of China and East Asian countries with a Confucian cultural heritage has shifted dramatically from an enormous obstacle to a competitive advantage. In *The Religion of China: Confucianism and Taoism*, Max Weber (1919/1951) asserts that the Confucian rationality has resulted in adjustment to the world as it is or the preservation of tradition, which makes a Confucian society unable to innovate and adapt sufficiently to bring about the enormous social changes required by capitalist industrialization. He states, "The legal forms and societal foundations for capitalist 'enterprise' were absent in the Chinese economy" (p. 85). Also, in *The Protestant Ethic and the Spirit of Capitalism* (Weber, 1904/1996), one of the most renowned, and controversial, works of modern social science, Max Weber also doubts the Oriental ability to generate a moral dynamism in economic activity comparable with that characteristic of the spirit of Occidental capitalism. This pessimistic view of the economic impact of Confucianism, also held by Gunnar Myrdal (1968), has dominated scholarly thinking for almost the first two thirds of the twentieth century.

Since the late 1970s, however, a growing body of literature has emerged that correlates Confucian philosophy with the fast-growing East Asian economies in a positive way, coining terms such as "Confucian challenge," "Confucius connection," "Confucian dynamism," "post-Confucian hypothesis," and "neo-Confucian culture" (Berger & Hsiao, 1988; Bond & Hofstede, 1989; Franke, Hofstede, & Bond, 1991; Hicks & Redding, 1983a, 1983b; Hofheinz & Calder, 1982; Hofstede & Bond, 1988; Kahn, 1979; MacFarquhar, 1980; Naisbitt, 1996). As a whole, these authors contend that Confucian values, such as family, ordering relationships, having a sense of shame, education and learning, community responsibility, loyalty, thrift, and persistence, provide a work ethic that has bestowed upon the Chinese and other East Asian societies a superb self-confidence with which to challenge the West. Herman Kahn (1979) is the first scholar who provides the overarching idea of the neo-Confucian hypothesis. He writes,

> Since the crucial issues in a modern society increasingly revolve around these equity issues and on making organizations work well, the neo-Confucian cultures have great advantages. . . . We believe that both aspects of Confucian ethic—the creation of dedicated, motivated, responsible, and educated individuals and the enhanced sense of commitment, organizational identity, and loyalty to various institutions—will result in all the neo-Confucian societies having at least potentially higher growth rates than other cultures. (p. 122)

Nevertheless, in the wave of Confucian challenge, Wei-Ming Tu (1984), the world's leading authority on Confucianism, remains reluctant to agree with the "Confucius connection." He argues that intrinsic to the Confucian traditions lies moral development rather than economic interest, and that "there is no causal relationship" between the "Confucian ethic" and the "East Asian entrepreneurial spirit." Tu writes,

> First of all, I do not think that a mono-causal relationship is the only way to understand the linkage between the Confucian ethic and the East Asian entrepreneurial spirit. Quite the contrary. This is misleading. I do not want to be misinterpreted as having argued that there is a narrowly specified causal relationship between the Confucian ethic and economic success. In fact, my argument is precisely the reverse. If one is totally committed to the Confucian ethic of the highest kind, one will cultivate one's sense of righteousness, not one's desire for profit. The pursuit of righteousness would hardly lead to the maximization of profit defined purely in economic terms. Therefore, there is no causal relationship. (p. 88)

Indeed, careful study reveals that Confucianism is a moral teaching that honors righteousness instead of profit. According to Confucius, a gentleman understands righteousness, and the inferior man understands profit. Confucius himself "fished with a line but not a net" (see the section on Moral Cultivation earlier in this chapter). Therefore, it does not seem to be totally "fair" to use such Confucian annotated terms as the Confucian connection and "the cash value of Confucian value" (Bond & Hofstede, 1989; Hofstede & Bond, 1988) to explain economic activities in East Asia, although Confucianism has its by-product contribution to the profit motivation and moneymaking mentality in Chinese culture (see the Family Orientation section).

Although viewing Confucianism as one fundamental force behind the East Asian economic miracles, Berger (1988, p. 8) writes, "At the same time, I strongly suspect that Confucianism is by no means the only cultural and religious factor in play. Other factors will have to be explored." Berger speculates on other factors such as Buddhism, Taoism, Shinto, and "folk religion." Hicks and Redding (1983b, p. 22), concluding their survey of a variety of literature on possible reasons for East Asian economic miracles, write, "As yet little work has been done on this fascinating and perplexing question and a final answer may be ten years or more into the future but it will be worth striving for." Fukuyama (1995) challenges the Confucian familism as a positive force for industrialization. He asserts that the Confucian family value constitutes an obstacle to the institutionalization and professional management of a company. Given the dramatic shift in perceptions of the impact of Confucian culture on Chinese economic growth from hindrance to competitive advantage, Fukuyama (1995, p. 326) holds that "we need to be cautious about the role of culture if more parsimonious explanations exist."

Although the Confucian emphasis on family, education, community responsibility, thrift, and so on certainly sheds much light on our understanding of the East Asian economic performance, I believe that the greatest contribution that Confucianism has made is to have provided East Asian business people with a relationship-based and cooperation-oriented business philosophy. Recent years have witnessed a development of the Western theory and practice of marketing toward the relationship marketing approach. Marketing scholars and practitioners have suggested that business relationships need to be considered as ongoing exchange processes; the essence of marketing is relationship marketing (Christopher, Payne, & Ballantyne, 1993; Grönroos, 1992; Gummesson, 1987; Håkansson, 1982; McKenna, 1991; Turnbull & Valla, 1986; Webster, 1979). Relationship marketing is the art of not only creating customers but also keeping them in the long term; it is a new marketing paradigm that integrates customers systematically into the company's product and process development and quality assurance process. It has taken several decades for the transaction cost-minded Western academics to realize the relevance of long-term interpersonal relationships for business. When ordinary people in East Asia are asked what business or marketing is all about, however, they will answer without hesitation: "It's about relationships."

In the field of strategic management, two contrasting strands of works have emerged: "market-oriented" theory and "resource-based" theory. The PIMS Principles (Buzzell & Gale, 1987), Five Forces (Porter, 1980), and so on are examples of the market-oriented paradigm in strategic management, whereas Core Competence (Prahalad & Hamel, 1990), Learning Organization (Senge, 1990), Resource-Based Competitive Advantage (Grant, 1991), Competence-Based Competition (Hamel & Heene, 1994), and so on are representative of the resource-based paradigm. By analogy, Confucianism, with its teaching on moral development, education and learning, family and group orientation, the importance of interpersonal relationships, harmony, and so on, offers a resource-based business strategy, which helps build the core competence required to meet the challenges in volatile business competitions. Chinese stratagems, which teach us how to use human wisdom to cope with various difficult situations, can be called a market-oriented competition strategy. Hence, the Chinese are culturally equipped with both resource-based and market-oriented strategies. In negotiations, Confucianism offers a cooperation-oriented win-win negotiation strategy based on long-term trusting relationships between the parties (see the discussion of negotiation strategy in Chapter 2).

Implication of Chinese Stratagems

Traveling within East Asia, Western visitors can hardly fail to notice a shared phenomenon: Almost everywhere in fast-growing East Asian economies (e.g., mainland China, Hong Kong, Japan, Singapore, South Korea, Malaysia, and Taiwan), local books and articles on business strategies seldom mention the name of Confucius; rather, they speak of the name of Sun Tzu and teach readers how to use Sun Tzu's *Art of War* to do business. In business life, it can also be observed that business people in China and other East Asian countries with a Chinese cultural heritage tend to use military talk or war terminology to describe their business situations. For example, the phrases "We must win this battle!" and "This battle is difficult to fight" actually mean "We must win this business!" and "This business is difficult to do or handle," respectively. How can East Asian people, the descendants of Confucius, sound so militant?

This interesting phenomenon enables us to doubt Confucianism as the only cultural explanation of East Asian economic miracles and leads us to think of Sun Tzu as well. In the book *The Asian Mind Game*, Chu (1991) emphasizes that strategic thinking is deeply ingrained in the Asian mind, and specific strategies to deal with all kinds of life situations have been developed, refined, and studied for thousands of years. She elucidates the "Asian mind game" by referring to the strategies[28] from *Art of War* and *The Thirty-Six Stratagems*.

Chinese stratagems have far-reaching influence on Japanese and Korean management styles (Chen, 1995; Chu, 1991). In *Asian*

Management Systems: Chinese, Japanese and Korean Styles of Business, Chen (1995) writes,

> Sun Tzu's *Art of War* has been regarded as the most influential classical strategic thinking in East Asia. Together with Confucianism and other classical Chinese thinking, Sun Tzu's strategic thinking was introduced to Korea and Japan and had significant influence on their native strategists, such as Japan's Miyamoto Musashi. Throughout history, it was a required textbook for the military academies in the three countries. In the era of post-Second World War economic development, the Japanese have systematically studied and applied Sun Tzu's strategic thinking to their management and business strategy-making. Sun Tzu's book is often used in the training seminars of Japanese companies. (p. 40)

It is observed that the basic principles of Japanese management are deeply rooted in Sun Tzu's *Art of War* (Hsiao et al., 1990; Li et al., 1986; Wu, 1991). The late Japanese entrepreneur and scholar Takeo Ohashi dedicated much of his life to applying *The Thirty-Six Stratagems* and *Art of War* in Japanese business management and achieved spectacular results (Ohashi, 1993). Robert March, a specialist in Japanese negotiating style and management philosophy, suggests that Japanese business strategy and negotiation style cannot be comprehended without a consideration of Sun Tzu. March (1988) writes,

> In any discussion of the Japanese businessman's ideas about business strategy and negotiation, it is useful to look at an Oriental philosophy of behaviour, that of the noted Chinese military strategist Sun-tzu (Sonshi in Japanese). Sun-tzu lived during the early fourth century B.C., but his ideas still prevail in Japan today and are much in evidence in books and magazine articles. A stickler for discipline, Sun-tzu continues to point the way for leaders in business and government, and his ideas are consonant with deep currents in Japanese culture. (p. 29)

March (p. 30) associates the Japanese way of doing business with Sun Tzu's strategic thinking—for example, managing "one's own resources and capabilities" and "intelligence about the field of battle and the enemy's strength, patience, and whatever dissembling is necessary to deceive and catch the enemy off-guard."

Rosalie Tung (1994a), a leading expert in East Asia business studies, published an article in which *Art of War*, *The Thirty-Six Stratagems*, *Three Kingdoms*, and Miyamoto Musashi's *The Book of Five Rings* are highlighted as the basic "ancient works from which East Asians generally draw their business philosophies" (p. 55). She singles out the following themes regarding the "East Asian approach to business" (pp. 58-59): (a) the importance of strategies, (b) transforming an adversary's strength into weakness, (c) engaging in deception to gain a strategic advantage, (d) understanding contradictions and using them to gain an advantage, (e) compromising, (f) striving for total victory, (g) taking advantage of an adversary's or competitor's misfortune, (h) flexibility, (i) gathering intelligence and information, (j) grasping the interdependent relationship of situations, (k) patience, and (l) avoiding strong emotions. As can be seen, there exists a great similarity between Tung's list and Sun Tzu's 15 principles discussed previously (see the section A Visual Model of *Art of War* earlier in this chapter).

Perhaps due to the Westerners' overemphasis on Confucianism[29] or the language barrier that has unfortunately prevented a body of literature on Chinese stratagems available in the Chinese language from being published in international journals, Chinese stratagems as a source of competitive advantage of the East Asian economies are poorly known in the West. As the descendants of Sun Tzu who are adept in all kinds of *ji*, Chinese and other East Asian business people share an important quality that makes them a shrewd business people: They are always able to work out skillful solutions to business problems of even the most subtle and daunting nature without causing destructive effects to the parties involved. Their capability at this microeconomic level contributes to their performance at the macroeconomic level. To recapitulate earlier discussion, Chinese stratagems provide a market-oriented competition strategy. In negotiations, Chinese stratagems offer a competition-oriented win-lose business negotiation strategy: win-lose without bringing about many "casualties" and win-lose as a Chinese way to the ultimate win-win solutions (see the discussion of negotiation strategy in Chapter 2).

Market Conditions

No explanation of a country's economic performance is complete without a sufficient account of that country's market conditions—that is, political, economic, legal, technological, demographic conditions, and so on. Hofheinz and Calder (1982) point out that a stable political system and market-oriented economy are more relevant factors than culture in explaining the East Asian economic miracles. This is particularly true, for example, in the case of China if she is examined from an historical perspective. The Confucian tradition and the notion of Chinese stratagems have been in place in the Middle Kingdom for more than 2,000 years. China, however, has not boasted a strong economy since the time of Confucius or Sun Tzu. Without the open-door policy in the late 1970s, China would not have been able to develop its economy at all, not to mention produce economic miracles. The current financial turmoil sweeping East Asia shows that pure cultural interpretations without any reference to market indexes have weaknesses (see, e.g., Bond & Hofstede, 1989; Hofstede & Bond, 1988).

Here, we find a useful implication of the Chinese business culture framework proposed in this book: Apart from Confucianism and Chinese stratagems, we must also study the PRC condition, the Japanese condition, the Korean condition, the Singaporean condition, the Taiwanese condition, and so on to explain the performances of these economies. Examination of the current market conditions of these economies shows that they share a number of features: strong governmental control, a market or market-oriented economy, increasing technological progress, a relatively well-educated and skilled workforce, a high saving rate, and so on (Cao et al., 1997; Rohwer, 1996; Shirk, 1993; Thomas & Wang, 1997). East Asians appear to be attempting to develop a new economic paradigm that is different from laissez-faire. It is of both academic and practical value to follow the future development of the market conditions in East Asia.

A Positioning Map

The discussion so far allows us to sketch a map to position studies on Chinese business negotiating style in terms of sociocultural explanations (Figure 3.5). The positioning of the works is based on my interpretation of the degree of orientation in their sociocultural explanations of Chinese business negotiating style regarding the PRC

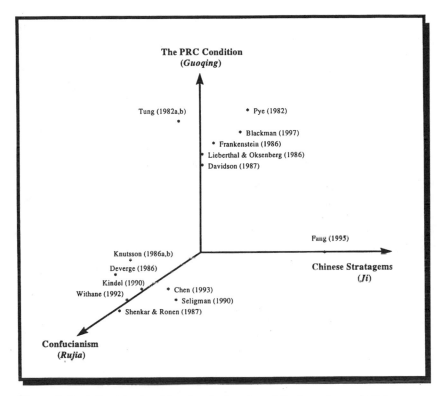

Figure 3.5. A Positioning Map for Sociocultural Explanations of Chinese Business Negotiating Style

condition (*Guoqing*), Confucianism (*Rujia*), and Chinese stratagems (*Ji* or *Jimou*).

For example, Pye (1982) translates Chinese negotiating behavior principally from the vantage point of Chinese bureaucracy. Pye has also made a significant contribution to the area by drawing attention to various Chinese negotiating tactics. Pye's cultural explanation of Chinese behavior, however, is rather weak. In addition, Pye has not provided a deep cultural explanation of the Chinese negotiating tactics he has discovered, making his cultural analysis of Chinese negotiating tactics a semifinished product (see the section in Chapter 2, Critique of Existing Literature). All this helps determine Pye's "vector" in my three-dimensional map, with a high "projection" on the PRC condition, a medium projection on Chinese stratagems, and a low projection on Confucianism.

Near Pye (1982) on the map are authors such as Blackman (1997), Davidson (1987), Frankenstein (1986), Lieberthal and Oksenberg (1986), and Tung (1982a, 1982b). The works of Davidson (1987) and Lieberthal and Oksenberg (1986) do not discuss traditional Chinese cultural and strategic issues in Chinese business negotiation but rather focus on how Chinese bureaucracy and China's basic conditions affect Chinese negotiating style. The latter is more intensified than the former in discussions along this vein. Blackman (1997), Frankenstein (1986), and Tung (1982a, 1982b) deal with how China's bureaucratic or institutional arrangements influence Chinese negotiating behavior. They distinguish themselves, however, by way of a somewhat strategic orientation by Blackman (1997) and Frankenstein (1986) and of a cultural orientation by Tung (1982a, 1982b). From the major theme running through all these works, we label these contributions from the Chinese bureaucracy school, the PRC condition school, or the *Guoqing* school.

Another cluster of writings form the Confucian school. For example, Kindel (1990) and Withane (1992) interpret Chinese negotiating behavior by referring solely to Confucian values, whereas a distinction can be made between scholars (Deverge, 1986; Knutsson, 1986a, 1986b) who devote space to a bureaucratic description of the Chinese and scholars (Chen, 1993; Seligman, 1990; Shenkar & Ronen, 1987) who combine the Confucian understanding of Chinese negotiating style with a discussion about Chinese negotiating tactics.

Chinese stratagems offer a perspective that explains Chinese business negotiating style in terms of *ji*. The strategic principles from *Art of War* and *The Thirty-Six Stratagems* provide the platform on which the strategic Chinese negotiator is understood. Chinese stratagems are a new dimension on which relatively little research has been performed. They form the strategic component of Chinese culture that helps the reader to better understand Chinese negotiating tactics. One of my earlier papers (Fang, 1995), which introduced the concept of *ji* into the area of Chinese business negotiating style research, provides an initial penetration into this dimension.

In my opinion, a comprehensive understanding of Chinese business negotiating style should be one that directs efforts toward presenting a three-dimensional "holographic" picture—that is, trying to seek answers from the PRC condition, Confucianism, and Chinese stratagems. This systematic approach provides hints for us to decode even the negotiating style of overseas Chinese business people: Instead of the PRC condition, we need to examine the market condition of the country or region in which they live, together with a standard analysis of the influence of Confucianism and Chinese stratagems.

In summary, I have discussed Chinese business culture in this chapter. Three fundamental forces driving Chinese negotiating style— that is, the PRC condition, Confucianism, and Chinese stratagems— were identified, reasoned, and discussed. The PRC condition is a changing force, whereas Confucianism and Chinese stratagems are enduring forces, driving Chinese business negotiating behaviors and tactics. Using shipping terminology, I call the PRC condition the deck, Confucianism the engine, and Chinese stratagems the electric parts of Chinese business culture. Together, they define the Chinese way of doing business and their style of negotiating. Chinese negotiation strategy can be both cooperation-oriented and competition-oriented, depending on the degree of trust in the interactions between the negotiating parties. In my opinion, the Chinese are "coop-comp" negotiators who use both cooperative and competitive strategies in negotiations (Fang, 1997c).

Notes

1. Yan (1994) published an article on *guoqing* that is broadly interpreted to include even traditional Chinese thought such as Confucian values. My conceptualization of *guoqing*, which is somewhat different, is based on the contemporary usage of the term in the PRC.

2. In Chinese, these four points are as follows: (a) *Geren fucong zuzhi*, (b) *Shaoshu fucong duoshu*, (c) *Xiaji fucong shangji*, and (d) *Quandang fucong zhongyang*.

3. If Taiwan is included as a province, based on Qin (1994).

4. Today, China's foreign exchange reserve exceeds $140 billion, the second highest in the world. China is still not a rich country, however; the lack of capital to develop its economy, to vitalize its SOEs, and to promote science and education remain major challenges (Wang, Shang, & Xu, 1998; "Zhu Charts," 1998).

5. Strictly speaking, China's economic reform is not without political significance. It was initiated by the ruling party itself.

6. The number of ministries and commissions has been reduced from 40 to 29, a reform carried out by Zhu Rongji, China's premier, newly elected at the Ninth National People's Congress in Beijing in March 1998 ("Top Leaders," 1998).

7. Shenkar and Ronen (1987) and Kirkbride, Tang, and Westwood (1991) are among a few exceptions.

8. W. T. Chan, *A Source Book in Chinese Philosophy*, © 1963, Princeton University Press; quotations from Chan reprinted by permission by Princeton University Press.

9. Compiled by Dai Sheng during the West Han Dynasty (206 B.C.-A.D. 8).

10. The Chinese language has four different tones that are capable of differentiating meanings. Differences in tone convey different meanings to otherwise identical or similar syllables. The syllable *li* ("pears") has a second tone that differs from another *li* ("etiquette," "courtesy," etc.) that is on the third tone in Chinese pronunciation.

11. China is moving rapidly upward in the ranking of Ericsson's markets. Today, China is Ericsson's second largest market after the United States. Bo Landin (1996), Ericsson's senior vice president responsible for corporate markets, believes that "China will probably be the largest single telecommunications market within a few years."

12. Here we also find a clear Taoist influence.

13. In Sun Tzu (1963/1982), *ji* is translated by Samuel Griffith as "strategy."

14. In Chiao (1981), *ji* is translated as "strategy."

15. See, for example, the use of the terms *zhanlue* (strategy) and *zhanshu* (tactics) by Mao Zedong (1965) in *Selected Military Writings of Mao Tse-Tung*.

16. For variation and simplicity, I use the terms *stratagem(s)* and *Chinese stratagem(s)* interchangeably.

17. The Chinese version of Harro von Senger's (1991a) *The Book of Stratagems* is titled *Zhimou* (see von Senger, 1991b).

18. Sun Tzu, *The Art of War*, translated by Samuel B. Griffith. Translation © 1963/1982 by Oxford University Press, Inc. Used by permission of Oxford University Press.

19. Interested readers are referred to Chu (1991), Gao (1991), Sun (1991), and von Senger (1991a) for a detailed historical and legendary account of *The Thirty-Six Stratagems*.

20. There is an abundant indigenous Chinese literature that deals with *ji* in all spheres of life. One article, "Negotiating Techniques for Economic Contract Negotiations," is found in Chen and Xiao (1992, pp. 445-459). This article, written by an unknown Chinese scholar, discusses how to use *The Thirty-Six Stratagems* to negotiate with foreign business people.

21. At a high cognition level, strategic behaviors may also be called rational or logical behaviors.

22. In Chinese, *yin she chu dong*. Similar stratagems can be found in Stratagems 15 and 16 in Appendix A.

23. My maternal grandfather, a graduate of Peking University, died miserably as a "rightist" in 1959.

24. *Laozi*, in Chinese, means both Laozi the philosopher and "father." Mao intended both meanings. [This note was provided by Z. S. Li]

25. The Western term *marketing* was finally translated into Chinese as *shichang yingxiao*, a term suggesting the meaning of "doing business and selling in the market" (Mei & Zhang, 1990, p. 30).

26. "The Five Stresses" stand for stress on civilization, etiquette, hygiene, discipline, and morality; "The Four Beauties" stand for beauty in mind, language, behavior, and environment.

27. "East Asia" is used to refer to both East and Southeast Asian countries and regions with an influence of Chinese culture heritage. Personally, I do not prefer to use the term *miracles* to describe the East Asian economies. The term is borrowed from a large body of literature on "East Asian miracles."

28. In Chu (1991), *ji* is translated as *strategy*.

29. The Western overemphasis on Confucianism can be found in most writings on Chinese and East Asian business management in Western publications that I have read, and little attention has been paid to *ji* or Chinese stratagems and their fundamental influence on Chinese and East Asian business mentality.

4 Illustrations and Analyses

Illustration 1

Western negotiator:[1] "The Chinese government is the biggest boss." (Figure 4.1)

I have negotiated with the Chinese on many projects. . . . It is very difficult to negotiate joint ventures in China, because your Chinese partner does not represent himself. Instead, he represents the Chinese government. You must never forget this point. All Chinese enterprises must follow the government's plan in doing things. They have to follow the plan. Therefore, your Chinese partner is merely an agent, the government's agent. For example, the government authority may say: "This won't work, that condition is not OK." Your partner always has to come back to renegotiate with you. Therefore, you must be very clear in your mind from the very beginning that when entering a joint venture project in China, you are not negotiating with your partner but with the Chinese government. But the problem is, you are not allowed to

Figure 4.1. "The Chinese Government Is the Biggest Boss."
SOURCE: Cartoon by Björn Böke; copyright 1998 by Tony Fang.

negotiate terms and conditions directly with the government. You have
to negotiate with the Chinese government via the agent—your partner.
. . . All foreign ventures in China, whether joint ventures or solely owned
foreign subsidiaries, by definition are "Chinese" enterprises. They have
to operate in conformity with the Chinese government's policies. I
should put it this way; for all the companies in China, no matter whether
they are state-owned Chinese enterprises, joint ventures, or solely
owned foreign subsidiaries, the highest decision makers are not the
board of directors. Instead, the Chinese government is the biggest boss.
The board of directors in China has very limited power. This is one
important difference [between China and the West]. . . . You want to
break it? They will break you. Because you are in China.

Illustration 1 indicates important features of the political dimension of Chinese negotiating style: The real negotiator is not the negotiating Chinese organization but rather the Chinese government. This is
determined by the People's Republic of China (PRC) condition; Chinese
enterprises are appendages of the Chinese government and lack independent decision-making power (see the two sections in Chapter 3,
Politics and Economic Planning). This also implies that negotiation with

the Chinese may take a long time. When embarking on a venture in China, foreign firms must recognize the importance of studying the Chinese government's economic policies and plans and view the Chinese government as the ultimate negotiator or customer toward whom marketing and lobbying activities are directed. In summary, Illustration 1 shows the following:

◆ Chinese business negotiating style has a political dimension.

◆ Chinese companies are not the real negotiator. The unseen Chinese government authority is the real negotiator or the ultimate decision maker.

◆ Chinese companies do not have decision-making power; they are the "agent" of the Chinese government. As a result, negotiation with Chinese may take a long time.

◆ Chinese companies must follow the government's plans for doing things.

◆ Chinese may renegotiate old issues with you many times because of pressure from government authorities.

◆ Enterprises in China, whether Chinese or foreign, all operate under the control of the Chinese government, whose policies, rules, and regulations must be complied with.

Illustration 2

Western negotiator: "Finally, it was the then Chinese premier who made the buying decision."

If your technology and product can help China to resolve its problems, then [your success] depends mainly on whom you introduce your technology to. It often serves no purpose to present it merely to your end users. Why? Because for some types of projects, you have to introduce your technology to high-ranking officials. I once did a project, selling to China a complete paper packaging production line. We had tried for many years but failed. It seemed that at that time China did not foresee the potential demand. Nobody dared to make a decision. Finally, it was the then Chinese premier who made the buying decision during his visit to Sweden in 1984. We sat and discussed for about one and a half hours and settled the project. Now, you see paper packaging products being used all over China. This is the outcome of my negotiation with the Chinese premier.

Illustration 2 provides another example of the influence of the PRC condition, showing how important and effective it is to market one's products directly to, and negotiate directly with, high-ranking Chinese government officials. The case shows the personalized rule at the top of the Chinese bureaucracy: Top government leaders are the key to setting the political climate for negotiations and for approving large projects (see the section in Chapter 3, Chinese Bureaucracy). Negotiation with the Chinese is often described as being characterized by delays, delays, and delays. This case suggests, however, that Chinese business negotiations involving even large industrial projects may take only a few hours to conclude; identifying the real Chinese decision maker is the key. Another implication is that foreign firms can take advantage of Chinese government officials' foreign visits to nurture contacts and negotiate contracts quickly. In short, Illustration 2 can be summarized as follows:

◆ Negotiation with China involving large industrial projects may take only a few hours.
◆ "Negotiating" directly with key Chinese government officials will help secure positive outcomes.
◆ Chinese government officials' foreign visits may lead to large business contracts.
◆ The key to effective negotiations with China lies in identifying the real Chinese negotiators and negotiating at the right time.

Illustration 3

Western negotiator: "You must make it easy for them to *jiaochai*."

As far as negotiation with the Chinese is concerned, you must above all be familiar with *zhongguo de zhidu* ["China's system"]. I was making jokes with them [the Chinese negotiators] that we have our boss and they have theirs. But theirs is bigger than ours. Their boss is the

Chinese government. After you have become familiar with China's system, you know that their negotiators are of the *jiaochai* ["report to the leadership after accomplishing a task"] type who *bu qiu you gong dan qiu wu guo* ["would prefer making no mistakes to making achievements"]. This is the most fundamental point. You must make it easy for them to *jiaochai*. If you can satisfy them in this regard, negotiation will go smoothly. I can give you one example. In 1983, the Chinese came to Hong Kong and purchased a machine to use in an extended project. The machine was later burnt up in an operation. The Chinese complained that the machine had broken down because of a short circuit in the design. We found, however, that the accident was most probably caused by the operator's careless performance. I knew that the Chinese had difficulties in reporting to their boss. And it was unwise if we kept on accusing one another of faults, which might result in endless negotiations. So, I told them that A [the Swedish company] would compensate them with spare parts valued at about SEK 200,000-300,000. When they said they had no money to pay, I replied, "free of charge" and "I'd be glad if you could remember that you owe me a piece of *renqing* ['favor'] this time." What I did was to let them be able to *jiaochai* at ease. Later, the word spread within the industry and A's reputation in China was enhanced. The Chinese said they felt secure when purchasing from A, because we took responsibility for our products from beginning to end. As a result, I received many orders from Chinese organizations. When doing business in China, you must work on a long-term rather than short-term basis.

Illustration 3 shows how the PRC condition and Confucianism together influence Chinese business negotiating behavior. The illustration points out that the Chinese government is the "big boss" and emphasizes that this is a distinctive characteristic of "China's system." The Chinese phrases *jiaochai* and *bu qiu you gong dan qiu wu guo* demonstrate the core of Chinese bureaucracy: "He who does nothing makes no mistakes" (see Chapter 3, Chinese Bureaucracy). Helping the Chinese negotiators "*jiaochai* at ease" is to help them cover their bureaucratic "tails," which may be vulnerable to future criticism (see Chapter 2, The Chinese Bureaucracy School). The illustration implies that if foreign negotiators can satisfy the Chinese bureaucratic need to cover their tails, negotiation will go smoothly and result in repeated business deals in the long run. By helping the Chinese partners *jiaochai* at ease, the Swedish negotiator also helped save face for the Chinese side, which resulted in closer *guanxi* between the two sides. The orders the Swedish company received afterwards reflect precisely the Confucian notion of reciprocity in handling interpersonal relationships and "the rule of *renqing*" (see Chapter 3, Importance of Interpersonal Relationships). This also confirms what Pye (1982, p. 89) noted: "[A] great deal can be gained by helping the Chinese to win face." The case also shows the power of the Chinese "word of mouth" to spread one's reputation quickly within the whole industry. In summary, Illustration 3 suggests the following:

◆ To negotiate effectively with the Chinese, foreign firms must become familiar with the PRC condition (China's system in this illustration); the Chinese government is the big boss.

◆ Chinese negotiators are afraid of being criticized because of the influence of Chinese bureaucracy and face consciousness.

◆ Foreign negotiators will gain much if they can help their Chinese partner save and win face; closer *guanxi* can therefore be established with the Chinese because the Chinese owe the negotiators *renqing*.

◆ The Chinese view *guanxi* essentially as a reciprocal exchange of *renqing* (favors) to each other; good *guanxi* can lead to loyal customers and repeat business.

◆ The Chinese word of mouth can be spread quickly within the whole industry through the mechanism of Chinese bureaucracy.

◆ Helping your Chinese negotiators *jiaochai*—that is, to devise "language" that can be accepted by their decision makers—is a key to successful negotiation with China.

Illustration 4

Chinese negotiator: "We read the copy of the contract in the archives at the ministry."

That was around 1990 and 1991. We were considering the likely foreign partner for our projected joint venture. We knew X [American company] and S [Swedish company]. . . . I went to Beijing to talk to X's

China president. He gave me three points, very candidly. First, welcome. Second, he was right now negotiating with Chinese Plant C, an industrial equipment plant under the ministry. Third, he could not offer me better terms than he was offering to Plant C if he was to negotiate with me. After we had learned that X had recently signed the contract with Plant C, we tried to get to know the contents of the contract. We read the copy of the contract in the archives at the ministry. We found out that the terms offered by X were very unfavorable to the Chinese side. Among other things, the SKD [semi-knocked-down] price was so high that it even exceeded the system price! So, it was X's China president's third point that upset us and made us decide that we would not negotiate with X anymore. . . . We had a number of key ministry-affiliated plants across the country. Frequently, we exchanged experiences with one another at national gatherings. Joint venture contracts, after signature, were all placed in the archives and kept at the ministry. We could read the contracts at the ministry for the purposes of reference only. But we were not permitted to make a copy of them or take them home.

In Illustration 4, the PRC condition, Confucianism, and Chinese stratagems combine to shape Chinese negotiating style. The illustration indicates that Chinese bureaucracy provided opportunities for Chinese negotiators to get access to any information about foreign companies in China and therefore there were actually no "secrets" in China (during 1990 and 1991). Chinese companies are controlled by the Chinese government through industrial ministries, and all the Sino-foreign business contracts are also at the disposal of government authorities (e.g., specific ministries). This institutional arrangement, together with the lack of a legal concept by Chinese people, poses a threat to the protection of foreign technology and company secrets in China. Because of the "socialist responsibility" or so-called *daguofan*, Chinese organizations have become accustomed to free distribution and transfer of technology and information within the Chinese system (see Chapter 3, Technology). If one compares Chinese companies operating under a ministry with "members" of a "family" in Confucian terms, then one can see that this mutual exchange of favors reflects the obligation of the family members to help each other (see Chapter 3, Family Orientation). The disconcerting implication for foreign negotiators is that unless the people's legal concept and China's legislation framework are significantly improved, there is reason to be sympathetic to the anxiety of foreign companies regarding protection of technology in China. The illustration also shows that the Chinese pay much attention to collecting information—a Chinese stratagem (see Sun Tzu's Principle 15 [Espionage] in Chapter 3 or Stratagem 31 in Appendix A). The strategic Chinese thinking is wonderfully facilitated by the "umbrella" of Chinese bureaucracy. In short, Illustration 4 implies the following:

◆ The Chinese attach great importance to collecting strategic information about a foreign partner prior to negotiations.

◆ The Chinese bureaucracy provides an umbrella under which Chinese organizations can efficiently gain access to information about foreign suppliers and exchange it with other Chinese "brotherly" companies within the industry.

◆ Some Chinese people's awareness of law is blunt.

◆ Unless China's legislation framework and the legal concept of the average Chinese people are improved significantly, there is reason to believe that foreign technology and trade secrets cannot be effectively protected in China.[2]

Illustration 5

Western negotiator: "Five to ten minutes later, he came back with a fax."

In China, everyone knows what is going on with the negotiation. We do not involve anyone outside G [Swedish company] in the negotiation. But, in China, it is common that people from various government departments and commissions [e.g., planning, economic, and foreign trade commissions] are found sitting in the negotiation room. You have visits from ministerial or provincial officials. Your partners report not only to their corporate chiefs but also to the provincial government and the like. The Chinese must receive permits from the province. By contrast, it is up to G to decide everything we want to do. We don't have to go to our government to request any sort of permit. Then, the Chinese have a very big contact network over provincial borders. After some time, you come to know that these could be their old schoolmates or party colleagues sitting in different positions in different provinces in, for example, Guangdong, Jiangsu, and Liaoning. The distance to these places is "only" several thousands of miles and the Chinese we have negotiated with know each other well, with the results that agreements reached with one province quickly become known to other neighboring provinces. The Chinese can utilize the key persons in the network. Once in Laoning in North China, we said that we had previously made a similar agreement which was approved and filed by the SPC [State Planning Commission]. Then, a guy [Chinese negotiator] rose up from the negotiation table and went out. Five to ten minutes later, he came back with a fax. He had probably contacted someone in Beijing and received verification of what we had said. So the Chinese have contacts among the government authorities and they can quickly verify things much more easily than we can.

Illustration 5 can be interpreted from both the PRC condition and the Confucianism perspectives. The illustration reveals that Chinese bureaucracy can function "efficiently" to protect Chinese interests. The flow of information among Chinese organizations can be facilitated by Chinese *guanxi* networks webbed across the Chinese bureaucratic borders. This mechanism may be understood as a type of family existing within Chinese bureaucracy. Within the Chinese family, members exchange "the greatest communistic cooperation and mutual help." Distrust between non-family members is a typical symptom of Chinese familism (see Chapter 3, Family Orientation). Therefore, the Chinese distrust of a negotiating partner can be understood as a kind of "coldly indifferent" Chinese attitude toward "strangers." The illustration shows the rule of Chinese bureaucracy—He who does nothing makes no mistakes. The power of precedence is valued by the Chinese (see Chapter 3, Chinese Bureaucracy). Therefore, nothing is as reassuring as strong evidence showing that other brotherly Chinese companies have already agreed to the same or similar contractual provisions. The illustration again displays that Chinese companies' business is the Chinese government's business. One reason why Chinese negotiating teams tend to be large is because they may involve members from various departments of the government authorities. In brief, Illustration 5 shows the following:

- ◆ The Chinese negotiating team tends to be large and may involve people from various government organizations.
- ◆ Chinese companies must receive a permit from the Chinese government to do business with foreign firms.
- ◆ China is a "continent," but the flow of information within Chinese bureaucracy can be unbelievably quick due to the Chinese *guanxi* network.
- ◆ The Chinese show a distrust of their negotiating partners and may verify their words with the help of Chinese bureaucracy and *guanxi*.
- ◆ It is important that foreign negotiators enter the negotiation room armed with previously signed or approved contracts or both to gain the power of precedence.

Illustration 6

Chinese negotiator: "It is common to see that the Chinese negotiating team is large."

Why our team is large? First of all, Chinese do not have as many modern advanced communication conveniences as do foreigners. I have discovered that the frontline foreign negotiators, though only a few persons, had a large number of supporting people at home as backup. They communicated with each other frequently and effectively. Second, China has a problem. That is, when it comes to negotiation of a large project in which various departments are involved, if you do not ask each of these departments to come, they will probably make complaints and won't support your work very much in the future. This phenomenon exists. Therefore, in order to coordinate our work, we asked every department to send one representative to form our negotiating team. We kept on discussing internally if any problem arose. Since you represented your department and you were now present at the negotiating table, you would not be allowed to cause trouble in the future. Things could be done more smoothly because you did not have any excuse for not cooperating. The bottom line was that if any opportunity arose to go abroad for study or training, you could be included in the delegation, since, in China, chances of going abroad to study are rather few and people fight for them. If you are not asked to participate in the negotiation, you might probably have some *xiangfa* ["opinions"] and say, "Since you do not allow us to participate in the negotiation, we are not well informed, and therefore cannot cooperate well." In general, in our team, apart from technical people, we have people from the planning department, international or foreign affairs department, personnel department, etc. . . . Now, we are making a proposal that when forming a negotiating team, some departments need to be included, but not all. That you are not invited does not necessarily mean that your cooperation is not required. It is common to see that the Chinese negotiating team is large.

Illustration 6 sheds light on the impact of infrastructure and intraorganizational relationships within Chinese enterprises on Chinese negotiating style. It shows that the "large Chinese team" phenomenon is caused, in part, by China's poor infrastructure and communications facilities (see Chapter 3, Backwardness). In this illustration, the Chinese negotiator explains that the Chinese negotiating team has to be large so that people from different departments do not have reason not to cooperate with each other on the project—an explanation seldom found in the existing literature but that can be understood from the PRC condition perspective. The Chinese enterprise has poor communication between functional departments due to highly vertical dependence on "mothers-in-law" (see Chapter 3, Economic Planning). The Chinese inability to cooperate with people outside family and group networks can culturally be attributed to the narrow interpretation of the Confucian value of family (see Chapter 3, Family Orientation). In addition, the illustration demonstrates the bargaining nature of Chinese organizations. In summary, Illustration 6 suggests the following:

◆ The Chinese team tends to be large because it represents divergent interests from different functional departments. Bargaining is part of the Chinese bureaucratic culture.

◆ China's poor infrastructure also contributes in part to the fact that the Chinese team is large.

◆ Communication and cooperation between different Chinese departments are generally poor.

◆ Negotiation may take a long time because of the internal clashes between Chinese organizational departments.

◆ The Chinese negotiation team is a consensus-making group of people with different interests.

Illustration 7

Western negotiator: "You see varied Chinese behavior across China."

You see varied Chinese behavior across China. A Guangdong Chinese is very straightforward. In Guangdong, people are certainly most knowledgeable about Westerners and Western countries because the economy is most advanced there. In negotiations, they touch the points directly and demand more openness. But in Beijing and in North China, people are more tactful. They do not say directly what they actually mean but instead express themselves in other ways. They may not say anything at all. Shanghai is situated in the middle. Shanghai Chinese have a little "younger brother complex": Beijing has always been the big capital during the times after the revolution, while Guangdong has stood for the biggest economic development, and Shanghai lies somewhere in between. But in Shanghai, the Chinese claim themselves to be number one in the country, and this is more or less true. I cannot rank these places in order of preference. But I would say Beijing Chinese are very formal. The nearer one is located to the central power, the more formal one becomes and the more strictly one follows the law. For example, when negotiating with the Chinese, you need to know if your Chinese partner actually has the permit [business license] granted by the government authorities to start up negotiation with Western firms. In Nanjing and Beijing, the Chinese are rightly quick in showing the government's permit, while in Guangdong, the Chinese merely say, "This will be settled by us" or "We have the permit and we need not show it." They jump directly into the negotiations. In Shanghai, Beijing, and Liaoning, the Chinese negotiating partners involve government authorities in negotiations all the time, saying that the authorities cannot approve of this and that, while in Guangdong, people want to keep the authorities as far away as possible.

Illustration 7 demonstrates one aspect of the PRC condition—great size (see Chapter 3, Great Size). It suggests that due to geographical difference as well as differences in economic development between different regions in China, negotiating style varies between the northern and southern Chinese. Northern Chinese follow the government's rules and regulations more strictly than do southern Chinese. Negotiations taking place in northern China are characterized by stronger "political color," with more frequent involvement from government officials, than those occurring in southern China. Previously, I discussed the different regional characters of the Chinese. Beijing Chinese are described as "straightforward," whereas Guangdong Chinese are described as "full of stratagems" (Hu, 1994). This illustration, however, suggests almost the opposite: The former are "tactful," and the latter are "open." This illustration has implications for the study of the Chinese business negotiating style at the national culture level: The Chinese national sociocultural forces—that is, the PRC condition, Confucianism, and Chinese stratagems—may have a varying degree of explanatory power when applied to different regions of China. In summary, Illustration 7 suggests the following:

- ◆ Due to China's vastness and imbalance in economic development, the Chinese in different regions may have varied negotiating styles.
- ◆ Northern Chinese may be more "political," strictly following the rules of the central government, whereas southern Chinese may be more straightforward and matter-of-fact.
- ◆ In northern China, government authorities may be more frequently involved in business negotiations than in southern China.

Illustration 8

Chinese negotiator: "However, your ministers were on summer holidays when we were there."

We were visiting Sweden this summer. Our delegation was headed by the party secretary of our province. We visited B [Swedish company] in Västerås because B was one of the foreign bidders competing for our city's subway project worth billions of RMB.[3] No decision had yet been made as to who would win the project. That's why our provincial party secretary led the study trip to Sweden. We were very impressed by B. At B we saw workers working attentively on the shop floor and how quality was achieved. We met B's managers and exchanged opinions. We knew B's intention and ambitious plan, but we had not heard anything from your [Swedish] government. The subway project is so big that we must have your government's opinion. We must know how your government felt and supported the project. That's why we wanted to meet the Swedish industry and commerce minister or finance minister or ministers in the areas concerned. However, your ministers were on summer holidays when we were there. What a pity! You know, our provincial party secretary is the highest decision maker in our whole province. You would have had a wonderful opportunity to collect information about foreign investment policy and whatever you wanted, and this would also have been a wonderful opportunity for you to establish *guanxi*. At last, we learned that the Swedish agriculture minister would like to meet us instead. Feeling that the agriculture minister was not the person in charge of the issues in which we were interested and also because of our tight schedule, we declined the meeting and went home. . . . We have learned and understood that the summer holiday is very special in Sweden, but still, can you consider adjourning your holiday a little bit when you have an important visit? It seemed that Swedes did not quite understand this point. You know, should our provincial party secretary visit Japan, the Japanese would return from their holidays anywhere in the world within hours.

Illustration 8 describes a "culture shock" that a Chinese delegation headed by the provincial party secretary experienced in Sweden[4] and how the PRC condition or, more specifically, Chinese politics and economic planning, influences the Chinese attitude toward foreign partners (see Chapter 3). As shown in Illustrations 1 through 5, there is a significant "political dimension" in Chinese business negotiation and negotiating style: The Chinese government is the biggest boss, and Chinese bureaucracy directly influences Chinese negotiating style. Because of the all-pervasive influence of Chinese politics on Chinese business, it is natural to the Chinese to believe that, in the West, government is also the "biggest boss" and involved in a company's business negotiations. This is a Chinese misconception—one of many problems that may occur when people from different social systems negotiate with one another. This "Chinese style" contrasts directly with the "Swedish style." The Swedish companies have the final say in doing business and do not have to obtain a "permit" from the Swedish government (see Illustration 5). Of particular interest in this illustration is that although the Chinese delegation was kept informed of the difficulty on the part of the Swedish host in arranging a meeting with the Swedish ministers at that time of the year, the Chinese still expected to have the meeting on their arrival in Sweden. The Chinese felt uncertain when they did not hear "any opinions" from the Swedish government ministers. Reading between the lines, one can sense that the Chinese guests were rather disappointed because they were not received by the Swedish government officials with whom they expected to hold talks. According to the Chinese, the Japanese are more flexible than the Swedes in handling the kind of situation described here. The illustration concerns the issue of how people from different sociocultural backgrounds can adapt effectively to each other's way of doing business. In short, Illustration 8 implies the following:

◆ Chinese business is strongly influenced by Chinese politics; the provincial party secretary and governor are the highest decision makers in the province.

◆ Chinese business delegations appreciate holding talks with foreign government officials.

◆ Cultural adaptation poses a challenging issue for negotiating parties.

Illustration 9

Chinese negotiator: "The lawyers were *most troublesome!*"

We did not wish [foreign] lawyers to participate in negotiation. The lawyers were *zui taoyan* ["most troublesome"]! They were picking up the bone in the egg [Chinese saying], finding fault by splitting hairs. This was a sheer waste of time. The joint venture was to be set up in China. It should be negotiated on the basis of Chinese law. However, foreign lawyers hardly knew Chinese law. What they knew was to help the foreign party and were biased against the Chinese party. So, the more you talked, the more I disliked it. The presence of lawyers only served the opposite purpose, indeed. . . . It would be OK if you dispatched your lawyers to talk with a small *danwei* ["work unit"]. But no way here. We are also a large company and we know the policy. We would not accept that you sent your lawyers to negotiate with us. If you sent your lawyer here, we would also send our lawyer; the outcome would certainly be two lawyers biting each other. . . . The key [to effective negotiation] rests on *chengyi* [sincerity].

Illustration 9 is quoted from my interview with a chief Chinese negotiator involved in a Sino-Swedish joint venture negotiation. The Chinese interviewee was a division head in a Chinese national industrial corporation. He had a technology management background and a wealth of experience negotiating with foreign companies since the early 1980s. The illustration shows signs of the legal dimension of Chinese behavior and illustrates a typical "Confucian attitude" toward business negotiation (see Chapter 3, Moral Cultivation). Chinese generally do not use Chinese lawyers in face-to-face negotiations; they view foreign lawyers as troublesome persons in negotiations; they emphasize that business relationships should be based on sincerity rather than reliance on lawyers. The Chinese hope to gain more bargaining power by emphasizing that they are a large *danwei*—a PRC concept inextricably linked to the Confucian concept of family (see the two sections in Chapter 3, Chinese Bureaucracy and Family Orientation). The illustration also implies that if a foreign lawyer is very familiar with Chinese laws and regulations and takes care of the Chinese interest, the Chinese negotiators will not reject his presence (cf. Illustration 11). In short, Illustration 9 demonstrates the following:

◆ Chinese business negotiating style has a legal dimension.

◆ The Chinese attach great importance to the other party's sincerity during negotiations.

◆ Chinese lawyers generally do not attend business negotiations.

◆ The Chinese view foreign lawyers as troublesome persons in negotiations.

◆ The Chinese may criticize the foreign lawyers' lack of knowledge about Chinese laws and regulations.

◆ A large Chinese *danwei* bargains harder than a small one.

Illustration 10

> **Chinese negotiator: "How could we plan for divorce when we were just talking about marriage?" (Figure 4.2)**
>
> Foreigners just loved to work on the contract text. This was like calculating family property in preparation for future divorce at the time when we were just beginning to fall in love. How could we plan for divorce when we were just talking about marriage? I respect the foreign party's intention to seek legal protection. They are accustomed to placing emphasis on it. But, we really cannot agree to this practice. . . . In my opinion, when negotiating a joint venture contract, we must first grasp the core issues, for example, equity share, composition of the board of directors, distribution of power, payment of various key charges, pricing, and financing. We must look at the foreign party's technology, market, and economic strength. These are the points which we should by no means forget. Once we have got the OK on these points, the contract is basically workable. After we have signed the contract, we mainly rely on the spirit of cooperation to do things. What is most important is not to do things according to the contract but on the basis of mutual cooperation, of the spirit of cooperation. . . . For example, let us say the contract is now signed. How could we turn over the pages to check what is restricted by the contract? It's absolutely impossible. Most probably, the contract file would be locked into the drawer and nobody would read it anymore. After the opening of the joint venture, people would be doing what is actually required by reality, which will not necessarily be the same as specified by the provisions of the contract. As long as the parties have the spirit of cooperation, the project can be operated well.

Illustration 10 again demonstrates the legal dimension of Chinese negotiating style, reflecting the Confucian aversion to law held by the Chinese negotiator (see Chapter 3, Moral Cultivation). In Confucian terms, negotiation is not haggling but a problem-solving cooperation based on a high level of mutual trust. A contract is but an initial "framework" on which deeper mutual trust and understanding are built to solve unforeseen problems that can crop up at any time. In other

Figure 4.2. "How Could We Plan for Divorce When We Were Just Talking About Marriage?"
SOURCE: Cartoon by Björn Böke; copyright 1998 by Tony Fang.

words, the Chinese view a business contract essentially as a manifestation of the parties' commitment to initiating a long-term business relationship. The Chinese believe that problems can certainly occur beyond the scope of the contract (see Chapter 3, Backwardness; the Chinese do not believe in planning on paper). As long as parties have established a high degree of mutual trust or "the spirit of cooperation," however, the business venture will operate smoothly. The "marriage and divorce" metaphor shows a kind of nonlegalistic Chinese negotiating behavior, which, if handled properly, is very positive. This mentality, however, also implies that contracts are likely to be renegotiated throughout the course of the project life, and that the Chinese propensity for renegotiation can be a non-tactical Confucian behavior. The illustration also shows that the Chinese give high priority to issues such as technology, price, and financing. When teaming with foreign companies, the Chinese search for ones that are technologically and financially strong. In summary, Illustration 10 indicates the following:

◆ Chinese negotiators view the contract as a commitment to initiating a long-term business relationship. The Chinese are the "problem-solving" type of negotiators.

◆ The Chinese propensity to renegotiate seems to be inevitable given this Confucian problem-solving attitude toward a business contract, the details of which can be renegotiated throughout the course of the project's life.

◆ The Chinese place high priority on technology, pricing, financial issues, and so on when negotiating a contract.

Illustration 11

Western negotiator: "I have met Chinese lawyers only once."

In 1983, that's when I started negotiating in China. During the early 1980s we negotiated six licensing agreements. At that time there was not even a Chinese law regulating licensing. That law came in the spring of 1985.[5] Prior to that, when a legal framework didn't exist, we had already entered into six licensing agreements. The Chinese who were to negotiate with foreigners were given a "book," with examples of contractual rules, terms, and with comments. But the book was not a law. Someone from the top, from the government, had given the book as advice and guidance but, of course, the Chinese perceived the book to be very much the same as a law. But there is a big difference between the book and a law. I can read a law, but I was not given the book. So I didn't know what was in it. As for law, everyone can read the law, whether you are Chinese or Swedish. But here, what the Chinese saw as the law was only a book that was not permitted to be read. That was fine, however. I never felt that this was a negative thing when negotiating. And in another sense, it was a limitation of the possibility of the Chinese party to be flexible. They had only one understanding of the rules in that book and that understanding, in some cases, did not fit our project. Since they only had access to the strict rules in the book, they felt that we could not make the required adaptations. And that was a problem.

Since then I have been negotiating in China on a regular basis. Now, we also have several joint ventures there. One thing which is extremely positive and has helped us a lot—both the Chinese party and ourselves— is the fact that throughout these years in negotiating with the Chinese I have met Chinese lawyers only *once*. And that was in Changchun in Manchuria, during a joint venture negotiation. One day, two Chinese lawyers from a law firm in Changchun were brought in. But the following day, they did not come. So I asked the Chinese party: "Where are the lawyers?" Then they said, "We trust you. Because you know the Chinese rules much better than they." When I negotiate, I always bring with me the text in Chinese of the Chinese laws and, on the other side, the English translation. So when the lawyers started arguing with me about the law, I said, "You're wrong, please read the law." Several times they had to back off [laughter]. Then, the Chinese party said, "It's better we stick to the Swede. Because he seems to know Chinese law better than our own lawyers do." We always apply Chinese law in our contracts; always only Chinese law. So I have to know the Chinese law and to be able to understand as well as I can. In some cases I am the only one around the table who has read the Chinese law. . . . Yes, they trusted me. Because I did not try to alter Chinese law, but could show the wording of it. Everything in the contract is governed by Chinese law. So I have an interest in not being in conflict with Chinese law. People often say it is very difficult to negotiate with China, and they spend weeks doing it. But we usually come to a conclusion very quickly. Another thing, I always make the draft of the contract. The Chinese accept it, because it is based on the Chinese format, adapted to our project. . . . As to production technology, probably thousands of Chinese factories have been fooled into believing that if they get drawings, they can make the products. They can't. We, on the other hand, tell the Chinese honestly what we can give and what we cannot in terms of production technology, in particular. Honesty is very important. If you are not honest, why start a cooperation? This is my attitude and the attitude of our company. Honesty is an important part of our strategy in negotiating with the Chinese. . . . Throughout the years, we have never had any real conflicts with any of our Chinese partners. . . . The only serious problem I have had in China is the language problem. Many times it has happened that the demands from the Chinese party have sounded very tough. We have talked about prices and other terms and conditions. But if you penetrate the issue and really ask them why they argue and think the way you find tough, usually you find that it's just a question of communication. It is the translation that has made things sound worse than what they really are.

Illustration 11 is a senior Swedish lawyer's perception of Chinese negotiators. It illustrates both political and legal dimensions of Chinese business negotiating style that are influenced by the PRC condition and Confucianism. First, China's legal framework is young and developing rapidly. Foreign firms entering the China market may find that there is no Chinese law to regulate certain aspects of the business, a situation that also "forces" the Chinese to rely on trust and relationships in doing business. Second, the Chinese perception of law is a political book—the government's rules and regulations, many of which remain open to negotiation (see Chapter 3, Economic Planning and Legal Framework). Third, Chinese lawyers seldom participate in face-to-face negotiation, a typical Confucian attitude toward contracting (see Chapter 3, Moral Cultivation). This Swedish negotiator viewed the absence of Chinese lawyers in face-to-face negotiation as "extremely positive." It seems that the Confucian "absence of lawyer" in negotiation may provide an ideal working state: Both parties have great mutual trust and use a cooperation strategy in negotiation—a "win-win" working environment. Fourth, a foreign negotiator who is well versed in the Chinese law book— governmental rules and regulations—will not be rejected by the Chinese; instead, he will receive much respect from his Chinese partners (cf. Illustration 9). This is also where his bargaining power comes into play because in-depth knowledge of the Chinese system enables the foreign party to say "No" to the Chinese. Fifth, honesty is important in Chinese negotiation, and it is beneficial from the foreign manager's point of view. Respecting the Chinese system, but being one's self, is important (e.g., in this illustration, saying "No" and letting the Chinese know what the Swedish company can and cannot offer). For example, the Swedish negotiator respected the Chinese system by accepting and studying the political book (law), and he became an expert in it; he also remained himself, however, by saying "No" to the Chinese: "You're wrong, please read the law." An important implication is that the Chinese did not believe they had lost face but instead had gained trust and confidence in the Swedish negotiator. The higher the level of honesty among the parties, the easier the negotiation will be because honesty is a major consideration in Chinese decision making (see Chapter 3, Moral Cultivation). Honesty is the main reason why this Swedish company has never had any real conflicts with any of its Chinese partners throughout the years. Finally, language seems to be the biggest problem in negotiations with the Chinese. Translation may serve only to make things worse. To summarize, Illustration 11 shows the following:

- The Chinese rely on trust in negotiations because of the lack of a legal framework in China.
- Chinese perceive law as political rules and regulations from the Chinese government.
- Foreign negotiators who are very familiar with the Chinese legal system and government regulations will earn great respect and trust from their Chinese partners.
- When negotiating with the Chinese, it is important to respect the Chinese system but at same time be one's self.
- Saying "No" to the Chinese in a proper manner and letting them know what one can and cannot offer will most likely win the Chinese partner's trust.
- Honesty plays an important part in Chinese negotiations; honesty pays off.
- A major problem in negotiating with the Chinese is the language barrier.

Illustration 12

Western negotiator: "If they do not want to negotiate something, they can simply say that it is required by the government authorities."

Chinese law is fairly new and very difficult to interpret. Therefore, there is a lot of room to negotiate with your Chinese partner. The joint venture law is relatively new and not so well developed. It is hard to know what is encoded in the law, which you have to follow, and what remains open to negotiation between the parties. The Chinese can utilize this situation to their advantage. If they do not want to negotiate something, they can simply say that it is required by the government authorities. We have gradually learned this negotiation technique and demand that they show the government law text, even if it is in Chinese. If they can't, there may not be any law. It may simply be a pure negotiation technique which they are employing.

In Illustration 12, the Chinese display a strategic negotiating behavior: playing the "government card" or strategically utilizing immature Chinese law to their advantage (see Appendix A, Stratagems 3 and 29). Both the PRC condition and Chinese stratagems are at work in the illustration. The Chinese can turn the Chinese bureaucracy to their advantage. In short, Illustration 12 demonstrates the following:

♦ The Chinese legal framework is quite new, and issues may remain open to bargaining.
♦ The Chinese can strategically manipulate the immature Chinese legal framework to gain bargaining power at the negotiation table.

Illustration 13

Chinese negotiator: "We hope to have arbitration, if any, in China."

In our opinion, we hope to have arbitration, if any, in China. Disputes should also be handled in China. We had not insisted on this point previously. Now and in the future we shall insist on it. It is written in the final contract that arbitration, if any, shall take place in a neutral place, for example, Switzerland. However, as a matter of fact, Switzerland might not be favorable for us either, because no matter who the lawyers are, they are part of the European system, that is, they are culturally closer to Sweden than to China. If a third place is to be chosen, why not Hong Kong, for example? Hong Kong is closer to us. The reason that arbitration should take place in China is twofold. First, we should believe that the Chinese arbitration organization is impartial, since it is also an internationally accepted organization that performs its functions according to international principles. Next, the joint venture is in China and governed by Chinese law. Wherever you hold the arbitration, in Stockholm, Switzerland, or elsewhere, you still have to make the judgment based on Chinese law. If arbitration is held in China, I am of the opinion that the Chinese arbitration system would perceive the Chinese law more deeply and clearly. . . . Reluctantly, however, we finally agreed to the "arbitration in Switzerland" clause, because we believed that these foreign institutions would make their verdicts fairly.

Illustration 13 indicates that the Chinese also use a legalistic approach in business negotiation—for example, the arbitration clause. The Chinese tend to insist that "arbitration in China" be written into the contract. This legalistic Chinese approach might be understood as being influenced by both the PRC condition and the Chinese stratagems. In Illustration 11, it is shown that Chinese negotiators perceive Chinese law more as government policies, rules, and regulations than law in a Western sense. A primary Chinese motivation for holding arbitration in China is that the Chinese arbitration system knows the Chinese law better than do foreigners. This may be true in the sense that the Chinese legal regime is young and developing and with a constant influx of government rules and regulations (see Chapter 3, Legal Framework). Thus, the illustration points to the importance of the foreign party becoming an expert on Chinese law—a theme also empirically supported by Illustration 11. The Chinese behavior of insisting on arbitration taking place in China may also be interpreted as a strategic Chinese behavior (see Appendix A, Stratagem 4; this point is discussed further in Illustration 36). In summary, Illustration 13 shows the following:

◆ Chinese negotiators adopt a legalistic approach in business negotiations—for example, they would insist that arbitration, if any, is to be held in China.
◆ The Chinese worry about the foreign party's knowledge of Chinese law. It is important, therefore, that the foreign party become an expert at Chinese law.

Illustration 14

Western negotiator: "Chinese society is changing very fast."

[About Chinese law and lawyers] It is difficult to make generalizations. It depends on the complexity of the project. I have negotiated some projects that did not involve any lawyer. I have also negotiated some other projects in which the lawyers were the chief negotiators. The most complicated project I did was an aircraft leasing project. It was a large project. It involved four airplanes, valued at more than U.S.$100 million, and the leasing time spanned almost 10 years. I only signed the memorandum of understanding with the Chinese. Then, the rest of the negotiations were done mainly between my lawyer and the lawyer from the Chinese party, because the project was complicated, involved a large amount of capital, and was to last almost 10 years. These kinds of contracts, the leasing contract, are very complicated. Of course, you cannot discuss them because you are not capable of discussing them. That is why my lawyer talks to their lawyer. We didn't even need to sit there, because you didn't need to understand what they were talking about. If a project is quite simple, why bother to use a lawyer? You can't answer that question, so you have to see what type of projects you are in. . . . The status of lawyers in Chinese society is still quite low, but it is improving. The same as that of doctors, but also improving. In the old Chinese society, lawyers and doctors were not important people. I mean the whole Chinese society is changing now. For example, some years ago, you couldn't find a qualified accountant, because it was not good to talk about money, the papers, and the figures, which were equated with cheating the government. Chinese society is changing very fast. Today, they are the highest paid local Chinese in all foreign companies.

Illustration 14 is a reminder of the changing aspect of Chinese legal behavior in business negotiations. It can be expected that more Chinese lawyers will appear in face-to-face negotiation sessions in the future. Chinese negotiators are becoming more mature, accepting international common practice in negotiations, because of the rapid changes taking place in China (see Chapter 3, Rapid Change). Illustration 14 suggests the following:

◆ Chinese negotiators are becoming more mature, and international common practice in doing business will be more respected in China.

◆ More Chinese lawyers will participate in face-to-face negotiations in the future.

Illustration 15

Chinese negotiator: "We wanted to be backed by a big mountain."

Our intention is to import the most advanced technology and to cooperate with the large, world-famous foreign corporations. Because the life cycle of a technology is short, we, to a certain extent, pay even more attention to the suppliers' *houjing* ["reserve strength"] for continuous technological development. . . . Judging from these criteria, we considered E [Swedish company] a truly fine partner. . . . We knew that E is a very large internationally famous company. And in China, by the end of 1993, E's analogue cellular mobile system [TACS standard] had already occupied China's *banbi jiangshan* ["half of the territory"]. E's remarkable performance had really attracted special attention from the MPT [Ministry of Posts and Telecommunications][6] and PTIC [China National Posts and Telecommunications Industry Corporation]. It could be said that having a chance to cooperate with such a large company as E has been an urgent demand from the very beginning. . . . It can be illustrated by one unofficial phrase we used at that time: *Women xiang beikao dashan* ["We wanted to be backed by a big mountain"].

Illustration 15 is from my interview with a Chinese chief negotiator in a negotiation about technology transfer from the Swedish company (E) by means of joint venture. The illustration shows features of the technical dimension of Chinese business negotiating style. Where foreign technology transfer to China by means of joint venture is concerned, the Chinese side wants to receive the most advanced technology and team up with large, world-famous foreign firms. Not only must the technology be the most advanced but also it must be a continuously new one with research and development (R&D) capability (so-called *kaifa jishu* or "development technology"). The Chinese partner wants to be backed by a big mountain. This Chinese behavior reflects the influence of (a) the PRC condition: China needs technology. The ongoing transfer of advanced foreign technology to China is one major Chinese motivation to form a Sino-foreign joint venture (see the two sections in Chapter 3, Technology and Backwardness); (b) Confucianism— that is, face can be gained when doing business with large firms (see

Chapter 3, Concept of Face); and (c) Chinese stratagems—that is, relying on a strong partner to survive and develop (see Appendix A, Stratagem 14). In brief, Illustration 15 shows the following:

◆ Chinese business negotiating style has a technical dimension.
◆ The Chinese want to purchase the most advanced and R&D-oriented technology.
◆ The Chinese want to cooperate with large, world-famous firms.

Illustration 16

Chinese negotiator: "Our state policy is to exchange market for technology."

Our state policy is to exchange market for technology. We have given you the market free of charge, why do we have to pay for your technology? As a matter of fact, we haven't got the real "development technology" yet. We know clearly that the foreigners can earn big money on, for example, selling CKD [complete knocked down] kits and parts. They have their way of making money, if not here, then some other places.

Illustration 16 provides a Chinese answer to the Western observation that the Chinese want to buy the best technology but show no appreciation for the monetary value of knowledge (Pye, 1982). The illustration indicates that the Chinese know the value of technology exactly in the way that they know the value of the Chinese market. The deep-seated Chinese thinking is to exchange the great Chinese market for advanced foreign technology, a policy that Deng Xiaoping has repeatedly emphasized (see Chapter 3, Great Size). Again, the Chinese show a strong desire to obtain development technology. In short, Illustration 16 suggests the following:

◆ The basic Chinese attitude toward foreign technology transfer to China is to exchange the Chinese market for foreign technology.
◆ The Chinese are expected to drive a hard bargain on the price of technology.

Illustration 17

Chinese negotiator: "If I had money, why would I come to you?"

We are very poor, indeed, and we are short of capital. That is why we need a foreign partner. If I had money, why would I come to you? I have such an abundant resource, such a vast market, but why you? The simple truth is that we have no money. Thus, you'd better not press me to pay for your technology. I really cannot afford it. This is the *point* that we are negotiating about. For cooperation, you can take it or leave it. I simply cannot contribute that much money to satisfy your requirement. That's all.

Illustration 17 indicates that because China is short of foreign exchange (see Chapter 3, Backwardness), negotiation with China may be called the price negotiation. Price is the very issue that the Chinese negotiate about (cf. the two elements of negotiation in Chapter 2, What Is Negotiation?). The illustration suggests a key feature of the commercial dimension of the Chinese business negotiating style: Chinese negotiators are very price sensitive. Such price sensitivity may also be explained from Confucianism (i.e., haggling to win face; see Chapter 3, Concept of Face) and from Chinese stratagems (see Appendix A, Stratagem 17). It is interesting that the negotiating Chinese organization is introduced in its annual report of 1995 as "a national group in the industry in China with powerful economy and technology" with a total property value exceeding RMB 7 billion. The Chinese, however, did not want to pay for the technology, as shown in this illustration, because China is "very poor" and "short of capital." Playing the "China's backwardness" card to gain bargaining power is an effective Chinese negotiating tactic (see Appendix A, Stratagem 34). It can also be justified in Confucian tradition: In the Chinese family, those with wealth and power have obligations to less fortunate relatives (see Chapter 3, Family Orientation). In summary, Illustration 17 indicates the following:

◆ Chinese business negotiating style has a commercial dimension.
◆ Negotiation with the Chinese is essentially price negotiation; Chinese negotiators are very price sensitive.

◆ The Chinese may emphasize China's backwardness, such as a lack of foreign exchange, to gain bargaining power.

Illustration 18

Western negotiator: "Instead of saying 'Good night!' the Chinese were saying 'Lower your price tomorrow morning!' "

Later, we had been discussing price with the Chinese, of course. It is so easy for the Chinese to say that everything is too expensive, and the price is too high. This has been applied by the Chinese to expatriates' salary, travel, allowances, product value, GSM prices, terminal prices, kits prices, and whatever. The Chinese assumed that everything they were going to buy was too expensive. This has become a generic Chinese negotiating strategy. They just bargain like that during the whole negotiation. Instead of saying "Good night!" the Chinese were saying "Lower your price tomorrow morning!" at the end of a meeting. They play the game in this way: Either your technology or quality is too poor, or the price is too high. They drive price versus quality bargaining. We have resisted a great deal of this tactic. We know what the market price is. Therefore, we know we have a suitable price level anyway.

Illustration 18 provides an example of Chinese price sensitivity. In this case, the saying "Lower your price tomorrow morning!" was actually delivered by the Chinese in good humor. The Chinese "price is always too high" tactic fits neatly into the pattern of the Chinese stratagems (see Appendix A, Stratagem 7). The "price versus quality bargaining" can also be understood from the Chinese stratagems perspective (see Appendix A, Stratagem 19). In short, Illustration 18 reveals the following:

◆ The Chinese never stop haggling.

◆ The Chinese can use the "price is always too high" tactic: The opponent's price is always too high.

◆ The Chinese can drive price versus quality bargaining: They attack one's price if one's quality is high and attack one's quality if one's price is low.

Illustration 19

> ### Chinese negotiator: "If you offer 100, I will counter-offer 50."
>
> That [Chinese are price sensitive] is simple. Taken as a whole, the living standard of Chinese people is not very high. As a result, money is very very important to everybody. Since you are not living an affluent life, you must *jin da xi suan* ["carefully calculate and plan your economy"]. Another important factor is that there is a bad phenomenon in our society today. Some people do not respect business morals, and their commercial reputation is low. They are only after *baoli* ["dishonest profit"]. This is virtually an immature commercial behavior. Capitalist society might probably have looked like this in its primitive stage. Today, in our society, some people are really making dishonest "extreme profit." Their price contains too much *shuifen* ["water content"]. Naturally, I must bargain about price with him. I know that his cost is not as high as he says and his profit is not as low as he claims. Of course, I must ask him to go down in price rather than accept it as it is. Gradually, this phenomenon [of making extreme profit in a dishonest way] becomes so rampant in the society that I become accustomed to "cutting" your price in the first place. To put it in our own words, *lan yao xian kan yi dao* ["stop you by cutting your price in the first place"]: If you offer 100, I will counteroffer 50. I know that most probably you will still earn a lot on my 50. This becomes a game played by both buyer and seller. For the seller, because he well anticipates that you are going to cut his price, he therefore sets a great margin in advance, so much so that even if the price is cut by 50%, he could still have a considerable amount of profit to earn. This business atmosphere is prevalent nowadays. I believe that, step by step, things will be improved in pace with the progress of our society.

Illustration 19 is a Chinese answer to the foreign perception of Chinese price sensitivity. When explaining this frequently mentioned Chinese negotiating behavior, the Chinese negotiator refers to the PRC condition. First, the "not very high" living standard makes the Chinese calculate money carefully or so-called *jin da xi suan*. Next, the "bad phenomenon"—that is, the rampant illegal and immoral practice pursued by dishonest business people in China (see the two sections in Chapter 3, Legal Framework and Why Do the Chinese Use Stratagems?)—

makes the Chinese generally assume that any price one quotes must have a great margin (*shuifen* or water content in this illustration) included in it. As a result, the Chinese will automatically *lan yao xian kan yi dao* ("stop you by cutting your price in the first place"). The mechanism behind the Chinese tactic of cutting one's price in the first place without any regard for whether or not one's price is realistic can be seen in "Create something out of nothing" (see Appendix A, Stratagem 7; see also Illustration 18). This tough bargaining culture does not exist, for example, in Sweden and other Scandinavian countries in general in which people seldom bargain when buying goods in the market (except for buying a house or an automobile). The Chinese behavior can therefore frustrate Scandinavian business people. In short, Illustration 19 shows the following:

◆ The Chinese have an overriding tendency to assume that any price must have an excessive water content (margin) built into it.
◆ Fear of cheating by the other party is a reason for the Chinese haggling behavior.
◆ It is not unlikely that Chinese negotiators may ask one to drop one's price by 50%.

Illustration 20

Chinese negotiator: "The ministry told us, 'If you ask me to support you, you must have the majority control in the prospective joint venture.' "

Since the signing of the MOU [Memorandum of Understanding] in March 1993, the two parties had made a number of contacts. We had widespread discussions about how to design and operate this joint venture: the equity shared by each party, the products to be manufactured, whether or not T [technical specification] was to be considered, and so forth. Take the equity share issue as an example. We had a big brawl with V [Swedish company]. When establishing a Chinese-foreign joint venture, the Chinese partner, particularly those like us, being a large important industrial enterprise directly affiliated with the ministry, will insist on having the majority equity. . . . First, we are a ministry-affiliated enterprise. Second, our enterprise has a good market background. Besides, we have always had the support of the ministry in terms of industrial policy, and so much so that the ministry told us, "If you ask me to support you, you must have the majority control in the prospective joint venture." This is the opinion on which the ministry has always insisted. The issue is also associated with the state's sovereignty, which is considered critically important.

Illustration 20 concerns a major contentious issue involved in a Chinese-Swedish joint venture negotiation. The Chinese strongly desired to have a majority control in the joint venture—a marked commercial behavior of Chinese negotiators. The PRC condition (see the two sections in Chapter 3, Politics and Economic Planning) is at work in this illustration. The Chinese negotiator referred repeatedly to the instructions of the "ministry." What the Chinese side did was nothing more than the execution of the "opinion" of the ministry. In short, Illustration 20 shows the following:

◆ The Chinese wish to have the majority share of equity in Sino-foreign business joint ventures.
◆ What the Chinese insist on is nothing more than the execution of the instructions of the Chinese government (e.g., industrial ministries).

Illustration 21

Western negotiator: "Business is done not in a conference room or in an official negotiation, but rather over the mah-jongg table at home or in a hotel room."

Business in China is very much personal-chemistry steered and relationship driven. I think that people here always do business with relationships. It is always the persons in the companies who have relations who develop business processes with each other. In China, this is more prominent than in Sweden. You may be an expert in other Asian markets and able to tackle problems in one country after another, but China is by no means the same. . . . There are two kinds of relationships in China. One is the relationship in which people feel empathy, i.e., people know each other as persons. This type of relationship is probably not so common actually. A common relationship which I have perceived is when people feel mutual benefit. People build relationships upon the fact that they need and depend on each other and also have reciprocal joy from each other. . . . Another important point which I believe is that we Westerners, that is, we who do not speak Chinese, will always remain "visitors" and "secondhand people." We will not be on-site when business is done. Business is done not in a conference room or in an official negotiation, but rather over the mah-jongg table at home or in a hotel room. It is very much a question of language and also a question of culture. . . . I don't know if you met P [local Chinese]. He is in a totally different situation. Although we have the same position, he can go out and do business with customers, but I can't. I can start up and define the project and so on, but do business, no.

Illustration 21 is refined from my interview with a marketing manager of a Swedish company in China. It offers insight into understanding the Chinese way of doing business. First, Chinese business negotiating style has a social dimension—that is, Chinese negotiators attach great importance to interpersonal relationships or *guanxi* in business negotiations. *Guanxi* can be established through informal social activities beyond the negotiation table. *Guanxi*, as discussed previously (see Chapter 3, Confucianism), is essentially a reciprocal exchange of favors. Therefore, good *guanxi* between the negotiating parties would help smooth the negotiation and conclude the business easily. Second, there exists a pre-negotiation phase in the Chinese business negotiation process. That is, prior to the formal face-to-face negotiation, the Chinese try to size up (a strategic behavior; see Appendix A, Stratagem 31) and get familiar with the other party (a Confucian behavior; see Chapter 3, Moral Cultivation) mostly through informal social activities, such as playing mah-jongg, as witnessed in this illustration. Trust and *guanxi* play key roles. The illustration even suggests that business in China could be concluded without formal face-to-face negotiation sessions at all as long as parties have good *guanxi* and great mutual trust. Finally, the illustration suggests that, from the point of view of foreign companies, it is important to use local Chinese employees in doing business with China. Why could the Swede in this illustration not do business as effectively as did his local Chinese colleague? The answer is because Chinese society is familistic and the Chinese are family-minded people (see Chapter 3, Family Orientation). Trust can be established easily among family members, which is usually not the case for non-family members. The Chinese customer and the local Chinese colleague shared some common cultural identity (e.g., both are Chinese, from the same region, and speak the same language; see Illustration 23). This helped create a "quasi-family" atmosphere in which they felt comfortable doing business with each other. In addition, the local Chinese employees can be a great asset in communicating with the Chinese side and dealing with Chinese bureaucracy due to their obvious cultural and language advantages. In summary, Illustration 21 indicates the following:

◆ Chinese business negotiating style has a social dimension.
◆ The Chinese attach great importance to becoming familiar with the other party's style, personality, and sincerity through social activities beyond the negotiation table.
◆ There exists a pre-negotiation phase in the Chinese business negotiation process; business can largely be decided in the informal prenegotiation phase.
◆ Local Chinese employees are an asset in doing business in China; foreign firms should actively train and use their local Chinese resources.

Illustration 22

Western negotiator: "The Chinese want to get acquainted with you first."

They [the Chinese] are friendly, I think. You are well received [by the Chinese]. They probably consider meeting us foreigners interesting. Even when you, as a lone Westerner, go for a walk in town and in the local department store, the Chinese find it fun to watch you. They are very curious. They could be almost impertinent toward you, but always in a pleasant way, as I see it. . . . Social contact is important in Asia. Swedes are, generally speaking, poor at making social contact. While we would rather do business straight ahead, at once, the Chinese want to get acquainted with you first. And most probably, you may not achieve anything in the first meeting, which is more of a social gathering. But then, when you have met them at least twice, you become a friend. Afterwards, the atmosphere becomes better and you can begin negotiating with them in real terms.

Illustration 22 demonstrates the social dimension of Chinese business negotiating style. It indicates the importance of the Chinese getting to know the other party through social activities before formal negotiation commences. The Chinese want to make friends with the members on the other team and try to create a friendly atmosphere before negotiating on real terms. They generally do not go straight to detailed discussions but instead try to get acquainted first to establish a feeling of trust in the other party. Therefore, the first meeting tends not to be a business meeting. This is a typical Confucian negotiating behavior (see the two sections in Chapter 3, Moral Cultivation and Importance of Interpersonal Relationships). Briefly, Illustration 22 indicates the following:

- ◆ Social activities pervade the Chinese business negotiation process, particularly in the prenegotiation phase.
- ◆ The Chinese do not go straight into business negotiations but rather try to get acquainted with the other party first to establish mutual trust.
- ◆ One may not achieve anything in the first meeting with the Chinese.
- ◆ Patience is of vital importance in negotiating successfully with the Chinese.

Illustration 23

Chinese negotiator: "A friend coming to us to explain would always be much better than the same work performed by a *laowai*."

Another very important reason that we finally chose M [Swedish company] was that it had *zhong jian ren* ["middleman"], that is, Hong Kong-based company X and M's Chinese employee, L. X's boss has very good *guanxi* not only with our provincial government leaders, but also with leaders of our enterprise. . . . L was a Shanghainese working for

M China at that time. He was on the Swedish team and contributed a lot to the success of this project. He was a good friend of ours. He knew and had good *guanxi* with both sides. He was like the "matchmaker" in marriage. You know we are all people who have feelings. Whenever the negotiations deadlocked, L came to explain between the parties. A friend coming to us to explain would always be much better than the same work performed by a *laowai* ["foreigner"]. This is, in effect, a question of *trust*.

Illustration 23 shows that Chinese business negotiating style has a social dimension in which *guanxi* and trust are key variables. It emphasizes the importance of establishing trust and *guanxi* in business negotiations with China. The illustration concerns a joint venture negotiation in southeast China in 1991 in which the Swedish company M was competing with an American company for the project. One "very important" reason that the Chinese picked the Swedish company M was the matchmaker, or more specifically, *guanxi*. The Hong Kong-based firm, X, was working as a consultant in this project. X's good *guanxi* with the provincial political leaders as well as with the leaders of the Chinese company played a key role. The illustration demonstrates the awareness of the Swedish company M of the impact of the PRC condition and Confucianism on Chinese business negotiating style. The local Chinese employee L's "friendship" with the Chinese team and his "Shanghainese" identity[7] helped create trust and harmony in the negotiation. The illustration also indicates that, in case of deadlock, the Chinese prefer to use a friend of both sides to act as a mediator because a friend means trust, which can help break the impasse. This behavior mirrors the Confucian notion of family members helping each other, avoiding conflict and achieving harmony (see Chapter 3, Confucianism). In brief, Illustration 23 demonstrates the following:

◆ Trust and *guanxi* are key social elements in Chinese business negotiation.

◆ Good *guanxi* with the Chinese government officials and company executives is crucial to effective negotiation with China.

◆ The Chinese tend to use a trusted go-between in communicating with the foreign party when the negotiations run aground.

◆ The foreign company's local Chinese employees can make significant contributions to the success of negotiations with China.

Illustration 24

> **Western negotiator: "Chinese do business with you, *not* with your company."**
>
> I did not come to live in China until February last year [1994]. But I had lived in Hong Kong since 1983 and in Singapore since 1979. I have worked with Chinese all the time, and I like to work with the Chinese. If you have got a Chinese as your friend, he is your friend for life. Business in China is not about doing business between organizations, but about doing business between people. If people are business partners, they get to know each other and become personal friends who visit each other frequently. So, you have business when you have established an interpersonal relationship. This is what Swedish companies find difficult to comprehend. Therefore, you cannot change your people frequently. Your successor does not automatically inherit your friends and relationships. As I perceive, Chinese do business with you, *not* with your company. You have a certain influence over how your company functions. The company does what you promise, for example, deliver in time. . . . You can't be blue-eyed and believe that you have made friends through one or two deals. It takes a little more time.

Illustration 24 demonstrates that business relationships in China are essentially interpersonal relationships between the people involved. This is not strange because Confucianism has not defined any interorganizational relationships. Instead, Confucius created five sets of human relationships, the so-called "Five Cardinal Relationships," all of which are family-oriented (see the two sections in Chapter 3, Importance of Interpersonal Relationships and Family Orientation). Relationships are person specific and cannot be transferred. It follows that Chinese negotiators will naturally take a people-oriented approach toward negotiations; they "do business with you, not with your company." This is, according to the Swedish interviewee in this illustration, what Swedish companies find difficult to understand. The illustration also implies that a genuine Chinese friend is your friend for life. This is well in line with the Confucian notions of trust and family. In China, a trusting friendship between people takes time to cultivate; organizational trust is built largely on individual trust (see Chapter 3, Moral Cultivation). Therefore, continuity is critical; frequent rotation of members on the foreign team would make the Chinese feel confused and disappointed and cause negotiations to be less effective or more time-consuming. In summary, Illustration 24 indicates the following:

◆ There is a strong people orientation in the Chinese approach to business negotiation; the Chinese view business relationships between organizations essentially as interpersonal relationships between the people in the organizations; organizational trust follows individual trust.

◆ A genuine Chinese friend is your friend for life; it takes time, however, to make friends and establish rapport with a Chinese.

◆ From the vantage point of establishing a firm, trusting interpersonal relationship with the Chinese, continuity is critical; the foreign side must maintain a consistent team without frequent rotation of the members.

Illustration 25

Chinese negotiator: "Negotiations should be held between people of similar age and rank."

The big difference in age [between negotiating partners] should be avoided as much as possible. We made a mistake, though unintentionally. Once, a Swede came whose rank was something like vice general director in charge of the terminal department, I cannot remember exactly now. He is a senior person of great age. From our side, at that time, we could only send a 20-year-old, or so, young man to talk to the Swede. I do not know how the foreigners see this matter. In our opinion, what we did was very impolite, but we really had no other alternatives at that time. It might have been OK to send another person of an age similar to that of the Swede, but then he could probably have negotiated nothing. Still, I must apologize for this matter. I have not expressed our apology to date [to the Swedish party], but I feel that we should apologize. No matter what the foreigners' opinion is, we Chinese consider it very impolite. We think that negotiations should be held between people of similar age and rank. We do our best to choose [negotiators] among our people. . . . If a 20-year-old foreigner came to negotiate with our 50-year-old, we would also consider that this was not very suitable.

Illustration 25 indicates that Chinese negotiators are highly conscious of the age and rank of members on the foreign team. From the Chinese point of view, a large difference in age and rank between the negotiating counterparts must be avoided. The Chinese would consider it "impolite" and "not very suitable" for one party to send a young person to negotiate with an old person from the other party. This Chinese negotiating behavior is a direct product of the Confucian respect for age and hierarchy (see Chapter 3, Respect for Age and Hierarchy). From the Chinese stratagems perspective, the Chinese propensity to negotiate with the "big guns" can be interpreted as a stratagem (see Appendix A, Stratagem 18). My view is that, in this particular illustration, the Chinese seemed to have been driven fundamentally by Confucianism rather than by the Chinese stratagems. That the Chinese select negotiators according to their age may sound ridiculous to Westerners. "Age," however, is an important element in the Chinese business negotiations, as shown in the illustration. This influences directly how a foreign firm selects its people who are to work in China or negotiate with the Chinese. In brief, Illustration 25 indicates the following:

- ◆ Chinese negotiators are highly conscious of the age and rank of members of the other party.
- ◆ For foreign companies, it is vitally important to send the right people to China for negotiations; age and rank are two considerations.

Illustration 26

Western negotiator: "If you behave yourself, the Chinese behave themselves as well."

On my first trip to China, someone said that one must show a "poker face" and sit stiffly when dealing with the Chinese. I said that this was not my style. I have discovered that if you behave yourself, the Chinese behave themselves as well. This is rather simple. If you are natural, so are they. Should you play the game, then there will never be any people so intelligent as the Chinese to penetrate your posture and your way of expressing yourself to see if you are sincere. The Chinese have thousands of years of experience in it. You can never come in the vicinity of the Chinese regarding the analysis of people and of how you react, whether you are yourself or playing happy. If you play the game and if you are not sincere, then I have a feeling that the Chinese will have a terribly good memory. If you change your ideas all the time without any reasonable justifications, the Chinese will draw the conclusion that "I cannot trust him."

Illustration 26 is extracted from my interview with a senior Swedish negotiator with decades of negotiating experience with the Chinese. The illustration raises a central and subtle question about the holistic understanding of the Chinese business negotiating style: What is a Chinese negotiator? Is he a "sincere" Confucian gentleman or a "tactful" "Sun Tzu-like" strategist? This Swedish negotiator's experience provides an answer: It depends on how you behave yourself in front of the Chinese. The Chinese will behave as gentlemen when you behave as a gentleman; they will employ stratagems when you play the games. Why? The answer is because the Chinese notion of relationships is highly reciprocal. The Chinese are a people who will *bao* ("respond," "repay," or "retaliate") everything you do (see Chapter 3, Importance of Interpersonal Relationships). They are shaped by both Confucian-type cooperation and Sun Tzu-type competition (see Chapter 3, Chinese Business Culture and East Asian Economic Miracles). As is also shown in Illustration 11, honesty plays an important part in Chinese business negotiation. Honesty is a shrewd strategy that foreign companies should use for effective negotiations with the Chinese. It helps pull one's relationship with the Chinese toward the "cooperation" Confucian working state in which the parties do business on the basis of great mutual trust and cooperation. To summarize, Illustration 26 demonstrates the following:

◆ Chinese negotiators can behave both sincerely and tactfully; the other party's attitude toward the Chinese side is a vehicle affecting the behavior of the Chinese.

◆ The Chinese will behave as gentlemen when one behaves as a gentleman; they will employ stratagems when one plays games.

◆ Honesty is crucial to successful negotiation with the Chinese because it helps pull one's relationship with the Chinese toward the Confucian cooperation working state.

▓ Illustration 27

Western negotiator: "The Chinese are very suspicious."

The Chinese are very suspicious. It takes a long time to convince a Chinese that you are really telling the truth rather than trying to cheat him. This is probably why negotiation often takes a long time. Second, I believe that it is also a negotiating tactic of the Chinese side to push and see where your limit lies when you become impatient and irritated. You must be prepared for this. You must be aware that the more time it takes with the Chinese, the greater the chance your business turns out well. I also believe that if we want to convince the Chinese that we are serious, we must show that we are prepared to put time into business and not expect a big deal quickly. I even believe that even if you could persuade a Chinese within a day, he would feel that he had done a bad business and been cheated.

Illustration 27 deals with the social aspect of Chinese business negotiations. It shows that one reason Chinese business negotiation often takes time is suspicion. Suspicion is a rather typical Confucian attitude toward strangers or non-family members (see Chapter 3, Family Orientation). China is a familistic society in which there is a strong distrust of outsiders (non-family members), and it takes considerable time to build trust between non-family members. This traditional Chinese behavior has been reinforced recently by the Cultural Revolution, which resulted in people being less trusting toward others (see Chapter 3, Politics). As a result, the Chinese distrust fast talkers who want to make quick deals (Pye, 1982). Moreover, suspicion and prudence may also come from the typical Chinese intelligence and alertness that are deeply seated in the Chinese stratagems (see Chapter 3, Sun Tzu Principle 7, and Appendix A, Stratagem 33). Illustration 19 also shows that rampant illegal and immoral practices in China make the people highly suspicious of any price offered; they assume that there is a substantial water content, or large margin, in any offer price. China is on a steep learning curve in international business due to its relatively new opening to the rest of the world. There have been many cases in which the Chinese were fooled by foreigners in business negotiations due to the Chinese lack of international commercial experience (e.g., as shown in Illustration 11). Therefore, Chinese suspicion can well be expected in business negotiations in which the Chinese are not familiar with the other party. The illustration also points to the possibility that Chinese negotiators may use delaying tactics to pressure and wear down the other party (see Appendix A, Stratagem 4). The illustration shows that time is an important element in Chinese business negotiations. Linking Chinese negotiating style with time or the negotiation process is important for a holistic understanding of the Chinese behavior. Therefore, the negotiation process should be involved as a building block in the model of Chinese business negotiating style this book intends to construct (see Chapter 5, A Model of Chinese Business Negotiating Style). Finally, the illustration indicates that successful negotiation with China calls for great perseverance and patience on the part of Western negotiators. To summarize, Illustration 27 demonstrates the following:

◆ The Chinese tend to be suspicious of the other party in the beginning of negotiations.

◆ Time is an important element in Chinese business negotiations.

◆ The Chinese tend to regard good business as a time-consuming process; they do not believe in a quick big deal.

◆ The Chinese may use delaying tactics to wear the other party down.

◆ Great perseverance and patience are called for when negotiating with the Chinese.

Illustration 28

Western negotiator: "Language has caused enormous problems."

I made it clear very early that I must always have my own qualified person with me who knew both technology and the Chinese terminology. For there is a problem in China within technical areas. You may get an array of translations even from the same English expression. In English, it means the same thing regardless of which technical issues you are working with, but, in Chinese, it has a totally different translation. Therefore, if you did not have the technical knowledge, you would not have the least idea what people were actually talking about. Language has caused enormous problems. Swedish technicians and engineers often say that Chinese technical people are a bit stupid or backward, since they express themselves in stupid terms. This is because the interpretation is poor. I am profoundly convinced that the Chinese engineers think exactly the same as the Swedish engineers do. Many times I asked myself, "It is strange. How can he say things like that?" But it all depends on the interpreter. I had negotiated via an unknown Chinese interpreter with 15 to 20 Chinese sitting in the negotiation room. They did not introduce the negotiating team leader. It didn't matter. I recognized you after a while when you were talking about and looking askance at the interpreter. I used to do this when I felt the interpretation sounded strange: I told and showed the interpreter that I couldn't understand what he was talking about. So, people all came up to the blackboard and drew pictures instead. Then, we could understand each other and our discussion could continue. We could reach agreement even though we didn't understand each other's language, because everyone understood the pictures. Electricians understood the electric circuit diagrams. Had we continued our discussion via the interpreter, nobody would have understood anything.

Illustration 28 demonstrates the social aspect of Chinese negotiation—language and communication. Language constitutes a formidable barrier in Chinese-foreign business negotiation (also evident in Illustration 11). The poor foreign language ability on the part of the Chinese side might be ascribed to the PRC condition that the education level on average is rather low. Nevertheless, as shown in this illustration, problems of a linguistic nature also exist. The same English words may have different versions of interpretation or different terminology when translated into Chinese. This can be a source of misunderstanding even in the situation in which the interpreter is "perfect" in the sense of language per se but without special knowledge about the technology in question. The illustration shows that language is so important in Chinese negotiations that it can sometimes help one identify the Chinese chief negotiator. The illustration also shows that saying "No" to the Chinese (i.e., telling the truth that you do not understand what the Chinese interpreter is talking about) is necessary and important so that effective communication and discussion between the parties can be ensured and the Chinese may not feel they have lost face (see Illustration 11). In short, Illustration 28 indicates the following:

- ◆ Language is a major barrier in Chinese-foreign business negotiations.
- ◆ Language can sometimes help one identify the Chinese chief negotiator.
- ◆ It is important to employ a qualified interpreter in Chinese business negotiation who knows both language and the technology in question.
- ◆ Saying "No" to the Chinese is necessary and important so that effective communication and discussion between the parties can be ensured.

Illustration 29

Chinese negotiator: "If he still works as interpreter, we will not negotiate anymore."

BB [an American Chinese, approximately age 30, bilingual, and working as an interpreter and consultant on the Swedish team] is a very intelligent person. However, after months of working with him, many of us felt that he was too arrogant and that he did not care about Chinese etiquette. In translation, he frequently added his own opinions. For example, he often prevented us from saying what we liked to say. He persuaded us not to do this and that, boasting there was nothing in the world he had never seen. Whenever we wanted to gain more power, he stopped us and said, "Why contend for power?" He asked us to do nothing but to sit quiet and receive money. . . . Once, at the dinner table, no sooner had our CEO even touched his chopsticks than BB was already starting to serve himself. This was just horribly impolite! . . . That's why Lao Z [chief Chinese negotiator] said, "If he still works as interpreter, we will not negotiate anymore."

Illustration 29 sheds light on Confucian ethics in Chinese business negotiation. The Chinese respect age and hierarchy (see the section in Chapter 3, Respect for Age and Hierarchy), attach great importance to etiquette (see the concept of *li* in Chapter 3), and show the need for moderation and harmony (see Chapter 3). In Chinese society, "No beard, no business" prevails. A Confucian passages states, "In the concluding feast, honored places were given to people with white hair, so as to follow the order of seniority" (see Chapter 3, Respect for Age and Hierarchy; see also the sections *Li* and *Keqi*). It seems that BB's "arrogance," "boasting," and "not caring about Chinese etiquette" violated the Chinese codes of etiquette and hurt the Chinese negotiators, which resulted in BB being rejected by the Chinese as an interpreter in the later phases of negotiations. The author also interviewed BB and found that he was a straightforward, fast-speaking, and matter-of-fact person who had constructive and helpful ideas for the Chinese as well as the Swedes. I found that BB had plenty of guts to say "No"—a very positive quality for effective negotiation with the Chinese (see Illustrations 11, 28, and 34). The problem, however, was that BB's way of expressing his ideas and his behavior seemed too direct and sharp (perhaps unintentionally) so the Chinese found it uncomfortable to accept, at least at the face-to-face level. I guess that if he had used an indirect way of saying "No" to the Chinese, he would have remained as the interpreter in the negotiations. The illustration also points to the fact that having an overseas Chinese on a foreign negotiating team may not bring about an automatic advantage; it depends on the person's personality, cultural sensitivity and adaptability, and communication skills, not merely on language ability. In short, Illustration 29 indicates the following:

◆ The Chinese pay special attention to *li* (etiquette, courtesy, ceremony, etc.) in business negotiations.

◆ The Chinese have disdain for an opponent's arrogant and aggressive behavior.

◆ Being courageous and saying "No" to the Chinese is a good trait; however, "No" should be expressed in a proper manner.

◆ A careless, unintentional violation of the Chinese codes of etiquette may jeopardize business opportunities.

◆ Having an overseas Chinese on a foreign team may not bring about an automatic advantage; it depends on the person's personality, cultural sensitivity and adaptability, and communication skills, not merely on language ability.

Illustration 30

Western negotiator: "There was only water in his glass!"

I have many funny things to tell you about the Chinese. Let me just recall some for you. We have had a lot of fun with the Chinese when having dinner with them. The Chinese from northern China drink more than the Chinese from southern China. Guangdong Chinese seldom drink; while Liaoning Chinese drink more than we Swedes do. In the banquets, we sometimes encountered some Chinese with a "dirty little trick." They poured [wine] out of their glasses instead of drinking it up. They poured in water and the like in the glass. We have actually got to know a trick there. Once a man [Chinese negotiator] was sitting there, clinking his glass with each of us. He never became drunk; but we were already feeling dizzy. Then, before his eyes, we exchanged glasses with him: We took his and he took ours. There was only water in his glass! He was forced to drink from our glass. . . . When you are uncertain about a Chinese, you must always exchange your glass with his.

Illustration 30 demonstrates the interesting scene of a Chinese business banquet. Eating is important in China. Chinese people treat food as "heaven," as the following Chinese proverb states: "For the people, food is heaven." Therefore, eating and banquets always accompany Chinese business negotiations. Banquets can be viewed as being driven by a Confucian motivation—to get to know people, cultivate friendship, and strengthen *guanxi* (see Chapter 3, Importance of Interpersonal Relationships). From the Chinese stratagems perspective, however, the banquets also provide a good opportunity for the Chinese to size up the other party's traits. This is where "water in his glass" could happen—a stratagem whose prototype can be found in Stratagems 8 and 25 in Appendix A. The Chinese purpose is to test and size up the personality of the other party in social activities (see Appendix A, Stratagem 31). In fact, competing and pretending to be a big drinker by secretly drinking water instead of wine is an accepted form of table manners not uncommon at all at the Chinese dining table. This reminds one of the definition of *ji* (stratagems) as "a socially allowed though not necessarily encouraged scheme" (see Chapter 3, Chinese Stratagems).

What seems most inspiring is the point made by the Swedish negotiator: "When you are uncertain about a Chinese, you must always exchange your glass with his." It implies that, as a foreigner, one cannot fully imitate the "Chinese way" of drinking, thinking, and behaving; rather, one should be aware of the Chinese way of drinking, thinking, and behaving but be oneself. Honesty and openness pay off in dealing with the Chinese (see Illustrations 11, 28, and 34). To neutralize the Chinese tactics, we must "raise the issue explicitly" (see Chapter 2, Negotiation Strategies). In summary, Illustration 30 demonstrates the following:

◆ Eating and banquets always accompany Chinese business negotiations.

◆ The Chinese are both Confucian gentlemen and Sun Tzu-like strategists; banquets and social activities are a way for Chinese to both establish friendly *guanxi* with the other party and size up its personality and style.

◆ It is important to respect Chinese culture but be oneself—"When you are uncertain about a Chinese, you must always exchange your glass with his."

Illustration 31

Western negotiator: "Chinese want to 'win-lose' you."

Chinese employ negotiating tactics, of course. For example, we were invited to Beijing several times for negotiations just 1 week before Christmas Day. . . . In negotiation, *ji* thinking constitutes absolutely far more than 10% [of Chinese mentality]. I believe it accounts for more than 50%. I agree that *ji* is built into the Chinese mentality and the Chinese can adopt it *xia yi shi* ["unconsciously"]. . . . Furthermore, I believe the "win-lose" type of Chinese negotiators makes up the larger proportion. As a matter of fact, the Chinese set out to win and want to see the other party lose. That is, in my words, the Chinese want to "win-lose" you, though the intended margin may vary from situation to situation and from people to people. However, with the deepening of negotiations, it may turn out to be a "win-win" situation or even "lose-win" situation. Nevertheless, whether it is "win" or "lose," the Chinese always have their ways to please their *lingdao* ["superiors" or "leaders"] from certain perspectives, claiming that they are the *winner*. Otherwise, they may be blamed for being incompetent and not being able to accomplish their task.

Illustration 31 is cited from my interview with a senior Swedish negotiator (local Chinese) in a Swedish multinational's subsidiary in Hong Kong who has a wealth of negotiation experience from dealing with mainland Chinese since the 1970s. The illustration implies that there is a strategic dimension to Chinese business negotiating style: The Chinese do employ tactics in business negotiations, intentionally or unconsciously or both. *Ji* or Chinese stratagems are a cultural phenomenon that permeates the socialization process of Chinese people (see Chapter 3, Chinese Stratagems). In the interviewee's words, "*Ji* is built into the Chinese mentality and the Chinese can adopt it unconsciously." The invitation to conduct negotiations in Beijing 1 week prior to Christmas Day is just one example of using the Chinese stratagems (see Appendix A, Stratagem 22). The reason that the Chinese want to win-lose you can be translated from the perspectives of both the PRC condition (see Chapter 3, Chinese Bureaucracy) and Confucianism (see Chapter 3, Concept of Face). For the former, the Chinese can show their *lingdao* (superiors and authorities) that they are the winners and are not to be blamed for being incompetent. For the latter, although not indicated in the illustration (but see Chapter 3, Legacy of Confucianism?), the Chinese gain face when they believe they have won. Therefore, it seems culturally necessary to, for example, pad one's price to the level that one can give away the margin to the Chinese to let them gain face and show they are the winner. The percentage of Chinese who are win-win or win-lose negotiators is a matter of debate. At the national sociocultural level, I believe that the Chinese are both win-win and win-lose negotiators who use both cooperation and competition strategies in negotiation depending on the circumstances (e.g., *guanxi*, personalities, and situational factors). In brief, Illustration 31 demonstrates the following:

◆ Chinese business negotiating style has a strategic dimension.
◆ The Chinese may employ tactics in business negotiation intentionally or unconsciously or both.

◆ The Chinese " 'win-lose' you" bargaining can result from the Chinese motivation to please superiors and gain face in front of them.

◆ It seems culturally necessary to, for example, pad one's price to the level that one can give away the margin to the Chinese to let them gain face and show they are the winners.

◆ The Chinese are both win-win and win-lose negotiators who use both cooperation and competition strategies in negotiation; which strategy is used depends on the circumstances (e.g., *guanxi*, personalities, and situational factors).

Illustration 32

Western negotiator: "The Chinese said, 'Before the negotiation, we had divided our work internally.' " (Figure 4.3)

That was in Beijing in 1986. We were negotiating with *zhongcan* [Headquarters of the General Staff of the People's Liberation Army] about selling our products. The contract was not large, valued at under U.S.$100,000. In the midst of one face-to-face negotiation, one Chinese team member whom I did not know at all suddenly stood up, shouting angrily at me, "YY [full Chinese name of the interviewee]! You cannot cheat me! I am from Guangdong, I know your price there. . . . " I had totally lost myself. I didn't know this person at all. How could he be so rude to me? . . . It was exactly 2 years after this encounter that we met each other again at a dinner party. We had gotten acquainted with each other during the years due to the business we did. We were there chatting quite friendly. When we recalled that past unpleasant encounter, the Chinese said, "I am sorry. It was not my intention to attack you personally, you who I did not know. Before the negotiation, we had *fen gong* ["divided our work"] internally. If you came up with a price above our line, I would stand up and shout. If not, my colleagues would play the game differently."

Illustration 32 tells a story of how the Chinese manipulated tactics in a business negotiation. It shows that the Chinese negotiators did their homework well. They went to great lengths to collect information about the other party prior to the negotiation (see Appendix A, Stratagems 31 and 33). During the face-to-face meeting, members of the Chinese team

Figure 4.3. "The Chinese Said, 'Before the Negotiation, We Had Divided Our Work Internally.'"
SOURCE: Cartoon by Björn Böke; copyright 1998 by Tony Fang.

coordinated with one another in a way commonly known to the Chinese as playing "red face" (tough) and "white face" (soft) (see Appendix A, Stratagem 11). The Chinese attacked the other party by borrowing or referring to the external force—that is, the other party's price offered in Guangdong previously (see Appendix A, Stratagems 3 and 29). They showed their anger openly in front of a foreign negotiating team, hoping to shame and shatter its personality and confidence (see Appendix A, Stratagem 13). The illustration also suggests that the Chinese tend to behave rather "rudely" toward and haggle "ruthlessly" with strangers. Once the negotiating parties become familiar with each other and become friends, however, a Confucian family type of atmosphere will be created in which secrets seem to be nonexistent (see Chapter 3, Confucianism). In summary, Illustration 32 indicates the following:

- ◆ Chinese negotiators plan negotiations and do their homework well.
- ◆ The Chinese go to great lengths to collect intelligence information about the other party.

◆ The Chinese tend to haggle ruthlessly with strangers.

◆ The Chinese can show anger openly in front of the foreign negotiating team.

◆ The Chinese can play red face and white face in business negotiations.

Illustration 33

Western negotiator: "They told us that things must be ready on Saturday when the mayor would come to the banquet."

A tactic that I believe that the Chinese employ is that the middle managers have agreed with those at higher levels, perhaps not only at the level of the company they represent, but also at provincial or municipal level, that they set the "deadline" on a certain week and arrange a banquet long before the contract is actually ready. They told us that things must be ready on Saturday when the mayor would come to the banquet. In this way the Chinese applied pressure on us to reach an agreement. This was common. We learned that this was a mere trap, because if we didn't go in and accept their terms, they had to cancel the banquet anyway. You became a little disappointed the first time you came across such a situation. But, after a while, when you recognized the same thing happening again in other places, you knew that it was a tactic.

Illustration 33 presents a Swedish negotiator's perception of how the Chinese tried to apply pressure on the other party by setting a deadline on the negotiating schedule—the banquet was arranged and politicians would be coming. This tactic can be interpreted from Stratagem 22 in Appendix A. The illustration suggests that the Chinese try to control the pace of negotiation to their advantage (see Appendix A, Stratagem 4). What seems unique for the Chinese case is that the tactic might produce a magic effect for the Chinese given foreigners' general knowledge about the Chinese decision-making process and bureaucracy (see Chapter 3, The PRC Condition). Again, the illustration implies that the best strategy that foreign negotiators can use is to honestly let their Chinese partner know what they can and cannot offer the Chinese. Honesty pays off and can neutralize the Chinese stratagems in negotiations, which is also suggested in Illustrations 11 and 30. In brief, Illustration 33 indicates the following:

- ◆ The Chinese try to control the pace and agenda of business negotiations to their advantage.
- ◆ The Chinese can set a deadline on negotiations and apply pressure on the other party.
- ◆ The best way to withstand the Chinese tricks is honesty; honesty pays off.

Illustration 34

Western negotiator: "He utilized *face*, I would say."

I can give an example of how face influences our business environment. We have a director [Chinese] as our customer. His demands are often high, and he has ideas about doing things his way. I understand that one should never say "No" to a Chinese. It's just impossible and it won't work. This ["No"] is a word that one does not use here. It happened that Director C [Chinese negotiator] took advantage of our silence. He treated it as a confirmation, a "Yes." He interpreted more than what we actually promised. Then he went out, talking to all the subbureaus and local operators under his control that A [Swedish company] would be doing this and that. Afterwards, when we presented our plans which turned out not to be the ones he had demanded, he "lost face" because he had promised everyone and everywhere. Therefore, he put very much pressure on us to live up to his demands. Furthermore, he had to make sure that everyone knew that it was the fault of A that did not live up to its promise. . . . He had not misinterpreted anything. On the contrary, he interpreted it as he liked, and it was clear that he did this on purpose. He utilized *face*, I would say. This influenced our business situation. He had had a major influence on our working and business environment. . . . To deal with the Chinese, you need patience, patience, and patience.

Illustration 34 shows that foreigners' stereotypical image of China and the Chinese can be strategically used by Chinese negotiators to their advantage. The case of face is just one example. Earlier, I discussed the Chinese concept of face and its significance in business negotiations (see Chapter 3, Concept of Face). The Chinese avoid saying the word "No" to maintain the face of the parties involved. Many experts on Chinese business negotiating style advise that one will gain much if one helps a Chinese save face, and one will lose more if one does not, no matter how unintentional. Empirical material indicates that Pye's advice is valuable (see Illustration 3). This illustration, however, suggests the opposite. A significant implication offered here is that respecting Chinese face and never saying "No" to the Chinese is advisable only within the domain of business relations between Confucian gentlemen working in an amicable Confucian working atmosphere. Chinese negotiators can culturally be not only Confucian gentlemen but also Sun Tzu-like strategists (cf. Chapter 2, A Wonderful Way of Life; see also the section in Chapter 3, The PRC Condition, Confucianism, and Chinese Stratagems: An Interplay). Therefore, never saying "No" to a Chinese could be dangerous when it is practiced in dealing with a Sun Tzu-like Chinese strategist. Then, as shown in this illustration, one's shyness to say "No" can be taken advantage of by the Chinese strategist. This is exactly where a fair amount of previous studies on Chinese business negotiating style have failed. Without systems thinking, and failing to distinguish between the cooperative (Confucian-type) and competitive (Sun Tzu-type) Chinese negotiating strategies, many provided advice that can be misleading and even dangerous. Technically, the tactic that the Chinese "director" in this illustration employed, whether deliberately or inadvertently, exemplifies the Empty City Stratagem (see Appendix A, Stratagem 32; see also Appendix B): The Chinese director did not actually have as many cultural reflections weighing on his mind as his Swedish counterpart had imagined; he simply manipulated and used the Swedish "silence." In other words, he manipulated the Swedish blue-eyed "imitation" of the Chinese way. The illustration suggests that one must not be shattered by Chinese face. Face, like other frequently mentioned Chinese cultural traits (e.g., *guanxi*), can be a myth. One must dare to explode the myth of face and honestly say "No" in a proper way, when it is required, to a Chinese in business negotiations. Following blindly the Chinese way does more harm than good. The best one can do is to respect Chinese sociocultural traits, on the one hand, but be oneself, on the other hand. It is important to dare to say "No" to a Chinese when circumstances require it. As suggested by Illustrations 11 and 28, saying "No" to the Chinese and letting them know what one can and cannot offer or understand will most likely win one's Chinese partner's trust and facilitate communications. Likewise, it is important to dare to create a distance to *guanxi*. Vulgarized *guanxi* results in nepotism that will harm a healthy and efficient working environment. Technically, one can say "No" to the Chinese in a very polite and acceptable manner—for instance, "I am sorry that I find it very difficult to accept your terms, due to . . . (our difficulties)." To express one's opinions candidly is of vital importance to thwart Chinese tactics, as was suggested in Illustrations 30 and 33. Finally, at the end of the interview, when asked for the most important advice for dealing with the Chinese, the Swedish negotiator's answer is three words: patience, patience, and patience. Patience is a popular piece of advice that can be found in almost all the business guides in dealing with the Chinese. What is new with this Swedish negotiator's patience is that this advice is valuable in the light of the Chinese stratagems: One must have great patience and persever-ance to deal with Chinese strategists. In short, Illustration 34 shows the following:

◆ The Chinese may take advantage of foreigners' stereotypical image of China and the Chinese (e.g., face).

◆ Face and other frequently mentioned Chinese cultural traits (e.g., *guanxi*) can be a myth. Foreign business people should learn both to practice them and to distance themselves from them.

◆ It is absolutely important to be courageous and say "No" to a Chinese when circumstances require it.

◆ A good foreign negotiator is a master of the art of respecting Chinese sociocultural traits while being himself; to express one's opin-ions honestly is of great importance to thwart Chinese negotiating tactics.

◆ Great patience and perseverance are required to deal with the Chinese strategists.

Illustration 35

Chinese negotiator: "Nobody would forget that sandwich day!"

Claims that we engage in "protracted war" to deal with foreigners are *absolutely* not true. On the contrary, we sometimes feel foreigners are trying to wear us down. We have no intention to conduct marathon-type negotiations. You know, we are not physically stronger than foreigners. And we do not have the habit of *kai yeche* ["working round the clock"]. I can still remember that we were negotiating with D [Swedish company] twice in Beijing, working as late as until 1 o'clock the next morning for the first meeting, and 4 o'clock for the second. We never moved out of that "basement room" in the hotel after we sat down there about 9 o'clock in the morning. What's more, we were stuffed with sandwiches all day! I myself was relatively used to such cold and uncooked stuff. But most of my colleagues were strangers to Western food and felt very uncomfortable. That day we did not finish our meeting until 1 o'clock the next morning. What a bitter experience! Nobody would forget that sandwich day! . . . . When we finally came back to our representative office in Beijing after midnight, each of us was offered a bowl of warm *zhou* [porridge] with *zhacai* [salted preserved vegetables]. What a relief and refreshment after a whole day's meeting and sandwiches! What a hard and uncomfortable night! We would never negotiate that way in the future.

Illustration 35 provides a Chinese disagreement with the allegation that the Chinese use protracted war or attrition tactics (see Appendix A, Stratagem 20) in Sino-foreign business negotiations. Two reasons that the Chinese negotiator gave are reasonable. First, the Chinese cannot wear others down in a physical way; a Chinese is not physically stronger than a foreigner. Also, working late at night is not a Chinese habit. During my investigation, I learned that the so-called "sandwich" meeting was actually designed and successfully executed by some "China hand" working on the foreign team—using Chinese stratagems (see Appendix A, Stratagems 4 and 20) to deal with the Chinese! Second, many Chinese managers told me that they were actually "chased" so hard by the end users to deliver the ordered systems and equipment that they earnestly wanted to *su zhan su jue* ("fight quickly"—another example of Chinese using war terminology in a business context; see Chapter 3, Implication of Chinese Stratagems). Any delay in delivery of equipment caused by prolonged negotiations means a great loss of money and reputation for the Chinese party. The illustration suggests that although the Chinese are in part Sun Tzu-like strategists, they are not always obsessed with manipulating tactics. They are in part Confucian gentlemen as well, without any regard to ploys. Therefore, unreliable exaggeration about *ji* or Chinese stratagems must be avoided.[8] I believe that explaining Chinese behavior by referring purely to *ji* (see, e.g., Chu, 1991) is incomplete. *Ji* is the "third explanation" or an alternative to the PRC condition and Confucianism in explaining and understanding Chinese business negotiating style. Furthermore, the Western claims of Chinese negotiating tactics—for example, those classified under the 36 Chinese stratagems in Appendix A—must be substantiated and verified based on more empirical evidence. Finally, we should never forget other variables contributing to Chinese negotiating behavior, such as situational factors and individual personalities. The illustration also suggests that more research in the future should be directed toward listening to what Chinese negotiators think, perceive, and feel to obtain a more complete picture of Chinese business negotiating style. In brief, Illustration 35 indicates the following:

◆ The notion of Chinese stratagems must not be exaggerated; it is an alternative to the PRC condition and Confucianism in explaining Chinese business negotiating style.

◆ Western claims of Chinese negotiating tactics need to be substantiated and verified based on more empirical evidence.

◆ Foreign business people should abandon two extreme attitudes toward *ji*: ignorance and overcaution.

◆ Generally, the Chinese are not used to eating Western food.

◆ More research is called for in the future that is directed toward studying how Chinese negotiators perceive themselves.

Illustration 36

Chinese negotiator: "It is not our intention at all to play home court."

It is *not* true that we did this [negotiation taking place in China] *intentionally*. Negotiation often takes place in China because of our financial limitations. It is really not very easy for a Chinese to *chuguo* ["go abroad"]. I would actually feel happy to negotiate in Sweden. I could then have an opportunity to travel in Sweden [laughter]. I had participated in the negotiation on this project countless times, but I have never been to Sweden. To be frank, we do not have the financial resources to travel abroad frequently, particularly for a large team. If negotiating abroad, we would only be able to dispatch very few people, perhaps only one or two persons, wouldn't we? But the situation might actually require four or five persons. And it would be the enterprise rather than the State that would bear all the costs. . . . I can fully understand foreigners saying that we "play home court," and that we take advantage of favorable *tianshi he dili* ["heavenly and terrain conditions"]. Nevertheless, it is not our intention at all to play home court. But, at the same time, I admit that it would be more favorable for China if negotiation takes place in China. After all, you feel strange and insecure when you travel abroad and work in a new environment. This is just like in a sports event. The probability of winning is larger when playing at home, because there are *environmental* and *psychological* factors at work.

Illustration 36 suggests that the so-called playing home court Chinese negotiating tactics (see Appendix A, Stratagem 4), as emphasized by Pye (1982) and Seligman (1990), may be more an outcome of the PRC condition than a deliberate strategic maneuver. China's lack of foreign exchange (see Chapter 3, Backwardness) poses an administrative hurdle for the Chinese negotiating abroad. In this illustration, the Chinese enterprise did not have the financial resources to negotiate abroad. Internal communication within Chinese bureaucracy was another consideration for the Chinese. If negotiating abroad, the Chinese would, as a rule, require a rather large team (see Illustration 6). The illustration suggests that negotiation in China will not only save money but also facilitate internal communication for the Chinese party. Also, there is another obvious reason largely unknown to Westerners: Few Chinese have passports that would allow them to freely apply for a visa for traveling abroad. In China, arranging passports and entry visas involves daunting bureaucratic procedures and is extremely time-consuming. The great majority of Chinese have not been to the West, and generally they are keen on having a chance to travel to Western countries even for reasons of curiosity.[9] Chu (1991, p. 5) stated bluntly that "foreign travel is the most prestigious and sought-after perk available to a Chinese official." Therefore, from this viewpoint, negotiation outside China does not seem completely impossible if the PRC condition is improved (i.e., financial and administrative barriers are removed). At the same time, as the Chinese negotiator also admitted, the Chinese will certainly gain environmental and psychological advantages if the negotiation takes place inside China. The illustration once again indicates that Chinese negotiating style is a product of, and must be understood from, three different sociocultural forces—the PRC condition, Confucianism, and Chinese stratagems. In summary, Illustration 36 indicates the following:

◆ That negotiation often takes place in China may be more an outcome of the PRC condition than a deliberate strategic maneuver.

◆ Chinese negotiating style must be examined and understood in terms of different sociocultural forces—the PRC condition, Confucianism, and Chinese stratagems.

◆ The Chinese negotiators' viewpoint would be helpful for a complete understanding of Chinese negotiating style.

◆ It seems that negotiation outside China is not impossible if the PRC condition is improved (i.e., financial and administrative barriers are removed).

Illustration 37

Chinese negotiator: "What we did was *huo bi san jia.*"

What we did was *huo bi san jia* ["Comparing three vendors when buying goods"]. We talked with J [Japanese company], A [American company], and S [Swedish company] at the same time. First, we crossed off J, mainly because its price was higher and also its reputation was not as good. Then, we tried to make a decision between A and S. This was in 1990. We traveled all the way to visit these two companies, first to the USA and then to Sweden. As a matter of fact, we had different opinions internally. We had to collate our trip findings to conduct further investigation and research. Both A and S were acceptable from the technological point of view, and the main focus was therefore the *price*. Just when we were right in the middle of the discussion about the two suppliers, S's offer came, which was higher than A's. . . . We finally chose A.

Illustration 37 can be interpreted from the Chinese stratagems, the PRC condition, and Confucianism perspectives. *Huo bi san jiu* ("Comparing three vendors when buying goods") is a common Chinese saying that can be understood as another version of "Kill With a Borrowed Knife" (see Appendix A, Stratagem 3). This Chinese behavior of comparing three vendors when buying goods is particularly evident during the early stages of negotiation. The PRC condition, such as the lack of technology and foreign exchange (see the two sections in Chapter 3, Technology and Backwardness), makes Chinese business negotiation basically a technology and price negotiation. That the Chinese attached great importance to the other party's reputation is a Chinese mentality deeply ingrained in Confucian morality (see Chapter 3, Moral Cultivation). In short, Illustration 37 shows the following:

◆ The Chinese tend to compare three vendors when buying goods.
◆ The Chinese examine mainly technology and price in business negotiations.
◆ Reputation is a main criterion by which the Chinese select foreign suppliers.

Illustration 38

Chinese negotiator: "What was important was to let them feel they were being put in a *comparison situation.*"

At that time, we had arranged, rather *ingeniously,* the timing of the meetings with these two companies so that they would not clash with each other. That is, the timing allowed us to negotiate with both companies comfortably at different times. . . . After we signed the feasibility study report with F [foreign company], our factory's deputy director came personally to the negotiation table, giving the news to the S [Swedish company] people. He said we were prepared to sign a similar report with S. . . . Our method was neither too implicit nor too explicit. What was important was to let them feel they were being put in a *comparison situation.* The same rule was applied to both S and F, making both of them feel uneasy and uncertain in their heart, while keeping alive their hopes. . . . From my point of view, we should not hide what did not need to be hidden. Open and frank talking would yield greater profit.

Illustration 38 provides an example of Chinese stratagems: The Chinese were adroit at playing off rival businesses against one another (see Appendix A, Stratagem 3). The Chinese were conducting parallel negotiations intentionally and carefully—negotiating with two foreign companies. They deliberately informed the Swedish company about the progress of their negotiation with another foreign company and vice versa. The Chinese put the two competing partners to a tough psychological test, applying calibrated pressure to both to make them feel uneasy and uncertain. Briefly, Illustration 38 shows the following:

◆ The Chinese can employ stratagems intentionally in negotiations.
◆ The Chinese schedule negotiations carefully.
◆ The Chinese pit competing negotiating partners against each other.

Illustration 39

Chinese negotiator: "Lao Han often appeared absent-minded, not listening to his counterpart, or just keeping silent, as if he didn't understand anything."

Both Lao Han[10] and I are able to *understand* English quite well. There is no big problem for us to understand and read English. Yet, it's true that we are no good at spoken English. . . . *Laowai* ["foreigners"] often judge us at face value and believe that we do not understand English. In the meeting, they explained again and again to us, even with pictures. . . . As a matter of fact, we knew at quite an early stage what the counterpart meant. We merely did not want to state our opinions in a rush. This is a *celue* ["stratagem"]. For instance, Lao Han often appeared absentminded, not listening to his counterpart, or just keeping silent, as if he didn't understand anything. Sometimes he went so far that I became bewildered and couldn't help interrupting him. That's why Lao Han lost his temper with me. Afterwards, I listened to Lao Han's explanation and realized that my interruption was childish indeed.[11]

Illustration 39 demonstrates how Chinese negotiators used translation of language strategically in business negotiations. Given the PRC condition, few Chinese speak foreign languages. Problems of a linguistic nature also exist (see Illustration 28). Chinese negotiators, however, as this illustration suggests, may be able to understand English well (i.e., in terms of listening and reading abilities), even though they are generally poor at spoken English. If this is the case, the Chinese negotiators can, but not necessarily do, use the situation strategically (see Chapter 3, Rational Versus Strategic Patterns of Chinese Negotiating Style). The illustration affords many clues for understanding *ji* (Chinese stratagems), the subtle art of Chinese negotiating—for example, *celue* (see Chapter 3, What Is Ji?), feigning absentmindedness (see Appendix A, Stratagem 27), and keeping silent (see Appendix A, Stratagem 13). In brief, Illustration 39 demonstrates the following:

◆ The fact that Chinese negotiators do not speak but understand English gives them the advantage in negotiations; Chinese negotiators will have twice the response time compared with that of the foreign counterparts.

◆ The Chinese behaviors, such as "being absentminded" and "understanding nothing," can be a strategic game.

Illustration 40

Zhang Xingsheng, Ericsson China:[12] "To do things, you must first 'do people.' "

[Tony Fang: I saw you talking with friends in an ad which I found very interesting. But the only thing missing was a woman!]

Ladies had actually been planned from the beginning. You know, customers often kid me, for I have many beautiful girls working here in my department [business development]. Should our girls really appear in the picture, they would say: "Aha, *Nü Se Ji!*"[13] That's too much [laughter]. . . . The other three in the picture were arranged by the advertising firm. They symbolize the government as well as the customers. After the picture was prepared, we set out to select our slogan. I picked *Zuo shi xian zuo ren* ["To do things, you must first 'do people.' "] as the theme to mirror Ericsson's corporate image. That is, we not only develop science and technology but also attach importance to *renji guanxi* ["interpersonal relationships"]. . . . *Networking* [his own word] or *guanxi* is a major concern in doing business not only in China but also in other parts of the world. Lobbying also exists abroad. If you want to sell your ideas to the government and ask for acceptance, you must lobby. In China and East Asia, this "color" is even stronger. . . . We chose "*zuo* ['do'] *shi* ['thing'] *xian* ['first'] *zuo* ['do'] *ren* ['people']" because we mean to imply that here "*zuo ren*" means not only "become a morally developed person" but also *zuo ren de gongzuo* ["working with people" or "do people"]. We in Ericsson must see to it that we are able to "do people" and do business better than any of our competitors.

Illustration 40 regards a highly publicized ad that appeared in China during 1995 and 1996. The case is specially documented to highlight the central message of this book: Chinese negotiating style is a product of the interplay of the PRC condition, Confucianism, and the Chinese stratagems. To do business effectively with the PRC, foreign firms must be keenly aware of the central role the Chinese government plays in Chinese business negotiations, the dynamics of personal relationships (*guanxi*), and the strategic Chinese thinking (*ji*). It is interesting to me that my line of thought was supported by Mr. Zhang's opening words. Mr. Zhang viewed the Chinese government essentially as a business partner and a direct marketing and lobbying target (i.e., the persons in the ad symbolize the Chinese government as well as customers); he talked about *ji*—a Chinese cultural phenomenon (i.e., the beautiful woman stratagem; see also Appendix A, Stratagem 31), and he emphasized *guanxi* and the people-oriented approach required to do business with China (i.e., do people). It is interesting to observe that Mr. Zhang used the English word *networking* interchangeably with the

Chinese word *guanxi*. He viewed Chinese business essentially as networks of various actors and resources interacting with each other, suggesting that marketing in China is about relationship marketing. Furthermore, this illustration also implies that too much preoccupation with *ji* may not be wise (see also the discussion of a Volvo case in Chapter 3, The Uniqueness of Chinese Negotiating Tactics). As Mr. Zhang said, "That's too much." I also note that running away from *ji*, or negotiating without *ji*, is probably the best *ji* for doing business successfully in China. In short, Illustration 40 indicates the following:

◆ Government, *guanxi*, and *ji* pervade Chinese business practices.

◆ It is important to view the Chinese government as a major business partner and a direct marketing and lobbying target when doing business with China.

◆ Business in China is about working with people, and marketing in China is about relationship marketing.

◆ Too much preoccupation with *ji* may not be a wise *ji*.

Notes

1. Here and throughout the illustrations in this chapter, the term *Western negotiator* refers to "Swedish negotiator."
2. The case described here took place in approximately 1990 and 1991. As noted earlier, China has been steadily improving its record in recent years regarding the protection of intellectual property rights (see Chapter 3, Technology).
3. The Chinese currency is called the *renminbi*, here symbolized by RMB.
4. I was told by the Swedish host that the Chinese delegation's visit to Sweden was carefully prepared. The Chinese were well informed in advance that it would be difficult for them to meet several ministers due to the Swedish summer vacation. One Swedish provincial governor actually broke his summer holiday to meet the Chinese upon their arrival.
5. The "law" refers to "Regulations on the Administration of Technology Import Contracts," which was promulgated by the Chinese government (the State Council) on May 24, 1985.
6. The MPT has been replaced recently by Ministry of Information Industry ("Top Leaders," 1998).
7. The Chinese organization in this case is located within the Yangtze delta, with Shanghai as the geographical center. The Chinese interviewee is also a Shanghai Chinese.
8. My experience with some Westerners indicates that they are either ignorant or overcautious about *ji*. I think we need to abandon both "half-baked" attitudes. Chinese stratagem classics, such as *Art of War, The Thirty-Six Stratagems*, and *Three Kingdoms*,

have gradually been placed on the required reading list of Western business people. When studying Chinese stratagems, it is well to bear in mind the following Chinese admonition: "A heart hostile to others is inexcusable; but a heart wary of others is indispensable." I share the stance of Chen and Ying (1994, p. 27) that "foreign investors should not think that every Chinese businessperson is out to swindle them. However, they must be careful to avoid being reeled in by the fishermen [unscrupulous businessmen] who do exist."

9. The number of Chinese going abroad in 1995 grew by 21% compared with 1994—to 4.5 million ("Asians at Play," 1996, p. 87).

10. The Chinese name Lao Han is fictitious.

11. I also got the chance to interview Lao Han, the chief Chinese negotiator in this case. Lao Han said, "I understood *thoroughly* the meaning of my Swedish counterpart. No sooner had my interpreter finished her translation than I was already prepared to answer the question without a hitch."

12. In October 1995, I was on a local Chinese plane flying from Hong Kong to the mainland. I was attracted by a full-page ad in *CAAC Inflight Magazine* (Issue 5, No. 75, 1995) that I found in the cabin. The ad was from Ericsson China. In the picture, four middle-aged Chinese men are sitting and chatting pleasantly together, one of whom is Mr. Zhang Xingsheng, now Ericsson China's vice president. There are no suits, no ties, and no piles of documents and office duties; they are drinking tea in a cozy traditional Chinese home environment. The picture conveys a plain but profound atmosphere, suggesting somewhat the Swedish passion for nature. In particular, the heading caught my attention: "*Zuo shi xian zuo ren,*" a popular Chinese saying that commonly means "To do things, you must first behave yourself upright." This Chinese expression is a pun that can also be translated as "To do things, you must first 'do people.' " By "do people," the Chinese mean cultivating relationships with people and working with people. "What an ad!" I said to myself. Unfortunately, there was no woman in the ad, a practice that seems neither Swedish nor Chinese in flavor. Out of curiosity, I raised the question as to "Why?" with Mr. Zhang to open my interview with him in Beijing on October 30, 1995.

13. In Chinese, *Nü Se Ji* is equivalent to *Mei Ren Ji* (The beautiful woman stratagem; see Appendix A, Stratagem 31).

5 Conclusions

In this chapter, I summarize theoretical and empirical findings and offer managerial implications. I also discuss the limitations of the book and make suggestions for future research. The most important finding of the book is that the Chinese negotiator is a blend of "Maoist bureaucrat," "Confucian gentleman," and "Sun Tzu-like strategist." Broadly speaking, the negotiating style of a Chinese, whether a People's Republic of China (PRC) citizen or a non-PRC citizen, can be understood as being shaped by the interaction between Confucianism, Chinese stratagems, and the contemporary conditions of the social systems of the countries and regions in which he lives.

Theoretical and Empirical Findings

The purpose of this book is to provide an in-depth and systematic understanding of Chinese business negotiating style in a Chinese sociocultural context. The theoretical and empirical analyses enable achievement of the research purpose and answer the questions raised in Chapter 1.

Six Dimensions of Chinese Business Negotiating Style

In this section, I answer the following research question: What are the primary patterns of Chinese business negotiating behaviors? Western literature distinguishes between three dimensions of business negotiations and negotiating style—that is, technical, commercial, and social dimensions (see the section in Chapter 2, Dimensions of Business Negotiation). The empirical materials of this book, however, suggest that Chinese business negotiating style can be divided into six dimensions: political, legal, technical, commercial, social, and strategic dimensions. These six dimensions represent six primary patterns of Chinese business negotiating behaviors: Political behavior concerns how the Chinese business decision-making process is influenced by Chinese politics; legal behavior deals with the Chinese attitude toward contracting and other legal arrangements; technical behavior concerns the Chinese attitude toward technology, technical specification, quality, and so on; commercial behavior refers to how the Chinese bargain about price and other economic arrangements; social behavior refers to how the Chinese establish trust toward the other party through personal contacts and other forms of social interactions both verbal and nonverbal during the negotiation process; and strategic behavior shows how the Chinese manipulate various negotiating stratagems.

This dimensional analysis also suggests that Chinese business negotiating style involves both rational and strategic patterns. In theoretical terms, political, legal, technical, commercial, and social patterns or dimensions represent rational Chinese negotiating behaviors, whereas the strategic pattern or dimension constitutes strategic Chinese negotiating behaviors—Chinese negotiating tactics. The empirical evidence for the six dimensions is shown as follows based on the illustrations and analyses presented in Chapter 4:

Political Behavior

◆ The Chinese government is the real negotiator, customer, and ultimate decision maker; Chinese companies must follow the government's plan to do business (see Chapter 4, Illustrations 1-3, 5, 8, 20, and 40).

- The frontline Chinese negotiators have a limited mandate and fear criticism; intraorganizational communication within the Chinese negotiating organization is poor, and the Chinese negotiating team tends to be large (see Chapter 4, Illustrations 1, 3, 5, and 6).
- Business in China, whether Chinese or foreign, is under the control of the Chinese government; Chinese business is governed by the "political book"; Chinese partners are protected under the "umbrella" of Chinese bureaucracy (see Chapter 4, Illustrations 1, 4, and 11).

Legal Behavior

- The Chinese view contracting as an initial intention and an ongoing problem-solving framework rather than a one-off nicely wrapped legal package (see Chapter 4, Illustrations 10 and 11).
- The Chinese awareness of law is blunt, and its legal system is young. Chinese lawyers seldom participate in face-to-face meetings, although recently they have begun to increasingly appear (see Chapter 4, Illustrations 4, 9, 11, 12, and 14).
- The Chinese tend to insist that arbitration, if any, is to be held in China (see Chapter 4, Illustration 13).

Technical Behavior

- The Chinese want to cooperate with large, technologically strong companies (see Chapter 4, Illustration 15).
- The Chinese want to buy the most advanced and research and development-oriented technology; apart from price, technology is the other major issue in Chinese business negotiation (see Chapter 4, Illustration 15).
- The basic Chinese attitude toward foreign technology transfer to China is to exchange the Chinese market for foreign technology (see Chapter 4, Illustration 16).

Commercial Behavior

- The Chinese tend to choose large and financially strong foreign companies with which to cooperate (see Chapter 4, Illustration 17).

- ◆ The Chinese are extremely price sensitive; Chinese business nego-
  tiation is essentially a negotiation about price and technology (see
  Chapter 4, Illustrations 10, 16-19, and 32).
- ◆ The Chinese insist on having the majority share of equity in a
  Sino-foreign business joint venture (see Chapter 4, Illustration 20).

Social Behavior

- ◆ There is a pre-negotiation phase in the Chinese business negotiation
  process in which the Chinese try to establish trust and confidence in
  the other party through information gathering, personal contacts, and
  other social activities (see Chapter 4, Illustrations 21 and 22).
- ◆ The Chinese attach great importance to sincerity and reputation on
  the part of the foreign side (see Chapter 4, Illustrations 9, 10, 21,
  and 22).
- ◆ Chinese negotiating style is people-oriented and permeated with
  such Confucian notions as *guanxi*, *renqing*, face, family, age, hierarchy, harmony, and *li* (etiquette) (see Chapter 4, Illustrations 3, 5,
  8, 21, 23-25, 27, 29, 34, and 40).
- ◆ Language is a major barrier in Chinese-foreign business negotiation
  (see Chapter 4, Illustrations 11 and 28).

Strategic Behavior[1]

- ◆ *Ji* or "Chinese stratagem" exists in the mentality of Chinese negotia-
  tors.
- ◆ The Chinese may employ negotiating tactics deliberately or inad-
  vertently.
- ◆ Chinese business negotiating tactics empirically evident in this
  book include the following:[2]
  - ➤ Information gathering and intelligence (see Chapter 4, Illustra-
    tions 4 and 32; see also Appendix A, Stratagems 33 and 31)
  - ➤ The "price is always too high" tactic (see Chapter 4, Illustrations 18
    and 19; see also Appendix A, Stratagem 7)
  - ➤ "Price versus quality bargaining" (see Chapter 4, Illustration 18;
    see also Appendix A, Stratagem 19)
  - ➤ "Red face/white face" manipulation (see Chapter 4, Illustration 32;
    see also Appendix A, Stratagem 11)

➤ "Pre-Christmas Day push" (see Chapter 4, Illustration 31; see also Appendix A, Stratagem 22)

➤ Referring to a third party, borrowing external force, and playing the government card (see Chapter 4, Illustrations 12 and 32; see also Appendix A, Stratagems 3 and 29)

➤ Shaming and showing anger technique (see Chapter 4, Illustration 32; see also Appendix A, Stratagem 13)

➤ "Mayor will come to the banquet" (see Chapter 4, Illustration 33; see also Appendix A, Stratagems 4 and 22)

➤ "Your silence means 'Yes' " (see Chapter 4, Illustration 34; see also Appendix A, Stratagem 32)

➤ "Water in glass" manipulation (see Chapter 4, Illustration 30; see also Appendix A, Stratagems 25 and 31)

➤ Comparing three vendors when buying goods and playing competitors off against each other (see Chapter 4, Illustrations 37 and 38; see also Appendix A, Stratagem 3)

➤ "Espionage" (see Chapter 4, Illustration 4; see also Appendix A, Stratagem 31)

➤ "The Chinese arbitration organization is impartial" (see Chapter 4, Illustration 13; see also Appendix A, Stratagem 4)

➤ "Rest on big mountain" (see Chapter 4, Illustration 15; see also Appendix A, Stratagem 14)

➤ "We are very poor, indeed" (see Chapter 4, Illustration 17; see also Appendix A, Stratagem 34)

➤ "Absentminded negotiator" and "Keep silence" (see Chapter 4, Illustration 39; see also Appendix A, Stratagems 27 and 13)

When comparing the six dimensions of Chinese business negotiating style with the Western theory of business negotiation discussed previously, there are stark contrasts in the political, legal, and strategic dimensions of Chinese business negotiating behaviors. Most remarkable is the strong political feature in Chinese business negotiation. The decisive influence of the Chinese government and Chinese bureaucracy on the behavior of Chinese negotiators constitutes a major difference between Chinese and Western business negotiating styles. As discussed in Chapter 3, the centralized hierarchical Chinese bureaucracy owes as much to Confucian traditions as it does to the Communist and Maoist ideologies. The legal dimension of Chinese business negotiating style has been fundamentally shaped by Confucian traditions and reinforced by the PRC condition. The strategic Chinese negotiating style has been molded by *ji* (Chinese stratagems)—a peculiar Chinese cultural phenomenon rooted in Taoist principles. The study has also found that Chinese business negotiation is essentially a negotiation about technology and price (see Chapter 4, Illustrations 10, 15-19, and 32), and that Chinese negotiators use a people-oriented approach (see Chapter 4, Illustrations 3, 5, 8, 21, 23-25, 27, 29, 34, and 40).

The six dimensions of Chinese business negotiating behavior are incorporated as the "what" elements in the model of Chinese business negotiating style to be proposed later in this chapter.

Three Fundamental Components of Chinese Business Culture Driving Chinese Business Negotiating Style

In this section, I answer the following research question: What are the fundamental Chinese sociocultural traits underlying Chinese business negotiating style? On the basis of theoretical reasoning in Chapters 2 and 3 and supported by the empirical evidence in Chapter 4 (see the 40 illustrations and the analyses thereof), I have identified three fundamental components of Chinese business culture that drive Chinese business negotiating style: the PRC condition, Confucianism, and Chinese stratagems.

The PRC condition (*guoqing*) refers to the distinctive characteristics of China's social system and conditions. Specifically, it involves variables such as Chinese politics, China's socialist planned economic system, technology development, great size, backwardness, and rapid change. The central theme under the PRC condition is Chinese bureaucracy, characterized by centralized decision making, internal bargaining, bureaucratic red tape, and quick buying. The empirical data related to the PRC condition are shown in Illustrations 1 through 17, 19, 20, 28, 31, 33, 35, 36, 37, 39, and 40 in Chapter 4.

Confucianism includes six basic values: moral cultivation; importance of interpersonal relationships (concepts of *guanxi, renqing,* and *li*); family and group orientation; respect for age and hierarchy; avoidance of conflict and need for harmony; and concept of face.

Confucianism is demonstrated in Illustrations 3, 4, 5, 7, 11, 15, 17, 21 through 27, 29, 31, 32, 35, 36, 37, and 40 in Chapter 4.

The Chinese stratagem is a strategic element in Chinese culture with its philosophical origins in the Taoist Yin Yang and Wu Wei principles. *Art of War* and *The Thirty-Six Stratagems* are the two best introductions to the strategic facade of the Chinese mind. Inherent in various Chinese stratagems lies the strategic Chinese thinking of "subduing the enemy without fighting." Chinese stratagems assert the superiority of using human wisdom and indirect means rather than resorting to direct pitched battle to cope with various situations and to gain advantages over the opponent. The highest principle of Chinese stratagems is flexibility. Chinese stratagems are discussed in Illustrations 4, 7, 12, 13, 15, 17, 18, 25, 26, 27, 30, 31, 33 through 39, and 40 in Chapter 4.

In this book, both theoretical reasoning and empirical materials show that the PRC condition, Confucianism, and Chinese stratagems, as a whole, provide a useful framework with which to understand Chinese business negotiating style socioculturally. The "contrasting" findings provided by Illustrations 35 and 36 in Chapter 4 regarding Chinese stratagems and Illustration 3 and 34 concerning the Chinese concept of face serve to reinforce, to a broad extent, the standpoint I have attempted to convey: A comprehensive understanding of the idiosyncratic nature of Chinese business negotiating style should be one that attempts to seek answers from the PRC condition, Confucianism, and Chinese stratagems, systematically (see Chapter 3, A Positioning Map). The Chinese can follow different teachings to enrich each aspect of their life (see Chapter 2, Chinese Culture). This implies that the PRC condition, Confucianism, and Chinese stratagems can both separately and interrelatedly influence Chinese negotiating behavior. The Chinese are of a mixed personality.

The framework of Chinese business culture has an important theoretical implication for our understanding of the overseas Chinese negotiating style—that is, the negotiating style of the Chinese living outside mainland China. As noted earlier, Confucianism and Chinese stratagems represent the profound Chinese cultural forces salient to all Chinese no matter where they choose to live. Therefore, the negotiating style of overseas Chinese can be understood as being driven by the interplay between the enduring traditional forces—that is, Confucianism and Chinese stratagems—and the changing contemporary force—that is, the conditions of the social systems of the countries and regions in which they live. Hence, the Chinese style of negotiating is both classic and modern, both enduring and changing.

The three fundamental components of Chinese business culture or sociocultural traits mentioned previously are the "why" elements in the model of Chinese business negotiating style to be proffered later in this chapter.

The Chinese Negotiator: A Blend of Maoist Bureaucrat, Confucian Gentleman, and Sun Tzu-Like Strategist

In this section, I answer the following research question: Why do the Chinese negotiate in different ways? or How can Chinese negotiating style be understood in Chinese sociocultural context? The study has found, based on theoretical and empirical analyses in Chapters 2 through 4, that there is a close link between Chinese business negotiating style and Chinese sociocultural traits. In fact, the research question (why or how) raised here was answered in the analysis of each of the 40 illustrations in Chapter 4. Here, I emphasize that the way in which Chinese negotiators, both as individuals and as a group, behave and interact with foreign negotiating counterparts in Sino-foreign business negotiation processes is influenced fundamentally by the interplay between the PRC condition, Confucianism, and Chinese stratagems; a given Chinese negotiating behavior may have a combination of these sociocultural driving forces.

For example, the Chinese proclivity to renegotiate is often viewed as a strategic move (e.g., "revisiting old issues" in Seligman [1990] and "unending negotiation" in Pye [1982]). This is true in the sense that "mooching," or expecting something extra, when buying goods is a strategic Chinese behavior embedded in Chinese stratagems (Chu, 1991; see also Appendix A, Stratagem 12). It must not be forgotten, however, that the Chinese propensity for renegotiation may be caused by hierarchical pressure from the Chinese bureaucracy, a feature of the PRC condition rather than a strategic move, as shown in Illustration 1 in Chapter 4. Moreover, the Chinese behavior of renegotiating may also be a non-tactical Confucian behavior as implied in Illustration 10 in Chapter 4. The Chinese tendency for renegotiating, regardless of motivations, is an important feature of Chinese business negotiating style, which in turn results in the fact that, in dealings with the Chinese, negotiation and renegotiation move in circles.

The phenomenon that the frontline Chinese negotiators are not the real negotiators and the real negotiators or decision makers normally do not participate in face-to-face negotiation sessions has been noted both in the literature (Pye, 1982, Seligman, 1990) and in this book (see Chapter 4, Illustrations 1 and 2). In a more generalized sense, this phenomenon can be viewed as being shaped by the PRC condition, Confucianism, and Chinese stratagems. The PRC condition indicates that the Chinese political culture contributes to this Chinese bureaucratic practice; the Chinese company's chief negotiators are "career negotiators" rather than important executives or decision makers (see Chapter 3, Chinese Bureaucracy). The Confucian perspective reminds one of the Chinese respect for hierarchy and need for face as another reason behind the Chinese behavior. Top Chinese executives tend to view negotiation more as an operational activity rather than a strategic managerial task; their status is reserved to control the negotiation outcomes instead of handling the negotiation process. Therefore, they consider that their heading a negotiation team would not be in harmony with their status (Chen & Faure, 1995). Their weakness will never be exposed to the opponent, and their face can thus be saved if they remain behind the scene. The Chinese stratagems perspective allows us to uncover a Chinese negotiating tactic: By keeping a physical distance from the negotiation table, the real Chinese negotiators have greater flexibility to "subdue" the opponent "without fighting" (see Appendix A, Stratagem 11).

"Play home court" is another example. That negotiation always occurs in China is explained at great length by Pye (1982) as a deliberate Chinese tactic. This is true also in the sense that "awaiting leisurely the exhausted enemy" is seated in the domain of strategic Chinese thinking (see Appendix A, Stratagem 4). Nevertheless, as implied by Illustration 36 in Chapter 4, this common Chinese behavior of conducting negotiations on Chinese soil may be more a product of the PRC condition (i.e., Chinese lack of foreign exchange, requirement for hierarchical reporting, and administrative obstacles) than a strategic maneuver.

"What on earth constitutes the Chinese style of negotiating?" is a question that has not been answered in the existing literature. Chinese negotiators have an inherent advantage at the negotiation table because their negotiating behaviors and tactics come naturally from their distinctive sociocultural system. The idiosyncratic Chinese sociocultural traits have shaped a style of the Chinese negotiator that I describe as follows: The Chinese negotiator is a blend of Maoist bureaucrat, Confucian gentleman, and Sun Tzu-like strategist. I emphasize that it is this "three-in-one" Chinese style that makes Chinese business negotiating style unique; it is this three-in-one Chinese style that perplexes many Western business people in dealings with the PRC.

As a Maoist bureaucrat, the Chinese negotiator does nothing but follow his government's plans for doing business. He gives first priority to China's political interest and never separates business from politics. He avoids taking initiatives, shuns responsibility, fears criticism, and has no final say. Currently, he lacks international business experience but is moving upward on the steep learning curve. He is no doubt a shrewd and tough negotiator because he is trained daily in Chinese bureaucracy in which bargaining is an integrated element (see Chapter 3, The PRC Condition; Davidson, 1987; Lieberthal & Oksenberg, 1986; Pye, 1982; see also Chapter 4, Illustrations 1-3, 5, 8, 14, 16, 20, 31, and 40). His negotiating style can be militant given Mao's doctrine: "A revolution is not a dinner party." He is the most "elusive" or "inscrutable" negotiator because of the changing nature of the PRC condition. His negotiation strategy comes naturally from his old culture, which can be called a mix of Confucian-type cooperation and Sun Tzu-type competition.

Being a Confucian gentleman, the Chinese negotiator behaves on the basis of mutual trust and benefit, seeking cooperation or "win-win" solutions for everybody to succeed. He places high value on trust and sincerity on his own part and that of the other party as a human being. For him, cultivation of righteousness is far more important than the pursuit of profit. He shows a profound capacity to conclude business without negotiating. He simply does not like the word *negotiation*; he prefers to say "discussion" because "negotiation" suggests somewhat disagreeable connotations of conflict, which must be avoided at all costs. He does not like lawyers to be involved in face-to-face discussions. He is well mannered and generous; a mere handshake or exchange of business cards implies a lifelong commitment. He views contracting essentially as an ongoing relationship or problem-solving process rather than a one-off legal package. He associates business with *guanxi* and friendship. He is group-oriented, self-restrained, conscious of face, age, hierarchy, and etiquette, and suspicious of "non-family" persons. He can be a daunting negotiator, for example, when he revisits old issues in the light of a changing market situation to seek well-balanced mutual benefits for both parties and when he bargains toughly in the interests of his "family." His negotiation strategy is characterized basically by cooperation (see Chapter 3, Confucianism; Deverge, 1986; Kindel, 1990; Seligman, 1990; Shenkar & Ronen, 1987; Withane, 1992; see also Chapter 4, Illustrations 9-11, 21-27, and 40).

As a Sun Tzu-like strategist, the Chinese negotiator believes everything is a "zero-sum game" and that the marketplace is like a battlefield (see Chapter 3, Chinese Stratagems; Chu, 1991; Mun, 1990; Pye, 1982; Tung, 1994a). He sets out to "win-lose" you. He never stops bargaining. He is a skillful negotiator, endowed with a formidable variety of Chinese stratagems from his ancestors. At the heart of his bargaining technique lies Sun Tzu's secret: "To subdue the enemy without fighting is the acme of skill." He seldom wages a physical war; rather, he is keen on a psychological wrestling of wit to manipulate one into doing business his way. His actions tend to be deceitful and indirect. He often creates favorable situations to attain his objectives by utilizing external forces. He is always ready to withdraw from the bargaining table when all else fails, but this is only a Chinese stratagem for fighting back. The general pattern of his negotiating tactics is compared to that of Tai Chi—a "soft" form of Chinese martial art (kung fu). Tai Chi is often perceived as water; nothing is as weak as water. When water advances, however, attacking something hard or resistant, then nothing withstands it. By the same token, the Sun Tzu-like strategist adopts apparently soft but essentially tough tactics in negotiations. His negotiation strategy is characterized by competition (see Chapter 4, Illustrations 31-34 and 37-39).

In summary, the metaphor that the Chinese negotiator is a blend of Maoist bureaucrat, Confucian gentleman, and Sun Tzu-like strategist broadens our perspectives to predict and analyze Chinese negotiating style. My formula is that a Chinese negotiator is basically a Confucian gentleman as well as a Sun Tzu-like strategist; the degree of trust in the other party determines the role he is going to play. When mutual trust is high, he negotiates as a gentleman; when mutual trust is low, he manipulates as a strategist! The Chinese negotiator is also a Maoist bureaucrat, particularly so when the "Beijing wind" changes.

The metaphor also affords a clue to understanding the negotiating style of the Chinese in a more generalized sense—that is, the Chinese inside and outside mainland China. Regardless of where he lives, a Chinese negotiator is, above all, a blend of Confucian gentleman and Sun Tzu-like strategist. His negotiating style is also influenced by, for example, the political, economic, legal, and technological factors of the society in which he settles.

The "Coop-Comp" Chinese Negotiation Strategy

What is the nature of Chinese negotiation strategy? Western negotiation theory provides two generic negotiation strategies: cooperation and competition. The former is often referred to as a win-win strategy, whereas the latter is considered a win-lose strategy (see Chapter 2, Negotiation Strategies). The conventional wisdom tends to produce a stereotype: Cooperation and competition are but two universal concepts without any regard to specific cultural values and motivations. This stereotype fails to show the reality that indigenous cultural values, norms, and habits may have contributed greatly to the shaping of patterns of cooperative and competitive behaviors among people in a specific culture and society. This book shows that cooperation and competition—the two generic Western negotiation strategies— find their Oriental counterparts in the traditional Chinese culture: Both win-win (Confucianism) and win-lose (Chinese stratagems) elements exist in the traditional Chinese culture that underlie Chinese negotiating style.

Chinese negotiators can take the problem-solving or cooperation approach, on the one hand (see Chapter 4, Illustrations 9-11), and the zero-sum or competition approach, on the other hand (see Chapter 4, Illustrations 31-34 and 39). In other words, they use both the

Confucian-type cooperation strategy and the Sun Tzu-type competition strategy in negotiations (see Chapter 4, Illustration 26)—a strategic mix that I call the coop-comp Chinese negotiation strategy.[3] The term *coop-comp* suggests that Chinese negotiators can negotiate both cooperatively and competitively because they are driven by both cooperative and competitive sociocultural traits. This explains why Chinese negotiators are often described as contradictory, strange, and inscrutable.

I believe that Chinese negotiators "for centuries . . . have known few peers in the subtle art of negotiating" (Pye, 1986, p. 74) because Confucian tradition and Chinese stratagems have bestowed on the Chinese a superb culturally embedded coop-comp strategy with which to negotiate both sincerely and deceptively with Westerners.

The following question arises, however: When do the Chinese use the cooperation strategy and when do they use the competition strategy? This is a good question. I believe it depends on *guanxi* or, ultimately, trust between the negotiating parties (see Chapter 3, Importance of Interpersonal Relationships). The empirical illustrations in this book indicate that when *guanxi* between the negotiating parties is fine and trust is great, the negotiation will be smooth and the business will be done rather quickly (see Chapter 4, Illustrations 3, 11, and 21-23). When the parties do not have any *guanxi* (e.g., when foreign negotiators are strangers to the Chinese), however, the Chinese feelings of distrust and suspicion will be strong; the Chinese will probably use various stratagems to manipulate the foreign party into doing things their way (see Chapter 4, Illustration 32), and the negotiation is most likely to be circumscribed by a volatile haggling atmosphere.

Generally, the Chinese will examine and evaluate the state of *guanxi* and trust between the parties at the outset of negotiation, and then they will calibrate their negotiation strategies in dealing with the other party based on the Confucian principle of reciprocity (see Chapter 4, Illustration 26). Therefore, it is of strategic importance, on the part of the foreign party, to attempt to create and maintain a genuine *guanxi* and a high degree of trust with its Chinese partner so that negotiations can take place in what I call the Confucian working environment, in which both parties use the cooperation strategy to ensure that both win (see Chapter 4, Illustrations 11 and 26).

A Model of Chinese Business Negotiating Style

In this book, I have attempted to make my contribution to the understanding of Chinese business negotiating style by constructing a conceptual model—a model that will allow a systematical analysis of Chinese negotiating behaviors in a sociocultural context. First, the three Chinese sociocultural traits—that is, the PRC condition, Confucianism, and Chinese stratagems—provide a Chinese sociocultural context in which Chinese business negotiating style is understood (answering the "whys").

Next, the six dimensions of Chinese business negotiating style— that is, political, legal, technical, commercial, social, and strategic dimensions (see illustrations in Chapter 4 and the section on Six Dimensions of Chinese Business Negotiating Style, earlier in this chapter)—are used to describe Chinese business negotiating behaviors (answering the "whats").

Finally, a detailed examination of Chinese negotiating behaviors must involve the negotiation process—that is, an examination of how Chinese negotiating style unfolds during the process of negotiation from the parties' initial contacts to their cosigning the final contract. This study has demonstrated that there is a pre-negotiation stage in the Sino-foreign business negotiation process (see Chapter 4, Illustrations 21 and 22). Drawing on the discussion of negotiation phases in Chapter 2, I incorporate prenegotiation, face-to-face interaction, and postnegotiation into my model of Chinese business negotiating style.

As shown in Figure 5.1, the model of Chinese business negotiating style takes shape by involving "what," "why," and process variables. The model visually synthesizes the theoretical and empirical findings of this book. Its offers a systematic approach to the subject by addressing the various components of the whole of Chinese business negotiating style and their relationships. The model suggests that given the interplay of the Chinese business culture (i.e., the PRC condition, Confucianism, and Chinese stratagems), six dimensions of Chinese negotiating style (i.e., political, legal, technical, commercial, social, and strategic) can be found in the Chinese business negotiation process (i.e., pre-negotiation, face-to-face interaction, and post-negotiation).

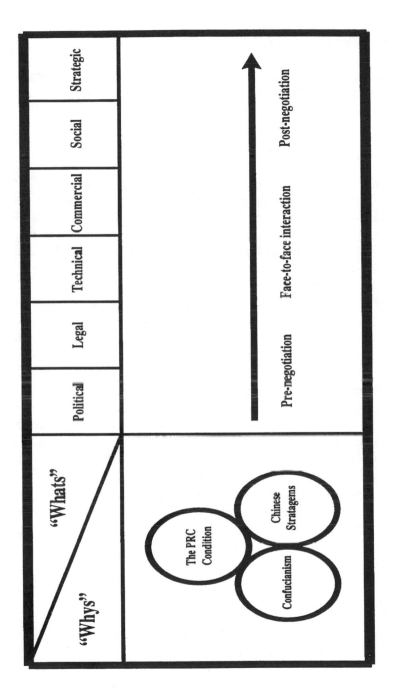

Figure 5.1. A Model of Chinese Business Negotiating Style

▓ Managerial Implications

On the basis of theoretical and empirical findings, I offer 12 pieces of advice to Western business people who are negotiating or preparing to negotiate with the Chinese.

Send the Right Team to China

Sending the right team to negotiate in China is vitally important. The status of your team members will directly affect the attitude of the Chinese host organization toward your company. The Chinese would regard it as impolite, feel insulted, and be dubious of your sincerity if you dispatched a young and low-ranking employee to negotiate with them. This most probably will result in the Chinese party also sending a young, low-ranking, no-mandate official to "match" you rather than to negotiate with you (see Chapter 4, Illustration 25). Your team leader should be a person who is old enough, with charismatic charm, a patient personality, credibility, and sufficient authority to make key decisions. Technical and financial specialists must always be included on your team to be able to answer technical and financial questions raised by the Chinese counterparts, who are technology and price sensitive (see Chapter 4, Illustrations 10, 15-19, and 32). Your lawyer, if participating in face-to-face meetings, should be well versed in Chinese law and government regulations and prepared to negotiate according to the Chinese "political book" (see Chapter 4, Illustrations 11 and 13). Your Chinese-speaking colleague (native or ethnic Chinese, etc.) can be a great asset in bridging cultural and language gaps between the parties (see Chapter 4, Illustration 23) if he possesses an agreeable personality, high cultural sensitivity, and good communication skills (see Chapter 4, Illustration 29).

Show Political Support

The all-pervasive influence of Chinese politics on Chinese business (see Chapter 4, Illustrations 1-6, 8, 11, 20, and 40) results in the fact that Chinese decision makers tend to take it for granted that the government is also the "biggest boss" in the West, and its involvement in the company's business negotiations is unquestioned. By recalling their domestic practices and experiences, the Chinese may simply doubt your company's stability, reliability, and credibility if your government does not support your company (see Chapter 4, Illustration 8). Therefore, it is of crucial importance to show the Chinese the political support and governmental backing behind your China missions, especially when negotiating large and high-risk projects in China. Large business contracts can be secured and problems resolved if leaders of your government and business community work hand in hand in doing business with China.

Identify Real Chinese Negotiators

When embarking on a China venture, make sure you know the real Chinese negotiators. Despite the large Chinese team with many participants, the real Chinese negotiators usually are absent from the negotiation room. Those who are actually running and influencing the negotiation tend to be high-ranking officials from the government ministries or commissions or senior executives of the Chinese companies or both (see Chapter 4, Illustrations 1-3, 5, 8, 12, 20, and 23). Never miss the chance, if any, to "negotiate" directly with the top leaders of the Chinese government at central and local levels to gain their personal support and endorsements for your project (see Chapter 4, Illustration 2). By identifying and negotiating with the real Chinese negotiators, you can, as a Chinese proverb states, "get twice the result with half the effort."

Take a People-Oriented Approach

The Chinese do not believe legal packages; they believe people. The common Western ideal of an effective negotiator—one who has powerful verbal persuasive flair and is always ready to turn to legal proceedings as his first course of action—would be frowned on by his Chinese negotiating partner as superficial, imprudent, and even insincere. The deeply ingrained Confucian aversion to law allows the Chinese to associate law with coercion, troubles, and failure of the relationship and to link lawyers with "troubles" (see Chapter 4, Illustration 9). From the Chinese perspective, the intangible "cooperation spirit" and trust are far more significant than a tangible contract (see Chapter 4, Illustration 10). To negotiate effectively with the Chinese, Western managers should take a people-oriented approach to negotiation, never expecting one-off legal agreements to bring about the planned outcome. Chinese business negotiation is distinctively people-oriented, and the Chinese do business with you and not with your company (see Chapter 4, Illustrations 21, 22, 24, and 40). It pays off to cultivate *guanxi* and friendship through social activities with a view to establishing mutual trust even before formal face-to-face interaction commences. Make sure to avoid settling disputes through litigation, which must always be used as the last resort. As a Chinese saying states, "Never display the family shame to outsiders."

Use Local Chinese

Local Chinese nationals are a great asset for your China ventures. Illustrations 21 and 23 in Chapter 4 show that a foreign company's local Chinese employees can make remarkable contributions to the success of its negotiations with China. China is a "familistic society," in which trust is high inside and low outside the family border (see the two sections in Chapter 3, Moral Cultivation and Family Orientation; see also Chapter 4, Illustration 27). Given this characteristic, Chinese negotiations tend to be tough, and the Chinese negotiators tend to haggle "ruthlessly" when negotiations are held between parties who are strangers (see Chapter 4, Illustration 32). In this context, your local Chinese employees will be able to help you penetrate into the Chinese family and establish a trusting family relationship with your Chinese customers more effectively than would be the case otherwise. In summary, given their cultural and language advantages, local Chinese nationals are valuable in communicating with Chinese customers, circumventing Chinese family borders, dealing with Chinese bureaucracy, sensing Chinese stratagems, and formulating counter-strategies. Like in other markets, the success and failure of your long-term footing in China hinges eventually on your ability to recruit and keep the loyal service of a team of talented local Chinese nationals. In the Middle Kingdom, given the Confucian tradition, Chinese loyalty is tricky because it is not a universal notion but a highly reciprocal business, depending on how fair and trustful you are perceived in the eyes of your Chinese partners. A Chinese is your "friend for life" and behaves as a gentleman when you behave as a gentleman; he employs tricks and ploys when you play games (see Chapter 4, Illustrations 24 and 26). Currently, many Western companies recruit local Chinese based merely on their English language proficiency. Language is but one of many qualifications that constitute what I call China market penetration ability. A human resource policy that suggests any distrust of the local Chinese nationals would serve only to make your first-rate Chinese candidates shy away from you. Trusting, motivating, training, and using your local Chinese human resources to help you penetrate the "Invisible Great Wall" and contribute actively to your China market development strategies is an issue of strategic importance if you want to secure a long-standing foothold in the Chinese market.

Maintain a Consistent Team

Maintaining the same team throughout the negotiation process is an essential means of gaining trust from the Chinese side. Remember that the Chinese do business with you as a person and not as a company; your successor does not automatically inherit your friends and relationships (see Chapter 4, Illustration 24). Trust, *guanxi*, and friendship that took time to build up may be undermined overnight if you frequently rotate members of your team. Therefore, it is important to retain a consistent team as much as possible when negotiating with the Chinese, allowing the same persons to deal with each other as long as business continues. This point has an implication for foreign corporations' expatriate policies. Regular rotation of managers is common among large multinational corporations as a means to train managers and enrich their international experience. This practice, although important in many respects, must be adapted to Chinese business culture. Given its sociocultural characteristics, the China market requires relatively long sojourns of expatriates so that they have time to create a robust working relationship with Chinese partners and customers and secure a firm foothold in the market. Therefore, managers doing business with China should not be withdrawn from their China operations too quickly.

Pad Your Price Reasonably

Bargaining is a Chinese way of life, both politically and culturally (see Chapter 4, Illustrations 1, 6, 18, and 19). The Chinese always believe that any price you quote must have some "water content" (see *shuifen* in Chapter 4, Illustration 19). Therefore, Chinese negotiators set out automatically to squeeze out the water content. By doing so, a Chinese can not only gain face but also show that he is the "winner" in front of his superiors (see Chapter 4, Illustration 31). Therefore, it is necessary to pad your price to a culturally reasonable level that allows you to give away some margin to the Chinese to help them gain face and satisfy their bureaucratic needs and wants. I do not mean to encourage cheating in negotiation with the Chinese, however. Honesty wins the Chinese heart (see Chapter 4, Illustration 11).

Help Your Chinese Counterpart

In China, those who make decisions tend not to be technical people but bureaucrats. Therefore, it is important to help your Chinese negotiating counterparts get around the bureaucratic obstacles and become less susceptible to any would-be criticism of their dealings with you (see Chapter 4, Illustration 3). You should put yourself in the position of your Chinese partner and devise language and solutions to enable him to have the agreement approved by his superior. You may show the Chinese that the same contractual clauses or conditions have previously been accepted by other Chinese negotiators (see Chapter 4, Illustration 5). Nothing is as reassuring to the Chinese as evidence that other Chinese colleagues agreed to the same or similar contractual provisions, given the notorious Chinese fear of making mistakes. Sometimes your symbolic concessions to produce the atmosphere of reciprocal benefit must be made so that the Chinese negotiators can sell the "package" smoothly within the Chinese bureaucracy. Never assume that the Chinese team has a unanimous voice. Members of the Chinese team often have differing internal interests (see Chapter 4, Illustration 6). Helping the Chinese design bureaucratic languages to satisfy the divergent internal interests is a key consideration in negotiating effectively with the PRC.

Invite the Chinese to Negotiate Abroad

Much has been written about the Chinese negotiating tactic of playing home court (see Appendix A, Stratagem 4). This book indicates, however, that the Chinese would be pleased to travel abroad for business talks if the financial and administrative barriers were removed (see Chapter 4, Illustration 36). Inviting and helping the Chinese to visit your country for some of the negotiating sessions could be a smart and rewarding strategy not only for the obvious reasons of cost,[4] time, and strategy but also because your kindness in assisting the Chinese to travel abroad will not be forgotten by them. On the basis of the *guanxi* principle, it will be reciprocated later. Even if you pay for the trip, the payment would be well worth the cost. A visit to Sweden, for example, would allow the Chinese to experience the Swedish culture and business ambience. The Chinese, who come from a country in which bargaining is a way of life (see Chapter 4, Illustrations 6 and 19), would reflect on and probably alter their bargaining strategies after they notice that deals are seldom made on a bargaining basis in the Scandinavian culture. Besides, never miss the chance, if any, to meet and hold courtesy talks with high-ranking Chinese government officials during their visit to your country. Access to high-ranking Chinese officials is far easier in your own country than in China, as suggested by Illustrations 2 and 8 in Chapter 4.

Design "8-Numbered" Products for China

China is known as a "land of etiquette." Chinese society is shaped by a set of norms, rules, habits, symbols, and moral obligations different from those of Western societies. For example, the number 8 is adored in Chinese societies (see the section in Chapter 3, Chinese Social Customs, Taboos, and Symbolism) but means nothing special in the West. A careless unintentional violation of the Chinese codes of etiquette may risk losing business opportunities, as suggested by Illustration 29 in Chapter 4. Therefore, I use "Design 8-numbered products for China" as a metaphor[5] to enunciate the importance of respecting and learning Chinese sociocultural traits. Your products and people should avoid a 4-numbered identity when entering the Chinese market.

Be Patient

"Be patient" is advice so popular that it can be found in almost all books and articles on doing business with China. New with my advice is a systematic approach. Patience is required given the fundamental influence of the PRC condition, Confucianism, and Chinese stratagems on the Chinese business negotiation process. From the perspective of the PRC condition, China is such a large country that problems of various types are bound to crop up (see the two sections in Chapter 3, Great Size and Backwardness; see also Chapter 4, Illustration 10). The formidable Chinese bureaucracy (see Chapter 2, The Chinese Bureaucracy School, and Chapter 3, Chinese Bureaucracy; see also Chapter 4, Illustration 3), poor infrastructure, and so on (see Chapter 4, Illustration 6) often invite marathon negotiations. From the perspective of Confucianism, China is a familistic society in which it takes time to build trust between non-family members (see the two sections in Chapter 3, Moral Cultivation and Family Orientation). "The Chinese distrust fast talkers who want to make quick deals" (Pye, 1982, p. 92). Remember the Chinese expressions: "Good things come out of many tribulations" (*Hao Shi Duo Mo*) and "More haste results in less speed" (*Yu Su Ze Bu Da*). Remember that "Kung Fu" also means "time" in Chinese. From the vantage point of Chinese stratagems, you must have great patience and perseverance to deal with Chinese stratagems and strategists (see Chapter 4, Illustration 34). In summary, do not forget that the Chinese character for patience or tolerance means "the edge of a knife mounted on the top of the heart," as shown in Figure 5.2. Believe that by being patient, tolerant, calm, persistent, and honest in dealing with the Chinese, you will eventually win the Chinese heart and trust.

Explode the Myth of Face

Face is one of the most significant mechanisms in Chinese social psychology. The Chinese are face conscious; they can go to great lengths to avoid saying the word "No" (see Chapter 3, Concept of Face).

Figure 5.2. The Chinese Character "Patience" or "Tolerance"
SOURCE: Calligraphy by Tony Fang; copyright 1998 by Tony Fang.

Experts on Chinese business negotiating style universally advise that
you will gain much if you help a Chinese save face, and you will lose
more if you do not (Brunner & Wang, 1988; Pye, 1982). This book,
however, suggests that respecting Chinese face and never saying "No"
to a Chinese is advisable only within the domain of business relations
between Confucian gentlemen or in a pure Confucian working environment. Chinese negotiators can culturally be both Confucian gentlemen and Sun Tzu-like strategists (see the section in Chapter 3, The
PRC Condition, Confucianism, and Chinese Stratagems: An Interplay). Therefore, the advice that you should never say "No" to a
Chinese could be dangerous when it is practiced in front of a Sun
Tzu-like Chinese strategist. Then, as shown in Illustration 34 in
Chapter 4, your reluctance to say "No" can be taken advantage of by
the strategist. Therefore, it is strategically important not to be shattered by the Chinese face. You must dare to explode the myth of face.
Saying "No" to the Chinese is extremely important to communicate
and negotiate effectively and efficiently (see Chapter 4, Illustrations 11

and 28). Therefore, I recommend that you say "No" honestly, but in a proper manner, to the Chinese in business negotiations when the circumstances require it. Honesty (e.g., let the Chinese know what you can and cannot offer) is a rewarding strategy that can be used to neutralize Chinese stratagems (see Chapter 4, Illustrations 30 and 33). In a more generalized sense, you must have guts to explode not only the myth of face but also the myths of *guanxi*, Chinese bureaucracy, and Chinese stratagems. A skilled negotiator is a master of the art of keeping a good balance between designing 8-numbered products and exploding the myth of face or a balance between learning Chinese sociocultural traits and being himself. Pye (1982) is absolutely correct in suggesting that we should not imitate the Chinese way blindly: "Try to understand Chinese cultural traits, but never believe that a foreigner can practice them better than the Chinese" (p. xii). Therefore, my ultimate advice for negotiating and dealing with the Chinese is to respect Chinese culture but be yourself.

Limitations and Future Research

It must be noted that this book has limitations. Future research should take into consideration a number of theoretical and methodological issues. First, this book tackles the subject at a national sociocultural level. Although this macro-sociocultural explanation of national negotiating style is insightful, other factors, such as regional cultures, situational factors, and individual personalities, that are not particularly discussed in this book should by no means be deemed insignificant. A team of cross-cultural negotiation style researchers (Graham & Sano, 1986, p. 71) suggest that "in business negotiations personalities may be even more important than cultural norms."

Second, communication is an important issue in negotiation style research. In fact, negotiation and communication are inherently intertwined (Putnam & Roloff, 1992). The empirical illustrations in this book suggest that language is a major problem in Chinese business negotiation (see Chapter 4, Illustrations 28 and 29), and it can be used strategically by Chinese negotiators (see Chapter 4, Illustration 39). This book, however, has not given sufficient attention to this aspect.

Chinese culture is a high-context culture in which meanings may not be perceived in the coded, explicit, and transmitted part of the messages but rather found in the context. The Chinese communication process possesses a number of characteristics, such as implicit communication, listening centeredness, and politeness, and it is insider focused and face directed (Gao, Ting-Toomey, & Gudykunst, 1996). Further research examining the verbal and nonverbal communication patterns of the Chinese negotiators would be interesting.

Third, this book used the emic approach to analyze Chinese negotiating style. In future research, the etic approach, or a comparative perspective, should be combined to achieve an even fuller understanding.

Fourth, the efforts to involve a Chinese voice in the debate have been marked in this book. Although audible, the Chinese voice is still not loud enough. Future research should try to link Chinese and Westerners to each other in the form of a direct dialogue occurring in the negotiation process.

Finally, I believe a study of Chinese negotiating style beyond the Sino-Western negotiation context is necessary. I hypothesize that the Chinese may negotiate differently with people other than westerners. Paul Kreisberg's (1995) study of Chinese diplomatic negotiating style shows that the foreign perceptions of Chinese negotiators vary considerably from country to country. Although Americans often identify the Chinese haggling style and use of horrifying tricks and ploys, a Zambian diplomat with rich negotiating experience with the Chinese during the 1960s through the 1980s found (as quoted in Kreisberg, 1995, p. 470) "Chinese negotiators consistently cooperative, friendly, forthcoming, and open. They were unconcerned about bargaining, simply agreeing to remedy any problems that arose in negotiations." Don't the Chinese haggle anymore? No. Political considerations can be a reason, but cultural factors may also exist. Chinese negotiators are still Chinese negotiators, but the context has changed: In this case, the Chinese are dealing with a Third World "brother" instead of a "Western power." It has been shown in this book that Chinese moral standards are not universal but highly reciprocal, situational, dynamic, and context-related (see discussion of Confucianism in Chapter 3). The senior (e.g., ruler and the older) and the junior (e.g., subject and the younger) play different roles in a dyadic hierarchical relationship. Therefore, it is very likely that the Chinese adopt different negotiating styles to deal with people of different political and economic backgrounds.

Notes

1. The term *strategic* is used as an adjective form of *stratagem*.

2. At the same time, however, there are two cases (Chapter 4, Illustrations 35 and 36) in which Chinese disagreed with the foreign claims of Chinese using attrition and playing home court tactics.

3. The term *coop-comp* is coined to mean "cooperation-competition."

4. China is one of the world's most expensive places for foreign business people to sojourn. Beijing, for example, is the leader of all the cities in the Asia-Pacific region in terms of average monthly rent for a 180-square meter luxury apartment—$12,780 (Richard Ellis Ltd., as cited in Ness, 1996, p. 41).

5. By the metaphor, design 8-numbered products for China, I also mean a practical tip for marketing your products in all the markets with a Chinese cultural heritage; by using 8-numbered automobiles, mobile telephones, or engine series, for example, these products will help launch themselves in the market.

Appendix A

The 36 Chinese Stratagems and Chinese Business Negotiating Tactics

Stratagem 1: Cross the Sea Without Heaven's Knowledge *(Man Tian Guo Hai)*

Deceive the Emperor (Heaven) into sailing across the sea by inviting him into a seaside city that is in reality a huge camouflaged ship. Hide the deepest secrets in the most obvious situations.

◆ Deception of investors: Some Chinese state-owned enterprises attracted "unethically" unwary foreign business people for investment by covering up their dismal internal problems and exaggerating the competitive advantage that their facilities can provide (Chen & Ying, 1994).

◆ The Chinese may not give an overt indication that negotiation has moved from discussion stage into the final rounds (Seligman, 1990).

◆ Frequent misunderstandings and misinterpretations, half truths, or white lies can be found on the part of Chinese negotiators (Knutsson, 1986a, 1986b).

◆ Using false authority: The Chinese may allude to supposed local practices or government "secret regulations" to push the foreign negotiator to give what they want; what the Chinese say may be based simply on rumor or on the desires of their group (Blackman, 1997).

Stratagem 2: Besiege Wei to
Rescue Zhao (Wei Wei Jiu Zhao)

Save the state of Zhao by besieging the state of Wei, whose troops are out attacking Zhao. Avoid the strong to attack the weak.

◆ Identify and attack the adversary's vulnerabilities in either his position or his personality (Kazuo, 1979; Seligman, 1990).

Stratagem 3: Kill With a
Borrowed Knife (Jie Dao Sha Ren)

Make use of outside resources for one's own gain.

◆ Play competitors off against each other: The Chinese have been known to invite several competing suppliers for negotiations at the same time, often in the very same building (Pye, 1982; Schnepp, von Glinow, & Bhambri, 1990; Seligman, 1990).[1]

◆ Chinese are diabolical note takers, and they consider it fair game to throw your words back in your face whenever it serves their purposes (Seligman, 1990).

◆ The requirement that all joint venture contracts must be approved by the Ministry of Foreign Relations and Trade gives the Chinese a formidable "government card" to play: The Chinese negotiator can threaten that unless the foreign company accepts the Chinese requests, the transaction in question will not be approved by the government institutions (Chang, 1987).[2]

Stratagem 4: Await Leisurely
the Exhausted Enemy (Yi Yi Dai Lao)

Relax and preserve your strength while watching the enemy exhaust himself.

◆ Play home court; important negotiations always take place on Chinese soil (Pye, 1982; Seligman, 1990).[3]

◆ The Chinese are skilled at controlling the schedule and timing of the negotiation (Pye, 1982; Seligman, 1990).[4]

◆ The Chinese arbitration organization is impartial: The Chinese insist that disputes be arbitrated in Beijing before the Foreign Economic and Trade Arbitration Commission of the China Council for the Promotion of International Trade (Chang, 1987).[5]

◆ The Chinese negotiating team usually outnumbers that of the foreign counterpart (Seligman, 1990).

Stratagem 5: Loot a Burning House
(Chen Huo Da Jie)

Take advantage of the opponent's trouble or crisis.

◆ Use the Chinese "fishing" tactic—that is, take advantage of foreign business people's lack of knowledge of the local market (Chen & Ying, 1994).

◆ Exploit the opponent's uncertainty, inconsistency, and divergent interests.

Stratagem 6: Clamor in the East but Attack in the West *(Sheng Dong Ji Xi)*

Devise a feint eastward but launch an attack westward.

◆ Chinese negotiators are frequently less than candid about their actual needs at the initial stage (Seligman, 1990).

◆ The Chinese deliberately discuss small matters or make unexpected and ridiculous demands, and spend much time arguing about them, thereby drawing the other party off the main course (Blackman, 1997).

Stratagem 7: Create Something out of Nothing *(Wu Zhong Sheng You)*

Make the unreal seem real. Gain advantage by conjuring illusion.

◆ "The Chinese negotiator's job was not to evaluate the merits of a particular position and work out solutions. His job was to say no for as long as possible" (Lavin, 1994).

◆ The "Price is always too high" tactic: The seller's price is always too high.[6]

Stratagem 8: Openly Repair the Walkway but Secretly March to Chen Cang (An Du Chen Cang)

Play overt, predictable, and public maneuvers (the walkway) against covert, surprising, and secretive ones (Chen Cang).

◆ Chinese negotiation is full of surprises; the Chinese tend to make sudden demands and changes (Stewart & Keown, 1989).

◆ The Chinese negotiate openly with one supplier but secretly with another (Seligman, 1990).

Stratagem 9: Watch the Fire Burning From Across the River (Ge An Guan Huo)

Master the art of delay. Wait for favorable conditions to emerge.

◆ The Chinese are masters of the art of stalling while keeping alive the other party's hopes; they freely use stalling tactics and delays (Pye, 1982).

◆ Time is on the Chinese side. They can use it to wait you out (Seligman, 1990).

◆ One of the mild bluffs that the Chinese occasionally employ is a posture of "We can wait until the time is ripe" (Kazuo, 1979).

Stratagem 10: Hide a Knife in a Smile (Xiao Li Cang Dao)

Hide a strong will under a compliant appearance, win the opponent's trust, and act only after his guard is down.

◆ "Foreign friends speak first" (Knutsson, 1986a, 1986b); "You are our old friend" (Blackman, 1997).

◆ The Chinese notion of friendship and hospitality is a double-edged sword (Worm, 1997); the graciousness and the bountifulness of Chinese hospitality make it awkward on the part of foreign negotiators to be too business-like in starting negotiations (Pye, 1982; see also Stratagem 31).

◆ Chinese negotiators seem to have a double-sided personality— both obstinate and flexible and both aggressive and conciliatory (Pye, 1982).

◆ Chinese hospitality causes many foreign business people to make unrealistic promises (Pye, 1982; see also Stratagem 16).

◆ The Chinese often use the "friendly" banquet to put one to the test (Dunung, 1995).

Stratagem 11: Let the Plum Tree Wither in Place of the Peach Tree *(Li Dai Tao Jiang)*

Make a small sacrifice to gain a major profit.

◆ The frontline Chinese negotiators tend to take a sharper position than that of their superiors, who usually are involved at the beginning and the final phases of negotiations (Pye, 1982).

◆ The Chinese team is a combination of the "white-face" (good-guy) and "red-face" (bad-guy) people.[7]

◆ The Chinese have been known to exploit the rotation of new faces on the foreign team. The newcomers on the foreign team may find it very hard to refute the Chinese claims of previously "established understanding" (Chen, 1993).

Stratagem 12: Lead Away a Goat in Passing *(Shun Shou Qian Yang)*

Take advantage of opportunities when they appear.

◆ "Mooching" is a popular and accepted form of behavior among the Chinese; the Chinese often expect something to be tossed in for free when they buy goods. This expectation of a little something extra extends to international trade (Chu, 1991).

◆ The following is an example of Chinese trying to get more than originally agreed: After the agreement, the Chinese had gone through every contract signed with the foreign company in any part of China during the previous 7 years and wanted all the items ever given in those contracts included in the current one. They said everything was OK, except that the foreign company should provide four service vans (Blackman, 1997).

◆ The Chinese frequently reopen negotiations in an attempt to press out additional profit (Eiteman, 1990; Pye, 1982; Schnepp et al., 1990; Seligman, 1990).

◆ The Chinese view negotiation as an opportunity to elicit as much information as possible and train themselves (Seligman, 1990; Warrington & McCall, 1983).

Stratagem 13: Beat the Grass to Startle the Snake (Da Cao Jing She)

Use direct or indirect warning and agitation.

◆ Keep silent: It is fundamental to the Chinese negotiating style to insist that the other party reveal its interests first while the Chinese mask their interests and priorities (Pye, 1982).[8]

◆ The Chinese typically do not prepare a Chinese draft until they have received the first one in English (Schnepp et al., 1990).

◆ Apply pressure to the other party and test the reactions (Seligman, 1990).

◆ The Chinese often ask many probing questions, encouraging you to tip your hand (Seligman, 1990; Yuann, 1987).

◆ Use "shaming" technique, showing anger and so on: The Chinese genuinely believe that people will be shattered by the shame of their faults, and they will attempt to use ostensible transgression to embarrass one into doing things their way (Pye, 1982; Seligman, 1990).[9]

Stratagem 14: Borrow a Corpse to Return the Soul (Jie Shi Huan Hun)

According to popular Chinese myth, the spirit of a deceased may find reincarnation. Revive something "dead" by decorating or expressing it in a new face.

◆ "Rest on big mountain" tactic: The "dying" Chinese companies view teaming up with a foreign partner in a joint venture as a means to solve their financial, technological, and management problems (Chen, 1996; Chu, 1991).[10]

Stratagem 15: Lure the Tiger to Leave the Mountains *(Diao Hu Li Shan)*

Draw the opponent out of his natural environment from which his source of power comes to make him more vulnerable to attack.

◆ Control negotiation location, schedule, and use China's ubiquitous standard form contracts (see Stratagems 4 and 22).

◆ When negotiations take unexpected turns and they need time to sort out their own position, the Chinese can declare a day of rest and send the other party off sightseeing (Seligman, 1990).

Stratagem 16: In Order to Capture, First Let It Go *(Yu Qin Gu Zong)*

The enemy should be given room to retreat so that he is not forced to act out of desperation.

◆ Chinese hospitality causes foreign business people to make unrealistic promises (Pye, 1982; see also Stratagem 10).

◆ A Chinese "offensive tactic" is calling the other side's initial concessions or flexibility "a certain progress" and urging him to offer further concessions (Kazuo, 1979).

Stratagem 17: Toss out a Brick to Attract a Piece of Jade *(Pao Zhuan Yin Yu)*

Trade something of minor value for something of major value in exchange.

◆ The Chinese are extremely price sensitive; price is uppermost in the minds of Chinese negotiators (Frankenstein, 1986; Pye, 1982).

◆ "Double standard" tactic: The Chinese tend to apply a double standard to contract compliance; they tend to be specific and deal with concrete matters only if they affect the Chinese, whereas issues of concern to foreigners are dealt with at the general level (Frankenstein, 1986). The Chinese are extremely interested in the contract language; in a joint-venture negotiation, the Chinese team may push hard to get one to guarantee to export a "fixed percentage" of the product produced, but for its own part may promise only to make its "best effort" to install the production line at the same factory (Seligman, 1990).

Stratagem 18: To Capture Bandits, First Capture the Ringleader *(Qin Zei Qin Wang)*

Deal with the most important issues first.

- ◆ The Chinese deal only with the "best": They do business only with the best firm and buy the most advanced technology (Chu, 1991; Knutsson, 1986a, 1986b; Pye, 1982).
- ◆ The Chinese expect to open negotiations with "big guns"—the top foreign business executives (Pye, 1982).
- ◆ The Chinese are unwilling to negotiate with opponents who are much younger or have a lower position than that of the Chinese.[11]

Stratagem 19: Remove the Firewood From Under the Cooking Pot *(Fu Di Chou Xin)*

Avoid confronting your opponent's strong points and remove the source of his strength.

- ◆ A former Chinese manager in the joint venture set up a rival company across the street and diverted materials from the joint venture to his new company to produce the same products (Roberts, 1997a).
- ◆ The "quality versus price" tactic: Attack your price if your quality is high; attack your quality if your price is low.[12]

Stratagem 20: Muddle the Water to Catch the Fish *(Hun Shui Mo Yu)*

Take advantage of the opponent's inability to resist when put in a difficult and complicated situation.

- ◆ "Attrition" tactics: Engage a variety of programs and protracted negotiations, causing physical and psychological inconveniences on the part of the opponents; "The Chinese subjected us to verbal and almost physical bashing. They really do work at getting you angry and wearing you down and getting you to agree to what are pretty unreasonable terms" (Blackman, 1997, p. 113).[13]

◆ "Excessive entertaining in the evening can also take the edge off a foreign negotiator's attentiveness" (Hinkelman, 1994, p. 169).

◆ A tactic that the Chinese use is to reshuffle elements of the deal in a rapid and complex way so as to confuse you (Knutsson, 1986a, 1986b).

Stratagem 21: The Golden Cicada Sheds Its Shell *(Jin Chan Tuo Qiao)*

Create an illusion by appearing to present the original "shape" to the opponent while secretly withdrawing the real "body" from danger.

◆ If the Chinese have chosen not to pursue further negotiations with you, they may communicate this only indirectly by putting excessive demands on you, making you the breaching party (Seligman, 1990).

◆ It is common that after weeks of negotiations, the foreign company receives a telephone call from the so-called "information link" in Hong Kong or China who can offer the inside information and support but asks for commission of 2% or 3% of the contract value. It is believed that the money is shared by the Chinese negotiation team leaders (Leijonhufvud & Engqvist, 1996).

Stratagem 22: Shut the Door to Catch the Thief *(Guan Men Zhuo Zei)*

Create a favorable enveloping environment to encircle the opponent and close off all his escape routes.

◆ A common tactic that the Chinese use is to ask you, upon arrival, the date and time of your departure flight (Dunung, 1995); if the Chinese know when you intend to leave, they can manipulate the schedule to squeeze you by concentrating the haggling over the most important issues into the last day or two (Seligman, 1990).

◆ The Chinese propose the negotiation "deadline" by announcing that the signing ceremony and banquet to be attended by high-ranking government officials have already been arranged on a certain date and then time press the opponents.[14]

◆ "Pre-Christmas Day push": The Chinese invite you to come to China for negotiation 1 week before Christmas Day.[15]

◆ The Chinese strategy was to dispute everything and wait until the last minute to make even the smallest concessions (Lavin, 1994).

◆ Initiate with agreement on general "spirit" or "principles" (e.g., letter of intent). Later, press the counterpart to comply with the spirit or principles (Pye, 1982).

◆ Foreign firms are often forced to use the ubiquitous standard form contracts or "model contracts" provided by Chinese government authorities and organizations (Chang, 1987; Seligman, 1990).

Stratagem 23: Befriend the Distant States While Attacking the Nearby Ones (Yuan Jiao Jin Gong)

Deal with the enemies one by one. After the neighboring state is conquered, one can then attack the distant state.

◆ The Chinese may try to split a foreign team by befriending subordinate members of the team; they may use information gained from the subordinate members to unsettle the chief negotiator and the foreign team (Blackman, 1997).

Stratagem 24: Borrow the Road to Conquer Guo (Jia Dao Fa Guo)

Deal with the enemies one by one. Use the nearby state as a springboard to reach the distant state. Then remove the nearby state.

◆ In establishing a joint venture, a primary Chinese motivation is to use the foreign partner's proprietary technology and international marketing, sales, and distribution networks to facilitate export from China (Chen, 1996; Farhang, 1994; Mann, 1989).

◆ The Chinese may be less interested in concluding a deal than in gleaning information that they can put to use in parallel negotiations with the competition (Seligman, 1990).

Stratagem 25: Steal the Beams and Change the Pillars *(Tou Liang Huan Zhu)*

In a broader sense, this stratagem refers to the use of various replacement tactics to achieve one's masked purposes.

◆ It is not uncommon for the Chinese to switch negotiators and to change the terms of a deal even after a long period of discussion (Dunung, 1995).

◆ To destabilize the foreign negotiator when discussions are not heading in their favor, the Chinese side will change both negotiators and the location of the negotiation. When a new negotiator is brought in, negotiations start again from the beginning, and former understandings are negated (Blackman, 1997).

◆ "Water in glass" manipulation.[16]

Stratagem 26: Point at the Mulberry Tree but Curse the Locust Tree *(Zhi Sang Ma Huai)*

Convey one's intention and opinions in an indirect way.

◆ Feign anger: Chinese negotiators sometimes use displays of temper to try to get what they want. The Chinese may go so far as to pack up their papers with a flourish and storm out of the negotiating room (Chang, 1987; Seligman, 1990).

Stratagem 27: Play a Sober-Minded Fool *(Jia Chi Bu Dian)*

Hide one's ambition to win by total surprise.

◆ Pretend to be an "ignorant" (Mann, 1989) or absentminded negotiator.[17]

◆ The Chinese steel themselves against feelings of empathy and are quick to move aggressively if they sense that the other party has problems (Pye, 1982).

◆ The Chinese can keep 5 minutes of total silence, making the other party volunteer an answer (Schnepp et al., 1990).

Stratagem 28: Lure the Enemy Onto the Roof, Then Take Away the Ladder *(Shang Wu Chou Ti)*

Lure the enemy into a trap and then cut off his escape route.

- ◆ Take advantage of the adversary's time schedule: Squeeze him out and sign the contract shortly before his scheduled departure for the airport (Mann, 1989).
- ◆ The Chinese sometimes push you to the brink of terminating the negotiations to determine your true bottom line (Seligman, 1990).

Stratagem 29: Flowers Bloom in the Tree *(Shu Shang Kai Hua)*

One can decorate a flowerless tree with lifelike but artificial flowers attached to it so that it looks like a tree capable of bearing flowers. One who lacks internal strength may resort to external forces to achieve his goal.

- ◆ Use the "external force" (e.g., "government approval" and "internal regulation") to gain bargaining power (Chang, 1987; Seligman, 1990).[18]
- ◆ The Chinese employ "swaying tactics" (Kazuo, 1979) to undermine the position and prestige of the other negotiators: They will not hesitate to discuss historical, political, and personal issues if they sense that these may be effective (Kazuo, 1979; Seligman, 1990). They also link international political issues with commercial negotiations (Frankenstein, 1986).
- ◆ The Chinese insist that to keep good governmental relations the level of business must be increased (March, 1994).
- ◆ The Chinese can use interpreters strategically—for example, an English-speaking Chinese negotiator may use the translation process to observe the other party's nonverbal behaviors and to get twice the response time (Graham & Herberger, 1983).
- ◆ Borrow the foreign partner's strength to deal with Chinese bureaucracy (Seligman, 1990).

Stratagem 30: The Guest Becomes the Host *(Fan Ke Wei Zhu)*

Turn one's defensive and passive position into an offensive and active one.

- ◆ Play the card of "the last big market on the planet"; it is always the foreign business people who are seeking favors from China (Eiteman, 1990; Pye, 1982).
- ◆ Use China's economic weakness as a bargaining point: The Chinese try to get a Westerner to understand their problems and then push him for a concession, and they will not hesitate to point out that the foreign company has far greater resources than the Chinese party (Frankenstein, 1986; Seligman, 1990).

Stratagem 31: The Beautiful Woman Stratagem *(Mei Ren Ji)*

Use women, temptation, and espionage to overpower the enemy: Attach importance to espionage, intelligence, and information collecting.

- ◆ Capture your feeling of kindness; manipulate friendship and obligation (see Stratagem 10).
- ◆ Use social activities (i.e., banquets, sightseeing, karaoke bar, and gifts) to size up the other party.[19]
- ◆ Espionage: A Chinese organization will collect all the information it can about a foreign company from other Chinese organizations (Yuann, 1987).[20]

Stratagem 32: The Empty City Stratagem *(Kong Cheng Ji)*

If you have absolutely no means of defense for your city, and you openly display this vulnerable situation to your suspicious enemy by just opening the city gate, he is likely to assume the opposite. A deliberate display of weakness can conceal the true vulnerability and thus confuse the enemy. The stratagem also implies a situation in which the opponent is manipulated with "emptiness" and can also be used to mean something with a grand exterior but a void interior.

◆ "Your silence means Yes": The Chinese may make use of foreigners' stereotypes about China (e.g., cultural complication and political bureaucracy) to their advantage. They "consciously" misinterpret anything one says and turn things around to their way (Knutsson, 1986a, 1986b).[21]

◆ The Chinese often say, "If you give us this product at a very low price, your future success in China will be guaranteed" (Knutsson, 1986a, 1986b).

◆ "Along the way, the Chinese negotiators offered a series of empty concessions" (Lavin, 1994, pp. 19-20).

▨ Stratagem 33: The Counterespionage Stratagem (Fan Jian Ji)

When the enemy's spy is detected, do not "beat the grass to startle the snake" but furnish him with false information to sow discord in his camp. Maintain high intelligence and alertness.

◆ The Chinese do their homework (i.e., planning and information collecting) well (Schnepp et al., 1990).[22]

◆ The Chinese are suspicious of everything; they seem to always be worried that foreigners are trying to cheat them (Knutsson, 1986a, 1986b).[23]

◆ Apply calculated pressure to the ethnic Chinese (or Chinese-speaking persons) on the foreign team, making them not an automatic advantage for the opponents; overseas Chinese on the foreign team are far more likely to be pressed for kickbacks from the Chinese side and may be treated poorly when they fail to comply (Chen, 1993; Seligman, 1990).

▨ Stratagem 34: The Self-Torture Stratagem
(Ku Rou Ji)

Display one's own suffering to win sympathy from others.

◆ The "We are very poor, indeed" tactic: "Frank" exposure of China's backwardness (e.g., lack of foreign exchange) to gain a bargaining advantage—China is a very poor country and cannot afford to pay the price foreigners ask (Seligman, 1990).[24]

◆ The Chinese have every expectation that it is only right for the better off or richer partner to bear the heavier burden without protest (Pye, 1982; Seligman, 1990). The Chinese expect that people are somehow quite naturally going to help them and, equally naturally, want to do it for nothing (Schnepp et al., 1990).

▨ Stratagem 35: The Stratagem of Interrelated Stratagems *(Lian Huan Ji)*

This stratagem combines various stratagems into one interconnected arrangement. It is also the deliberate planning of a series of stratagems

◆ A number of Chinese stratagems might be at work at the same time; several tactics are systematically used by Chinese negotiators, such as controlling location and schedule, utilizing weaknesses, using the shame technique, pitting competitors against each other, feigning anger, rehashing old issues, and manipulating expectations.

▨ Stratagem 36: Running Away Is the Best Stratagem *(Zou Wei Shang Ji)*

"A good fighter flees from the danger of the moment": Run away when all else fails. Endure temporary disgrace and losses to win ultimate victory. Run away to gain bargaining power.

♦ The Chinese generally try to avoid or postpone direct confrontation (Chen, 1993).

♦ "The Chinese said, 'You cannot threaten us. This will hurt you more than it will hurt us. We have lived without trade with the United States for five thousand years, and we will do so for five thousand more, etc.' " (Lavin, 1994).

♦ The "everything is in China" perspective or the "long-term" negotiating tactic: The technology will remain in China, and the foreign partner will be gone after a period of years (Seligman, 1990).

♦ "The real problems don't come in negotiating the deal—the real problems start after you sign the contract" (Hendryx, 1986, p. 75).

Notes

1. Evident in this book (see Chapter 4, Illustrations 37 and 38).
2. Evident in this book (see Chapter 4, Illustrations 12 and 32; see also Stratagem 29).
3. Not evident in this book (see Chapter 4, Illustration 36).
4. Evident in this book (see Chapter 4, Illustration 33).
5. Evident in this book (see Chapter 4, Illustration 13).
6. Evident in this book (see Chapter 4, Illustrations 18 and 19).
7. Evident in this book (see Chapter 4, Illustration 32).
8. Evident in this book (see Chapter 4, Illustration 39).
9. Evident in this book (see Chapter 4, Illustration 32).
10. Evident in this book (see Chapter 4, Illustration 15).
11. Evident in this book (see Chapter 4, Illustration 24). A Confucian explanation, however, is more reasonable in this case.
12. Evident in this book (see Chapter 4, Illustration 18).
13. Not evident in this book (see Chapter 4, Illustration 35).
14. Evident in this book (see Chapter 4, Illustration 33).
15. Evident in this book (see Chapter 4, Illustration 31).
16. Evident in this book (see Chapter 4, Illustration 30).
17. Evident in this book (see Chapter 4, Illustration 39).
18. Evident in this book (see Chapter 4, Illustrations 12 and 32; see also Stratagem 3).
19. Evident in this book (see Chapter 4, Illustrations 21 and 30).
20. Evident in this book (see Chapter 4, Illustrations 4 and 32; see also Stratagem 33).
21. Evident in this book (see Chapter 4, Illustration 34).
22. Evident in this book (see Chapter 4, Illustrations 4 and 32; see also Stratagem 31).
23. Evident in this book (see Chapter 4, Illustration 27).
24. Evident in this book (see Chapter 4, Illustration 17).

Appendix B
The Empty City Stratagem[1]

Figure B.1
SOURCE: Drawing by Tony Fang; copyright 1998 by Tony Fang.

During the Three Kingdoms period (A.D. 220-265), Kung Min sent his troops to battle. His city was left without good protection. His greatest enemy, Si Ma, the commander of the army of Wei, made an unexpected approach while Kung Min was in this vulnerable position. But Kung Min used the empty-city strategy to defend the city. He sent an old man to open the city's front gate and sweep the entranceway. Kung Min then went to his tower to prepare food and wine. He played a musical instrument and sang poetry as if he had not a care in the world. Commander Si Ma approached the city gates, but hesitated to enter. He was wary of tricks and feared a trap was waiting because of this obvious lack of security. Si Ma ordered his troops to retreat and wait so he might discover the true situation. While Si Ma waited and wondered, Kung Min's soldiers returned from their campaign and the city was once more defended.

—Chu (1991, pp. 71-72)

Note

1. A detailed story of the empty city stratagem can be found in *Three Kingdoms* (Luo, 1994, pp. 1137-1150).

References

Adler, N. J. (1991). *International dimensions of organizational behavior* (2nd ed.). Boston: PWS-Kent.

Adler, N. J., & Bartholomew, S. (1991). Academic and professional communities of discourse: Generating knowledge on transnational human research management. *Journal of International Business Studies, 23*(3), 551-569.

Adler, N. J., Brahm, R., & Graham, J. L. (1992). Strategy implementation: A comparison of face-to-face negotiations in the People's Republic of China and the United States. *Strategic Management Journal, 13*(6), 449-466.

Adler, N. J., Campbell, N., & Laurent, A. (1989). In search of appropriate methodology: From outside the People's Republic of China looking in. *Journal of International Business Studies, 20*(1), 61-74.

Angelmar, R., & Sten, L. W. (1978). Development of content analytic system for analysis of bargaining communication in marketing. *Journal of Marketing Research, 15*(1), 93-102.

Asians at play: A good day out. (1996, December 21). *The Economist,* 87-90.

Bagozzi, R. P. (1978). Marketing as exchange: A theory of transactions in the market place. *Journal of Marketing, 39*(4), 32-39.

Baker, H. (1993). Symbolism in cross-cultural trade: Making Chinese symbols work for you. In T. D. Weinshall (Ed.), *Societal culture and management* (pp. 271-278). Berlin: de Gruyter.

Barnouw, V. (1979). *Culture and personality.* Homewood, IL: Dorsey.

Berger, P. L. (1988). An East Asian development model? In P. L. Berger & H.-H. M. Hsiao (Eds.), *In search of an East Asian development model* (pp. 3-11). New Brunswick, NJ: Transaction Books.

Berger, P. L., & Hsiao, H.-H. M. (Eds.). (1988). *In search of an East Asian development model.* New Brunswick, NJ: Transaction Books.

Berry, J. W. (1980). Introduction to methodology. In H. C. Triandis & J. W. Berry (Eds.), *Handbook of cross-cultural psychology* (Vol. 2, pp. 1-28). Boston: Allyn & Bacon.

Björkman, I. (1994). Role perception and behavior among Chinese managers in Sino-Western joint ventures. In S. Stewart (Ed.), *Advances in Chinese industrial studies* (Vol. 4, pp. 273-283). Greenwich, CT: JAI.

Blackman, C. (1997). *Negotiating China: Case studies and strategies.* St. Leonards, NSW, Australia: Allen & Unwin.

Bo, Y. (1992). *The ugly Chinaman and the crisis of Chinese culture.* St. Leonards, NSW, Australia: Allen & Unwin.

Boisot, M., & Xing, G. L. (1992). The nature of managerial work in the Chinese enterprise reform: A study of six directors. *Organization Studies, 13*(2), 161-184.

Bond, M. H. (1991). *Beyond the Chinese face: Insights from psychology.* Hong Kong: Oxford University Press.

Bond, M. H. (Ed.). (1996). *The handbook of Chinese psychology.* Hong Kong: Oxford University Press.

Bond, M. H., & Hofstede, G. (1989). The cash value of Confucian values. *Human Systems Management, 8,* 195-200.

Bond, M. H., & Hwang, K.-K. (1986). The social psychology of Chinese people. In M. H. Bond (Ed.), *The psychology of the Chinese people* (pp. 213-266). Hong Kong: Oxford University Press.

Bond, M. H., & Wang, S. (1983). China: Aggressive behavior and the problem of maintaining order and harmony. In A. P. Goldstein & M. H. Segall (Eds.), *Aggression in global perspective* (pp. 58-74). New York: Pergamon.

Bonoma, T. V., & Johnston, W. J. (1978). The social psychology of industrial buying and selling. *Industrial Marketing Management, 7*(4), 213-224.

Brislin, R. W. (1983). Cross-cultural research in psychology. *Annual Review of Psychology, 34,* 363-400.

Brislin, R. W. (1993). *Understanding culture's influence on behavior.* Fort Worth, TX: Harcourt Brace.

Brislin, R. W., & Hui, C. H. (1993). The preparation of managers for overseas assignments. In L. Kelley & O. Shenkar (Eds.), *International business in China* (pp. 233-258). London: Routledge.

Brislin, R. W., Lonner, W. J., & Thorndike, R. M. (1973). *Cross-cultural research methods.* New York: John Wiley.

Brown, L. R. (1995). *Who will feed China? Wake-up call for a small planet.* New York: Norton.

Brown, R. C. (1993). The role of the legal environment in doing business in the People's Republic of China. In L. Kelley & O. Shenkar (Eds.), *International business in China* (pp. 63-87). London: Routledge.

Brunner, J. A., & Taoka, G. M. (1977). Marketing and negotiating in the People's Republic of China: Perceptions of American businessmen who attended the 1975 Canton Fair. *Journal of International Business Studies, 8*(2), 69-82.

Brunner, J. A., & Wang, Y. (1988). Chinese negotiating and the Chinese concept of face. *Journal of International Consumer Marketing, 1*(1), 27-43.

Buzzell, R. D., & Gale, B. T. (1987). *The PIMS principles: Linking strategy to performance.* New York: Free Press.

Campbell, N., & Adlington, P. (1988). *China business strategies.* Oxford, UK: Pergamon.

Cao, Y. Z., Fan, G., & Woo, W. T. (1997). Chinese economic reforms: Past successes and future challenges. In W. T. Woo, S. Parker, & J. D. Sachs (Eds.), *Economies in transition: Comparing Asia and Eastern Europe* (pp. 19-39). Cambridge: MIT Press.

Carver, A. (1996). Open and secret regulations and their implication for foreign investment. In J. Child & Y. Lu (Eds.), *Management issues in China: Volume II* (pp. 11-29). London: Routledge.

Chai, Y. Q. (1992). *The bank of stratagems.* Nanning, China: Guang Xi People's Press. (In Chinese)

Chan, W.-T. (1963). *A source book in Chinese philosophy.* Princeton, NJ: Princeton University Press.

Chang, J. (1991). *The Tao of love and sex: The ancient Chinese way to ecstasy.* New York: Penguin.

Chang, J. (1992). *Wild swans: Three daughters of China.* New York: Anchor.

Chang, J.-L. J. (1991). Negotiation of the 17 August 1982 U.S.-PRC Arms Communiqué: Beijing's negotiating tactics. *China Quarterly, 125,* 33-54.

Chang, T.-k. (1987). The great battle of the forms. *China Business Review, 14*(4), 7-11.

Chen, D. R., & Faure, G. O. (1995). When Chinese companies negotiate with their government. *Organization Studies, 16*(1), 27-54.

Chen, M. (1993). Tricks of the China trade. *China Business Review, 20*(2), 12-16.

Chen, M. (1995). *Asian management systems: Chinese, Japanese and Korean styles of business.* London: Routledge.

Chen, M. (1996). *Managing international technology transfer.* London: International Thomson Business Press.

Chen, M., & Ying, W. J. (1994). Beware the fisherman. *China Business Review, 21*(3), 26-27.

Chen, S., & Xiao, X. W. (Eds.). (1992). *Comprehensive handbook of Sino-foreign enterprise management and contract negotiating.* Beijing: Hua Wen Press. (In Chinese)

Cheng, S. K. K. (1990). Understanding the culture and behaviour of East Asians—A Confucian perspective. *Australian and New Zealand Journal of Psychiatry, 24*(4), 510-515.

Chiao, C. (1981). Chinese strategic behaviors: A preliminary list. In *Proceedings of the International Conference on Sinology* (pp. 429-440). Taipei: Academia Sinica.

Child, J. (1990). Introduction: The character of Chinese enterprise management. In J. Child & M. Lockett (Eds.), *Advances in Chinese industrial studies* (Part A, pp. 137-152). Greenwich, CT: JAI.

Child, J. (1994). *Management in China during the age of reform.* Cambridge, UK: Cambridge University Press.

Child, J., & Lu, Y. (1990). Industrial decision-making under China's reform. *Organization Studies, 11*(3), 321-351.

Child, J., & Lu, Y. (1996). China and international enterprise. In J. Child & Y. Lu (Eds.), *Management issues in China: Volume II* (pp. 1-8). London: Routledge.

Child, J., & Markoczy, L. (1993). Host-country management behavior and learning in Chinese and Hungarian joint ventures. *Journal of Management Studies, 30*(4), 611-631.

The Chinese Culture Connection. (1987). Chinese values and the search for culture-free dimensions of culture. *Journal of Cross-Cultural Psychology, 18*(2), 143-164.

Christopher, M., Payne, A., & Ballantyne, D. (1993). *Relationship marketing: Bringing quality, customer service and marketing together.* Oxford, UK: Butterworth-Heinemann.

Chu, C.-N. (1991). *The Asian mind game.* New York: Rawson.

Chu, C.-N. (1992). *Thick face black heart: The path to thriving, winning and succeeding.* Beaverton, OR: AMC.

Churchman, C. W. (1968). *The systems approach.* New York: A Delta Book.

Cohen, R. (1991). *Negotiating across cultures.* Washington, DC: Institute of Peace Press.

Constitution of the Communist Party of China, The. (1982). In J. C. F. Wang, *Contemporary Chinese Politics,* (pp. 356-380). Englewood Cliffs, NJ: Prentice Hall.

Cooper, J. C. (1990). *Taoism: The way of the mystic* (Rev. ed.). San Bernardino, CA: Borgo.

Dadfar, H. (1984). *Marketing progress and buyer behavior in the Middle-East: A deep structure approach* (Thesis No. 34). Linköping University, Department of Management and Economics, Linköping, Sweden.

Dadfar, H. (1988). *International business negotiation.* Unpublished manuscript, Linköping University, Department of Management and Economics, Linköping, Sweden.

Dadfar, H. (1990). *Industrial buying behavior in the Middle East: A cross national study.* Doctoral dissertation, Linköping University, Department of Management and Economics, Linköping, Sweden.

Davidson, M. (1995). *The transformation of management.* London: Macmillan.

Davidson, W. H. (1987). Creating and managing joint ventures in China. *California Management Review, 29*(4), 77-95.

Davies, D. (1984, June 21). How Britain fell for the Peking game-plan. *Far Eastern Economic Review,* 44-45.

Davies, H., Leung, T. K. P., Luk, S. T. K., & Wong, Y.-h. (1995). The benefits of "Guanxi": The value of relationships in developing the Chinese market. *Industrial Marketing Management, 24*(3), 207-214.

Dawson, R. (1995). *Roger Dawson's secrets of power negotiating.* Hawthorne, NJ: Career Press.

de Anzizu, J. M., & Chen, D. (1991). General management in China: An emerging and complex task. In N. Campbell (Ed.), *Advances in Chinese industrial studies* (Vol. 2, pp. 55-68). Greenwich, CT: JAI.

de Bary, W. T., Chan, W.-t., & Watson, B. (Eds.). (1960). *Sources of Chinese tradition.* New York: Columbia University Press.

de Bruijn, E. J., & Jia, X. F. (1993, January/February). Transferring technology to China by means of joint ventures. *Research Technology Management, 36*(1), 17-22.

de Keijzer, A. J. (1992). *China: Business strategies for the '90s.* Berkeley, CA: Pacific View Press.

de Mente, B. (1992). *Chinese etiquette and ethics in business: A penetrating analysis of the morals and values that shape the Chinese business personality.* Lincolnwood, IL: NTC Business Books.

Deming, W. E. (1993). *The new economics for industry, government, education.* Cambridge: MIT, Center for Advanced Engineering Study.

Deng, X. P. (1985). *Building socialism with Chinese characteristics.* Beijing: Foreign Languages Press.

Deng, X. P. (1987). *Fundamental issues in present-day China.* Beijing: Foreign Languages Press.

de Pauw, J. W. (1981). *U.S.-Chinese trade negotiations.* New York: Praeger.

Deverge, M. (1983). Understanding Confucianism. *Euro-Asia Business Review, 2*(3), 50-53.

Deverge, M. (1986). Negotiating with the Chinese. *Euro-Asia Business Review, 5*(1), 34-36.

Dubin, R. (1978). *Theory building* (Rev. ed.). New York: Free Press.

Dunung, S. P. (1995). *Doing business in Asia.* New York: Lexington Books.

Dutton, M. R. (1992). *Policing and punishment in China: From patriarchy to "the people."* Cambridge, UK: Cambridge University Press.

Eberhard, W. (1971). *Moral and social values of the Chinese: Collected essays* (Chinese Materials and Research Aids Service Center Occasional Series No. 6). Taipei: Cheng Wen Press.

Ebrey, P. B. (Ed.). (1993). *Chinese civilization: A sourcebook.* New York: Free Press.

Eitel, E. J. (1984). *Feng-Shui: The science of sacred landscape in Old China.* London: Synergetic Press. (Original work published 1873)

Eiteman, D. K. (1990). American executives' perceptions of negotiating joint ventures with the People's Republic of China: Lessons learned. *Columbia Journal of World Business, 25*(4), 59-66.

Fairbank, J. K. (1974). Introduction: Varieties of the Chinese military experience. In F. A. Kierman, Jr., & J. K. Fairbank (Eds.), *Chinese ways in warfare* (pp. 1-26). Cambridge, MA: Harvard University Press.

Fairbank, J. K. (1992). *China: A new history.* Cambridge, MA: Harvard University Press.

Fan, J. R., & Yan, T. F. (1990). Principles and skills for marketing negotiations. In H. Kuang (Ed.), *Encyclopedia of modern marketing* (pp. 623-648). Beijing: Economics and Management Press. (In Chinese)

Fang, S. (1992, February 24). On opening to the outside world and utilizing capitalism. *People's Daily* (Overseas ed.). (In Chinese)

Fang, T. (1993). *The model of the Chinese mind: A conceptual framework for understanding Chinese business negotiating behavior* (Working Paper No. LIU/ EKIWPS9306). Linköping, Sweden: Linköping University, Department of Management and Economics.

Fang, T. (1995). Chinese stratagem and Chinese business negotiating behavior: An introduction to *Ji.* In P. Turnbull, D. Yorke, & P. Naude (Eds.), *The 11th IMP International Conference proceedings* (Vol. 3, pp. 1369-1400). Manchester, UK: Manchester Federal School of Business and Management.

Fang, T. (1996). *A model of Chinese business negotiating style.* Paper presented at the 6th Nordic Workshop on Interorganizational Research, August 23-25, Norwegian School of Management, School of Marketing, Oslo.

Fang, T. (1997a). *Chinese business negotiating style: A socio-cultural approach.* Licentiate dissertation, Linköping University, Linköping, Sweden.

Fang, T. (1997b). *Chinese negotiating tactics: A study of Ji.* Paper presented at the 17th Strategic Management Society Annual International Conference, October 5-8, Barcelona.

Fang, T. (1997c). The "Coop-Comp" Chinese negotiation strategy. In F. Mazet, R. Salle, & J.-P. Valla (Eds.), *The 13th IMP International Conference proceedings* (pp. 187-216). Lyon, France: Lyon Graduate School of Business.

Fang, T. (1998). *Reflection on Hofstede's fifth dimension: A critique of "Confucian Dynamism."* Paper presented at the Academy of Management Conference, August 9-12, San Diego, CA.

Fang, T., & Timm, K. (1995). Book review: Chinese negotiating style. *Scandinavian Journal of Management, 11*(3), 299-300.

Farhang, M. (1994). *International inter-firm transfer of technology: Case studies from Swedish firms' joint ventures and licensing operations in China.* Doctoral dissertation, Luleå University of Technology, Luleå, Sweden.

Faure, G. O., & Sjöstedt, G. (1993). Culture and negotiation: An introduction. In G. O. Faure & J. Z. Rubin (Eds.), *Culture and negotiation: The resolution of water disputes* (pp. 1-13). Newbury Park, CA: Sage.

Fayerweather, J., & Kapoor, A. (1976). *Strategy and negotiation for the international corporation: Guidelines and cases.* Cambridge, MA: Ballinger.

Feng, J. C. (1996, March 12). Festival highlights life, culture. *China Daily,* p. 9.

Ferraro, G. P. (1990). *The cultural dimension of international business.* Englewood Cliffs, NJ: Prentice Hall.

Feuerwerker, A. (1990). Chinese economic history in comparative perspective. In P. S. Ropp (Ed.), *Heritage of China: Contemporary perspectives on Chinese civilization* (pp. 224-241). Berkeley: University of California Press.

Firth, A. (Ed.). (1995). *The discourse of negotiation.* Oxford, UK: Pergamon.

Fisher, G. (1980). *International negotiation: A cross-cultural perspective.* Yarmouth, MA: Intercultural Press.

Fisher, R., & Ury, W. (1981). *Getting to yes.* London: Hutchinson.

Foster, L. W., & Tosi, L. (1990). Business in China: A year after Tiananmen. *Journal of Business Strategy, 11*(3), 22-27.

Francis, J. N. P. (1991). When in Rome? The effects of cultural adaptation on intercultural business negotiations. *Journal of International Business Studies, 22*(3), 403-428.

Franke, R. H., Hofstede, G., & Bond, M. H. (1991, Summer). Cultural roots of economic performance: A research note [Special issue]. *Strategic Management Journal, 12,* 165-173.

Frankenstein, J. (1986). Trend in Chinese business practice: Change in the Beijing wind. *California Management Review, 29*(1), 148-160.

Frankenstein, J. (1993). Toward the Year 2000: Some strategic speculations about international business in China. In L. Kelley & O. Shenkar (Eds.), *International business in China* (pp. 1-28). London: Routledge.

Fukuyama, F. (1995). *Trust: The social virtues and the creation of prosperity.* London: Hamish Hamilton.

Fung, Y.-L. (1966). *A short history of Chinese philosophy.* New York: Free Press. (Original work published 1948)

Gao, G. P. (1993). International business in China. In L. Kelley & O. Shenkar (Eds.), *International business in China* (pp. 225-232). London: Routledge.

Gao, G. P., Ting-Toomey, S., & Gudykunst, W. B. (1996). Chinese communication processes. In M. H. Bond (Ed.), *The handbook of Chinese psychology* (pp. 280-293). Hong Kong: Oxford University Press.

Gao, Y. (1991). *Lure the tiger out of the mountains: The thirty-six stratagems of ancient China.* New York: Simon & Schuster.

Garston, N. (Ed.). (1993). *Bureaucracy: Three paradigms.* Boston: Kluwer.

Geertz, C. (1973). *The interpretation of cultures.* New York: Basic Books.

George, C. S., Jr. (1972). *The history of management thought.* Englewood Cliffs, NJ: Prentice Hall.

Ghauri, P. (1983). *Negotiating international package deals: Swedish firms and developing countries.* Doctoral dissertation, University of Uppsala, Uppsala, Sweden.

Ghauri, P. (1996). Introduction. In P. Ghauri & J.-C. Usunier (Eds.), *International business negotiations* (pp. 3-20). Oxford, UK: Pergamon.

Ghauri, P., & Usunier, J.-C. (Eds.). (1996). *International business negotiations.* Oxford, UK: Pergamon.

Goffman, E. (1955). On face-work: An analysis of ritual elements in social interaction. *Psychiatry, 18*(3), 213-231.

Goldenberg, S. (1988). *Hands across the ocean: Managing joint ventures with a spotlight on China and Japan.* Boston: Harvard Business School Press.

Gorman, T. D. (1986). China's changing foreign trade system 1975-85. In R. Delfs, T. D. Gorman, & O. D. Nee, Jr. (Eds.), *China* (pp. 81-100). London: Euromoney.

Graham, J. L. (1985a). Cross-cultural marketing negotiations: A laboratory experiment. *Marketing Science, 4*(2), 130-146.

Graham, J. L. (1985b). The influence of culture on the process of business negotiations. An exploratory study. *Journal of International Business Studies, 16*(1), 81-97.

Graham, J. L. (1986). The problem-solving approach to negotiations in industrial marketing. *Journal of Business Research, 14*(6), 549-566.

Graham, J. L. (1996). *Vis-a-vis* international business negotiations. In P. Ghauri & J.-C. Usunier (Eds.), *International business negotiations* (pp. 69-90). Oxford, UK: Pergamon.

Graham, J. L., & Herberger, R. A., Jr. (1983, July/August). Negotiators abroad—Don't shoot from the hip. *Harvard Business Review,* 160-168.

Graham, J. L., & Lin, C.-Y. (1987). A comparison of marketing negotiations in the Republic of China (Taiwan) and the United States. In *Advances in International Marketing* (Vol. 2, pp. 23-46). Greenwich, CT: JAI.

Graham, J. L., Mintu, A. T., & Rodgers, W. (1994). Explorations of negotiation behaviors in ten foreign cultures using a model developed in the United States. *Management Science, 40*(1), 72-95.

Graham, J. L., & Sano, Y. (1986). Across the negotiating table from the Japanese. *International Marketing Review, 3*(3), 58-71.

Graham, J. L., & Sano, Y. (1989). *Smart bargaining: Doing business with the Japanese* (Rev. ed.). New York: Harper Business.

Graham, J. L., Kim, D. K., Lin, C.-Y., & Robinson, M. (1988). Buyer-seller negotiations around the Pacific Rim: Differences in fundamental exchange processes. *Journal of Consumer Research, 15*(1), 48-54.

Granström, L. (1996). Packed and ready for Shanghai. *Contact* (No. 6, a newspaper of Ericsson). (In Swedish)

Grant, R. M. (1991). The resource-based theory of competitive advantage: Implications for strategy formulation. *California Management Review, 33*(3), 114-135.

Griffith, S. B. (1982). Preface. In S. B. Griffith (Trans.), *Sun Tzu: The art of war.* London: Oxford University Press. (Original work published 1963)

Grönroos, C. (1992). Quo vadis, marketing? Towards a neo-classical marketing theory. In H. C. Blomqvist, C. Grönroos, & L.-J. Lindqvist (Eds.), *Economics and marketing: Essays in honour of Gösta Mickwitz* (pp. 109-196). Helsinki: Swedish School of Economics and Business Administration.

Gu, Y. G. (1990). Politeness phenomena in modern Chinese. *Journal of Pragmatics,* *14*(2), 237-257.

Gudykunst, W. B., & Ting-Tommey, S. (1996). Communication in personal relationships across cultures: An introduction. In W. B. Gudykunst, S. Ting-Toomey, & T. Nishida (Eds.), *Communication in personal relationships across cultures* (pp. 3-16). Thousand Oaks, CA: Sage.

Gummesson, E. (1987). The new marketing—Developing long-term interactive relationships. *Long Range Planning, 20*(4), 10-20.

Hakam, A. N., & Chan, K. Y. (1990). Negotiations between Singaporeans and firms in China: The case of a Singaporean electronics firm contemplating investment in China. In N. Campbell (Ed.), *Advances in Chinese industrial studies* (Part B, pp. 249-261). Greenwich, CT: JAI.

Håkansson, H. (1982). *International marketing and purchasing of industrial goods: An interaction approach.* Chichester, UK: Wiley.

Hall, E. T. (1959). *The silent language.* New York: Doubleday.

Hall, E. T. (1981). *Beyond culture.* New York: Anchor. (Original work published 1976)

Hall, E. T., & Hall, M. R. (1989). *Understanding cultural differences.* Yarmouth, MA: Intercultural Press.

Hall, L. (Ed.). (1993). *Negotiation: Strategies for mutual gain.* Newbury Park, CA: Sage.

Hamel, G., & Heene, A. (Eds.). (1994). *Competence-based competition.* Chichester, UK: Wiley.

Handel, M. (1992). *Masters of war: Sun Tzu, Clausewitz and Jomini.* London: Frank Cass.

Harnett, D. L., & Cummings, L. L. (1980). *Bargaining behavior: An international study.* Houston: Dame.

Harris, P. R., & Moran, R. T. (1996). *Managing cultural differences.* Houston: Gulf.

Hart, B. H. L. (1982). Foreword. In S. B. Griffith (Trans.), *Sun Tzu: The art of war* (pp. v-vii). London: Oxford University Press. (Original work published 1963)

Hendon, D. W., Hendon, R. A., & Herbig, P. (1996). *Cross-cultural business negotiations.* Westport, CT: Quorum.

Hendryx, S. R. (1986, July/August). The Chinese trade: Making the deal work. *Harvard Business Review, 75,* 81-84.

Herbig, P. A., & Kramer, H. E. (1992). Do's and don'ts of cross-cultural negotiations. *Industrial Marketing Management, 21*(4), 287-298.

Herskovits, M. J. (1955). *Cultural anthropology.* New York: Knopf.

Hicks, G. L., & Redding, R. G. (1983a). The story of the East Asian "economic miracle": Part Two: The culture connection. *Euro-Asia Business Review, 2*(4), 18-22.

Hicks, G. L., & Redding, R. G. (1983b). The story of the East Asian "economic miracle": Part One: Economic theory be damned! *Euro-Asia Business Review, 2*(3), 24-32.

Hillier, T. J. (1975). Decision-making in the corporate industrial buying process. *Industrial Marketing Management, 4*(2/3), 99-106.

Hinkelman, E. G. (Ed.). (1994). *Chinese business: The portable encyclopedia for doing business with China.* San Rafael, CA: World Trade Press.

Ho, D. Y.-f. (1976). On the concept of face. *American Journal of Sociology, 81*(4), 867-884.

Ho, S. K. (1997). Competitive strategies through Sun Tzu's *Art of Warfare. Strategic Change, 6*(3), 133-147.

Ho, S. K., & Choi, A. S. F. (1997). Achieving marketing success through Sun Tzu's *Art of Warfare. Marketing Intelligence & Planning, 15*(1), 38-47.

Hofheinz, R., Jr., & Calder, K. E. (1982). *The Eastasia edge.* New York: Basic Books.

Hofstede, G. (1980). *Culture's consequences: International differences in work-related values.* Beverly Hills, CA: Sage.

Hofstede, G. (1991). *Cultures and organizations: Software of the mind.* London: McGraw-Hill.

Hofstede, G., & Bond, M. H. (1988). The Confucius connection: From cultural roots to economic growth. *Organizational Dynamics, 16*(4), 5-21.

Hofstede, G., & Usunier, J.-C. (1996). Hofstede's dimensions of culture and their influence on international business negotiations. In P. Ghauri & J.-C. Usunier (Eds.), *International business negotiations* (pp. 119-129). Oxford, UK: Pergamon.

Holmes, M. E. (1992). Phase structures in negotiation. In L. L. Putnam & M. E. Roloff (Eds.), *Communication and negotiation* (pp. 83-105). Newbury Park, CA: Sage.

Hoose, H. P. (1974). How to negotiate with the Chinese of the PRC. In W. W. Whitson (Ed.), *Doing business with China: American trade opportunities in the 1970s* (pp. 449-469). New York: Praeger.

Hsiao, F. S. T., Jen, F. C., & Lee, C. F. (1990). Impacts of culture and Communist orthodoxy on Chinese management. In J. Child & M. Lockett (Eds.), *Advances in Chinese industrial studies* (Part A, pp. 301-314). Greenwich, CT: JAI.

Hsieh, C.-H., & Liu, C. (1992). The importance of personal contact in trading with China. *Review of Business, 14*(2), 41-42.

Hsu, F. L. K. (1963). *Clan, caste, and club.* Princeton, NJ: Van Nostrand.

Hu, H. C. (1944). The Chinese concepts of "Face." *American Anthropologist, 46*(1), 45-64.

Hu, W. L. (1994). China's social custom and traditions in business relations. In J. Reuvid (Ed.), *Doing business with China* (pp. 234-241). London: Kogan Page.

Hu, W. Z., & Grove, C. L. (1991). *Encountering the Chinese: A guide for Americans.* Yarmouth, MA: Intercultural Press.

Huang, Q. Y., Leonard, J., & Chen, T. (1997). *Business decision making in China.* New York: International Business Press.

Huang, Y. S. (1996). *Inflation and investment controls in China: The political economy of central-local relations during the reform era.* Cambridge, UK: Cambridge University Press.

Hunt, R. G., & Yang, G. (1990). Decision making and power relations in the Chinese enterprise: Managers and party secretaries. In J. Child & M. Lockett (Eds.), *Advances in Chinese industrial studies* (Part A, pp. 203-225). Greenwich, CT: JAI.

Huntington, S. P. (1996). *The clash of civilizations and the remaking of world order.* New York: Simon & Schuster.

Hwang, K.-k. (1987). Face and favor: The Chinese power game. *American Journal of Sociology, 92*(4), 944-974.

Iké, F. C. (1968). *How nations negotiate.* New York: Praeger. (Original work published 1964)

Jackson, P. M. (1982). *The political economy of bureaucracy.* Oxford, UK: Philip Alan.

Jackson, S. (1992). *Chinese enterprise management reforms in economic perspective.* Berlin: de Guyter.

Jansson, H. (1994). *Industrial products: A guide to the international marketing economics model.* New York: International Business Press.

Jarillo, J. C., & Ricart, J. E. (1987). Sustaining networks. *Interfaces, 17*(5), 82-91.

Jiang: State-run firms are backbone. (1996, March 9). *China Daily,* p. 1.

Jin, L. N. (1994). *A grand look at Three Kingdoms.* Shanghai: Ancient Books. (In Chinese)

Kahn, H. (1979). *World economic development: 1979 and beyond.* London: Croom Helm.

Kao, J. (1993, March/April). The worldwide web of Chinese business. *Harvard Business Review,* 24-36.

Kazuo, O. (1979, September). How the "inscrutables" negotiate with the "inscrutables": Chinese negotiating tactics vis-a-vis the Japanese. *China Quarterly,* 529-552.

Keesing, M. R. (1974). Theories of culture. *Annual Review of Anthropology, 3,* 73-97.

Kennedy, P. (1993). *Preparing for the twenty-first century.* London: Fontana.

Kindel, T. I. (1990). A cultural approach to negotiations. In N. Campbell (Ed.), *Advances in Chinese industrial studies* (Part B, pp. 127-135). Greenwich, CT: JAI.

Kirkbride, P. S., & Tang, S. F. Y. (1990). Negotiation: Lessons from behind the bamboo curtain. *Journal of General Management, 16*(1), 1-13.

Kirkbride, P. S., Tang, S. F. Y., & Westwood, R. I. (1991). Chinese conflict preferences and negotiating behavior: Cultural and psychological influences. *Organization Studies, 12*(3), 365-386.

Kissinger, H. (1979). *White House years.* Boston: Little, Brown.

Kluckholn, F. R., & Strodtbeck, F. L. (1961). *Variations in value orientations.* Evanston, IL: Row, Peterson.

Knutsson, J. (1986a). *Chinese negotiation behavior.* Stockholm: Stockholm School of Economics, Institute for International Business. (In Swedish)

Knutsson, J. (1986b). Chinese commercial negotiating behaviour and its institutional and cultural determinants: A summary. In *Chinese culture and management* (pp. 18-31). Brussels: Euro-China Association for Management Development.

Kosenko, R., & Samli, A. C. (1985). China's four modernizations program and technology transfer. In A. C. Samli (Ed.), *Technology transfer: Geographic, economic, cultural, and technical dimensions* (pp. 107-131). Westport, CT: Quorum.

Kotler, P. (1994). *Marketing management: Analysis, planning, implementation, and control.* Englewood Cliffs, NJ: Prentice Hall.

Kotler, P., & Singh, R. (1981, Winter). Marketing warfare in the 1980s. *Journal of Business Strategy,* 30-41.

Kreisberg, P. H. (1995). China's negotiating behaviour. In T. W. Robinson & D. Shambaugh (Eds.), *Chinese foreign policy: Theory and practice* (pp. 453-477). Oxford, UK: Clarendon.

Kristof, N. D., & Wudunn, S. (1994). *China wakes: The struggle for the soul of a rising power.* New York: Times Books.

Kroeber, A. L., & Kluckhohn, C. (1952). *Culture: A critical review of concepts and definitions.* Cambridge, MA: Peabody Museum.

Kroeber, A. L., & Parsons, T. (1958). The concepts of culture and of social system. *American Sociological Review, 23,* 582-583.

Laaksonen, O. (1984). The management and power structure of Chinese enterprises during and after the cultural revolution; With empirical data comparing Chinese and European enterprises. *Organization Studies, 5*(1), 1-21.

Lall, A. (1968). *How Communist China negotiates.* New York: Columbia University Press.

Landin, B. (1996). We have to focus more on Asia! *Contact,* No. 4 (a newspaper of Ericsson). (In Swedish)

Lardy, N. R. (1994). *China in the world economy.* Washington, DC: Institute for International Economics.

Lavin, F. L. (1994). Negotiating with the Chinese: Or how not to kowtow. *Foreign Affairs, 73*(4), 16-22.

Lee, K.-H., & Lo, T. W.-C. (1988, Summer). American business people's perceptions of marketing and negotiating in the People's Republic of China. *International Marketing Review, 5*(2), 41-51.

Lee, S. M. (1995). *Spectrum of Chinese culture.* Selangor Darul Ehsan: Pelanduk.

Leijonhufvud, G., & Engqvist, A. (1996). *The dragon wakes: China Year 2000* Stockholm. Norstedt. (In Swedish)

Levinson, J. C. (1995). *Guerrilla marketing: How to make big profits from a small business* (Rev. ed.). London: Piatkus.

Lewis, D. J. (Ed.). (1995). *The life and death of a joint venture in China* (2nd ed.). Hong Kong: Asia Law & Practice.

Li, J., & Murray, V. (1992). Obstacles to the development of the field of organizational behavior in China. In W. C. Wedley (Ed.), *Advances in Chinese industrial studies* (Vol. 3, pp. 155-168). Greenwich, CT: JAI.

Li, L. Q. (1995). *Basic knowledge about utilization of foreign investment in China.* Beijing: CPC Central Party School Press. (In Chinese)

Li, S. J., Yang, X. J., & Tan, J. R. (1986). *Sun Tzu's art of war and enterprise management* (2nd ed.). Nanning: Guangxi People's Press. (In Chinese)

Li, V. H. (1980). A perspective on the new legalization drive. In N.-T. Wang (Ed.), *Business with China: An international reassessment* (pp. 37-43). New York: Pergamon.

Li, Z. S. (1994). *The private life of Chairman Mao.* New York: Random House.

Li, Z. W. (1997). *Thick black theory.* Beijing: Economic Daily Press. (In Chinese)

Lieberthal, K., & Oksenberg, M. (1986). Understanding China's bureaucracy: The first step to a better corporate strategy. *China Business Review, 13*(6), 24-31.

Lin, Y. T. (1939). *My country and my people.* London: Heinemann.

Lin, Y. T. (1981a). Confucius as I know him. In H. Shih & L. Yutang (Eds.), *China's own critics: A selection of essays* (pp. 146-159). Westport, CT: Hyperion.

Lin, Y. T. (1981b). What is face? In H. Shih & Y. T. Lin (Eds.), *China's own critics: A selection of essays* (pp. 127-131). Westport, CT: Hyperion.

Lin, Y. T. (1996). *The importance of living.* New York: Morrow. (Original work published 1937)

Lindén, P. (1997). Ericsson showed many products at the fair. In *Contact,* No. 4 (a newspaper of Ericsson). (In Swedish)

Lip, E. (1991). *Chinese tactics for success: 36 stratagems.* Singapore: Shing Lee.

Lip, E. (1995). *Feng Shui for business.* Singapore: Times Books International.

Liu, G. (1996). *Negotiating expert.* Beijing: China Economics Press. (In Chinese)

Liu, X. D., & Zhu, S. Y. (1991). Postscript to *Wisdom and stratagems* (Chinese version of von Senger's *Strategeme*) (X. D. Liu & S. Y. Zhu, Trans.). Shanghai: Shanghai People's Press. (In Chinese)

Liu, Z. L. (1996, April 15-21). Report on the implementation of the central and local budgets for 1995 and on the central and local draft budgets for 1996. *Beijing Review*, 20-21.

Lockett, M. (1988). Culture and the problems of Chinese management. *Organization Studies, 9*(4), 475-496.

Lockett, M. (1990). The nature of Chinese culture. In J. Child & M. Lockett (Eds.), *Advances in Chinese industrial studies* (Part A, pp. 269-276). Greenwich, CT: JAI.

Lu, H. Y. (1996a, April 15). Telecoms to fuel nationwide growth. *China Daily*, p. 5.

Lu, H. Y. (1996b, March 15). Reforms of firms intensify. *China Daily*, p. 1.

Lu, X. (1980). On "Face." In *Selected works* (Vol. 4, pp. 131-134). Beijing: Foreign Languages Press.

Lu, X. (1990). *Diary of a madman and other stories* (W. A. Lyell, Trans.). Honolulu: University of Hawaii Press.

Lubman, S. B. (1983). Negotiations in China: Observations of a lawyer. In R. A. Kapp (Ed.), *Communicating with China* (pp. 59-69). Chicago: Intercultural Press.

Luo, G. Z. (1994). *Three kingdoms*. Beijing: Foreign Languages Press.

Ma, C. G. (1996a, March 18). NPC session closes successfully: Top legislature adopts blueprint for future growth. *China Daily*, p. 1.

Ma, C. G. (1996b, March 13). Economic laws to be tackled. *China Daily*, p. 1.

MacDougall, C. (Ed.). (1980). *Trading with China: A practical guide*. London: McGraw-Hill.

MacFarquhar, R. (1980, February 9-15). The post-Confucian challenge. *The Economist*, 67-72.

Managing "big" is a strategic issue of economic development. (1997, September 8). *Baokan Wenzhai* [*Newspaper and Magazine Digest*], p. 1. (In Chinese)

Mann, J. (1989). *Beijing jeep: The short, unhappy romance of American business in china*. New York: Simon & Schuster.

Mao, Z. D. (1965). On individualism. In *Selected works of Mao Tse-Tung* (pp. 112-113). Peking: Foreign Languages Press.

Mao, Z. D. (1966). *Quotations from Chairman Mao Tse-Tung*. Peking: Foreign Languages Press.

Mao, Z. D. (1967). On protracted war. In *Selected military writings of Mao Tse-Tung* (pp. 187-267). Peking: Foreign Languages Press.

March, R. M. (1988). *The Japanese negotiator: Subtlety and strategy beyond Western logic*. Tokyo: Kodansha.

March, R. M. (1994). *"Inscrutables" negotiate with "inscrutables": Experience and lessons from Japanese negotiations with the Chinese* (Working paper No. 5/1994, Issue No. 1036-5613). University of Western Sydney, Nepean, Department of Marketing, Sydney, Australia.

March, R. M. (1997). *Managing business relationships with East Asia: Building and pilot testing a model of long-term Asia/Western business relationships* (Working paper No. 3/1997). University of Western Sydney, Nepean, Department of Marketing, Sydney, Australia.

McCall, J. B., & Warrington, M. B. (1984). *Marketing by agreement: A cross-cultural approach to business negotiations*. Chichester, UK: Wiley.

McDonald, G. M., & Roberts, C. J. (1990). The brand-naming enigma in the Asia Pacific context. *European Journal of Marketing, 24*(8), 6-19.

McKenna, R. (1991). *Relationship marketing: Successful strategies for the age of the customer.* Reading, MA: Addison-Wesley.

McNeilly, M. (1996). *Sun Tzu and the art of business.* New York: Oxford University Press.

Mei, R. H., & Zhang, H. (1990). Research on and application of modern marketing theory in China. In H. Kuang (Ed.), *Encyclopedia of modern marketing* (pp. 29-34). Beijing: Economics and Management Press. (In Chinese)

Merriam, S. B. (1988). *Case study research in education: A qualitative approach.* San Francisco: Jossey-Bass.

Ministry of Foreign Economic Relations and Trade (MOFERT). (1992). *Collection of laws of the People's Republic of China concerning enterprises with foreign investment.* Beijing: Department of Treaties and Law, MOFERT.

Mintzberg, H. (1973). *The nature of managerial work.* New York: Harper & Row.

Mintzberg, H. (1990). Strategy formation: Schools of thought. In J. W. Fredrickson (Ed.), *Perspectives on strategic management* (pp. 105-236). New York: Harper & Row.

Mintzberg, H., Quinn, J. B., & Voyer, J. (1995). *The strategy process.* Englewood Cliffs, NJ: Prentice Hall.

Modern Chinese-English dictionary. (1994). Beijing: Foreign Languages Teaching and Research Press.

Mohamad, M., & Ishihara, S. (1995). *The voice of Asia: Two leaders discuss the coming century.* Tokyo: Kodansha.

Moran, R. T., & Stripp, W. G. (1991). *Successful international business negotiations.* Houston: Gulf.

Moser, M. J. (1986). *Business strategies for the People's Republic of China.* Hong Kong: Longman Group (Far East).

Mun, K.-c. (1990). The competition model of Sun Tzu's *Art of War.* In H. Kuang (Ed.), *Modern marketing management encyclopedia* (pp. 930-935). Beijing: Economics and Management Press. (In Chinese)

Murray, D. P. (1983). Face to face: American and Chinese interactions. In R. A. Kapp (Ed.), *Communicating with China* (pp. 9-27). Chicago: Intercultural Press.

Myrdal, G. (1968). *Asian drama: An inquiry into the poverty of nations.* New York: Twentieth Century Fund.

Naisbitt, J. (1996). *Megatrends Asia: Eight Asian megatrends that are reshaping our world.* New York: Simon & Schuster.

Nalebuff, B. J., & Brandenburger, A. M. (1996). *Co-opetition.* London: HarperCollins.

Needham, J. (1954). *Science and civilization in China. Vol. I: Introductory orientations.* Cambridge, UK: Cambridge University Press.

Negotiating in China: Foreign perceptions and bureaucratic reality. (1986). *China Business Review, 13*(6), 29.

Ness, A. (1996). No longer a hardship post. *China Business Review, 23*(4), 40-45.

Nierenberg, G. I. (1981). *The art of negotiating.* New York: A Fireside Book. (Original work published 1968)

Officials outline policies regarding WTO, Taiwan. (1998, March 20). *China Daily.*

Ohashi, T. (1993). *The thirty-six stratagems from ancient times* (2nd ed.). Xi'an, China: San Qin Press. (In Chinese)

Pan, Y. G., & Schmitt, B. (1996). Language and brand attitudes: Impact of script and sound matching in Chinese and English. *Journal of Consumer Psychology, 5*(3), 263-277.

Pang, P., & Liu, Z. (1994). *The spirit of the traditional Chinese culture.* Shenyang, China: Liaoning People's Press. (In Chinese)

Patton, M. Q. (1990). *Qualitative evaluation and research methods* (2nd ed.). Newbury Park, CA: Sage.

Pheng, L. S., & Sirpal, R. (1995). Western generic business and corporate strategies: Lessons from the thirty-six Chinese classical strategies of war. *Marketing Intelligence and Planning, 13*(6), 34-40.

Pike, K. L. (1967). *Language in relation to a unified theory of the structure of human behavior.* The Hague, Netherlands: Mouton.

Porter, M. E. (1980). *Competitive strategy: Techniques for analyzing industries and competitors.* New York: Free Press.

Porter, R. (1996). Politics, culture and decision making in China. In D. Brown & R. Porter (Eds.), *Management issues in China* (pp. 85-105). London: Routledge.

Potter, P. B. (1995). *Foreign business law in China: Past progress and future challenges.* San Francisco: The 1990 Institute.

Prahalad, C. K., & Hamel, G. (1990, May/June). The core competence of the corporation. *Harvard Business Review,* 79-91.

Pruitt, D. G. (1981). *Negotiation behavior.* New York: Academic Press.

Pruitt, D. G. (1991). Strategy in negotiation. In V. A. Kremenyuk (Ed.), *International negotiation: Analysis, applications, issues* (pp. 78-89). San Francisco: Jossey-Bass.

Pruitt, D. G., & Rubin, J. Z. (1986). *Social conflict: Escalation, stalemate and settlement.* New York: Random House.

Putnam, L. L. (1990). Reframing integrative and distributive bargaining. In B. H. Shepard, M. H. Bazerman, & R. J. Lewicki (Eds.), *Research on negotiation in organizations* (Vol. 2, pp. 1-30). Greenwich, CT: JAI.

Putnam, L. L., & Roloff, M. E. (1992). Communication perspectives on negotiation. In L. L. Putnam & M. E. Roloff (Eds.), *Communication and negotiation* (pp. 1-17). Newbury Park, CA: Sage.

Pye, L. W. (1981). *The dynamics of Chinese politics.* Cambridge, MA: Oelgeschlager, Gunn & Hain.

Pye, L. W. (1982). *Chinese commercial negotiating style.* Cambridge, MA: Oelgeschlager, Gunn & Hain.

Pye, L. W. (1984), *China: An introduction.* Boston: Little, Brown.

Pye, L. W. (1985). *Asian power and politics: The cultural dimensions of authority.* Cambridge, MA: Harvard University Press.

Pye, L. W. (1986, July/August). The China trade: Making the deal. *Harvard Business Review,* 74-80.

Pye, L. W. (1988). *The mandarin and the cadre: China's political cultures.* Ann Arbor: University of Michigan Press.

Pye, L. W. (1992a). *The spirit of Chinese politics.* Cambridge, MA: Harvard University Press.

Pye, L. W. (1992b). *Chinese negotiating style: Commercial approaches and cultural principles.* New York: Quorum.

Qin, S. (1994). *China 1994.* Beijing: New Star.

Quan, Y. C. (1992). *Mao Zedong: Man, not God.* Beijing: Foreign Languages Press.

Raiffa, H. (1982). *The art and science of negotiation.* Cambridge, MA: Harvard University Press.

Redding, S. G., & Ng, M. (1982). The role of "face" in the organizational perceptions of Chinese managers. *Organization Studies, 3*(3), 201-219.

Ren, J. Y. (1986). *New interpretation of Lao Tzu* (Rev. ed.). Shanghai: Shanghai Gu Ji Press. (In Chinese)

Resolution on certain questions in the history of our party since the founding of the People's Republic of China (adopted by the Sixth Plenary Session of the Eleventh Central Committee of the CPC on June 27 (1981). In *Resolution on CPC History* (pp. 1-86). Beijing: Foreign Languages Press.

Ries, A., & Trout, J. (1986). *Marketing warfare.* New York: McGraw-Hill.

Roberts, D. (1997a, October 6). Cheated in China? *Business Week,* pp. 142-144.

Roberts, D. (1997b, February 24). Maybe guanxi isn't everything after all: Connections haven't helped a big Beijing project. *Business Week* (international edition), p. 23.

Roehrig, M. F. (1994a). The right time and place. *China Business Review, 25*(5), 8-9.

Roehrig, M. F. (1994b). *Foreign joint ventures in contemporary China.* London: Macmillan.

Rohner, R. P. (1984). Toward a conception of culture for cross-cultural psychology. *Journal of Cross-Cultural Psychology, 15*(2), 111-138.

Rohwer, J. (1992, November 28). When China wakes. A survey of China. *The Economist,* Special Report.

Rohwer, J. (1996). *Asia rising: Why America will prosper as Asia's economies boom.* New York: Touchstone.

Root, F. R. (1987). *Entry strategies for international markets.* Lexington, MA: Lexington Books.

Ropp, P. S. (1990). Introduction. In P. S. Ropp (Ed.), *Heritage of China: Contemporary perspectives on Chinese civilization* (pp. ix-xxi). Berkeley: University of California Press.

Rubin, J. Z., & Brown, B. R. (1975). *The social psychology of bargaining and negotiation.* San Diego: Academic Press.

Salacuse, J. W. (1991). *Making global deals: Negotiating in the international marketplace.* Boston: Houghton Mifflin.

Schell, O. (1992). Introduction. In L. Z. Fang, *Bringing down the Great Wall: Writings on science, culture, and democracy in China* (pp. xiii-xl). New York: Norton.

Schmitt, B. H. (1995). Language and visual imagery: Issues of corporate identity in East Asia. *Columbia Journal of World Business, 30*(4), 28-36.

Schmitt, B. H., & Simonson, A. (1997). *Marketing aesthetics: The strategic management of brands, identity, and image.* New York: Free Press.

Schnepp, O., von Glinow, M. A., & Bhambri, A. (1990). *United States-China technology transfer.* Englewood Cliffs, NJ: Prentice Hall.

Selected military writings of Mao Tse-Tung. (1967). Peking: Foreign Languages Press.

Seligman, S. D. (1990). *Dealing with the Chinese: A practical guide to business etiquette.* London: Mercury.

Selmer, J. (1997). *Vikings and dragons: Swedish management in Southeast Asia.* Hong Kong: Hong Kong Baptist University, the David C. Lam Institute for East-West Studies.

Senge, P. M. (1990). *The fifth discipline: The art and practice of the learning organization.* New York: A Currency Book.

Shen, B. N., Guo, Z. Y., & Li, L. Z. (1995). *Guidance for study of the documents of the 5th Plenary Session of the 14th Central Committee of the Communist Party of China.* Beijing: China Yan Shi Press. (In Chinese)

Sheng, R. (1979). Outsiders' perception of the Chinese. *Columbia Journal of World Business, 14*(2), 16-22.

Shenkar, O., & Ronen, S. (1987). The cultural context of negotiations: The implications of Chinese interpersonal norms. *Journal of Applied Behavioral Science, 23*(2), 263-275.

Sheppard, B. H., Bazerman, M. H., & Lewicki, R. J. (Eds.). (1990). *Research on negotiation in organizations.* Greenwich, CT: JAI.

Shi, Z. W. (1993). *Chinese: Go out of the dead lane* (Rev. ed.). Beijing: China Development Press. (In Chinese)

Shirk, S. L. (1993). *The political logic of economic reform in China.* Berkeley: University of California Press.

Shorter Oxford English dictionary on historical principles. (1975). Glasgow: Oxford University Press. (Original work published 1933)

Siebe, W. (1991). Game theory. In V. A. Kremenyuk (Ed.), *International negotiation: Analysis, approaches, issues* (pp. 180-202). San Francisco: Jossey-Bass.

Silk, M. A. (1994). Cracking down on economic crime. *China Business Review, 21*(3), 21-28.

Simon, D. F. (1989). China's drive to close the technological gap: S&T reform and the imperative to catch up. *China Quarterly, 118,* 598-630.

Snow, P. (1980). Receiving a Chinese delegation. In C. MacDougall (Ed.), *Trading with China: A practical guide* (pp. 57-75). London: McGraw-Hill.

Solomon, R. H. (1985). *Chinese political negotiating behavior.* Santa Monica, CA: RAND.

Solomon, R. H. (1987). China: Friendship and obligation in Chinese negotiating style. In H. Binnendijk (Ed.), *National negotiating styles* (pp. 1-16). Washington, DC: U.S. Department of State, Foreign Service Institute.

Stewart, S. (1990). Where the power lies: A look at China's bureaucracy. In N. Campbell & J. S. Henley (Eds.), *Advances in Chinese industrial studies* (Part B, 51-58). Greenwich, CT: JAI.

Stewart, S. (1994). A look at some PRC views on joint ventures in China. In S. Stewart (Ed.), *Advances in Chinese industrial studies* (Vol. 4, pp. 303-317). Greenwich, CT: JAI.

Stewart, S., Cheung, M. T., & Yeung, D. W. K. (1992). The latest Asian newly industrialized economy emerges: The south China economic community. *Columbia Journal of World Business, 27*(2), 30-37.

Stewart, S., & Keown, C. F. (1989). Talking with the dragon: Negotiating in the People's Republic of China. *Columbia Journal of World Business, 24*(3), 68-72.

Stone, R. J. (1992, November). Negotiating in China is not easy. *Hong Kong Business, 11,* 64-65.

Stover, L. E. (1974). *Cultural ecology of Chinese civilization: Peasants and elites in the last of the agrarian states.* New York: A Mentor Book.

Sun, H. C. (1991). *The wiles of war: 36 military strategies from ancient China.* Beijing: Foreign Languages Press.

Sun, L. (1995, December 10-16). Rampant fraud turns consumers off health food. *China Daily (Business Weekly).*

Sun Tzu. (1910). *Sun Tzu on the art of war* (L. Giles, Trans.). London: Luzac.

Sun Tzu. (1982). *Sun Tzu: The art of war.* (S. B. Griffith, Trans.). London: Oxford University Press. (Original work published 1963)

Sun Tzu. (1994). *Sun Tzu: The art of war* (R. D. Sawyer, Trans.). Boulder, CO: Westview.

Swidler, A. (1986). Culture in action: Symbols and strategies. *American Sociological Review, 51*(2), 273-286.

Szuma, C. (1979). *Selections from records of the historian* (H.-y. Yang and G. Yang, Trans.). Peking: Foreign Languages Press.

Tan, C. H. (1990). Management concepts and Chinese culture. In J. Child & M. Lockett (Eds.), *Advances in Chinese industrial studies* (Part A, pp. 277-288). Greenwich, CT: JAI.

Tan, H. K. (1993, January 21). Urban dwellers try to keep pace with reforms. *China Daily.*

Tang, Y.-J. (1991). *Confucianism, Buddhism, Daoism, Christianity and Chinese culture.* Washington, DC: Council for Research in Values and Philosophy.

Terpstra, V., & David, K. (1991). *The cultural environment of international business.* Cincinnati, OH: South-Western.

Thomas, V., & Wang, Y. (1997). East Asian lessons from economic reforms. In W. T. Woo, S. Parker, & J. D. Sachs (Eds.), *Economies in transition: Comparing Asia and eastern Europe* (pp. 217-241). Cambridge: MIT Press.

Ting-Toomey, S. (1988). Intercultural conflict styles: A face-negotiation theory. In Y. Y. Kim & W. B. Gudykunst (Eds.), *Theories in intercultural communication* (pp. 213-235). Newbury Park, CA: Sage.

Top leaders elected or approved by NPC (March 17-18). (1998, March 19). *China Daily.*

Triandis, H. C. (1982). Review of culture's consequences: International differences in work-related values. *Human Organization, 41*(1), 86-90.

Triandis, H. C. (1988). Cross-cultural contributions to theory in social psychology. In M. H. Bond (Ed.), *The cross-cultural challenge to social psychology.* Newbury Park, CA: Sage.

Triandis, H. C. (1994). *Culture and social behavior.* New York: McGraw-Hill.

Triandis, H. C. (1995). *Individualism and collectivism.* Boulder, CO: Westview.

Triandis, H. C. (1996). Foreword: Psychology moves east. In M. H. Bond (Ed.), *The handbook of Chinese psychology* (pp. v-vii). Hong Kong: Oxford University Press.

Trompenaars, F. (1994). *Riding the waves of culture: Understanding diversity in global business.* Chicago: Irwin.

Tsang, E. W. K. (1994). Strategies for transferring technology to China. *Long Range Planning, 27*(3), 98-107.

Tse, D. K., Francis, J., & Walls, J. (1994). Cultural differences in conducting intra- and inter-cultural negotiations: A Sino-Canadian comparison. *Journal of International Business Studies, 25*(3), 537-555.

Tu, W.-M. (1984). *Confucian ethics today: The Singapore challenge.* Singapore: Federal Publications.

Tu, W.-M. (1985). Selfhood and otherness in Confucian thought. In A. J. Marsella, G. DeVos, & F. L. K. Hsu (Eds.), *Culture and self: Asian and Western perspectives* (pp. 231-251). New York: Tavistock.

Tu, W.-M. (1990). The Confucian tradition in Chinese history. In P. S. Ropp (Ed.), *Heritage of China: Contemporary perspectives on Chinese civilization* (pp. 112-137). Berkeley: University of California Press.

Tung, R. L. (1982a). *U.S.-China negotiations.* New York: Pergamon.

Tung, R. L. (1982b). U.S.-China negotiations: Practices, procedures and outcomes. *Journal of International Business Studies, 13*(2), 25-37.

Tung, R. L. (1989). A longitudinal study of United States-China business negotiations. *China Economic Review, 1*(1), 57-71.

Tung, R. L. (1994a). Strategic management thought in East Asia. *Organizational Dynamics, 22*(4), 55-65.

Tung, R. L. (1994b). Human resource issues and technology transfer. *International Journal of Human Resource Management, 5*(4), 807-825.

Tung, R. L. (1996). Negotiating with East Asians. In P. Ghauri & J.-C. Usunier (Eds.), *International business negotiations* (pp. 369-381). Oxford, UK: Pergamon.

Tung, R. L., & Worm, V. (1997). East meets West: North European expatriates in China. *Business & the Contemporary World, 9*(1), 137-148.

Turnbull, P., & Valla, J.-P. (Eds.). (1986). *Strategies for international industrial marketing.* London: Croom Helm.

Tylor, E. B. (1871). *Primitive culture: Researches into the development of mythology, philosophy, religion, art, and custom.* London: Murray.

Usunier, J.-C. (1996). Cultural aspects of international business negotiations. In P. Ghauri & J.-C. Usunier (Eds.), *International business negotiations* (pp. 93-118). Oxford, UK: Pergamon.

Vanhonacker, W. (1997, March/April). Entering China: An unconventional approach. *Harvard Business Review,* 130-140.

van Zandt, H. F. (1970, November/December). How to negotiate in Japan. *Harvard Business Review,* 45-56.

Veith, I. (1972). *The yellow emperor's classic of internal medicine.* Berkeley: University of California Press.

von Clausewitz, C. (1984). *On war.* Princeton, NJ: Princeton University Press. (Original work published 1832)

von Senger, H. (1991a). *The book of stratagems.* New York: Viking/Penguin.

von Senger, H. (1991b). *Wisdom and stratagems.* Shanghai: Shanghai People's Press. (In Chinese)

Walder, A. G. (1989, June). Factory and manager in an era of reform. *China Quarterly, 118,* 242-264.

Wall, J. A., Jr. (1990). Managers in the People's Republic of China. *Academy of Management Executive, 4*(2), 19-32.

Walton, R. E., & McKersie, R. B. (1965). *A behavioral theory of labor negotiations: An analysis of a social interaction system.* New York: McGraw-Hill.

Wang, H. (1996, November 14). China's economy energizes the world. *China Daily.*

Wang, J. C. F. (1989). *Contemporary Chinese politics.* Englewood Cliffs, NJ: Prentice Hall.

Wang, N.-T. (1984). *China's modernization and transnational corporations.* Lexington, MA: Lexington Books.

Wang, Y., Shang, W., & Xu, Y. (1998, March 18). Zhu Rongji heads state council. *China Daily,* p. 1

Wang, Y. J., Zhang, Q., He, Q., & Zhang, Z. S. (1995). *Foreign investment in China: A question-and-answer guide.* Beijing: Zhong Xin Press. (In Chinese)

Warner, M. (1991). How Chinese managers learn. *Journal of General Management, 16*(4), 66-84.

Warrington, M. B., & McCall, J. B. (1983). Negotiating a foot into the Chinese door. *Management Development, 21*(2), 3-13.

Weber, M. (1951). *The religion of China: Confucianism and Taoism.* Glencoe, IL: Free Press. (Original work published 1919)

Weber, M. (1964). *The theory of social and economic organization.* New York: Free Press. (Original work published 1947)

Weber, M. (1996). *The Protestant ethic and the spirit of capitalism.* London: Routledge. (Original work published 1904)

Webster, F. E., Jr. (1979). *Industrial marketing strategy.* New York: John Wiley.

Weinshall, T. D. (Ed.). (1977). *Culture and management.* Harmondsworth: Penguin.

Weinshall, T. D. (Ed.). (1993). *Societal culture and management.* Berlin: de Gruyter.

Weiss, S. E. (1994a). Negotiating with the "Romans"—Part 2. *Sloan Management Review, 35*(3), 85-99.

Weiss, S. E. (1994b). Negotiating with the "Romans"—Part 1. *Sloan Management Review, 35*(2), 51-61.

Wheeler, E. L. (1988). *Stratagem and the vocabulary of military trickery.* Leiden: E. J. Brill.

Whetten, D. A. (1989). What constitutes a theoretical contribution? *Academy of Management Review, 14*(4), 490-495.

Williams, C. A. S. (1941). *Outlines of Chinese symbolism and art motives.* Shanghai: Kelly & Walsh.

Withane, S. (1992). A consensual framework for business negotiation: An analysis of the Chinese cultural and religious value system. In W. C. Wedley (Ed.), *Advances in Chinese industrial studies* (Vol. 3, pp. 63-76). Greenwich, CT: JAI.

The World Bank. (1996), *Poverty in China* (Press release No. 96/41/EAP; http://ftp.worldbank.org/html/extdr/extme/9641eap.htm).

Worm, V. (1997). *Vikings and mandarins: Sino-Scandinavian business cooperation in cross-cultural settings.* Copenhagen: Handelshojskolens Forlag.

Wu, D. Y. H. (1996). Chinese childhood socialization. In M. H. Bond (Ed.), *The handbook of Chinese psychology* (pp. 143-154). Hong Kong: Oxford University Press.

Wu, E. B. (1990). *Interpretation of the Four Books.* Changchun, China: Ji Lin Culture and History Press. (In Chinese)

Wu, T. G. (1991). Sun Tzu's art of war and marketing. In *Marketing theories and practices—Papers presented at the Conference of the Founding of Marketing Institute of China* (pp. 97-104). Beijing: China Business Press. (In Chinese)

Xu, Y. C. (1996, May). Good prospects for further expansion of Sino-Swedish trade and economic co-operation. In *China: Marketplace.* Stockholm: Grossistförbundet Svensk Handel.

Yan, R. (1994, September/October). To reach China's consumers, adapt to *Guo Qing. Harvard Business Review,* 66-68, 70-74.

Yang, L.-s. (1957). The concept of "Pao" as a basis for social relations in China. In J. K. Fairbank (Ed.), *Chinese thought and institutions* (pp. 291-309). Chicago: University of Chicago Press.

Yang, M. M.-h. (1994). *Gifts, favors, and banquets: The art of social relationships in China.* Ithaca, NY: Cornell University Press.

Yao, E. L. (1987). Cultivating *guan-xi* (personal relationships) with Chinese partners. *Business Marketing, 72*(1), 62-66.

Yao, W. (1983). The importance of being KEQI: A note on communication difficulties. In R. A. Kapp (Ed.), *Communicating with China* (pp. 71-75). Chicago: Intercultural Press.

Yau, O. H. M. (1994). *Consumer behaviour in China: Customer satisfaction and cultural values*. London: Routledge.

Yeung, I. Y. M., & Tung, R. L. (1996). Achieving business success in Confucian societies: The importance of *guanxi* (connections). *Organizational Dynamics, 25*(2), 54-65.

Yin, R. K. (1994). *Case study research: Design and methods* (2nd ed.). Thousand Oaks, CA: Sage.

Young, K. T. (1968). *Negotiating with the Chinese Communists: The United States experience, 1953-1967*. New York: McGraw-Hill.

Yuann, J. K. (1987). Negotiating a technology license. *China Business Review, 14*(3), 50-52.

Zakaria, F. (1994). Culture is destiny: A conversation with Lee Kuan Yew. *Foreign Affairs, 73*(2), 109-126.

Zartman, I. W. (1978). Negotiation as a joint decision-making process. In I. W. Zartman (Ed.) *The negotiation process: Theories and applications* (pp. 67-86). Beverly Hills, CA: Sage.

Zhou, S. L. (1992). Reform of the economic structure. In G. Totten & S. L. Zhou (Eds.), *China's economic reform: Administering the introduction of the market mechanism* (pp. 1-18). Boulder, CO: Westview.

Zhu charts development course. (1998, March 20). *China Daily*, p. 2.

Index

About the Author

Tony Fang is presently a PhD candidate of industrial marketing working at IMIE, Department of Management and Economics, Linköping University, Linköping, Sweden. He received his Licentiate of Economics degree in industrial marketing from Linköping University and his Master of Science degree in naval architecture and ocean engineering from Shanghai Jiao Tong University. Before moving to the West to pursue economics and management studies in 1991, he worked as a ship investment manager and seaman in the Chinese shipping and shipbuilding industries. He has been a visiting scholar at Massachusetts Institute of Technology. His current research, teaching, and consulting interests are industrial marketing and international management with a spotlight on China.